THINKING *of* YOU

D1453560

THINKING *of* YOU

The Weekly Columns from the *Catholic Standard*

Cardinal Theodore E.
McCARRICK

ave maria press AmP notre dame, indiana

© 2011 by Cardinal Theodore E. McCarrick

Founded in 1865, Ave Maria Press is a ministry of the Indiana Province of Holy Cross.

www.avemariapress.com

ISBN-10 1-59471-129-1   ISBN-13 978-1-59471-129-9

Cover image © AP Photo/Pier Paolo Cito.

Cover and text design by John R. Carson.

Printed and bound in the United States of America.

Library of Congress Cataloging-in-Publication Data
McCarrick, Theodore, 1930-
  Thinking of you : the weekly columns from The Catholic standard / Theodore E. McCarrick.
     p. cm.
  ISBN-13: 978-1-59471-129-9 (pbk.)
  ISBN-10: 1-59471-129-1 (pbk.)
1. Theology. 2. McCarrick, Theodore, 1930- 3. Catholic Church. Archdiocese of Washington (D.C.) I. Title.

BX4705.M4756A5 2011
282'.753090511--dc22
                        2010044270

INTRODUCTION

Fifty years ago, when I was a young priest, the Second Vatican Council reinforced one of the traditional roles of a bishop. The Council Fathers made it clear that the bishop needed to teach his people using all the means that modern media placed within his reach. Today, just about every bishop I know makes it a priority to reach out to the people entrusted to his care in an ever-increasing number of ways. From profound theological analyses to Facebook and other popular forms of communication, the bishop, at least in our country, tries to "stay in touch" with his faithful.

When Pope John Paul II gave me the privilege to serve as Bishop of Metuchen, I realized that personal communication was going to be essential in creating a family spirit among the four hundred thousand parishioners in the counties that made up that new diocese in central New Jersey. Of course, I needed to use the instrument of pastoral letters to try to pass on the great truths of Catholic teaching. Of course, I had always to be open to an invitation to speak on the radio or appear on television or give a talk at some occasion, since the more your people can hear or see you, the better your chance to share with them the wonders of their faith. But it seemed that those opportunities were still not enough.

As time went on and we began our own diocesan newspaper, that was clearly another chance to reach the people, and so, like many bishops before me, I started a weekly column. At first, I started to read what other bishops were writing about, their styles, their concerns, and their subjects. I soon realized that my brothers were as different in their writing styles as they were in their different personalities, and that I just had to find a way, as the great crooner would say, to try "to do it my way!"

Over the years, some particular goals for the columns presented themselves. Some were written carefully to make a specific point and others to develop a certain way of looking at the events of our day. In still others, I tried to tell folks about myself or my family, since the people you serve become, in a real sense, your own diocesan family and the more they know about you, the better. It became a challenge to put on paper every week something that would be interesting or uplifting or useful—or even just funny! I always made it short so they would be tempted to read it all and tried to vary the themes to make it current.

It got so that I looked forward to writing the columns, although there were days when the thoughts just wouldn't come. Perhaps the columns from those times were the best, since I was often surprised at the result of those efforts. The readers were wonderful. Sometimes they would say to me, "I always read your column first" and before I had a chance to be grateful for that kind remark, the person might add, "because I often disagree with you!" Other times, when I would write about a song whose lyrics I had forgotten, a half-dozen letters would come in with the full text. Or, when I complained about being tired in a column, a dozen remedies would arrive by mail.

By the time I arrived in Washington as archbishop, my writing program was established. For the better part of six years, I only missed one week. It was the week that the cardinals were locked in the conclave, from which Pope Benedict emerged as our pope. I guess I could have prepared a column the week before, but I thought that the historical significance of the conclave would be brought out clearly by my absence from writing that week.

All in all, these columns have been a narrative of the history of my years in Washington. They are the reflections of a bishop who really loved—and continues to love—his people, and whose joys, as well as his failings, are portrayed in these columns. I hope you will enjoy them—and pray for their author.

Cardinal Theodore E. McCarrick

2001

A New Beginning
January 4, 2001

Just a few days ago, I finished my last column for the Catholic Advocate of Newark, and here I am beginning again as I write to you. I called that column "Time to Say Goodbye" after that wonderful song that Andrea Bocelli sings so well. I was going to call this one "Time to Say Hello," but it really sounded awkward, and so the title is a more prosaic "A New Beginning," and I guess that says it all.

In the months and years ahead, however many God gives me to serve you, hopefully we will get to know each other pretty well. I will try to get around to all the parishes every couple of years, so at least I will have a chance to get to know the priests, deacons, and religious to some extent. If I don't get to know each of you who are the real life of the parishes by name, at least we will be praying together at Mass, and I will have the occasion to shake your hand. I am hoping that the pastoral councils in every parish will give me an opportunity to listen and to learn about the hopes and dreams, the concerns and the fears, of our people, so that I can understand and try to help.

From the extraordinary ministry of Cardinal Hickey, I know that you already are a Eucharistic people rich in love for the Blessed Sacrament, that awesome sign of God's love for us.

I know that you have a great devotion to Our Lady, one that is fostered in a special way by the presence of her beautiful National Shrine here in our midst. How fortunate we are in Washington to have the shrine so close to us as a constant reminder of Mary's caring love. I know, too, that under the cardinal's leadership, you have always reached out to the poor, the homeless, and the hungry. I want to do that too, and so we will work together to ease the burdens of these sisters and brothers of ours.

People are always asking about my priorities. I tell them that they are very simple. First and foremost, I need to know you in your parish settings, in your schools and your institutions, pastoral and charitable services. Secondly, I want you to help me and the vocations office of the archdiocese in our encouragement of priestly and religious vocations. A parish that is filled with faith and love is a parish that gives its sons and daughters to the Lord in lifelong, generous service. Pray for vocations, be on the lookout for those who have them, and don't be afraid to talk to young people—and those not so young—about service as priests and religious.

In the dioceses where I was privileged to serve in the past, I always called my column "Thinking of You." I'd like to use that title here in the Archdiocese of Washington, too. It is a real description of what I hope my life will be like as your bishop and your servant. In all the things I will try to do, I must always be thinking of you and your needs. Getting around to see you and to listen will help me to think of you all the time. You know, of course, that thinking of you guarantees that I will be praying for you all the time, too. That is a two-way street, isn't it? It comes with a plea that you will always pray for me.

Getting to Know You
January 11, 2001

It does seem a little corny—as we used to say—to use a line from an old musical to introduce a column like this. But it does say everything that I have been doing since I arrived last Tuesday.

I can't believe that I have been here in Washington a whole week. It seems just the day before yesterday that I drove down from Newark with a lot of boxes and a couple of suitcases, following a moving van with more boxes, an excercycle, and some paintings. I can't seem to lose the feeling that this is all happening in an altered state of consciousness. I told Bishop Lori—who by the way has been an extraordinary help, guide, and friend—that I still had the feeling that I am just working here on some project for a few days and then I'll have to head back to New Jersey!

The problem is unpacking. I have been so busy since I have arrived that my rooms are still a mess and I spend half the free time that I have looking for things I just put away somewhere. Once I get everything organized, it will be better. (Please God, I get everything put away by Easter!)

It is not that I haven't been working. You probably know that I have had several great visits to some of our parishes and neighborhoods. After Wednesday's evening prayer in the cathedral and the great Mass of Installation on Thursday in the National Shrine, I have offered Mass in seven of our churches, and had the chance to visit some five of our parishes in Anacostia last Saturday morning. Whenever I have been with the people, they have been truly wonderful. They have received me with great graciousness and love and made me feel very much at home. I look forward to visiting more of our parishes in the weeks ahead, either for a Sunday or Saturday Vigil Mass, or just for quiet early morning Mass on a weekday. Being with the people continues to be a special grace for me.

What a wonderful diocese this is! What great and beautiful churches we have and how blessed we are with the people who fill them. I want to visit all our churches, together with our schools and social service agencies, as time goes by. In fact, I could probably use eight or more days a week to do all the things I would like to do. Please pray for me that I can organize my life in the way the Lord wants me to and that, as I continue thinking of you, I may learn each day how to serve you better.

Thank You!
January 18, 2001

What a wonderful diocese this is! I am really so inspired by the priests and religious I have met, the great deacons and their families, and by all our people. They are from many nations, races, and ethnic groups and yet each has—as Saint Paul wrote in his epistle last Sunday—his or her own gifts to bring to the building up of this Church of Washington. All of you have been so very welcoming to me! It's not too soon to say thank you, and I do it with the deepest sense of how blessed I am to be here to serve you.

I am writing this in Leonardtown in St. Mary's County. It is 6:45 on Sunday morning and I just came back to my room in the rectory after praying for all of you in the little chapel in this historic house where I stayed last night. You will probably read of my journeys around our local Church in another part of today's *Catholic Standard*, but I am writing to you now so that you will be assured that in all these meanderings around the different parts of this archdiocese, you are always in my prayers. Whenever I offer Mass, it is always for you, and whenever I go to chapel to pray, I take you with me. (I wish I were a holier man so that my prayers would be more effective, so you must pray for me that God will give me the grace to be better!)

It is less than two weeks since I arrived on the day before the ceremony at St. Matthew's Cathedral. It has already been filled with enough memories to write a short book. The

Masses last weekend in St. Augustine and Sacred Heart, the visits to different parishes and convents each morning, this great weekend in Southern Maryland have all given me a sense of the Church of Washington, which fills me with gratitude for the extraordinary pastoral service of Cardinal Hickey and the remarkable spirit of cooperation and willingness to work together of everyone I met.

This is not to say that I understand it all already. That will take many weeks and months as I try to listen and try to learn. The only thing that I have asked already is that we must all concentrate more on praying for and working for vocations to the priesthood and religious life. This is a real concern for all of us, and I truly count on you to help both by your prayer and your willingness to raise the consciousness of our people so that it is on the front burner of our thoughts. From all of this, you can tell that just about all the time I am here, I am thinking of you and hoping that you are praying for me too.

On Many Things
January 25, 2001

I had planned to write about my visit to Southern Maryland again and especially to comment once more on that oyster stew! My friends in Leonardtown will be happy to know that I guarded it carefully and that it lasted for several suppers. I did share it with Bishop Lori on at least one occasion, however, and he, too, remarked on how good it was. The events of the last few days have changed the life of the Archdiocese of Washington again, as you well know, and I thought I probably should write to you about them and put off my further reminiscences about my most pleasant journey to our southern counties for a later date.

About my nomination as cardinal, much has already been written. From my statement, which appears in another part of our *Catholic Standard*, you know how honored I am by this most gracious appointment of our Holy Father and how I truly believe that in a special way Pope John Paul II is honoring the Archdiocese of Washington, which has become so extraordinary a local Church under the dedicated care of my truly beloved predecessor, Cardinal Hickey. As I tell the media every time they ask me about what this new designation means, I am still going to be the same person and still have as my number one priority getting to know you, to love you, and to serve all God's people here in the district and in the five counties of Maryland that make up our family. Of course, I will need your prayers all the more now, so please don't forget me!

For me, the most touching news was the Holy Father's appointment of Bishop Lori to the dynamic and growing diocese of Bridgeport. It is a great appointment, and Bishop Bill will be a wonderful shepherd of that young local Church. He brings so much goodness and enthusiasm and so much extraordinary experience from his tremendous service to the Church of Washington and, in a special way, from the great example and invaluable on-the-job training he received from working closely with Cardinal Hickey, one of the most pastoral and farsighted diocesan bishops of our United States Catholic Church.

But how I will miss him! Not a day has gone by since I was named to Washington that I did not speak to him and learn so much from his vast storehouse of knowledge and wisdom. Not only has he been an excellent guide, but also a wonderful friend and brother. I rejoice that our Holy Father is promoting him to the leadership of a diocese—he will be one of the youngest diocesan bishops in our country!—and I know that the Church of Bridgeport will be truly blessed.

As I look to the future and see all the things we have to do together, I count so much on our priests, our deacons, and religious, as well as all the great lay men and women of the Church of Washington to continue your already most generous and gracious help that I may learn more quickly and serve more effectively as a good pastor here. You know I'll be thinking of you all the time and counting on your good counsel and love.

Is God Calling You?
February 1, 2001

Years ago I had the great idea (at least *I* thought it was a great idea) of leasing outdoor advertising billboards for vocation recruitment. As a matter of fact, several Catholic dioceses around the country have already started doing it. The idea is to start people thinking about vocations to the priesthood and the religious life at a time when they might not be distracted by the multitude of other daily cares and concerns. A sign along a highway as someone is driving by or atop a building as someone goes walking along could do just that.

I had it all figured out what the billboard should say. It would be the catching question, "Is God Calling You?" Perhaps setting those simple words against a background of clouds or something like that. The only other wording would be the name and phone number of the archdiocese's vocation office. I never got to do it, probably because the costs up in the northeast would make it an expensive proposition and because my colleagues weren't overwhelmed by the idea.

That's why I thought it would be a good topic for this column. I have to warn you that I will be writing about vocations a lot since it is so very important to you and to me that we have the priests, sisters, and brothers to take care of our people in the years ahead. We have an excellent vocation program here in the Archdiocese of Washington, but it will only be successful if we all keep praying for vocations every day and if our families with children bring them up with openness to embrace and answer God's challenge to religious service when it comes.

Last weekend, I had the opportunity to be part of a discernment retreat for almost twenty young men from our area who are seriously considering what God has in mind for their lives. Most of them have not yet decided, and so the retreat was geared to give them a couple of days apart in prayer and reflection with priests available to listen and to talk to as needed. I was truly very impressed by the caliber of the men who were present, by their seriousness, and by their obvious deep faith. I pray that some of them at least will decide that God is calling them and that they will come to study for the priesthood in the Archdiocese of Washington.

I write to you all about this for many reasons. First of all, since I like you to know what is going on in this local Church of ours; second, in case someone reading this column might be inspired to contact the vocations office himself; and finally because I need your prayers and your own encouragement for this vital need of ours. We need to do the same thing for religious sisters and brothers, and with God's help we will redouble our efforts for every religious vocation. In all of this your participation is essential. That is why whenever I think of vocations I am thinking of you and even wondering, "Is God Calling You?"

El Salvador
February 8, 2001

Although I had hoped that I would not have to travel as much as archbishop of Washington as I did before, the terrible suffering of the people of El Salvador brought me to Central America last week. The ties that bind the Church of Washington to El Salvador are many and strong. Most of our Spanish-speaking Catholics come from that beautiful country and therefore it seemed right for me to bring the people of that land the prayers and the help of their relatives and neighbors here in Washington. It was a short visit—Wednesday to Friday—but one that I will not soon forget.

I had gone to El Salvador a couple of years ago on behalf of our bishops' conference after hurricane Mitch had done such tremendous damage to several Central American countries. Some of the neighborhoods in El Salvador that were hit by the hurricane were hit again by this earthquake. It will probably put the already fragile economy of that land back ten years or more. What is more troubling for the people is the fact that the after-shocks are still continuing—even after two weeks!

I was awakened from sleep last Friday at 2:15 in the morning by one of those after-shocks. It registered 5.4 on the Richter scale. Back home, we would have called it a sizeable earthquake by itself. There are houses that were damaged by the major earthquake but still considered safe to occupy. These strong aftershocks can change that and leave thousands more homes unsafe for occupancy. Many people have been living in makeshift tents and that will become a major crisis when the heavy rains of April and May start to fall.

Hundreds of churches have been destroyed and that also presents a problem in that the faithful will miss the chance to gather and pray together. The bishops are doing their best to cope, but we will all have to help. Then on top of all this, the devastating Indian earthquake with its thousands of people killed and hurt only stretches the capacity of the world's relief agencies to the utmost. I thank God for Catholic Relief Services and its ability, as a worldwide agency, to reach out to the vulnerable on so many fronts.

In spite of all the hardships in El Salvador, I sensed both a spirit of trust in the providence of God and a willingness to reach out to help a neighbor whose loss or suffering was even worse than one's own. All in all I left the country determined to keep helping, but thanking God for the gift of faith and confidence that those great people have. Of course, as I thank God for them, I am thinking of you as well.

The Priests of Washington
February 15, 2001

In the last ten days, I have buried three priests of the Archdiocese of Washington. Learning something about their lives of service and listening to the homilies at their funerals have given me a chance to reflect on the priesthood as it is lived by the diocesan priests of our local Church. I believe you will agree with me when I say that we have really been blessed by the dedication and the great ability of the priests who serve the faithful here in the archdiocese.

One of the priests I buried had a remarkable life of service in many diocesan ministries; the second had an outstanding reputation for holiness and was a sought-after confessor; while the third spent much of his priestly life as a military chaplain where his courage and devotion to those he served was outstanding. I was inspired, too, by the large numbers of our brother priests—young and old—who assisted at these three funeral Masses, not just a tribute to the deceased, but also a wonderful sign of their appreciation for the bonds of priestly friendship and support.

We have great priests here—not enough of them, as I have mentioned to you before—but fine men devoted to their people and faithful to the Gospel. I have gotten to know more than one hundred of them by now, and I hope I will soon be able to call all of them by name. I am inspired by their gracious welcome of me, by their sense of service and their sense of humor, and by the way they reach out to their people—and especially to the poor and the newcomers.

A good number of them are from our area—either from the District of Columbia or from the surrounding counties or southern Maryland, but others had their roots in different parts of the country—and the world! It is fun to see them together, even at a funeral, and to enjoy their friendship and their thoughtfulness as they speak about the Church. When we lose three priests over a short period we all grieve, but we take heart in the conviction that the Lord will not forget their labors and their lives of service to his people. When I see so many of the laity at the funerals of these priests, I thank God that they are remembered with love and, thinking of you, I pray that we will always have good priests to serve you and to help you on your own journey to the Lord.

On Becoming a Cardinal
February 22, 2001

Since we have become more or less family already, I feel that I can share some of the personal musings that are going through my head as I prepare to go to Rome for the consistory at which three of us Americans will become cardinals. When I was a youngster growing up in New York City, one never saw a cardinal, let alone greeted one. I remember when I was maybe eight years old, we heard that Cardinal Hayes had died. Everyone was talking about it with sorrow, although in those days before TV, most people had only seen his picture in the newspapers. Cardinals would come to a parish only for a major funeral or maybe once every twenty years for Confirmation.

Later, as a young man in college, I would drop in at St. Patrick's Cathedral now and then and would see Cardinal Spellman at a Mass, never imagining that I would ever be speaking with him personally. In the seminary he would come to visit a couple of times a year, usually when a visiting cardinal from overseas would be his guest. He would say a few words to the seminary community (usually the words we all strained to hear were "day off!") and then would have dinner with the faculty.

Cardinal Spellman was a very important person in my life since he ultimately ordained me a priest in 1958. He sent me to Puerto Rico and then to Catholic University here in Washington shortly afterwards. Several years later, when I became president of the Catholic University of Puerto Rico, I did get a chance to know him better and he was always very kind to me. Of course, Cardinal Terence Cooke, whom I served as secretary for seven years, was a great model and friend. His cause for beatification has already been received in Rome and he was for me an extraordinary example of kindness and simplicity and total dedication to the Lord and his people. He was a holy man and he demonstrated that it was possible even in our time to live a joyful life of total and generous commitment to the Lord. He died in his early sixties and though I have had more years than he, I have never been able to come close to his goodness or to the genuine virtues of his prayerful life.

In my days as a bishop in New Jersey, I was privileged to work with Cardinal O'Connor, who was my neighbor across the Hudson; with Cardinal Krol, my neighbor across the Delaware; and Cardinal Bevilacqua, who succeeded him. I think of all the present American cardinals as friends and I worked with several of them in different national apostolates for many years. I met Cardinal Hickey almost forty years ago and I do not have to tell you what an extraordinary example to all of us he has been.

My international responsibilities have brought me into contact with many cardinals from overseas, and I truly have been blessed by the chance of meeting many of these very special witnesses of God's love throughout the world. I have really been inspired by them as men of great learning, deep love for the Church and its people, and qualities of leadership that I wish I had.

And this week in Rome, I will be with the cardinals again. The only difference is that I'll be one, too! It happens because I am archbishop of Washington, I know, and not because of anything that I have done. But it will be an awesome thing as I look at the others and think of all the ones I have known. There have been cardinals for more than a thousand years and I wish I were like the holy ones! Pray that when they rank us all in heaven, your present archbishop will make the grade. That's important because you know that if I get there, I'll always be thinking of you.

Rome
March 1, 2001

The journey to Rome was wonderful! I am not really refer-ring to the excitement of the consistory and the new chance

I have to serve as a cardinal—although that had to be, of course, a once-in-a-lifetime experience. More than that, the chance to be with family and friends for a great week of prayer, of sunshine, and of so many new opportunities and new grace has truly been a wonderful blessing for me.

There must have been around seven hundred of us in our combined Washington/New Jersey crowd. A wonderful combination of old and new friends, of lay people and religious, of priests I had ordained and seminarians I hope I will ordain in the years to come. Everyone seemed to get along well and, in spite of a few unavoidable glitches that bedevil every large pilgrimage, it really went off smoothly until the last day.

I had hoped to return in our charter flight last Monday to the Washington National Airport. I was looking forward to spending some more time with the folks whose prayerful and truly gracious presence I had so much enjoyed for a week. When Father Charles Antonicelli, my secretary, came to my room at the North American College Monday morning on the way to the chapel for Mass, he told me of the mechanical problem that had sidelined the plane that was to take us home. He explained the new plan for the group, which would have them landing late in the evening on Monday. That would have been a real problem for me, since we had scheduled the annual dinner of the priests of the archdiocese for Monday evening at the pastoral center and I had to be there, both because I was the host and because it was such a great chance to be with them and to get to know more of them by name. To make a long story short, the travel agent was able to get me on a flight to Philadelphia and I made the party a little late.

But Rome was really wonderful! As you know, we had sunshine and comfortable weather for all the great ceremonies outside in the magnificent piazza of St. Peter's Basilica and the only real rain occurred in the evenings—just like the theme song of Camelot! In last week's *Catholic Standard* you could read about all the special celebrations and the audience with the Holy Father. They were historic moments and the homilies that the pope preached were eloquent and moving and very much worth meditating on—especially for a new cardinal! The presence of both Cardinal Hickey and Cardinal Baum at the ceremony was especially gratifying for me. Washington may be the only diocese in the whole world that now has three living cardinals!

Maybe for me, the best of all were the Masses we had together. We gathered as a pilgrim group in the chapel of the North American College, at St. Peter's Basilica at the Altar of the Chair, in Santa Susanna—Rome's American Church— and in the great Basilica of Santa Maria degli Angeli. That last church—always one of my favorites in Rome—is the titular church of one of my closest friends, Cardinal Keeler of Baltimore. Since I could not celebrate Mass this time in my own titular Church of Saints Nereus and Achilleus, the cardinal graciously offered me the chance to celebrate in his very large titular church. (In a column down the road I'll tell you something about the titular church. It is said to be very beautiful, although I have not gotten inside it yet.)

You know what I am going to add to my story now. Wherever I was, whatever I was doing, whenever I was praying, in all those exciting days, you were always in my heart and I brought you with me to the altar. You can be sure that throughout my time in Rome I was thinking of you.

The Church Alive
March 8, 2001

In the midst of the Atlantic Ocean, about ninety miles north of Haiti and Santo Domingo, there lies a group of

twelve islands called the Turks and Caicos. It is a British
Crown colony and has a fascinating history. Probably discovered by Christopher Columbus on his first or second voyage,
it was there that England settled the Loyalists who had lost
their lands in the thirteen colonies after the American Revolution. For some strange reason, the Catholic Church never
seems to have had a permanent presence on these beautiful
islands, although many Catholics lived there. About four
years ago, the Holy See asked me to take responsibility for
these islands as superior of the mission. As archbishop of
Newark, I did have a number of young priests who were
eager to accept a challenge like this and so I said yes. Newark
now has six men on the islands: three priests and three seminarians on their pastoral year. When the new archbishop of
Newark is named—probably in a few months—he will take
over that responsibility, but until then, I continue to have
oversight for the pastoral care of this area. Since we have
been trying to expand one of the churches and the rectory
in Providenciales, as well as swapping some property for a
new church that could serve the growing tourist population,
I went down there last week for what was probably my last
visitation.

I know what you are thinking! But it really wasn't four
days of sun and surf. I did get to the beach one afternoon
for a couple of hours, but the rest of the time was spent in
meetings with the priests, the government people, and the
lawyers and architects. My reason for devoting this column
to it was the wonder of God's grace in that very lovely part
of his world.

Four years ago, when we took responsibility for the Church
in the islands—there had not been a full-time priest there in
years—you would get fewer than twenty people for Sunday
Mass in Grand Turk, the capital, and another twenty or so
in the largest island, Providenciales. There was no constant
service to the visitors and very little parish life. Last week,

the reason for my concern to expand the church facilities was obvious and wonderful. I confirmed five youngsters in Grand Turk—the largest number in their history—and had more than twenty people for weekday Mass on Providenciales! The Sunday Masses are now standing room only, conversions are taking place, and the young priests are appreciated and making a difference in the life of the islands. They are serving the very poor Haitian community at the same time as they are discovering more and more Catholics among the expatriate community of English and Irish, Americans and Canadians. Before I left Newark, I was able to raise money for a new church near the area where the tourist hotels are located, and we are even wondering about the feasibility of a Catholic school!

How good God is! What a blessing to see this new growth and life in his Church! People are being touched by his grace to come back to the Church or to discover it! Catholics are being catechized and the sacraments administered. The presence of the Church has changed the lives of so many people. I was blessed to be part of it and I come back to Washington hoping that through the apostolic efforts of our own priests and people, we, too, can grow in grace and build on what our great predecessors have established. It is wonderful to see what the Lord will do when he has generous and joyful servants. As I am thinking of you, I know that we have them here at home!

The Church in Washington
March 15, 2001

Can I brag a little? I have gotten to know you somewhat in the past three months, and I really think you're wonderful. Of course, I'm prejudiced. You have all been so extraordinarily welcoming to me. It's even a little embarrassing. I wish I were a better person so I would deserve your remarkable kindness; but time after time in the parishes I visit and the ceremonies I attend, the warmth of your greeting and the joyful reception I receive come pretty close to being overwhelming.

Many people—including bishops—told me that I would meet a very fine presbyterate when I came to Washington, and so indeed it has been. We have so many great priests here, older men who have served the Lord for years and have never lost zeal, men in middle age whose wisdom and vision I treasure, and younger priests filled with a deep love of the Church and their people. I am proud to be one of them, and I know that their prayers sustain me.

Our community of deacons is impressive, too, not just in its numbers but also in the talent and generosity that is so apparent in their service. I have come to love the religious— both women and men—and to thank God for the presence of these consecrated lives and the apostolic work they do among us. Our seminarians are fine young men—and some not so young—all of whom seem happy about their vocations and the mysterious call to priestly ministry that they have received. We need many more of them, as I have been telling you just about every day since I came, but the men we have are good examples and I am glad we have them in our family of faith.

Most of all and best of all—as our priests would surely say—are you, the people of the Archdiocese of Washington. I can sense your love of the Lord and of the Church, your own longing to grow in holiness, and your great respect and affection for all of us whom the Lord has sent to serve you. It makes for a great combination and for a wonderful archdiocese, and I know how blessed and fortunate I am to be here.

I just visited my fifty-second parish last Sunday, thanks to my secretary and the young priests who drive me from time to time. I've come to love Southern Maryland; my first Con-firmation was at St. Michael's Parish in Ridge last week, and I'm fascinated by the beauty of our nation's capital. As I've gotten to know Prince George's and Montgomery Counties better, I almost can find my way on and off the beltway.

All of which is to say that you have really made me feel at home. And you know that now, whatever I'm doing, I'm thinking of you.

A Journey to Saudi Arabia
March 22, 2001

By the time you read this I will hopefully be completing my journey to Saudi Arabia. As you know, I am a member of the US Commission on International Religious Freedom. We have been studying the religious liberties of some of the nations of the world where persecution and discrimination on religious grounds still exists. It is our job to monitor this and then to make recommendations to the US Department of State as to what our own foreign policy should be with regard to these governments.

Saudi Arabia is a case in point. There are millions of very faithful Moslems living there who are really a great witness to their religion. They are very strict in their practice of their faith and take great pride in the fact that the Prophet Mohammed was from that area and began his preaching there. The difficulty is that, up until now, their government has not permitted any other religion to exist legally in that large and important country. It is a crime to celebrate or to attend Mass or any other Christian service. I am hoping to talk to government people in Saudi Arabia to see how these prohibitions can be changed.

Today it is estimated that close to a million Christians live in that nation, all being denied the chance to worship in their own way, according to their own conscience. I am not sure that I will have any success on my mission, but for the sake of all these people, it is important to try. So far, I have some hope since they did issue me a visa. We believe I may be the first Catholic bishop allowed to enter the country precisely as a bishop. Others have gone in dressed in civilian clothes and registering as tourists and the like. My photo on the passport on which they issued the visa makes it clear that I am a priest, so they know I'm coming and, since the commission made the arrangements, they know what I'll be talking about.

Wouldn't it be wonderful if something good could come from this journey? That is in the hands of God, of course, but please pray with me that I will say the right thing in the right way and perhaps make some progress. In the week that I'll be away in Arabia and in the Holy Land, I'll miss going to the parishes to have Mass with you. Even though you don't see me around, however, you know I'll be thinking of you.

Work and Play?
March 29, 2001

I have another confession to make. I have been saying yes to requests too much, too often. Last week, I was really beat and would have given a lot to have had just one day completely free. It's my own fault, of course. I can't blame it on my secretaries who are usually trying to talk me out of things I have agreed to do. The worst part of it is that some of these things I am doing are out of the archdiocese and I get the guilty feeling that I'm not serving you well when I am away.

About ten years ago, I had a conversation with Pope John Paul II when I was archbishop of Newark. I told him that I had accepted several responsibilities outside of the Archdiocese of Newark and that it was bothering me that they were taking so much time. I explained that some were for the bishops' conference, some for public bodies, and some for the Holy See. They were all good things to do—for refugees, for peace, for the poor around the world, and for helping some bishops in difficult areas. The Holy Father then proceeded to give me a truly beautiful meditation about the place of the bishop in his own diocese and how that was the real priority of all our lives.

I was just about to say to him, "Thank you, Holy Father, I will drop all these other things," when he then started to give me an equally beautiful meditation about the bishop's responsibility to the whole world and to the whole Church and not just to his home diocese. After he was finished, we just looked at each other and smiled. I said to him, "Your Holiness, I guess I should just keep doing what I'm doing, then?" Pope John Paul smiled again and shrugged his shoulders and then we moved to another subject.

Of course, I have to admit that my tiredness did go away, thank God. I find so much strength in you, the faithful of the Church of Washington. Over the weekend, my weariness pretty well disappeared as I talked to young adult parish leaders, to several men in their twenties and thirties who are considering a call to priestly vocation, to representatives of Hispanic young people gathering to get ready for a national meeting, and, best of all, to little children in our German-speaking Catholic mission as they were preparing for First Communion. All the events of this last weekend really gave me a wonderful boost, since seeing the faith-filled enthusiasm of all these folks made me more alive and more eager to work hard. I don't have to tell you that I am thinking of you and praying for you every day of the week even when the schedule makes it hard to get all my jobs done as I would want to do them.

Knowing Oneself
April 5, 2001

This may become one of those complicated columns, but it was provoked by something that happened to me on the way back from the Middle East last week. One of these days, when I have fully processed the experiences of my journey to that fascinating part of the world, I'll write you about it all, but this column is just one of the many stories that took place. First of all, I have to give you some background.

Years ago, when I was a young priest, I worked in Latin America. Part of that time, in the late 1960s, while I was president of the Catholic University of Puerto Rico, I was elected to one of the commissions of the International Federation of Catholic Universities that involved a lot of travel "South of the Border" and in those days, the tales of mislaid and misdirected luggage would stand your hair on end. The biggest problems occurred when you had to change planes and the checked baggage was supposed to change with you. Even when the baggage came, the sometimes long wait for checked baggage would drive me "up the wall" since I have always been woefully lacking in patience.

I developed a rule of life for myself: "Wash rather than wait" was my motto. It was better to take the time at night to wash your clothes than to waste a half hour or more for extra suitcases to arrive. (This works for me, but my secretaries found it quite challenging since they had to do the same. In fact, in the days that I could take nieces or nephews with me, it ultimately proved impossible as the young people would exclaim "But it's easy for you. You always wear the same thing!")

To make a long story short, this sometimes resulted—as it did last Thursday when I was leaving the Holy Land—in my carrying very heavy and occasionally somewhat unwieldy luggage. I had gotten through all the controls and the checks with my three pieces of luggage, my ticket, and my passport in my hand, when I tripped getting on the airport bus to the plane. I didn't hurt myself, thank God, except for my dignity, but I didn't realize that I had dropped my passport! When I arrived at my seat and made the usual check of my important articles, I realized that it was gone. What an awful feeling. Although I realized that landing in Newark where I knew so many of the customs and immigration people, they would somehow work it out for me, a passport is such an important document that I was really troubled. What made it worse was that it was my diplomatic passport since the journey was for the Federal Commission on which I serve.

Thank God, the Good Lord takes care of stray dogs and old archbishops, and so it all worked out. The folks at Continental Airlines were great, and I was able to describe where I thought I must have dropped it. They found it and I had it before we took off, but it really set me to thinking.

Socrates, the great Greek philosopher, believed that the real secret of a person's knowledge was his or her ability to know himself or herself truly. He had a saying, "Know thyself," which challenged his disciples to probe deeply into their own personalities and their own fundamental understanding of who they thought themselves to be.

We should be grateful to God that we don't need a document like a passport or an identity card to establish our own identity. Documents like that are important to catalogue our relationship with other people, with the state, or some other important entities, but we are who we are, children of God and of our parents, the products of a multiplication of relationships, some essential and many accidental. The old philosopher was right. We do not make progress on our life's journey without self-knowledge. Socrates may not have understood it perfectly, but self-knowledge begins with understanding our relationship with God and with our neighbors. So you see, during those important moments when I was worrying about my lost passport, I was also thinking of those deeper things and therefore also thinking of you.

Walking in Washington
April 12, 2001

Some of you may know that I lived in Washington many years ago when I studied for my doctorate at Catholic University. You would think that I would know the city and the surrounding area from that earlier time. The fact is that I really didn't get around that much in those days. Beside the courses I had to take at the university, I served as a university chaplain and then as dean of students. In those jobs, you tried to stay pretty much at the service of the young people and so the vast majority of your time was spent on campus. Once every couple of weeks, I would call another priest— a wonderful professor at the university who enjoyed good food—and we would go down to Blackie's House of Beef for dinner. But that was pretty much the sum of my "outside life."

Now that I am back in Washington, I am determined to get a real sense of this great city. Last week I had meetings downtown and found myself with a couple of hours free. I decided to take a walk, and it was the best decision I could have made. What a beautiful city this is! What wonderfully friendly people! I was impressed by the architecture of the buildings and in awe of the cherry blossoms, which had just begun to bud! As I walked down the streets, I was just like a little kid on vacation or a visitor from some foreign land. As I traveled along, I was impressed by the number of people who greeted me, not because they recognized me, but just because I was a priest who smiled at them.

We really have a treasure here. Thank God for it. Oh, I am not naïve. I know we have more than our share of poverty and a lot of people who have no jobs. I am very troubled by the functional illiteracy of too many of our people and by a lot of buildings where families should not have to live. The fact that this area is so beautiful should make us all the more determined to work on these problems, so that the folks who live here could really enjoy this truly special part of the world.

The spring is certainly a wonderful time of year. In spite of those frequent April showers, the sunshine in our parks and traffic circles is a very special gift. This is Easter weather! It is a time to thank God for the gift of a great corner of America and for so many fine families and good people who rejoice in the newness of life that Easter brings. I know it can get very hot here in the summer, and I recognize that a lot of us don't drive too well in the snow, but this is a fine place to live and I am very happy to be here. I hope I'll have more time to walk around town and thus get to know this city better. It will help me to keep on thinking of you.

St. Matthew's Cathedral
April 19, 2001

When I was serving as archbishop of Newark, I was blessed with a truly magnificent cathedral. It was dedicated to the Sacred Heart and so captivated the Holy Father that when he visited in 1995, he raised it to the dignity of a Minor Basilica, just as the National Shrine of the Immaculate Conception here in our city has been so honored. Sacred Heart Basilica is one of the largest churches in America and one of the most beautiful. It can hold three thousand people and it is truly an architectural wonder. I will never forget the great moments of deepest prayer that I experienced there in my fourteen years as servant of the Church of Newark. It is situated at the highest point in Newark, but unfortunately the growth of the city moved in different directions and so it is rarely filled.

The Cathedral of St. Francis in Metuchen, which was my first cathedral as a bishop, also has for me an unforgettable charm and holiness. It had been a large and beautiful parish church until 1981 when the diocese was established and I came as the first bishop. St. Francis Cathedral and I got there together, so it means very much to me. Yet it, too, is located in a smaller community of some fifteen thousand people and not, as we are, in the center of the world!

Here in Washington I have just lived through one of the great Holy Weeks of my life! I am not sure why it was that special. Perhaps it was the music, which was outstanding at every service. Perhaps it was the rhythm and the flow of the liturgy, which in every way taught and proclaimed the presence of God in each celebration. Perhaps it was the people, the faithful of Washington and other prayerful visitors from afar who expressed their love for the Lord and their faith in his loving care by their obvious devotion and respect for the holy actions in which they took part. Perhaps it was the Cathedral of St. Matthew itself, the mother church of this extraordinary Archdiocese of Washington, so awesome in its beauty and grace, so memorable in its history. Whatever it was, I found it quite overwhelming.

Msgr. Jameson, the rector of the cathedral, told me that these were the largest crowds we've ever had. The weather and the cherry blossoms helped to bring folks downtown and the Lord invited them to pray with us. And that they did! In song and sacrament, both in deep prayer and joyful celebration. I want to thank everyone who made it possible, from those who organized and guided the liturgies, to the sacristans and the ushers, without whom it could never have happened. And the Lord. Thank God who is so present and so good, that he invites us to worship, not just individually in the quiet of our hearts, but together as a praying people so that we can take strength from each other and give proper praise.

And worship we did last week. From the Mass of Palm Sunday, Monday's Mass of the Chrism where the sacred oils were blessed for all the parishes in the archdiocese, to our penance service on Tuesday and Tenebrae on Wednesday, and, finally, to the great liturgies of the Easter Triduum, it was really a time of prayer. Thanks be to God for our great cathedral and for all it means and signifies to us and to this Archdiocese of Washington. It is a great gift, not just for me as a priest, but for all of us as faithful people, since every time I go to the altar I take you with me and it is then more than ever that I am thinking of you.

Spring Cleaning
April 26, 2001

How do we collect so much stuff? Every year, spring comes around with its warm breezes and sunny days and its delightful invitation to go for a walk and enjoy the real wonders of God's creation. I get all ready to do that; I may even put on a light windbreaker and head for the door when I pass my office and see the piles of letters and documents I have not yet finished working on or—what is much worse—I pass my little apartment where I live in the Archdiocesan Pastoral Center and see those three boxes of things that I brought down here from New Jersey and have not yet found the time to open, let alone to put carefully away!

Does this happen to you? Every springtime, my conscience gets the better of me and I pledge solemnly to myself that I'll clean up my rooms and put everything in its proper place and finally get organized. Sometimes I even get most of it done. Most times, the summer comes and I am still looking at it with disappointment at my lack of follow-through. I suspect that one or two of you generous people who may be reading this are sympathetic to the point of thinking, "Maybe I'll volunteer to help the archbishop put things away!" I am very grateful for that thought, but it's not going to work, since in my mind I think I know where everything should go, only I don't put it there.

Why do we tend to be so procrastinating? It's not really that we're lazy, I think. Probably it's because time in our world doesn't stop and we are always adding new things to do, to read, to keep. If for a week no mail would come, I could catch up—I tell myself—and organize things in the proper order. But the mail and the faxes and the phone calls keep coming and they reduce my good intentions to nothing. I feel like Dagwood Bumstead in the comic strip, only he gets a chance for a good nap on his couch with some more determined frequency.

Perhaps it is the Lord telling us that we really should not expect to get everything in order here in this life, since this is not the place we will spend eternity! If we are always a little bit unfinished, it reminds us that we are journey men and journey women on this extraordinary road of life that ultimately is meant to lead us to the real peace and order of the Kingdom of God. I'd like to think that, since it helps a little when I consider the awful challenge of spring cleaning and I realize that while putting order in my room is important, it is more important to put order in my life! I am thinking of you as I write this and hoping that you are more successful than I am in meeting both these challenges.

"And How Is Washington?"
May 3, 2001

I think you would be surprised at how often I am asked the question: "How is Washington?" The interesting part of it is that the persons who ask the question range from my relatives to total strangers who meet me on a train and happen to recognize me as a relatively newly arrived resident in our community. Some folks ask to find out what I think about Washington itself—the city, the people, the weather, the politics of it all. Most, however, seem to ask the question to see whether I am settled in and happy here.

The reason I am writing to you on this theme now is that I just returned from a meeting in Rome and even there—except for the Holy Father—just about everyone began a conversation, either in English or Italian, by asking "And how is Washington?" We live in a fascinating part of the world. The district and the nearby counties, both in Maryland and in Virginia, are truly of interest to people in our country and beyond. (Wait until they discover the special magic of Southern Maryland! A lot of people still don't know how beautiful that is.) We are really fortunate to live in a place that conjures up a sense of history being made and decisions that can even change the future of the world. People never seem to tire of wondering about Washington, and even a newcomer like me gets more than a fair share of questions.

If the questioner is asking for the basic information on how beautiful the city and its suburbs are, or how unpredictable its weather and its politics, I try to respond factually, briefly, and with some sense of real satisfaction that I am now part of the population. If the question is probing my own reaction to the welcome I have received here, then I reply—as you already know—with a sense of awe on how wonderfully all of my new neighbors and my new Catholic family have made me feel at home. I tell them about the extraordinary beauty of our churches and the extraordinary faithfulness of our people, of good hard-working priests and exemplary deacons, of prayerful religious and great lay apostles, of how lucky—and blessed—I am to be here and how I hope I'll be able to carry on the work of my great predecessors. After I am finished answering their question, people usually nod their heads and agree that Washington must be a nice place, in spite of what the papers sometimes say!

You know I am very excited about being here—even at seventy! Of course, I haven't gotten through our summer yet and that may make a difference, but I'm hoping to spend a good deal of time then visiting the parishes in Southern Maryland and I look forward to that. So if anyone asks you, how does the archbishop like Washington, you can safely tell them that he has fallen in love with it and with all of you and in fact he's thinking of you all the time.

A Challenging Proposition
May 10, 2001

Have you read the Holy Father's letter on the challenges of this new millennium? I had read it quickly when it first came out at the beginning of this year, but I've started to re-read it carefully since it is truly filled with deep wisdom and a very thoughtful analysis of the years that lie ahead and the opportunities for the Church and for all of us in this new moment in the life of the world. It is not a long document and is rather easy to read. The Latin title, by which these letters are usually known, is *Novo Millennio Ineunte*, which translates as "At the Beginning of the New Millennium."

The first part of the letter reviews the great jubilee that we have all just celebrated, but characteristically Pope John Paul II always looks forward to the years to come and asks us to put into practice new resolutions and to develop new guidance for action in the future. Most of the letter deals with things that are always the concern of this extraordinary man who is our pope. He speaks of the purification of memory, which comes from asking pardon and forgiveness of our failings, not just from God, but from the people around us—especially those who should be closest to us—whom we may have hurt by our actions or our selfishness. He goes on to speak of young people, of those who suffer and those who need to see the face of Christ.

Toward the end of the letter is a rather remarkable statement. I already used it as a major point when I preached to my brother priests and to those gathered at the Chrism Mass last month. It is the place where Pope John Paul II writes of charity. He has just reminded us of the Gospel story of the Lord's identifying himself with the poor. You remember the text from Matthew's Gospel: "I was hungry and you gave me food, thirsty and you gave me drink," etc. What comes next in the Holy Father's letter is very powerful and worth quoting verbatim. He writes, "This Gospel text is not a simple invitation to charity: it is a page of Christology which sheds a ray of light on the Mystery of Christ. By these words, no less than by the orthodoxy of Her doctrine, the Church measures Her fidelity as the Bride of Christ."

That is probably the strongest call to the exercise of charity that I have ever seen. We know how dedicated this Holy Father is to the correct proclamation of the Gospel in keeping with the Church's tradition and teaching. Here he puts the care of the poor as an equal test of our fidelity to the Lord. He tells us that active charity to those in need is as important an element in our response to the Gospel as is the striving for unity in faith. That is a challenging proposition for me, I know, and probably also for you.

Let us meditate on the words of the Holy Father. They truly call us to holiness and service. They will hopefully make a difference in my own life. Pray that I take them to heart. Meanwhile, I promise that I shall do whatever I can to continue to build on the great works of charity founded by my predecessors with all of your generous help. When I see what has already been done and listen to the Holy Father's challenge, of course I am thinking of you.

A Graduation Memory
May 17, 2001

Last Saturday I was privileged to preside at the commencement exercises of The Catholic University of America (CUA). As you may recall, I graduated from the university back in 1963 with my doctorate in sociology. The graduation brought back a number of wonderful memories, some of them very funny. I spoke at last Saturday's exercises and began with a funny story that is still fresh in my memory after almost forty years!

A number of folks were kind enough to comment on the recounting of this somewhat embarrassing tale of long ago and mentioned that they had enjoyed it. I thought that I would share it with you, too, so that you might enjoy it also. It is a story that I remember somewhat vividly and it did have a happy ending.

It goes back to a CUA graduation, probably in 1964 or 1965. Lyndon Johnson was president of the United States at that time and he had been invited to address the graduates and to receive an honorary degree. At that time I was dean of students at the university and therefore I had a reasonably good place on the dais as a member of the administration. Graduations in those days were held in the gymnasium and the faculty and members of the university staff would sit in bleachers at the far end of that great hall. As a matter of fact, I was sitting two rows behind the president. I had never met a president of the United States before and this was an enormously exciting opportunity—or so I felt. When President Johnson finished his talk and went back to his seat a few rows in front of me, all those who were sitting around him shook his hand and congratulated him. I wanted to do the same thing and so I reached down two rows and congratulated him with a firm handshake too.

The only problem was that I lost my balance and, as I almost fell, took two or three of the more important members of the faculty with me. I will never forget the look of surprise on the president's face as three very distinguished university administrators or faculty all began to topple off their places in the makeshift bleachers. The surprise on his face was nothing compared to the looks of chagrin and disapproval that I got from the rest of the university administration, and in a special way from those faculty members who came close to losing their footing. The only one who didn't give me a dirty look was the chancellor, Cardinal O'Boyle, who just looked, shook his head, and laughed. He was certainly a great chancellor and I hope that I can measure up to his ability to roll with the flow as he did on that day almost forty years ago.

I thought it would be fun to share that funny story with you. It did bring back some fond memories of my days at the university when I served as chaplain and then as dean of students and then finally as assistant to the rector for development. That was in my first life in Washington and now that I am back here, a lot of those memories come back with real joy and a sense of belonging. I am very proud to be an alumnus of Catholic University. It is an extraordinary institution and in its history it has provided leadership to our nation and our Church in a very special way. I am honored to serve as its chancellor.

At the graduation last Saturday they mentioned that I am only the second chancellor to be an alumnus of the university and that pleases me very much. It is one of the responsibilities that the archbishop of Washington assumes when he takes on the service of this local Church. I do it with some awe because of the extraordinary contributions that the former archbishops have made. Cardinal Hickey in a special way was so wonderfully faithful to the university in his long years of service here. I pray that I can also make a contribution to the life of the university in cooperation with its excellent leadership and its very strong faculty. For me, it is a special joy to walk along the paths of that beautiful campus and to see the growth that this important university has had since my days here as a young priest.

All these opportunities for old reminiscences are, of course always joined to the wonderful blessing now of thinking of you.

Reading, Writing, and Life
May 24, 2001

Can I go back to my visit to Saudi Arabia once more? This time it is just to make a point. I have had this experience before, and I want to use it as background for what I would like to talk about today. Usually I'm pretty good at languages. At least I can usually figure out the street signs and the instructions on forms and notices. Even in places that use the Cyrillic alphabet like Russia, with a little extra work I can make out in general what the signs are saying. Unfortunately, I cannot read Arabic. It was always one of my hopes that some day I could learn that fascinating language. Well, it hasn't happened so far and I can't even read it.

The feeling of hopelessness when you can't read a street sign or a traffic indication is a real one for someone like me who always likes to be able to work things out. There is no "figuring it out," only the sense of gratitude that the taxi driver or the person who came to pick me up will know the way. I can't tell where I am from the signs. I can't even tell where I'm going! I'm lucky since when I travel there is usually someone who meets me and knows the way, but it would be very difficult if that were not the case.

All of this is a way of saying that not being able to read and write is both a great cross and a great handicap. It has to affect the way we think, the way we deal with other people, and the way we plan our lives. There are thousands of people in our area who can't read or write. I'm not speaking about children, but adults. They have jobs but their choices are always so limited in finding a livelihood. They are always at a disadvantage. They can't pass a test for a driving license; they can't always decipher an ad in the paper; they can't pick up a bible or a prayer book and find consolation and strength.

They often have to rely on their children to read and write for them, children who are sometimes embarrassed to admit to others that their mom or dad can't read.

We really have to try to do something to help them. I'm not sure how we would go about developing new literacy programs for the area we serve, but I really believe that it would be a good and necessary thing to do. Here in the Archdiocese of Washington we have so many facilities—parishes, schools, Catholic Charities agencies, and the like. There have to be many ways in which we can help make life better for those neighbors of ours who may be brilliant in so many ways but somehow never learned to read or write. The United States has one of the lowest illiteracy rates among the countries of the world and this is a blessing. We should try to erase illiteracy altogether, so that a new world of learning and experience can open up for all our neighbors. Thinking of them and thinking of you, I truly believe that this would be a great thing to do.

Using Time Well
May 31, 2001

I just had a couple of days without a schedule! I returned to Washington early to attend the funeral of a very remarkable man. Bill Abell was a very special person. A wonderful husband and father, an outstanding leader in our community, and a man of devout faith, he made a difference in the lives of thousands of people in our area and through his kindness and his vision he made an enormous contribution to the life of the Church. To be present at his funeral, I changed my travel plans and found myself with a couple of days without a schedule.

Now I always remind myself—and the poor secretaries who have to put up with me—that many of the saints made vows never to waste time and therefore that is a model and a good example for all of us. But even after I added Masses in six of our parishes and caught up—somewhat—with all the paperwork, I still had time left over. I knew what I had to do. The awful specter of spring cleaning rose up to accuse me. My rooms at the Archdiocesan Pastoral Center were a mess. There were things that I brought with me from New Jersey that I still had not put away. There were even three boxes on the floor, never opened since January.

I am really embarrassed to admit all of this. The only reason that I can present in my defense is that I suspect that several of you who read this column may even possibly have had the same experience once or twice in your lives. It is not laziness, I tell myself. It's just that there are so many things to do, and—I also tell myself—before I start arranging my things, I need to figure out where everything will go. Well, you must know from experience that such a plan is totally unrealistic. Neither you nor I can ever remember what is in those boxes, let alone figure out where to put them. So in the hopelessness of it all, I usually just put it off. The fact that we are all so busy helps us to rationalize that decision over and over again.

Well, this time—since spring is almost over—I forced myself to open all the boxes and to take the contents out. Some things, like a couple of clocks and some framed pictures, I could immediately put in a proper place. Others, like presents I bought on a trip to give to my nieces and nephews, I could transfer to another box and plan on bringing that collection to them one of these days. But there were those other things—things I haven't looked at for years—that brought back many memories or papers whose contents I had forgotten and which now on reading them take a lot of time to digest and clarify.

The few hours I had so cleverly put aside to put my room in order rapidly disappeared and left—you know what I am going to say now—a bigger mess than I had before, since now I did not have just some boxes on the floor, but half a floor covered with what was in the boxes! I confess that the last state is worse than the first! One of my secretaries advised me to throw all those things away—but you all know that no scavenger like I am could ever do such a thing. I'll just have to find another block of time to get it finished. I am afraid that it will have to be called "autumn cleaning" now!

Getting a room fixed up and in order is a good thing. Getting one's life in order is even better! I pray that you and I will learn from the awesome process of spring cleaning how right it is to organize our lives according to rules and standards and values that last. We know that God loves each one of us, even with all our faults and that in the midst of our uncertainties and our confusion, He is always thinking of you and me and giving us the strength to put our lives in order.

The Mystery of God's Providence
June 7, 2001

As I reflected on my ordination as a priest forty-three years ago last week, I remembered one of the prayer cards I had distributed on that occasion. It cited a mysterious reference from the Gospel of John that compared the Holy Spirit to the wind, whose direction can change suddenly without warning and without our knowing why. The role of the Holy Spirit in our lives and in the lives of those we love can sometimes seem like that.

There is a beautiful text in the Old Testament that reminds us that we can never here on earth fully read the mind of God nor can we ever presume to be his counselor. The mystery of good and evil, the old and deep uneasiness when bad things happen to good people, the whole story of sickness, natural disaster, and sin—all of this brings into striking focus the mystery of divine providence, the awesome realization that there are things that we will never really understand in this life.

How important it is then that we keep our sights on the Lord and that we never close our ears to his good news? When we pass through the shadows of darkness in our own lives or behold that awful passage in the lives of those we love, we can never forget the blessed assurance that God does indeed love us and that, as Saint Paul teaches us so well, for those who love the Lord, all things turn out for good. Sometimes we cannot see how this is possible because we watch with human eyes and judge with only mortal understanding. Wait a little while, and we will see God's hand in all of these things and trust that ultimately he does wipe all the tears from our eyes and leads us to become the happy people he has created us to be.

God's ways are not our ways, as scripture tells us. It is hard enough trying to read the signs of the times, let alone to fathom the mind of God. Let this be enough for us—that we know he loves us with an everlasting love and that his will toward us is only for our good and never for our harm. If we can always hang on to that truth, then the roiling waters of confusion will never reach us and we can rest secure on the rock of refuge where he places us to escape the storms of this life.

As I look back on the long years of my priesthood, I recognize the innumerable times when the Lord delivered me from evil and held me in the palm of his hand. How grateful I am for all those times of his special presence in my life. You have them too! Rejoice in them and thank the Lord for them. He does love you, and you can always be sure that not a moment goes by when he is not thinking of you.

Maybe
June 14, 2001

Ever since I was a seminarian (back in the days before electricity it seems!) I have tried to be dedicated to the promotion of vocations. At St. Joseph's Seminary in Dunwoodie, where I studied for the priesthood in the New York archdiocese, a few of us started a vocation guild, which published a newsletter on vocations and organized vocation days and visits to the seminary. As a young priest, and especially when I was chaplain at The Catholic University of America in the 1960s, that was one of the programs in which I was always deeply involved. Twenty years ago, when I first became a diocesan bishop, I started more seriously asking youngsters whether they thought that God was calling them to the priesthood or to the religious life.

In the early days of that questioning, I would probably get most young people to laugh and say no. Their parents were even sometimes annoyed at me for asking. Over the years, that changed somewhat and I started to get "maybe" as an answer from the young people and less of an objection from their parents. To each one who said "maybe," I always replied: "That's wonderful because God can work with a maybe. He just can't work with a no."

Here in Washington, I am amazed at the difference. So many young men will tell me that they have thought or are thinking about priesthood, and more young women than ever will smile and say "maybe" when I ask about religious life. If the youngsters are still in their teens and with their parents when the question is asked, I'm overwhelmed at the fact that so many parents will say "That would be wonderful" or "We are praying for that!" What a grace for Washington! What an extraordinary blessing for our archdiocese that we have people of faith like these young men and women and in a special way like those parents and families.

Last Saturday, at our truly imposing Cathedral of St. Matthew's, I had my first ordination to the priesthood as servant of this local Church. It was, as it always is, a moment of grace for me and a blessing for the future of this archdiocese. Four men were ordained, as you will read elsewhere in this *Catholic Standard*—good, prayerful men, full of zeal and joy at their new opportunity to serve God and to call their brothers and sisters to holiness and peace. But you know that I have already buried four priests this year and several will be retiring because of age or illness. We need forty new priests, not just four!

Pray with me for vocations. Encourage those in your families and your parishes. The forty potential seminarians are out there! In many cases, they already know that God is calling them. Pray that his voice is heard above the competing noises of the world. It is a life of challenge, of course, but it is also a life that, if lived deeply in the spirit of Jesus, can open the door to a relationship with Jesus like no other and a chance to serve God's people in a way that can give such fulfillment and peace. To those who are hearing God's call, even if it be ever so softly, when I pray for vocations, I am thinking of you!

A New Name
June 21, 2001

You may recall reading that just twenty years ago, I was sent by the Holy Father to establish a new diocese in Central New Jersey. The seat of the diocese was Metuchen, a small but centrally located town with a beautiful and large parish church which then became the cathedral. Well, a couple of weeks ago, they invited me back to celebrate my being named as archbishop of Washington and becoming a cardinal. I went with joy because you never forget your first love and my memories of those early years are still fresh in my mind.

When I went to Metuchen in 1981 as its first bishop, I had already served for four years as auxiliary to the servant of God, Cardinal Terence Cooke. He was a gentle, prayerful man who loved people and who guided the complex Church of New York with skill and dedication for fifteen years until he died of cancer in his early sixties. I learned much from him. How I wished I had learned even more! Metuchen was a wonderful challenge for me. In the four and a half years I served there, thirty-three new priests were ordained, five congregations of religious entered the diocese, and the lay people found a sense of unity that really brought the different parts of the diocese together. When I was transferred to Newark in 1986, I left Metuchen with a large piece of my heart still there.

The ceremony at the Cathedral of St. Francis was therefore really wonderful. I was amazed—and so pleased—that every seat in the cathedral was taken, that seventy-five priests were present, and that the Diocesan Festival Choir, which I started twenty years ago, was at the top of its form. Toward the end of the Mass, however, something happened that will make this "homecoming day" always unforgettable for me.

Bishop Vincent Breen, my second successor, announced that St. Mary's High School in South Amboy would now be called Cardinal McCarrick High School! I have never allowed anyone to name anything after me, but this time no one asked me, so I had nothing to say about it. I always felt that there were better names you could choose and that sometimes a naming opportunity can honor a major benefactor.

When I thanked the bishop and the people, I only made one comment. I told them that I could see the headlines in the high school sports pages and they terrified me. Imagine reading that "All Saints defeat McCarrick" or even worse, "Cardinal McCarrick overcome by Holy Spirit," or even still worse, "McCarrick best not good enough for Our Lady of Mercy"! Oh well, it will all work out. I was really honored and I just hope that those high school students don't mind the change. (I wonder what they'll call their teams now.) I'll have to follow all their games, of course, but not to worry, I'll still be thinking of you.

Time Out?
June 28, 2001

Last week, I actually heard someone say "It's almost July and the summer is already half over!" What a chilling thought that was. I haven't even finished planning my vacation! Of course, planning a vacation is probably at least half the fun. To put the calendar in front of you and to weigh those seemingly infinite possibilities of time away from work and responsibility—what a "neat thing" that would be, as the youngsters of my generation would likely say.

When I was a boy living in New York City, the dream vacation was a couple of weeks at the beach. For us, the beach was either Asbury Park or the Jersey Shore or, when things got a little better financially, a rental bungalow in Long Beach on the south shore of Long Island. For an eight-year-old, the train ride to Long Beach was already a great adventure. We didn't have to worry about missing our station since Long Beach was right on the ocean and the train couldn't go any farther.

I recall that when I was twelve, the family had a chance to buy that bungalow, but the outlay of cash—I think it was a thousand dollars—seemed too risky and we never had a chance to be real "property owners"! I learned how to swim—not too well—and to ride a bike down there. I made friends, and we went to the movies a lot. I remember *Robin Hood* was the great adventure film one of those summers. After the two or three weeks were over, it was back to the hot city again, but always with those great memories of a time at the beach.

It is good to get away, even for a few days, just for a change of pace, a break in the schedule, a chance to breathe, to smell the flowers, as they say. Workaholics like me—I like to think that I am a happy workaholic—will insist that they don't need the time off, but we know we do and are often too locked into a pattern of work to pull ourselves away. I do like to work, to see all the papers on the desk diminish, to hold out the dream that some day I'll be all caught up. In my heart, I confess that that will never happen, because each day brings its own share of new challenges and new adventures and I'll never really be totally up to date.

So this summer, I will take a vacation. It won't be overwhelming since I just promised some bishop friends to go for part of it to the Balkans to try to help them in their efforts for peace and stability. But it will be a few days in Southern Maryland and a few days at the Jersey Shore. I'm really looking forward to it, even though I know that the papers will be there in greater numbers waiting to greet me when I get back. I'm just not going to think about them when I'm away. As a matter of fact, I'll try not to think of the office at all—but whatever happens, don't worry, I'll still be thinking of you.

Rainy Weather
July 5, 2001

There was always one rainstorm that I could never forget. It was not one of those scary hurricanes that I experienced in the tropics, but one memorable one that occurred on October 5, 1995, in East Rutherford, New Jersey. It was the day of the pope's Mass at Giants' Stadium, and since it was in the Archdiocese of Newark, I was the host. We had already been preparing for that historic visit for months and the great stadium was packed to a record crowd of eighty-seven thousand! Cardinals and bishops, priests and religious, deacons and their wives, representatives from every parish in the Archdiocese of Newark, together with some forty thousand people from all the other dioceses of New Jersey, were all there—and early since they had to be in place a couple of hours before the Holy Father came.

About an hour before he arrived, the rains began. I had never experienced more steady heavy rain in my life. It lasted all through the Mass and everyone was soaked. The great part of it was that no one left! They sang, they cheered, they prayed. It was a wonderful moment of faith for the Archdiocese of Newark, and the Holy Father has always remembered it too. It was my most historic rainstorm—until last Friday!

As you know, I was just in Rome for a few days to receive the pallium last week—as well as to take possession of the ancient and historic Basilica of Saints Nereus and Achilleus, my titular church as a cardinal. The Mass of the Pallium was to take place in the evening of the great Solemnity of Saints

Peter and Paul. All day the clouds and the sunshine were fighting a pleasant duel to take over the sky. It was a nice day, all in all, and the sometimes-overcast sky had kept down the heat. There were some thirty-six archbishops who were going to receive the pallium. (You will see me wearing it at major celebrations in the archdiocese. It is a type of wool collar worn around the neck as a symbol of the authority of a metropolitan archbishop, as well as a sign of our local Church's unity with the Church of Rome.) By the time we arrived at St. Peter's Basilica for the Mass, a few drops were falling. Just a sun shower, we all said. It will keep us cool.

By the time the procession formed, it was spitting large drops on our miters and vestments. By the time we reached the altar and went to our assigned seats in the open air, it was a deluge! The red vestments we were wearing were brand new and they bled their color over our white albs and in some cases even down to our white shirts. Since your archbishop thinks he is smart, I had tucked my new white miter under my chasuble to keep it more or less dry. When I took it out to put it on a few minutes later, I found to my chagrin that it was now half red! Umbrellas were rushed out to us, but it seems that they only succeeded in collecting water. I was on the lower side of the upper square and the rainwater came rushing across the pavement at my shoes, covering them at times because of the density of the sudden downpour. It kept up for a half hour and then the clouds rolled away, leaving the almost two score of new archbishops looking like a poster for a clothing drive!

The good part of it is that I will never forget it. And since it was one of those special moments when I carried you all—priests, deacons, religious, and laity—in my prayers, my mind, and my heart, you shared that memorable experience, without ever getting wet! Receiving the pallium from the hands of the Holy Father—as I did fifteen years ago when I became archbishop of Newark—is always a special moment.

I'm always very much filled with a humbling sense of not being the best person for this responsibility and praying for the confidence that God will give me the grace to do it well. And because you are the ones for whom I carry this charge, I'm always thinking of you.

"O" Negative
July 12, 2001

Did you know that one type of blood is the most useful to have if you are a blood donor? It's blood type O negative, and it is called the universal donor because just about anybody can receive it in a transfusion. Actually, that's the blood type I have. It is probably very fitting because bishops should be able to take care of everyone anyway. After one donation a couple of years ago, the folks who were conducting the blood drive in New Jersey gave me a tee shirt that had the O negative symbol on it and read "O's are very compatible!" I've always liked that idea. To be able to help everybody, to be able to reach everyone, and to be able to share their hopes and dreams, their pains and problems—that's the work of a priest in a very special way. So being "compatible" really seems to say a lot to what I ought to try to become.

In a more down-to-earth sense, I'm writing about blood donations this week since I've been reading about a shortage that hospitals and blood banks are facing in our own area. It really seems to be a serious shortage and I wanted to call your attention to it in this column. I try to give blood several times a year. The body replenishes the supply, as you know, so that within a few weeks you are back to normal again—and you have the opportunity to do so much good.

There is a special sense of doing something very worthwhile in giving your blood for a blood drive. You never know who is being helped by your donation, but you are sure that somewhere a brother or sister in this great human family of ours is getting a chance for recovery—or even for life—because of something you did. I'm a fast bleeder and so it takes me less than a quarter of an hour to donate a pint of blood, and that small gift of time can actually mean a lifetime of new health or survival for another person. Thank God, I've never needed a transfusion, but if I ever did, I know how grateful I would be that someone made it possible for me by their donation.

I would like to encourage our parishes and institutions to consider the possibility of having a blood drive during the year, especially around those times of greater shortage, such as the holidays and the summer when people are so busy with other things. I would also like to encourage you individually to give thought to making a blood donation yourself. Someone who is interested can always contact the American Red Cross at 1-800-GIVE-LIFE (1-800-448-3543) or the blood bank in one of our hospitals. I know that as your bishop I must concentrate on your spiritual health, but for those who can do this, a blood donation can be a great corporal work of mercy as well as the gift of life. So you see, even when I read about physical health, I'm still thinking of you.

Thoughts on Vacation
July 19, 2001

The very fact that I am writing this on my vacation underlines the point that I want to make in today's column. I am sitting in my car at the side of a country road waiting for one of our priests, who is driving in from Washington to join me for a couple of days. So far everybody has missed the turn, so I figured I would stay at the crossroads and signal him when he drives up. I needed to find a little quiet time anyway, since I didn't want the week to go by without writing you and this seemed a good time to do it.

I'm in Southern Maryland, that magic land of which I am always talking! I love Washington. I truly believe that it is one of the most beautiful cities in America. I am fascinated by the burgeoning towns of Prince George's County and the near and far suburbs of Montgomery, but I have never really had a great amount of rural territory to serve as a bishop, and the rivers and streams, the forests and rolling hills of this part of the archdiocese are very special to me. Then, too, I am very conscious of the important history of this part of the Church in our country. In Newark, my oldest parish dated to the 1820s and yesterday I stopped in to pray at St. Francis Xavier in Newtowne, where a parish had already existed for a century and a half before that! You all know these things, of course, but for me, since I love history, it is all rather wonderful.

The weather has been great and the house where I am staying with some priest friends—due to the kindness of a Catholic family from the area—is a perfect place to get away. The only problem is that I can't stay more than four days. The archbishop of Washington tends to become involved in so many things that I can't seem to escape for too long. (I really fear that it is because my predecessors were not only holier and wiser men than I will ever be, but also much better administrators!) Part of my problem is that I have gotten to know too many people in the jobs I have had over the years.

When I was at the consistory in Rome a couple of months ago, some of the bishops from the Balkans, where the situation continues to be so difficult, insisted that I come stay with them so they could show me all their problems. I guess I should have said "no," but I haven't learned to do that quite yet. So, as you read these lines, I'll be in Sarajevo, Kosovo, or Albania instead of sitting back and fishing in one of the great backwaters of the Potomac. I'll try to find a week to get away again later in the summer, but I really believe that we pass this way but once—as the poets say—and we all have to do what we can for others while we're here. (Or maybe it's just that I can't say "no" yet.)

So please pray for my journey and thank God with me for these four great days of a less hectic life. I hope our priests don't give up on me. I think they know that I'll work as hard as I can in the years that God gives me. If only I could develop the eight-day week or the fourteen-month year, what great adventures I would undertake! Failing that, I'll do the best I can and keep thinking of you.

Traffic in People
July 26, 2001

Sometimes when I write to you, it is on light subjects or even on the funny things that happen in my life. Other times I need to tell you about problems that I encounter in my work or on my travels that I want to share with you to raise your own conscience or to enlist your help in solving a problem that faces our society. Today I am writing about one of those more serious themes.

I have always been troubled by the trafficking in human lives that goes on in some parts of the world. In fact, I made it a major point in my talk last month at the National Press Club luncheon. As I travel in the Balkans this week at the request of the bishop, I have become more and more aware of this terrible crime against the dignity of human beings, especially women and children.

In many countries of the world, particularly in the poorer countries of Asia and Eastern Europe, women and children are lured into a life of abject servitude by unscrupulous criminals who promise them glamorous and well-paying jobs through which they can escape grinding poverty and earn enough money to help their families back home. Unfortunately for them, these jobs do not exist, and by the time they find that out, they are in a foreign land without money or friends and with their so-called employment agent holding their passport as a guarantee that they will repay the enormous amount of money he claims to have advanced to pay for their transportation and his services.

You can imagine the jobs he finds for them and the circumstances in which they must live and work. It is really a life of slavery and it is estimated that thousands of people are trapped in it in Western Europe and in the Middle East—and perhaps on our own continent too! Sometimes it is fostered by corrupt politicians and/or police officials, but it is a growing problem, and the United Nations and the governments of the nations that are involved must come to grips with it before more thousands of lives are ruined. Three things must be done.

First, there must be laws with teeth in them directed against this dehumanizing traffic in people and they must be enforced with vigor. Secondly, in the countries where these young people are being recruited, government must sound the alarm and not allow these criminal entrepreneurs to exercise this callous trade. They must become more active in developing a campaign of information so that families become aware of the trap into which their children are being lured. Finally, religious groups and faith communities must organize so they can reach out to women who do find an escape from this form of slavery and give them a safe place where they can be secure from the criminals who have abused them and be prepared to start a new life either back in their own country or in the place where they are now.

Somehow we must galvanize our own public officials to be aware of this growing problem that harms so many women's lives and move our own country into taking the leadership in the abolition of this new form of slavery. Thinking of you and your deep respect for the dignity of every human person, I wanted you to reflect on this challenge with me.

Doors That Close and Open
August 2, 2001

By God's grace and your very warm and gracious welcome, I have now served in Washington for seven months. Sometimes it seems to me that I have always been here and other times it seems that it is only a few days since I arrived. Up until last week, there was a constant note that reminded me of my roots as a bishop in New Jersey; something that continued to draw me back from time to time to the Archdiocese of Newark, where I had served so long. That constant note was the fact that no one yet had been appointed to take pastoral care of that local Church. Therefore, my links with it—although now only in affection—were still very prominent in my mind.

I tell our priests the funny stories of my slips in talking about our own archdiocese by referring to it unconsciously as the "Archdiocese of Newark." The worst of these slips came when, by force of habit, I told our four newly ordained priests after their ordination last June that I was giving them "the priestly faculties of the Archdiocese of Newark"! It was only when I saw the surprised look on their faces that I realized my blooper. The priests of Washington probably understand what a challenge this is, because it has to be hard for them to pray for me in the Eucharistic Prayer of the Mass after they had become so used to mentioning the name of Cardinal Hickey, who served them and you with such love and effectiveness over a score of years.

Well now that door has closed, and in the appointment of Archbishop Myers, the Church of Newark starts another chapter in its long life. The priests of that local Church must become accustomed to praying for their Bishop John after fifteen years of praying for Theodore. Archbishop Myers is a good man, very warm and gracious, and very articulate. He will be a great teacher of his people and a good brother to his priests. A new door opens for them and, since all of us are different, a new opportunity for the loving service of God's people.

Do I miss New Jersey still sometimes? I would be dishonest if I said I never do. But as you know, I have really been overwhelmed by the welcome of our priests and people and I have really fallen in love with the Church of Washington. Not only am I inspired by the obvious life of fidelity of so many of our parishes and by the hard-working spirit of unity and friendship among our priests, but even the weather since I came has been milder and friendlier than I remember in my days here as a student priest. And, since my father's family had its roots in Virginia, in a sense I am really coming home!

Please pray for Archbishop Myers as he accepts the responsibility of leading the Church of Newark, and don't ever forget to pray for me as this door of service and opportunity opens wider for us all and together we dedicate ourselves with ever greater love and generosity to build up the Church of Washington, to serve and protect the poor and the vulnerable, to proclaim the good news and to walk together with Jesus in the years ahead. Now that there is no reason for me to be concerned about anyone else, you know that I'll be spending all my time thinking of you.

Growing Up
August 9, 2001

I was a bit embarrassed last week after the extraordinary full center-piece coverage of Uncle's Day! I'm not sure that anyone, except my relatives and friends, would be interested in the goings-on of my extended family. The pictures were great—as one would expect from a real professional like Michael Hoyt—and the commentary was excellent—as a first-class editor and reporter like Mark Zimmermann can produce. Both of them were a most pleasant addition to the gathering and were very popular, especially with the kids, who love to have their pictures taken, and who gave their names and ages to the "press" with great gravity and care. I was surprised by the number of folks whom I met over the last few days who said: "When are you going to write about the children?" and so I'll do it today.

We have been having Uncle's Day since I turned fifty and it has been a grace and a wonder to watch all these little girls and boys growing up! I am sure that many of our families in the Archdiocese of Washington have similar gatherings, so what I am going to say will hopefully strike a familiar note. For me these events are special.

First of all, they keep me in touch with my roots. I really don't get to see and visit with my natural family very much. Ever since I was named a bishop almost twenty-five years ago, 99 percent of my life has been with the spiritual families that God has given me to serve. You are my family now and I can never forget that! Any success I will have in my life from now on will be measured on how well I can call you to holiness, how clearly I can proclaim—and live—the good news of our savior, how nearly my life can become even a shadow of his loving and caring providence for all of you. That's a very big order, and once in a while it helps to step back and take stock of what you are and who you are, and moments like Uncle's Day can help to do just that.

Secondly, on the human side, I get a special joy at seeing the little ones grow up. You know how fast they change, not just in size and intelligence, but in personality too. One grand-nephew who was the hardest one to deal with at two and three, now at four has become my best friend. One grand-niece who, as a young child, thought her great-uncle to be a great hero, now as a preteen has already developed other interests and gives me just a demure "Hello." Do your families have youngsters like that too? I wouldn't be surprised. Growing up is a mystery, but also a wonderful, entrancing, somewhat scary part of life.

Perhaps, most of all, the greatest joy is seeing the little kids of yesterday grow up and become such remarkable parents today. Where did they get that patience, that painstaking attention to others' needs, that heroic spirit of loving, joyful service that we often looked for in vain when they were teenagers? When I see them with their own children, they are so wonderful. What a grace God gives to mothers and fathers! It always makes me want to try harder as, thinking of you, I know how blessed I am to serve you.

Seminarians
August 16, 2001

You know how I am always talking about vocations to the priesthood and the religious life. Well, this week I want to bring you some positive news. Now I don't want you to think that we are in any way out of the woods. That is really a long way ahead. Yet I did have a good meeting with all our seminarians last Saturday as they gathered for a day of prayer and orientation at Our Lady of Mattaponi, our retreat camp in southern Prince George's County. The numbers were not enough to satisfy our needs, although thanks to the opening of our new archdiocesan missionary seminary, we did go up 10 percent over last year, but the quality of these young men is impressive and their willingness to serve is obvious.

The most interesting thing about them is that like the priests of the Archdiocese of Washington whom, please God, they will join in caring for the pastoral needs of our people, they are all so very different. I think that is a good message for any young man who is thinking about a priestly vocation. God calls all types of people and men of many different personalities and backgrounds. It would be wrong to think that only a certain type of person could be called by God to serve his people.

Washington has always attracted seminarians from different parts of our country and that is still true today. Many of these new candidates were born and brought up elsewhere but came to this area for college or postgraduate studies or to work for the government or in the military, or because they had relatives who had settled here and they liked the atmosphere and the pace of our part of the country. The majority of our new seminarians now, however, have their roots here within the district or in Maryland, and so very often it was the example of one of our own priests who helped them to realize their vocation.

There are lawyers among them and former teachers and coaches, converts to the faith, and some who have been touched by the new movements that the Holy Spirit has stirred up in the Church today. Some were outstanding athletes; some had distinguished military service behind them. They are accountants, businessmen, and recent graduates, as well as men in their second careers. They are all shapes and sizes—but I note with real thankfulness that they are all making a determined effort to get and stay fit. I tell them constantly that the priesthood needs men who are healthy and can serve with singular zeal and enthusiasm the needs of God's people here in the archdiocese.

I am grateful to Father Bill Parent, our vocation director, and to the priests who work with him, in helping these men to discern God's call and to commit themselves so generously to the preparation for his ministry. I realize that each and every one of them will not continue to priestly ordination, but I know that whatever happens in their lives, the years in a seminary will be worthwhile as an opportunity to come closer to God and to build up a deep spirit of prayer and personal generosity.

I am very proud of our seminarians. You can be too. Please pray for them that God will strengthen their vocation and multiply their numbers. The future of our Church depends so much on an increase in priestly and religious vocations. When I am thinking of you and of our need to serve you in the years ahead, that is foremost in my mind and prayers.

Diet Crabs
August 23, 2001

Someone will have to invent diet crabs! Wandering around Southern Maryland this month is a wonderful grace for me. The people are so very warm and welcoming and love to share the great history of this area with travelers. I have already met folks whose ancestors came to America on the *Ark* and the *Dove,* the two sailing vessels that brought the first settlers to our New World in the early seventeenth century. The story of the development of the Church in the colony of Maryland is a fascinating one. It is filled with all the adventures of a new land and made more remarkable by the role it played in the beginning of Catholic life here. It is a history of sunlight and shadows and, since it is our history, it has become very special to me.

As you know, all this travel is situated within the framework of celebrating Mass in all our churches, visiting our Catholic communities, and getting to know our priests better. I finished Calvert County last week. (Of course, that was easy since we have only five parishes there.) During the next few days, I'll have visited just about every parish in Southern Maryland. Each one has its own special charm and story, and the people are rightfully so proud of what they have. The Catholics of Southern Maryland are not without their dreams, too, as they long for more educational opportunities for their children, and as they prepare to welcome their future and whatever changes it may bring. I believe that they take me on my word that this part of the Archdiocese of Washington will always be a special priority for me as I try to serve the entire length and breadth of our local Church.

There is a major highway in this area called Three Notch Road. I firmly believe that the notches in the name have to do with the notches on a man's belt after dining here a lot! As a result of this travel and the genuine hospitality of our people, my own belt needs to yield at least another notch, and I wonder, where are the diet crabs? I have had crab dishes from crab dip to crab cakes and everything in between, all of them delicious and all of them impossible to turn down. There is Diet Coke and diet vegetables, diet bread, and even diet pasta. Someone has to develop diet crabs before I have to go out and buy a new pair of pants!

It's really not my fault that the cooks are so good and the crabs so delicious. I know that part of my problem is lack of exercise and another part is that I just eat too much. But the food down here—crabs, stuffed ham, oyster stew—really strains a man's willpower and brings me back to the table again and again. And I didn't even mention the sausages!

Obviously, it's not only the food that makes this part of the world a delight. It's the scenery and the water, the people and the history too. As you drive from parish to parish and visit churches that were standing before this great nation was born, there is a sense of awe mixed with gratitude for our courageous forebears in the faith. As in so many things, we reap the rewards of their labors. Thinking of you as I journey, I pray that your faithfulness and mine will be an encouragement for those who come after us in the years that lie ahead.

Our Catholic Schools
August 30, 2001

I suspect that the only columns you all remember are the funny ones and, of course, I get a special joy over that. From time to time, however, I need to bring some more serious themes to your attention if I am really to be faithful to the promise I made to you and to all the people of the Archdiocese of Washington back in January when I was installed. Today I want to talk about Catholic education and more specifically about our Catholic schools.

When I was a youngster, back in the Dark Ages it sometimes seems, the majority of our Catholic girls and boys were able to get a rather solid Catholic elementary school education. Thanks to the unbelievable commitment and quality of our women religious and the equally heroic dedication of the lay teachers who joined them, the parochial school was a miracle to behold. It was built by the nickels and dimes of parishioners who were almost always just working-class people and these were both parishioners who had no children in the schools as well as those who did. The parish community took enormous pride in the school and rightly so when we look back at the myriad of its alumni who have made a place for themselves in the world.

The parochial school of the 1930s and 1940s was not without its difficulties and its problems, of course. My first grade class had seventy pupils in it. We sat three to a bench and when we sang out our alphabet or our addition tables, the sound would drown out any teacher trying to give lessons in the neighboring classrooms. The teachers were often without certification or experience, but somehow they got the message across and we did learn. I was one of those youngsters who never really liked school. Even now, so many decades after, when the autumn comes I can still feel that awkward melancholy about losing the freedom of the summer. But the lessons we all learned there have survived during life. We learned reading, writing, and arithmetic and in the atmosphere of a Catholic school, we also learned about God and faith and goodness and how to treat our neighbors—as well as how to accept responsibility for ourselves.

I truly believe in our Catholic schools here in the Archdiocese of Washington, both those in the inner cities and those in our suburbs and rural areas. I wish I could find the money to keep their tuition lower so that money would never be an obstacle to a boy or girl enrolling. I wish congregations of sisters could be inspired to accept again the challenge of teaching in our parochial schools—understanding that this could only be done in the context of our present inter-relationships and the partnership that follows from it.

But when all is said and done, I do want to say to our parents that there is no better lasting gift you can give to your children—and grandchildren—than a Catholic school education. I tell you without hesitation that it is worth the sacrifice and, as I am thinking of you now, I pray that you will accept the challenge for the good of your children and the future that lies ahead.

A Clean Desk!!!
September 6, 2001

Do you know what it feels like to have a clean desk? I confess that it is not a feeling I get that often. As a matter of fact, I saw the top of my desk without papers covering it for the first time on the Friday before Labor Day! That's eight months of clutter, eight months of always being behind. When I arrived here the first week of January, my desk was already cluttered with notes of congratulations and best wishes. Those were really too much to be answered personally, more than a thousand in all—and I hope that my very gracious well-wishers understand that—but there is a certain feeling of guilt that comes from not answering a letter even if it comes, as many do, without a return address.

As soon as I was installed, the congratulation letters gave way to business correspondence, letters seeking solutions to problems, letters of concern or suggestions, and the mountains of invitations to events of every imaginable variety. I hit the desk around 6:00 a.m. every weekday morning and stay there until I eat breakfast with the priests at 8:00 a.m. unless I go out early for Mass. Except for prayer and for meetings, which happen frequently every day, and meals, which I sometimes ought to skip, I'm at the desk until 10:00 p.m. when I get ready for bed. And even with all of that, the mountains of mail never cease to avalanche over me. So you can understand how pleased I was finally to clean my desk.

Now there is a legendary story—which I do not believe for a minute—about an archbishop who would sweep all the mail off his desk into the wastepaper basket saying "If it's important, they'll write again!" First of all, I could never do that in case someone had sent the archdiocese a check! Secondly, I'm probably too much of a workaholic not to want to read the mail. That doesn't mean I can read every newspaper or magazine that comes across my desk, or some advertisement for growing hair or recovering memory loss (although those kinds of ads would certainly be of interest). But I do try to read and answer, or ask someone close to me to answer, all the serious letters and invitations that come across my desk.

My secretaries have developed an excellent pattern for making sure that I see all the essential things right away. They leave them on my chair and I have to notice them immediately or I can't sit down. That's why the Friday before Labor Day was so wonderful. There were no papers on my desk or on my chair! It won't last, of course, but it's nice to know that once in a while it can really happen. There is a lesson in all of this—as I guess there always is. If we keep our heart and our will in good order and in accord with God's will, we will learn that the greatest priority is loving God and everything else falls into place. Thinking of you as the summer ends, I pray that all of us will always have that same priority.

When Does the New Year Begin?
September 13, 2001

When I grew up, America was a family-oriented society. Today, partly because families are smaller and partly because modern society continues to drift away from the fundamental values of family and marriage, our perceptions and our priorities have changed. For families with children, the new year seems to begin in early fall or late summer when school opens again. The summer may have gotten busier for many of us—I surely have been living that way for years—but when the school bell starts to ring again, there is a perceptible change in our behavior and in our lives.

This phenomenon touches not only younger families whose children are currently in school, but grandparents, single aunts and uncles, and the vast array of businesses who deal in providing the things needed for a nation to go back into the "school is open" mode. I don't know what will happen if we ever go into a year-round educational system, but until we do, the subtle signals of "back to school" do still affect our thinking, our industries, and our lives.

Last week I wrote you about the extraordinary value of our Catholic school system. I repeat that now since I truly believe it is the best preparation for life you can give to your children, but today I want to reflect on the sense of new beginnings that the opening of another school year brings us. In a real sense, as we get the feeling of a "new year" at the start of school time, we should think of how to prepare for it in the best possible way.

Let me start with basics. I believe that every Catholic home ought to have three essential things: a bible, a crucifix, and a copy of the *Catechism of the Catholic Church*. Now I don't want you to think that I am selling these things. I do want you to know that I think they are most important for our lives. I have been saying in my homilies recently that all of us ought to take five minutes a day to read the New Testament and another five to reflect quietly on what God is saying to us in what we have read. After Mass last week, someone came up to me and said, "It's good you are telling us to read the scriptures. You ought to tell us to have them in our homes!" Well, the lady was right, of course, and I want to do that now. And while we're at it, let's get a crucifix to hang in a prominent place and a copy of the *Catechism of the Catholic Church* so that we will know what we believe and be able to express it clearly.

If I'm right and the beginning of school gives most of us a sense of starting up again, whatever our age might be, then let's celebrate the new beginning by making some "New Year's Resolutions" now. I'll write more about these three essential items in the weeks ahead, but thinking of you now, I can't imagine that our Catholic home would not have a bible, a crucifix, and that catechism close by.

The Mother Church of Washington
September 20, 2001

Have you been in St. Matthew's Cathedral recently? If you have, you surely have noticed the face-lift that is taking place in this mother church of the Archdiocese of Washington. To say face-lift is really not accurate. What is taking place is a very major restoration of this most central and historic spot in our archdiocese. It is the most extensive renovation we have undertaken since the construction of the great church was begun in 1893. Unfortunately, it is not just a cosmetic face-lift, but a most necessary repair.

A couple of years ago, Msgr. Jameson, who is the rector of the cathedral, discovered that several ceiling tiles had fallen down. Immediately a full-scale assessment was made of the problem and safety considerations made it necessary to begin a full-scale restoration at once. Since that date, the entire copper dome has been replaced and the roof structurally reinforced, the slate repaired, and the outside brick-work repointed and waterproofed. Now we have started the interior work. This includes securing and cleaning mosaic tiles, updating wiring, retrofitting fire and safety systems, repairing plaster, and restoring paintings.

I'm sure you are surprised that I know all these things, since you do know that when it comes to construction projects—like with a lot of other things—I am really usually lost in the woods. The critical difference here is that this is really our home, yours and mine, as the family of this local Church. Here is where most of our priests have been ordained, most of our bishops installed; here is where the oils are blessed at the Mass of Chrism every year and then are sent to every parish in the archdiocese for the sacramental anointings of Baptism, Confirmation, and the Anointing of the Sick. Besides all that, our cathedral is truly one of the wonders of American Catholic architecture and you remember that it took its place in history when so many of the leaders of the world came to it for President Kennedy's burial in 1963.

For me, it has always been a special place, even long before it became the place of my episcopal chair as archbishop of this Church of Washington. Even in my first life in this area, when I studied for my doctorate at Catholic U, I would come often to pray here. I still do it from time to time when I have some time downtown. It is a holy place, especially in the quiet of reflection. It is an awesome place when great ceremonies are taking place, when the great music and the wonderful rhythm of the liturgy carry us very close to the sense of God's presence there in his magnificent house. You and I are really blessed to have St. Matthew's as our cathedral.

It is going to cost us about eight million dollars to complete the work now in progress to restore St. Matthew's Cathedral. Approximately $1.3 million has been raised by the extraordinary efforts of St. Matthew's parish community, and another $4.4 million has been raised through the Stewards of St. Matthew's and other most-generous gifts. To complete the project we must still raise about two million dollars. I have approved the recommendation of our council of priests to have a special second collection at every parish in the archdiocese on the weekend of September 22–23 to help with this important work.

All of us who love the cathedral, especially the priests of the archdiocese and I, know that you will do your best to be as generous as you can in this collection. This mother church of Catholic Washington is very, very special to all of us and thinking of you and of all those who pray here, one really hopes that it will always be so.

Yes and No
September 27, 2001

I was going to title this column "Don't Say It," but I figured that such a beginning would be more than I wanted to say. It all started when someone said to me: "Well, life goes on"—referring to the tragedy that our country and so many of our families have suffered. There is, of course, a sense in which life must go on, but there is another sense in which it will never be the same.

Here in the Archdiocese of Washington, we all have no choice but to continue to try to serve as God calls us to do, with generosity and courage, with humility and zeal, with an eye on the life to come and our steps on the road that lead to creating a better world here on earth.

Our children, thousands of them, are back in school after the summer vacation, learning the three Rs in the context of the vast technological advances that modern education offers. Hopefully, both in our own schools and in the religious education programs for those who do not attend Catholic schools, the youngsters are learning more than the secular subjects that prepare them for promotion from grade to grade. We pray that they are also learning how to grow in grace in the kingdom of the God who is love and how to reach out to their neighbors who are poor or in need.

Our parishes, experiencing these days an increase in the number of the faithful at Mass, continue to be the place where our people come to kneel in prayer before the God who saves us, or to sit in silence in his presence and strain to hear the words of blessing that he whispers in our hearts. Our agencies of charity spread throughout the district and the surrounding five counties of Maryland, our Catholic hospitals, and our many homes for the elderly continue to open their doors to those who need healing or comfort or shelter. Throughout the length and breadth of our local Church of Washington, life does go on and service continues to be rendered to all who seek it, of whatever race or ethnic group or nation they may represent. In that sense things never change, and trauma and tragedy make them all the more necessary.

But, in another sense, life does not go on in the same way. There are empty places at our tables and empty places in our hearts. There are voices we long to hear again and smiles we will never see in this life anymore. For some, even as the great preface prayer reminds us, life is changed although not ended, and when this earthly dwelling lies in death, we gain an everlasting dwelling place in heaven. So yes, we are still here in the valley of struggles praying for deeper faith, for lively trust in God, for vocations to come for the needs of the faithful, and for the charity and good works to help the Church and its family of faith to grow. And no, it is not really the same. Life is changed for many. It goes on in a different way. Thinking of you and thinking of those who have gone on to God, this is a lesson we learn by heart.

Bingo!
October 4, 2001

There are 145 churches and public chapels in the Archdiocese of Washington. Some of them are large, open spaces for the worship of a great congregation; others are smaller, lovely country places where a small congregation feels very much at home. Some are melting pots of several races and nationalities; others are still national Churches that serve a single group of faithful. Some are historic, having their roots into the 1600s; others I have been privileged to bless in the nine months of my service here. In their own way, they are all very beautiful and beautifully different.

The happy news about them for me is that by this coming Sunday I will have visited and celebrated Holy Mass in each one! I saved St. Peter Claver Church in Saint Inigoes for last. There are three reasons for this. One is that Mass is celebrated there usually only on a Sunday and it is therefore more manageable to go to others with weekday Masses first. These last weekends, I have been visiting the churches where Sunday Mass is the only weekly celebration, as is the case in several of our parishes that serve different national groups such as our Portuguese and French congregations. Secondly, this will be a special Southern Maryland weekend, since I'll finish the last parish in Charles County on Saturday when I offer Mass at Indian Head and then bless the fleet on Sunday at St. Clement's Island. But the main reason I chose to have St. Peter Claver be the final pearl in that long rosary of parishes is that even though it was formally established as a mission only about a hundred years ago, it has a special history of devoted and faith-filled people and I wanted to single them out in this special way. I guess another reason would be that St. Peter Claver is one of my special favorites and his life as a missionary and as an outstanding lover of the downtrodden and the poor has always been a tremendous inspiration to me.

I feel somewhat like my grandmother who was wonderfully addicted to bingo in the last years of her life, when even in her eighties she would shop around from one bingo hall to another to try her luck. At dinner at home, we would hear the great stories of needing just one number for a smashing prize or—somewhat more rarely—of the times when she had that one number and shouted out "bingo" with the same gusto as Christopher Columbus must have shouted "land ho!" when he found San Salvador. It will be great to have gone to all our churches and to have prayed for all of you in each and every one of them. It is a grace for which I thank the Lord, as I thank him every day, for giving our people such generosity in building and sustaining these holy places and in using them so faithfully and so well.

Some of our folks are asking me: "What will you do now that you have visited every parish?" I think you already know the answer. I'll start over again. This time, I want to make sure that I will be in every parish for a Sunday celebration, so I can get to see more of our people and pray with them. I want to get to the schools, too. I visited four schools so far this fall, and I'd like to try to see them all before too long.

That will be a slower project, since I do have to put in the time in the office or I'll get too far behind in my paperwork. But as long as it takes, if God spares me, I want to spend time praying with you and thinking of you because when all is said and done, I think that's why the Lord sent me here.

"A Strange Time"
October 11, 2001

These are strange days for all of us. The response that our nation has taken to root out the nests of terrorism in Afghanistan, the concern that other terrorist attacks here in our own country may still be very possible, the grieving that still goes on in so many families in our communities, all that creates a special shadow on these early days of autumn.

For some reason or other, fall has always been a time of nostalgia for me. There is even a little melancholy connected with the dying of the leaves and the coming of the chill breezes of October. Perhaps it is a deeper sense of the fragility of human beings and the consciousness that goes back to the earliest days of humanity and warns us that we cannot stop the seasons and must be prepared for the challenges of winter. That feeling, together with all the others I have mentioned, make this truly a strange time in our lives. Maybe it is more heightened here in Washington where the decisions of war and peace and the stark presence of the damaged Pentagon are so much with us.

How shall we handle these feelings of unease and uncertainty? I think President Bush's advice to get on with our lives and our work is probably fundamental. We cannot be caught in a sense of fear or a lack of confidence in the future. We have gone through these concerns before, although perhaps never with such a sense that there could be a "fifth column" of terrorists within our borders. And yet, our greater strength is in our ability to keep working, keep caring for others, keep producing those basic elements for a better world tomorrow. The Holy Father keeps reminding us that the Gospel tells us we must not be afraid. If God is with us, who can be against us? And we put our confidence in the providential love of our father in heaven, in the words of that great hymn, "We shall not be moved."

It is now nine months since I was sent to be the servant of this Church of Washington. What remarkable days they have been. Since, as you know, I celebrated Mass last Sunday in the final parish of the archdiocese, I have been reflecting on our life together in a special way. I know your faith and your great generosity. I have personal experience every day of your kindness and love. The Catholics of this Church of Washington are strong and good people. Let us always be united in our trust and confidence in the God who loves us. Let us serve him and each other with joyful enthusiasm even as we reach out to serve our neighbors and our country with courage and grace.

Thinking of you in these strange days of autumn gives me a lot of strength and hope.

Fasting
October 18, 2001

The *Catechism of the Catholic Church* (CCC) doesn't say much about fasting. It covers the subject when it speaks of the different forms of penance in the Christian life. It does make the point that both the scriptures and the Fathers of the Church insisted on three forms of penance above all the others: fasting, prayer, and almsgiving (CCC #1734). Each of the three has a different relationship; prayer relates to God; almsgiving to our neighbor. Fasting relates to ourselves. It is intensely personal and very often a secret between oneself and God.

These were some of the reasons I decided to ask our Catholic people in the Archdiocese of Washington to fast one day a week for peace in the world, from now until this strange war is over. The present rules for fasting are not that difficult. We are allowed one full meal a day and the other two meals taken together should not be the equal of a full meal. Some of us do that just about every day anyway, and others would not find it too difficult. For some, the hardest part would be not eating between meals and giving up the snack before going to bed.

I believe that all of us want to do something together to beg God's help at this very troubling time in the history of the free world. I know that we are all praying very hard for a just and speedy conclusion to this crisis. Some of you are attending daily Mass—which is probably the one best thing that we can do. For some people, due to their jobs or their locations, that is not possible. But almost everyone can fast one day a week!

The sick and the elderly are, of course, already exempted from the law of fast and therefore all the more I would not be asking them to take on this burden, but I truly feel that all the rest of us need to feel that we are helping and, even more importantly, begging God's help for the coming of peace. The opportunity to fast one day a week throughout the year for peace is more or less doable for most Catholics, and I hope that many will make use of it.

We know from the Gospel that Jesus fasted and that in imitation of him many saints of the Early Church were dedicated to that form of penance and petition. The poor people of the world are fasting every day with little hope of a good nourishing meal at the end. Our fasting, then, has many good points to it. We fast to beg God for peace; we fast to show solidarity with our sisters and brothers who are poor or starving in many parts of the world; we fast to put ourselves more in touch with who we are, with the inner person who can grow stronger and more at peace through a little sacrifice; and finally, those of us who like me recognize that we have offended God and our neighbor by our selfishness or our sins, can make up a little of our fault through this holy and simple act of penance.

I ask you to fast one day a week—at your own choice—for all these reasons. I will do it too, of course, and I'll be thinking of you as I ask the Lord to make this practice a blessing for you all.

The Faith of Alonso Manso
October 25, 2001

This may turn out to be a complicated column. I'm certainly starting it out with a catchy title. I'm writing it on a plane coming back from Puerto Rico. I flew down there yesterday and I'm on my way back now. As some of you may recall, many years ago when I was a young priest—back in the late 1960s—I served for five years as the president of the Catholic University of Puerto Rico. During that time, the university initiated an award to a Catholic layman and a Catholic clergyman named after the first bishop of Puerto Rico, Alonso Manso.

Bishop Manso's fame was not just that he was named bishop of Puerto Rico in 1509, but that when he arrived in his diocese in 1511, he was the first successor of the apostles to come to the New World! The gift of Manso, as the first bishop to set foot in America, was that he confirmed the faith here and set the stage for the evangelization of this great new continent, which still continues after half a millennium. But to return to the reason for my story, the university this year gave me the Manso Cross, which I helped to establish almost forty years ago!

I think often about Alonso Manso. The Church he found in the New World was so very different from the Church we serve in the Archdiocese of Washington today. It was very dependent on the Spanish Crown and, although it was blessed in the number of its missionaries, it was almost without places of worship and schools. Manso began to build a new church and in the years he spent here, he accomplished quite a lot. The wonderful thing about his mission was that he came to teach the same fundamental doctrine that we teach today, to celebrate the same sacraments, and to proclaim the same message of salvation through Jesus Christ our Lord. We may describe the faith in more modern and easier-to-understand terms for our society today, but it is still the same faith that we have received from the Lord that Bishop Manso taught in the Caribbean five hundred years ago.

One of these days I want to do a pastoral letter on faith. I have been hoping to do it for some time now, even before I came to Washington last January. I am convinced of its fundamental importance to each one of us and our ultimate destiny as children of God. Receiving the Manso Cross and thinking of the faith that he brought to America reminded me of that desire to share with you whatever reflections God gives me on the meaning of faith in our lives and on the problems that we face in our often faithless secular culture. Faith is even more important today when the concerns and fears of these times can cause us to lose our way and to forget that always and everywhere we are still in the hands of God. So you see, as this plane comes streaking back to Washington, I am still thinking of you.

Life and Death
November 1, 2001

Somewhere in the breviary we pray every day, there is a hymn that has a line that says "Death is all around us; Jesus be our life!" I looked for it unsuccessfully because I wanted to quote it accurately as I prepared this column. Sometimes it does seem that death is all around us. The important thing is that we also recognize that Jesus is our life.

Three circumstances have called my attention to this in a powerful way these days. The first was the funeral of Joseph Curseen, the postal worker who died last week. I offered his funeral Mass last Saturday in Anacostia. He was only forty-seven and had a wonderful reputation among all of his neighbors and colleagues and friends. His death was, in human terms, a real tragedy and the loss of a fine Catholic man. I grieve for him with his bereaved family and I am sure that the Lord must love him very much and will take care of him forever.

The second part of this somber reflection of mine is that we are just ending Pro-Life Month, and every day in October I thought of thousands of little children in their mothers' wombs who will never see the light of day because of the terrible scourge of abortion. The line in the hymn is so real here: "Death is all around us." We have become so used to this. We have seen so many people closed to life, even in our own Catholic communities. May Jesus truly be our life and call us to a deeper understanding of what we do when we destroy the unborn baby and, in this way, destroy part of ourselves in the process as well.

Finally the news of the murder of sixteen of our Christian brothers and sisters worshipping in a church in Islamabad, Pakistan, sends a chill into my heart. Those of you who have been with me at Mass know that as I pray the Prayer of the Faithful at the offertory time, I usually add an intercession for our sisters and brothers who are being persecuted for their faith, and who even that day may have been called to give their lives as martyrs because of their belief in Jesus Christ. That has happened in Indonesia and the other islands of Southeast Asia including the Philippines. It has happened in the Middle East and in Africa. Now it happens in the Indian subcontinent in this terrible way right before our eyes. We are blessed in that such a bloody persecution is not rampant in the New World today, although some of us can still recall the martyrdom of Catholics in Mexico in the first half of the twentieth century.

What do all these happenings say to us? They remind us that death is indeed all around us, and yet, on All Soul's Day we proclaim with deepest faith that the souls of the just are in the hands of God and no torment will touch them. We know that Jesus is our life and that he calls us in his own time and according to his own providence so that all of us may rest in his peace forever. It is the blessed assurance that we do matter to a God who loves us enough to send us his son to be our redeemer, who allows us to hold on to the hope and confidence that he will make all things new again. As long as we are here, we are called to proclaim life, a life of trusting in God, who is thinking of you and of me and both gently and powerfully guiding us to salvation.

Islam
November 8, 2001

I have a very good friend who is Moslem. I became acquainted with him when I served on the US Commission

for International Freedom of Religion and always found him
fair and open to discussion of all the religions of the world, as
well as always respectful of our own religious faith and that of
the Jewish people, the other "People of the Book"! He taught
me many things about Islam, and in fact taught me best by
his own prayerfulness and deep faith.

The other day when I had to go back to the commission's
office for a brief luncheon meeting, we had a chance to talk.
He was concerned about attitudes of some people in the
United States toward Islam in view of the war going on in
Afghanistan and the continuing worries here at home over
terrorism of different kinds. He mentioned that he had been
invited to talk to some non-Moslem groups and to explain
true Islam and its teachings to them. He said that the reaction of the people when he quoted from the Qur'an—the
holy book of Islam—was always one of some surprise and
appreciation that the teachings of the Prophet Mohammed
were in some ways very similar to the teachings of Jesus and
the prophets of the Old Testament.

One of the most interesting of the quotations from the
Qur'an has to do with Christian people. It is from the fifth
chapter of that Moslem holy book and it reads in part: "[A]
nd nearest among (mankind) in love to the believers wilt thou
find those who say 'We are Christians': because amongst these
are men devoted to learning and men who have renounced
the world, and they are not arrogant" [5:82]. There is great
respect for the Lord Jesus in the Qur'an and he is regarded
as one of the most important prophets. It is interesting that
the figure of Mary, his mother, is also highly esteemed in a
singular manner in the faith of Islam.

This does not mean that the two religions are that similar,
of course. Islam does not accept the Trinity, the sacraments,
or the Church and therefore there are more differences than
similarities in the profession of our faith and theirs. But it
does mean that in the faith of our Moslem brothers and

sisters there are many wonderful expressions of kindness, hospitality, and a call to holiness and sacrifice. I have known many Moslems who live up to this challenging code of prayer and service. I know that I could learn much from their devotion to prayer and fasting. I have seen that in my friend's life when, in the midst of a busy day, he would always faithfully take time out for the prescribed periods of prayer five times a day.

We know from personal experience that there are good people and bad in every religion. We must never allow any religion to be used as a caricature for evil or wrong conduct. We Catholics have suffered much over the centuries from those who tried to destroy us because they did not understand what we stood for or what we believed. We must never do the same to our sisters and brothers who profess any other faith. We acknowledge that we are all sinners and that a loving and forgiving God calls all of us to holiness and to love for each other, whether we believe the same things or not. The important thing is that we proclaim the good news of Jesus with our lives as well as our words, and the world will soon be changed by the power of that message of love and justice and peace. Thinking of you as the changing of the leaves moves us all to deeper thoughts, I pray that all of us may be good neighbors to everyone.

Bishops
November 15, 2001

Back in the late 1980s when I was archbishop of Newark, the National Conference of Catholic Bishops decided to hold its spring meeting at Seton Hall University in that archdiocese. We had been inviting the bishops' conference to come for several years since the university had built a number of fine new residence buildings and for the first time we were able to house such a group like that. When they decided to come to Seton Hall, our enthusiasm was high. What an honor for the university and what a grace for the Archdiocese of Newark and for the Cathedral of the Sacred Heart when all the bishops of the United States offered Mass there together during the meeting! I was so delighted and grateful for that historic Eucharist that I placed a memorial tablet in the cathedral right next to the one that celebrated Pope John Paul II's visit in 1995.

Here in Washington each November, we have the bishops coming every year to our home for their annual Plenary Meeting. Since this is the first time they will come during my service to this great local Church, I am really excited about it. We have about four hundred Catholic bishops in our country. Almost two hundred of them are diocesan bishops—that means those who are responsible for a local Church—and another one hundred or so serve as auxiliary bishops. There is also a large number of retired bishops, many of whom come very faithfully to the meetings where their voices are heard with great respect because of their experience and their wisdom.

I really love the bishops. I am always edified and even inspired by these good men whom God has called to be the shepherds and guides of his people. Sometimes, of course, we have disagreements about one issue or another, but it is always in the context of the deep faith and love for the Church that motivates us all. These questions almost always are about how we can care for our people better.

I used to know every one of the bishops and still probably recognize more than 90 percent of them. Since I will have been a member of the bishops' conference for twenty-five years next June, I have worked with many of them over the years and have never ceased to be inspired by their goodness and their zeal for the care of God's people.

I guess I am writing this week's column about our episcopal visitors because I want to remind you to pray for the bishops that God will bless us all with wisdom and grace and with the vision that is needed to serve the Church in our country at this time. Of course, perhaps the most important task of a bishop is to be a good listener to the voices of our people and to maintain and develop a warm and deep communion with the Holy Father and the universal Church. The example of Pope John Paul II in his constant care for all the Churches is a guide to each of us on how to serve with generosity and love.

Next week, when the bishops have all gone back to their own local Churches, may their memories of the Church of Washington be a good example to them of a faithful and devoted people, filled with confidence in God and love for neighbor. This way, they will also be thinking of you with the same kind of admiration and love I always have.

". . . From All Anxiety"
November 22, 2001

Right after the Our Father in the Mass, the priest goes on to pray that God will "protect us from all anxiety." I have always found that to be a most comforting prayer since in the responsibilities that I have had over the years, there always are anxieties about very basic things, like building up the faith of our people and the health of our priests, responding to the shortage of vocations and the financial needs to continue the work of our parishes and our works of charity, let alone all our schools.

All of us have anxieties. It is a natural concomitant of being human in a world that we cannot control or manage as we would like. That is why the Church invites us to pray that God in his faithfulness will protect us from these worries over which we have little control.

When I was thinking about the column I would write you around Thanksgiving time, I decided that I would write about anxieties and concerns because I believe that this touches all of us whatever our individual responsibilities may be. We all do have anxieties. The youngsters in school are anxious about the tests that are about to be taken; the teenagers are anxious about how they will grow up, how they will look, how they will succeed, who they will marry if marriage is the goal of their lives.

Newlyweds are anxious about how they and their spouse will handle those early crises that come into the life of every family. Grandparents look at their children with such great hope and love but also with concern that the world into which they grow will be a world of peace and opportunity. Older folks have the anxieties of their own health, their children's happiness, their own place in the world that is to come. You can build on this list yourselves as you reflect with me on all those moments of our lives that can give us the fears that future uncertainties can feed.

Some years ago at a priests' day of recollection, I mentioned my own anxieties to a priest who was hearing our confessions. He was a very wise man and he began to speak of that prayer in the Mass that I mentioned earlier. He said that the Church understands the weight of anxieties and even compares them to the burden of our sins, since, as you recall when you next go to Mass, in that prayer after the Our Father, we ask both to be free from our sins and protected from our anxieties. He made the point that God's peace and our happiness depends on working to be delivered from both those shadows—sins and anxieties—on the road of our lives.

It's funny that some things people say to us stay with us for years. I have never forgotten that confessor's words although I never knew his name. He was wise in his counsel that we must strive to be free from both sins and anxieties if we are truly to be the People of God.

How do we do this? We all know the answer but we hesitate to accept it. It is simply by putting our trust in a God who loves us, a God who guides us, a God who takes us by the hand if only we will let him. Jesus has said it for us so clearly. Do not be anxious about tomorrow, you are worth more than many sparrows and yet not one of them falls from the sky without the Father's will. Have confidence in God, and live in his love, and the concerns of tomorrow will melt away in the trust of today. I am thinking of you as you celebrate this Thanksgiving Day and I pray that more than anything you will be thankful for a God who loves you and who protects you from all anxiety.

One Year Later
November 29, 2001

On Tuesday, November 22, 2000, around 8:00 in the morning, a small group of priests arrived at Union Station to be met by Cardinal Hickey, Bishop Lori, and some other members of the staff of the Archdiocese of Washington. I was one of those priests who arrived in the nation's capital that day. It was the day my transfer had been announced by the Apostolic Nuncio. I was seventy years old, a priest for forty-two years, and a bishop for twenty-three. The priests who accompanied me here had worked with me for the almost fifteen years of my service as archbishop of Newark. Some people were surprised that someone my age was transferred to such an important see as Washington. I was too! That was a year ago.

What a year this has been! You have been so great to me. The priests have received me with so much warmth and acceptance; the laity with a truly overwhelming welcome. Throughout these twelve months, I have often been embarrassed at your kindness to me. I have often said that I wish I were a holier man so that I would better deserve so gracious a people. It has been a wonderful year for me. The Lord blessed me so much by sending me to Washington!

Sometimes I think that I have been here for years. I have gotten to know so many of you and have prayed in so many of your churches and chapels. Other times, I am conscious that I have only just arrived—as when I make a mistake and still refer to the Archdiocese of Newark! I am so grateful to Cardinal Hickey who served this local Church so devotedly and so well. If I can accomplish 10 percent of what he gave to the Archdiocese of Washington in his years of loving service, I will be more than content. His predecessors, too, Cardinal O'Boyle and Cardinal Baum, made an extraordinary mark on the Church in this part of the world, and they leave me a great challenge to continue their dedicated service.

One year later, I truly rejoice in the gift of our people. The rich diversity of the Church of Washington, the generosity of our faithful, rich and poor alike, the faith that you are handing on to your children, the values that you both profess and manifest—what a blessing for any archbishop. My first year has been marked with your accomplishments. I try to keep up with you and to be wise and prudent in helping to guide you. Any good things that have been accomplished so far have been because of your energy and your vision, and I have stood around and applauded.

I go to Rome this week for a few meetings, but most of all to thank the Holy Father for giving me the chance to work for you. Pray for me that in whatever time God gives me to serve here, I may do it well, conscious of my faults and my many deficiencies, but also realizing his wonderful forgiving love and grace.

Wherever I am, one year after my transfer to Washington, I think you know that I'll always be thinking of you.

"I Didn't Need Another Adventure"
December 6, 2001

I guess I've had my share of adventures. God has blessed me with a good deal of excitement in my reasonably long life. I was in Sarajevo during the bombings and in Bujumbura during the worst riots; I was probably the first bishop to be able to travel to the forbidden city of Lhasa in Tibet since the thirteenth century; and I will never forget chopper rides with Cardinal Cooke visiting the troops in Vietnam. So I didn't need another adventure last weekend when I was trying to get back home from Rome.

It had been six months since I had been in Rome for any meetings and I was overdue. So, last week I had a good visit to the Eternal City, including the special grace of a supper with the Holy Father. I saw all our Washington seminarians who are studying at the North American College and found them really doing well. I had a chance to stop in at many offices at the Vatican, and of course, I had more of my share of great Roman meals! So, last Saturday, I was ready to come home and continue this special adventure of being archbishop of Washington and trying to serve all of you.

I was scheduled to fly out of Rome at 9:35 on Saturday morning and return to Reagan National Airport around 3:30 after a brief stopover to change planes at Newark International. It was a journey I have done often in the past and

I was so confident of the schedule that I was planning to preside at evening prayer at St. Matthew's Cathedral to commemorate World AIDS Day and to pray for all our brothers and sisters who are fighting that dread disease. I didn't need another adventure.

About an hour out of Rome flying over the French countryside, the pilot came on the intercom to tell us that we had developed a mechanical problem and we were diverting to Gatwick Airport outside of London. Two hours later we were off again over the ocean with an estimated arrival time of 7:00 p.m. in Newark and hopefully back here at 9:00. Two hours over the Atlantic, it happened again! The captain announced that we were in mechanical trouble once again and he didn't want to take the chance to finish the crossing to North America. Well, to make a long story short, we landed back in London at 8:00 p.m., we all checked into an airport hotel, and now had an established take-off time for Sunday at 8:00 a.m.!

It gets even funnier. I thought I better get a good night's sleep, so just as I was getting ready for bed, the hotel alarm went off and we were all evacuated to stand in the London chill for an hour while they checked the hotel before letting us back to our rooms. I had to call home and cancel my Sunday Masses and any chance I had to catch up on the paperwork I missed while I was away.

Forgive me for sharing all these misadventures with you. What I really want to share is the wonderful realization that we get sometimes when we appreciate that our lives are truly in God's hands and that it is he ultimately who calls the shots. We do the best we can, and that is always our responsibility, but God has the final word and it is good to appreciate that constant truth. I had to learn it again last weekend and, as I was constantly changing my schedules, you know that I was thinking of you.

Ecumenism and the Church
December 13, 2001

I was delighted several months ago when I received an invitation to give the address at an ecumenical prayer service at the Rankin Memorial Chapel of Howard University. As far as I know, no cardinal had ever preached there and very few Catholic bishops and therefore I was very conscious of the real honor that was given to the Archdiocese of Washington when I was asked. The chapel was opened more than a century ago, and some of the most influential protestant preachers of our nation have spoken from its pulpit.

They laughed when I told them that they made me feel very much at home not only by the gracious way they received me but also by the fact that when I saw how the chapel was filled from the back pews first, I almost felt that I was back at home in one of our Catholic churches! The chapel was crowded and the growing Cardinal Newman Association of the university's Catholic community was very much in evidence, thanks to an excellent Catholic chaplain. The service was one of hymns, powerfully sung by an excellent choir, scripture readings, and prayers, and even though my presence meant that I was only able to visit two Catholic parishes this Sunday, I believe it was still important for the archdiocese that I accepted their very kind invitation.

The reason I write about this is both that I like to share with you all the different things I do as servant of this Church of Washington, since you are so essential a part of my life, but also to make the point of how important it is for us Catholics to continue the ecumenical thrust of the Second Vatican Council. Pope John Paul II is always reminding us that the Church must have an ecumenical dimension if it is going to be faithful to the Gospel of Christ.

There are four great marks of the Church, as we know. It is one, holy, catholic, and apostolic. These we learned in catechism class. There are also other essential elements in its life that continue to identify it as God's true family, namely that it must always be concerned about the poor and the stranger, the children and the aged, the sick and the sinner, and that it must always strive to promote Christian unity, respectful dialogue with all other faith traditions, the protection of life, and the values of the family.

If we look at how the current administration of the Church is organized at the Vatican as the result of the Second Vatican Council, we can see that there are offices concentrating on all these particular areas. As you may remember, I serve on the body that is dedicated to the promotion of justice and peace. These two great goals of humanity are the cornerstones of Catholic culture, and remind us that all the things for which the Church strives in Jesus' name are the building blocks of a better world for every human being. Understanding each other better and joining hands in prayer to the one God who is Father of us all is a good start toward the building of a better world for the human race. I was thinking of you while I prayed at Howard University and I wanted to share that significant moment with you.

The Peace of Jerusalem
December 20, 2001

I really gave a lot of thought to what I would write to you in this column. This will be the one that appears in the *Catholic Standard* right before Christmas. All kinds of thoughts went through my mind. I thought first that I would just make a list of all the blessings I have received this year from the

Lord. That would have been a long column since God has really been so kind and gracious to me in this first year of my service to the Archdiocese of Washington. All of you, with your deep faith and generosity, have been such a great part of that gift.

Then I thought I would try to write a funny column that the young people might enjoy, and take some credit for the turnaround of our Redskins and the extraordinary performance of our Maryland football team. Both of them, as you know, are coached by newcomers to our area and I thought I would try to ride on their star-wagon of success since I was new too! I figured that this approach could be dangerous, however, since the season was not over yet—although I still have great hopes for the Redskins and great confidence in the Terrapins for the Orange Bowl!

When all was said and done, the story of the Holy Father's extraordinary call to the bishops of the Holy Land to come to Rome together with bishops representing the powerful nations of the West decided the subject of the column I felt I had to write. As more and more blood is spilled in Palestine and Israel, we must all join in a heartfelt cry of anguish and a fervent prayer for the peace of Jerusalem. The situation there becomes more and more desperate each day, it seems, and we must stand with the Holy Father in calling on all the players in that awful game of history—including our own nation's leaders—to do more to bring an end to this intolerable cycle of increasing violence and retaliation on both sides.

In the declaration that was issued at the conclusion of last week's meeting, there were clear and strong indications of the critical nature of this special moment in the history of this most blessed part of the world made sacred by the birth of Jesus and by his life, death, and resurrection. One sentence summarized the deep concerns of the participants—as it also reiterated the constant and consistent stand of the pope's: "Peace between the two peoples (Israelis and Palestinians) in fact can only come about if the law and fairness are respected regarding certain fundamental questions: the security of the state of Israel, the birth of a state for the Palestinian people, the evacuation of the occupied territories, an internationally guaranteed special statute for the most sacred places of Jerusalem, and a fair solution for the Palestinian refugees."

I believe that this has to be the message in my Christmas column. Too much blood has spilled to be ignored. Too many opportunities for peace and justice have been squandered. The future of the Christian presence in the Holy Land is too intimately tied to the ending of violence there. As I think of the terrible and strange war in which our country is now still deeply engaged, and as I am thinking of you and your own need to be able to live in a peaceful and secure world, I ask you to pray with me this Christmas for the peace of Jerusalem, that only he who is the Prince of Peace can bring about.

The Grace of God
December 27, 2001

There is an ancient formula that the Church uses on special occasions when important decrees or blessings are given in a solemn, public way. It happens at Christmastime in the major Mass in a cathedral when the bishop is present and the Christmas indulgence is solemnly proclaimed. It really has a medieval sound to it. For us in this local Church it goes like this: "Theodore Edgar McCarrick, cardinal priest of the Holy Roman Church under the title of Saints Nereus and Achilleus, by the grace of God and the favor of the apostolic see, archbishop of this Holy Church of Washington"—and then it continues depending on the message or the blessing that is pertinent to the occasion. As Christmas was approaching last week, I thought of it and it struck me that the most powerful part of it was when it placed the basis of all that high-sounding language on the strength of five words—by the grace of God.

Saint Therese of the Child Jesus, the beloved saint of the turn of the last century who is affectionately known as the Little Flower, used to say "everything is grace" and in that way she reminded us of the words of the second epistle of Saint Peter where that teaching is first proclaimed. How true it is! We are nothing and can do nothing good except for the grace of God. It is by his grace that we come into being; by his grace that we believe; by his grace that we find peace and happiness in our lives on earth; by his grace that we are saved. There is a great line in one of the Sunday prefaces in the Mass that reminds us that even the desire to serve God is itself his gift. There is no good that we can ever accomplish in our lives without his help, without his love, without his grace.

As we look back on the year that is ending and count our blessings and our pains, this is a constant monitor that we should carry with us. Now, of course, this should not make us passive or indifferent, leaving everything to God's power and not cooperating with his divine will. The paradox of our lives of faith is that, as Saint Ignatius of Loyola taught us, we should pray as if everything depended on ourselves and work as if everything depended on God. (That, by the way, is the correct formulation of the great saint's dictum, not the other way around, since if we work as if everything depended on ourselves, we can lose sight of our utter dependence on God!) It is the power of God's grace that accomplishes all things in our lives and without his grace we are nothing, whether we happen to be an archbishop or a busboy. We are all servants of each other, by the grace of God.

How blessed we are that God loves us and gives us his grace to do good things and to avoid the things of evil. Many times, I don't accomplish all the good things that he asks me to do. When that happens I am putting an obstacle to his grace and in his gentle providence. He will never force me to accept his grace. The great combination comes when we willingly and lovingly accept his grace and strive, with his help, to do the good things—and even the great things—that he has in mind for us. The scriptures tell us that Mary was full of grace. We will never equal her love and her union with the will of God, but she is an example for us and a mother who longs to see us, her children, living and acting by the grace of God. As I am thinking of you these quieter moments of the holidays, I pray with all my heart that God's grace and peace will always be with you.

2002

"It's a Wonderful Life"
January 3, 2002

In the midst of the turmoil and concerns that we all share as this momentous year comes to an end, it would be terrible if we neglected to count our blessings as well as our fears so that we can approach the New Year with courage and perseverance—and maybe even with hope and joy. Every once in a while, something happens that reminds us—as the great film says—"it's a wonderful life."

The Holy Father, just before Christmas, gave you and me a wonderful reason to rejoice. In the appointment of bishops-elect Kevin Farrell and Francisco Gonzalez, the Archdiocese of Washington becomes stronger in grace and strength and more able and ready to meet the challenges of this special time in our lives. Many of you know the two new bishops well. If you do, you will also know how happy and privileged I am to have as close collaborators these two good and prayerful men, both filled with a love for God and his Church, and zeal for the proclamation of the Gospel and the pastoral care of God's faithful.

With this appointment, Pope John Paul II has once again raised the number of our assisting bishops to three. He has also given us a bishop who will be especially sensitive to the needs of the Hispanic community, even as Bishop Olivier has always been sensitive to the needs of our African American Catholics. They will serve the entire diocese, of course, as Bishop Olivier has always done, but it is good that young people of these major groups in our local Church have a role model and a "friend at court" who will always understand very personally their needs, their hopes, and their dreams.

Ever since I arrived to take up my new life in your service almost a year ago (Thursday, January 3, it will be a year), I

have counted on these two priests in a special way. I asked
them to assume new responsibilities and to be good guides to
me as I tried to learn the archdiocese. Together with my other
immediate collaborators in the service of this local Church,
both men and women, they have led and guided me carefully
so that I could try as best I might to take the place of that
marvelous shepherd, administrator, and pastor, my predecessor, Cardinal Hickey. (I'm still not sure how well I've done,
but if anything good is still happening, it is because of Bishop
Farrell and Bishop Gonzalez and those others who have done
so much to keep me from walking into a wall.)

So please pray for them—as you pray for me. It is an awesome thing to become a bishop and never so much as today
when a bishop must sincerely try to be all things to all people,
and ever faithful to God and to the Church. It will be so good
to work with them and to watch them grow in their new role
as bishops. I will probably learn more from them than vice
versa, but the whole process will be a real joy for us all. They,
as well as I, will always be thinking of you as they prepare for
their ordination. How good God is to bring all this about!

The Media
January 10, 2002

For some weeks now I have been wanting to do a column
on the media. As I am just beginning my second year of
service as archbishop of Washington, it seemed like a good
time to do it. Our local news media has really been very
good to me, and yet the media in general does present some
concerns.

In my homilies around the archdiocese, I have sometimes
been quite critical of some parts of the media. I often

complain that the commercials tend to paint a picture of true happiness as being very powerful, very comfortable, very beautiful, and very skinny! This is not what the Gospel tells us about the road to happiness. The Lord teaches us that it comes from being very kind, very patient, very faithful, and responsible and that this is the way to find happiness in this life and the grace to achieve the reward of everlasting happiness in the world to come.

I worry about the young people who see in the TV series and who read in the print media a continuous and sometimes not so subtle attack on the values that religious people—and especially Catholics—hold dear and essential for the well ordering and happiness of society. Promiscuity and treachery, violence and selfishness are often portrayed as the acceptable and the normal way of life. I find that worrisome and I am concerned about its effect on the moral tone of our country and even on the future of our world.

In spite of the fact that I feel I must sometimes be critical, I really must acknowledge how really good the media has been to me since I came to Washington a year ago. They have been honest and more than fair in their reporting. I believe that this has been good for our Catholic people and many other people of good will towards the Church. So often our folks write to me or stop me on the street to say: "I saw you on TV" or "I heard you on the radio" or " I saw your picture in the paper." Here in Washington where there is more news than there is space and time to cover it, this has been a special gift and I do want to say thank you for it.

The media is a powerful tool for good and for truth, an extraordinary instrument for building up the spirit of a community or of a nation. I have witnessed the truly great contribution the press, the TV, and the radio have made to carry us through the trauma of September 11. What a positive force they have been and how wonderfully they have sensed and supported the mood of the nation. With such tremendous influence goes tremendous responsibility, and the men and women who guide and direct this powerful force can surely count on my prayers for their awesome task. When I come across something in the media about myself, I usually begin thinking of you and hoping that you may find it helpful in the journey of your own lives. And that is what it is all about.

Not So Smart
January 17, 2002

I was trying to figure out a good title for this column. I wavered between "Awfully Kind" and the one I finally chose, "Not So Smart." The first would have referred to all of you who were too gracious and therefore awfully kind not to write in to comment on my lapse of scriptural knowledge. Not so smart is probably more to the point and it refers to me, who is really not so smart as I thought I was.

It all began a couple of weeks ago when I was doing that Thinking of You column on "The Grace of God." I remembered a wonderful line from the second epistle of Peter in which the great apostle concludes that when all is said and done, everything is a grace, because everything that comes to us, whether joy or sorrow, pain or promise, comes from a God who loves us. After I sent it over to our *Catholic Standard*, I mentioned the line to my secretary. He immediately replied, "Yes, it is a deep and beautiful teaching and how authentically the essence of Saint Paul!"

Saying nothing to him of course, when we returned home, I went quickly to the New Testament and found that he was right on target. The words come right from the fourth chapter of Saint Paul's Letter to the Romans, and Saint Peter never

mentions it in that epistle at all, despite my supposedly clear
memory of where I found it. Bottom line—in case you hadn't
already perceived it, your bishop really is "not so smart" and
you were awfully kind not to notice.

May I try to salvage something from this story? Some of
our Protestant and Jewish sisters and brothers have such a
great love for the Bible that they can cite passage after passage
of this greatest Holy Book. And yet the Bible belongs to all
of us who are people of the Book. It is the compendium of
the revelation we have all received from a loving God. There
are different translations, of course, and the Church tries to
make sure that the ones we use are accurate and well written,
but the basic message is the powerful call to holiness and to
sacrifice and to the love of God and our neighbors.

I always try to read the Bible every day—indeed the divine
office of the breviary is filled with scripture—but one of my
New Year's resolutions now will be to read it more slowly
and more carefully so that I will remember it and be able to
meditate on it better. I would be so happy if you would do
that too. Don't read it to finish it or to get through it. Just
take a chapter a day and ask God to speak to you through it.
I know I've told you about this before, but it is so important
and so filled with grace that whenever I do read it with loving
care, I am always thinking of you.

Open to Life
January 24, 2002

It's snowing today as I am writing this. I probably shouldn't
tell you this, but I really love snow. As a youngster, I lived in
Manhattan near the George Washington Bridge and in those
days we had lots of snow. Since I really never liked school,

snow was always a hoped-for respite from the classroom and a chance to play in the street, building dams in the gutters and forts on the mounds that snow plows left behind. Snow is one of God's great gifts to children.

But I'm not going to write about snow. I want to write about children, about life, about openness to life. I talk about it a lot, I guess, because I truly believe that our attitude on this precise issue influences the way we think about many important things on our own personal journeys.

When I use the phrase "open to life," I mean many things. I mean a deep respect for life as a gift that comes from God. It affects our attitude toward capital punishment and inclines us to want to find another way to protect society from criminals who have killed others, and it affects the decisions husbands and wives make about bringing children into the world. On that latter point, the opposite of openness to life is threatening to make humanity an endangered species in many parts of the Western world.

There are many countries in this world that are so committed to a contraceptive way of life that they are not producing enough children to survive as national groups. There are cities and provinces in some of the most developed nations of the world that can continue to exist only through foreign immigration, because the native inhabitants are so closed to life that children are not being born in sufficient numbers to take the place of today's adults. Obviously this saddens me as I see great cultures, many of them Christian, on a path to extinction. More than that, my sadness comes so much more since oftentimes the reason for excluding children is a desire for more comfort, for less responsibility, for the quest for a new car or a new vacation plan rather than a new child and all the deep joy as well as the demands that a new baby can bring.

The most awful thing of all, of course, is when the new baby is already present in its mother's womb and the conscious decision is made to end its life in a violent way through some form of abortion. This is also the most terrible result of building a society that is closed to life. When I see a little child carried in its mother's or father's arms as the parent comes up for Communion at Mass, I reach out to give a special blessing to the child and I say a silent prayer of gratitude for the parents who were open to life and brave and generous enough to give that little person the chance to come into our wondrous world and to enjoy the opportunity of making it better.

On a snowy day, as I pass the children playing, I am thinking of you and families throughout this archdiocese and thanking God for the love that brought you here.

"Waltz Across Texas"
January 31, 2002

Some of you know that I went to Texas last Thursday to give a talk. It was one of those crazy days that come into our lives from time to time. Instead of getting up at 5:00, which is my usual time, I got up at 4:00, offered Mass at 4:30 in my little chapel in the residence, and drove to Reagan National Airport for a 6:30 plane. I arrived in San Antonio about 11:00 their time, drove to the hotel, and then after a little bit of lunch, gave the keynote talk at the twentieth anniversary of the Catholic television station in San Antonio. (They were extraordinarily generous to us after September 11, helping both with their prayers and their almsgiving, so I really felt that I wanted to help them celebrate when they asked me to come.) After the talk, I returned to the airport and flew back to Baltimore-Washington International Airport arriving around 7:30 in the evening. It's great what you can do in a day, but I confess that the rapid turnaround—which was wonderful for me and my schedule—was not so great the following days.

But that was not why I entitled this column "Waltz Across Texas." I happen to be a great fan of country-western music. I not only like the melodies, but the words often have some great homespun philosophy that is the start of a homily or a good talk. A few years ago, someone gave me a CD by Ernest Tubb called *Waltz Across Texas*, which has some wonderful tunes in it. The title song, sung by him and some other country-western singers, has a very catchy melody and I just started to play it again since I got a new CD player as a Christmas gift this year.

The evening before the March for Life, many of the American cardinals come to Washington for a great Mass in the Basilica of the National Shrine here. I had the good thought to invite them for dinner and tried out my CD as we gathered around before going in to eat. It was a great hit! We had eight cardinals in my house and a few bishops, and they all were fascinated by my devotion to country music and by this particular fascinating tune. It could have been a great sing-a-long if they had only known the words. Of course, after it was over, most of them shook their heads and said "I didn't know you were so much into this kind of music!"

There is a moral to this story. Each of us finds beauty where he or she finds it. As long as something can, in its own way, reflect the goodness and the glory of God, it is a grace—as I wrote you a few columns ago. And we people are like that too. Beauty is often in the eye of the beholder or in the ear of the listener. (I must remember that when I criticize my nephews and nieces for their rock music. If only they could learn to appreciate it without playing it so loud!) But God gives us so much pleasure in the good things of his world. For me, as I am thinking of you, I know what a gift you are too!

Once Again, Faith
February 7, 2002

As we turn into February, still marveling at the "spring-time in January" we have just experienced, it may be time to review the New Year's resolutions we made—or wanted to make—a few weeks ago. I decided to do it myself last week as I realized how quickly the year was already passing by and that I was no better in 2002 than I had been in 2001!

I quickly remade all the usual resolutions—take a day off, be more thoughtful with those who work for me, get more time for daily meditation—knowing deep down inside that I probably wouldn't fulfill them, but happy that I would at least try once again. And then, the nagging thought came back to me that I had promised to do a pastoral letter on faith last year.

As I go about the archdiocese on my second round of parish visits, this time trying to add a visit to our high schools and elementary schools, I end up so often preaching about faith. For me, and for all of us, really, it is the foundation stone of who we are as Catholics, of what our life here and hereafter hinges on. It is our faith in a God who loves us, in Jesus who saved us from our sins and is present to us now as Word and Sacrament, in the Holy Spirit who guides and inspires the family of the Church—it is this faith that makes us special, that allows us to live a life of union with the living God and with one another in him.

Whenever anyone asks me what my greatest priority is, I always say that it is to build up the faith of our people. That is more important even than vocations to the priesthood and religious life, more important than all our wonderful programs of charity and education, of family life and justice. It is more important because all those other priorities and programs depend on it. No one gives his or her life to a God in whom they do not believe; no one is enriched by a program of goodness and holiness unless they have seen with the eyes of faith that this is what a living God is calling them to do.

And so, here is my resolution, all dusted off and wrapped in the bunting of 2002. I will try to write a pastoral letter on faith this year. I realize that it is dangerous to remind you that I promised to do it. Now I can't keep putting it off anymore. Say a prayer that the Lord will give me the thoughts and the words and that, when it finally gets done, it might be helpful. I guess that is the price I pay for the joyful privilege of trying always to be thinking of you.

A Bad Spin
February 14, 2002

I'm not sure how conscious we always are of the ways that brilliant public relations people can influence our attitudes by the careful and clever use of words. When we listen to the commercials on radio and television, we are usually not paying much attention to the words that are used to command our interest or to influence the way we respond to the message. Yet, we know how costly only several-second sound-bites like these can be and we should be aware of the impact that they can have on our own thinking. Every word is chosen carefully and every concept measured for maximum advantage. It is in the way a word is used that can put a particular spin on a sentence.

Let me give you a case in point. It has to do with our continuing struggle against abortion. When this is presented by those who dislike our position, the words used are never "pro-life" and "pro-abortion" but always "anti-abortion" and "pro-choice." Those who are against us have succeeded in making the positive-sounding term "pro-choice" cover a hideous procedure that destroys the life of an innocent little child.

Everyone can see the attractiveness of wanting to assure freedom of choice to every individual. When most of us hear the phrase, we think it applies to a choice between options that are both good, but in this case, the choice involves ending the life of another human being. There must be a limit to our own rights when these "rights" deny the more basic right to life of another person. This is a bad spin of language and sadly it is a spin that has now become the popular usage of so much of the media.

The reason I bring this up today is that I see another "bad spin" of language on the horizon. It is in the area of health care and hospitals, and the same anti-life coalition is behind it. Our nation has always respected freedom of conscience. Legally, we cannot be forced to do what our conscience tells us is morally wrong. This has been true both of individuals whose consciences are formed by their moral beliefs and of institutions that operate according to the moral principles of their founding organizations.

It was beyond the contemplation of the statesmen who drafted our Constitution that any person should have to choose between honoring God and honoring the secular law. The author of the First Amendment, later President James Madison, said that the demands of religion preceded any obligations of the state. This historic principle is now being attacked by those who want to force Catholic hospitals to perform abortions and other medical procedures that we believe to be forbidden by the law of God and the natural law.

The secret of their strategy is to ignore the constitutional protection of conscience, which is guaranteed by our freedom of religion. They want to spin the language to suggest that in following our own right of conscience, "we refuse" to accommodate the supposed rights of others to put unwanted children to death in their mother's wombs. "Refuse" is the word they use to spin their argument. According to them, freedom of conscience is not involved; it is our refusal to accommodate choice—a terribly wrong choice—that they attack. If they get away with that negative spin of words, it is we who will be on the defense for refusing the immoral procedures, rather than they for refusing to respect our right and the right of our institutions to follow the teachings of our faith.

I see this as a perilous development—a concerted attempt on the part of those who are opposed to our moral position to cripple our nationwide system of health and hospital services. It is a campaign whose rallying cry is a bad spin at language.

This is a heavy subject, I know, but it is one that could have terrible consequences for the future and so I wanted to share my concerns with you as I was thinking of you today.

A Very Ordinary Ordinary
February 21, 2002

Years ago, when the Holy Father transferred me from the diocese of Metuchen to work as the ordinary or the diocesan bishop of the Archdiocese of Newark, there was some curiosity in the North Jersey newspapers as to what the new archbishop was like. One of my cousins, who has been one of my closest relatives and friends for most of my life, was interviewed by an enterprising reporter. He summed it all up by calling me "a genial workaholic"! Now I really hope that I am genial, but I confess that I probably am a workaholic.

Almost a century ago, when the great Saint Frances Cabrini was suffering her last illness—a bout of pneumonia in 1917 that ultimately brought on her death—the doctors had given orders to the sisters at the orphanage in Chicago where she was staying to ensure that she had total bed rest and liquids. One afternoon as they brought her a cup of juice, they could not find her in her bedroom. The alarm went out and all the sisters went to look everywhere for the mother. Finally they found her in the chilly storage room, happily wrapping Christmas presents for the orphans. They scolded her—as much as you can do to a general superior who is also a saint—and reminded her that the doctors had wanted her to rest. The story is that Cabrini replied with great conviction: "Rest, no, no, no—work, work, work. There will be enough time to rest in Paradise!"

I don't have the same certainty of Paradise that this great modern saint possessed on her own earthly journey, but I have always thought that this reply of hers was a good rule of life for me and I have tried to live it with fidelity and hopefully with joy.

The reason for writing this to you this weekend is that people often ask me "What is your day like?" I'm embarrassed to tell you that it is not always that exciting, and usually it is filled with the same ordinary things that fill your own days. It seems that by now just about everybody knows that I get up at 5:00 in the morning. (I don't know how that word got around, but folks are always telling me—"I know that you get up at 5:00." On Saturdays I don't set my alarm, and often can sleep until 6:00!)

I'm in the chapel by 5:45 and at my desk or in the car by 6:30, depending on whether I have an early Mass outside the center. I usually eat breakfast at 8:00 if my Mass is later in the day or if I've had Mass in the house chapel, which is usually at 7:30. After breakfast I try to read the newspapers and then I'm back in my office by 9:00. From then on, it's pretty

much the same every weekday. Between the telephone, the
computer, and paperwork on the one hand and meetings and
visits on the other, with a little more prayer fitted in whenever I can (my chapel is right next to the office)—and meals
whenever necessary—that covers my day. Calendar meetings
are necessary evils since dozens of invitations seem to come
in every week and the mail gets to me toward the end of the
day after the staff sorts it out and throws away the advertise-
ments! I end up in the office until 10:00 in the evening and
I get to bed by 11:00.

Now you know the inside-out of the archbishop's day. It is
nothing really wonderful, except the times to pray. No really
great accomplishments, except the time I spend with you in
the parishes or the institutions, but all of it has a purpose. In
some way, according to the mysterious providence of God,
my work joins with yours and together we offer to the Lord
all that we can do for his glory and our own salvation, knowing that the ordinary things that make up our day—if we do
them in love—will have a great reward.

So when all is said and done, you have a very ordinary
Ordinary, but one who is always thinking of you.

An Unpleasant Task
February 28, 2002

There are certain things you don't want to write about.
They are too sad or too sordid or so strange that they give
you an uncomfortable feeling right in the pit of your stom-
ach. One of these is pedophilia or child abuse. It seems that
so many people are writing about this topic in the media
these days that another column would be unnecessary, but
the letters I get from some of you in my archdiocesan family

indicate that there are enough folks who would want me to talk about it, too.

What shall I say? A few weeks ago I was on a live news program on TV and the second question I got was about child abuse. The question caught me by surprise since I was supposed to be discussing another topic, but it did give me a chance to say what I felt from my heart. Hurting a child or a young person through sexual or physical abuse is always despicable and to be condemned whoever the offender is, but when the perpetrator is someone who is trusted by the child because of his role or his profession, the wrong that is done is multiplied and is all the more horrendous. My heart breaks at the suffering this causes the children and their families, and I want to add my own deep apologies for any and every crime of this kind by a priest or a minister of religion here or anywhere.

It is good for us to keep an historical perspective since many of the cases now in the media are from past decades. Fifty years ago it was probably considered by most people to be a grave moral fault but one that an individual could correct. Similarly in the medical profession, many also believed that this problem could be corrected. Later on, the psychiatrists and other mental health experts began to understand that it was really more serious than that. It was also a deep-seated psychological illness that could only be controlled by lengthy hospitalization and more comprehensive psychological treatment.

Society and the medical and legal systems of our country began to see that the risks of repeated offenses were greater than previously thought and therefore a more stringent policy had to be followed. Probably some offenders can be helped by intense therapy, but now we know that it is too great a risk to take a chance with the mental or physical health of our young people, and, even more to the point, with their relationship with a God who only wants their good. Once a clear case has been made, an offending individual should never be placed in a position of trust with children ever again.

I think there are three important points that I ought to make. First of all I want to assure you that the Archdiocese of Washington has one of the most comprehensive and stringent procedures to guard against child sexual abuse of any agency, religious or secular, in the country. Elsewhere in today's *Catholic Standard* you can find an article that points this out in detail. That should give a real sense of security to our people.

Secondly, I want to talk to you about the priests who serve in this archdiocese. You know them as well or better than I do. Think about them, for a moment. They are good, solid, hard-working men who love God and who love you. In the past fourteen months I have come to love them and respect them, and you can be as proud of them as I am. Finally it is important to put this problem, as horrible as it is, into context. Experts say that there is no evidence that priests are more likely to engage in sexual misconduct against minors than men in other professions.

Of course, the fact that even one priest might have this problem is already a source of sadness for us all. I promise you that the stringent policies already in place at the time of my predecessor, Cardinal Hickey, will be scrupulously followed in this Archdiocese of Washington, and I ask you to join me in prayer for the victims of this crime, for their families, and also for the sick and tragic men who have caused all this pain.

May the terrible scars of the children who have suffered—and who now in their adult life still feel the pain and the loss of trust—be made to heal by the love of their families and by the prayers of our community of faith. I hesitated to write you on this, dear friends, because we seem to run into these stories wherever we turn, but hearing from some of you and thinking of you all, I thought I should share my own sad thoughts with you.

Keep Praying
March 7, 2002

Last week I wrote to all our pastors and asked them to encourage our people to pray for rain. In view of the real danger of an impending drought in our area, like so many other people, I had begun to worry about the bad effect on our local environment of the critical shortage of rain in the counties of the Archdiocese of Washington these past several months. I'm sitting in my office here in the pastoral center and looking out the window and it's now raining "cats and dogs" as we used to say. I'm grateful to the Lord for that and I hope we will get a really good soaking. The only problem is that it's Saturday morning and it's going to be a wet weekend for folks who planned to do things out of doors! I guess we can begin to pray for rain on weekdays after this.

That brings to my mind some thoughts about prayer that I'd like to share with you. The first—and most important—is to pray with confidence. The second is to make our prayer a real conversation with God, and the final note is not to forget to say thank you. All these things we would do in our human conversations. The point I want to make is that we must pray to God in the same way.

Praying with confidence is really the key to prayer. It is really related to our act of faith in a God who cares for us. (That's on my mind especially these days as I am grateful for the many reminders from you that I must do that pastoral letter on faith!) If we do not believe that God hears us and listens to us with love, then our prayer has no real basis and it becomes only a string of words that we memorized long ago. But if we truly believe that God is a loving Father to whom we can turn in times of joy or need or pain, if we listen to the words of Jesus in the scriptures when he tells us of the Father's special affection for each one of us, then we can approach our heavenly Father with the confidence that he does hear and answer our prayers. I believe today's rain is his reply to those who begged him to send it.

Secondly, we need to pray not just with our lips but with our minds and hearts. I remember a great cartoon of some weeks ago—you all know that I am hooked on the comic papers. I don't know if it was the Family Circus or Dennis the Menace, but it shows the youngster kneeling on top of his bed in prayer and saying to God, "Now, I think you need to hear the other side of the story." For me that was a beautiful reminder that children, when they pray, often show that they sense God's personal presence and talk to him as he loves to be talked to, recognizing that he is truly present and listening.

Finally, we should always remember to thank the Lord for his answer to our prayer, even if that answer is not what we really expected. Going back to the point I made in the beginning, it is our faith that makes prayer possible, as it is that same faith that helps us to realize that everything we ask for is not always what is best for us in the light of the eternity of happiness with God to which we are called. So please keep on praying for all those things you hope for, all those things you really feel you need, and remember those other special intentions that I ask you to add from time to time—for vocations, for rain, and also for this poor servant of yours who is always thinking of you.

Helping Hands
March 14, 2002

By now I guess almost everybody has heard of my adventure! It was a really interesting experience, one that taught me a lot—especially that I can't fast and give blood on the same day. Some of the lessons I learned were very beautiful. I learned again what I have always known, that so many people are so very good. In a world that is often filled with bad news, this is something we ought to share.

It all started in Southern Maryland. As you know, I try to go down to that magic part of our Archdiocese of Washington at least once a month. It is so easy to get caught up in the busyness and the excitement of this federal city and its surroundings that I could lose sight of our three southern counties filled with so much Catholic history and so much beauty. I visited some of our schools, offered Mass for the Catholic students at St. Mary's College, and spent a good deal of time talking to our folks who guide the extensive Catholic Charities operations in that area. Incidentally, we run the only shelter for women and children in Southern Maryland and I was privileged to spend some quality time with the staff and the residents—many of whom are victims of domestic violence.

Well, to make a long story short, I left early on Wednesday morning, without eating anything, to come to DC for a meeting with the ecumenical patriarch and some other bishops. Thank goodness, I did have a muffin and a glass of orange juice at that gathering, because right after it I went to Holy Cross Hospital to donate blood. (You remember that I am O negative, the universal donor, so I really ought to give blood as often as I can.) When they asked if I had eaten, I said "yes" thinking of the muffin and the juice. The process took longer than I had anticipated and so I got back to my office around 2:30 in the afternoon. I figured that it was too late for lunch and I knew that I was going to have a good meal that evening, so I went right to my meetings until I left for dinner around 6:30.

Just as we were gathering at table before 8:00 p.m., in the middle of a conversation with a friend, I just passed out. (I had been feeling a little lightheaded before that, but I figured I would be fine once I sat down at table and started to eat.) When I came to, I was lying on a sofa and everyone was very kindly worrying about me. In a few minutes, the police, the fire department, EMS, and an ambulance were all there taking extraordinary care of me. More than anything, I was embarrassed that I had caused all that extra work for so many people—especially for my host and hostess!

The fun part of it was the ambulance ride to the hospital. It was like *ER* on television! I have been in ambulances accompanying people who were ill, but this was my first experience as a patient, strapped to a gurney, and getting IV on the way! How gently and carefully everybody took care of me! From the moment of my fainting to the emergency room of the hospital, helping hands and experienced guides were with me. How good God is to imprudent archbishops who think they are supermen when at seventy-one they are more like one of the seven dwarfs. (You can choose which one, but his name begins with a "D.") I am so grateful to all those who took such good care of me and got me on my feet and back home that night.

In a special way, I was touched by the coverage that the media gave to my "indisposition." I believe that this is due in greatest part to the loving and invaluable presence of Cardinal Hickey and my predecessors here in Washington. Because of them, the Catholic archbishop has become a real part of this great city and we can be proud of their accomplishments, which make us a vital part of the life of this community and its service to youth, to the poor, and to education. The media must have done a tremendous job because someone called my office from Hawaii to see how I was doing after she saw the news on a TV station there! I'm fine, thank God, and I am grateful to all of you for thinking of me even as I try always to keep thinking of you.

Numbers
March 21, 2002

Years ago, when I was studying for my doctorate in sociology at Catholic University, I took a course in statistics. I confess that I couldn't pass it now—and I suspect I barely passed it then. One of the things I remember about it was that, like all things in life, statistical conclusions are only as good as the data they are given to work on. I want to talk about that today.

The newspapers are giving a lot of scary statistics about priests who have abused minors. Sometimes the numbers make us shudder—and rightly so since even one such man who abuses a child is a disaster and a scandal for us all. However, it can help us to put the problem into a clearer context if we take a second look at what we are being told.

A week or so ago, a large diocese in the Northeast reported that thirty-five priests had credibly been accused of this crime. What was not stressed was that this covered a period of fifty years during which that local Church had more than two thousand five hundred priests serving its Catholic people. We can all do the math. It comes to less than 1.5 percent of the priests, a little more than one in a hundred! Even the terrible statistics that have come out of Boston do not add up to 2 percent of the priests in that huge archdiocese. I wonder what profession or group of men or women has a better record than that?

We don't have such careful statistics on other groups in our society, basically because the Church in the United States has tried—often too late, I am sad to admit—to take steps against this problem. If a person in a nondescript occupation abuses a minor, it is usually reported in the back pages of our newspapers. If, God forbid, it is a clergy person from another denomination, it gets up toward the front. But if it is a Catholic priest, it makes banner headlines. I am not really complaining about this last point. In a way it is a tribute to our priests that our society expects more of them than it does of others, and when we fail, it is so much more terrible. I just don't want you to think that these numbers are an epidemic. Less than 2 percent does not indicate that, although, I say it again, even one priest who harms a child is one too many.

I hate to write about this or even to talk about it, but I want to put these statistics into context and to assure you as the servant of this Church of Washington that your love and respect for our priests is not misplaced. Pray for them—and for me—during these very difficult days. Be sure that, in a very special way now, all of us are gratefully thinking of you.

The Passion of the Church
March 28, 2002

I am almost finished writing a pastoral letter to you and to all the Catholics of the archdiocese. No, it's not the one on faith that I have been promising. That had to be deferred in this time of turmoil. It is on the passion of the Church and it seeks to compare the Church's present passion with that of the Lord. His passion ended in resurrection, and I am praying that this troubled moment in our lives ends the same way too.

The Church, like every family, is a living organism. Just as families pass through moments of crisis, of pain, and disappointment, so does the Church—and so did the Lord. Can we imagine that his mystical body would not reflect his own life and that the troubles of his own disciples would never be mirrored—even though in starkly different ways reflective of a starkly different culture—by today's disciples, namely you and I and all those other men and women who accept the gift of faith and somehow try to pursue the road of holiness? The history of the Church is filled with moments of glory, for example, in the lives of the saints. It is also going to know moments of sorrow and disappointment.

But the Church is purified through these periods of pain, and just as our salvation follows Christ's death on the cross, so the body of Christ always returns to its roots in the Holy Spirit after a moment of uncertainty or loss. Hope is the virtue we need for these times, a hope built on a solid, loving faith, a hope that is founded on a real personal relationship with Jesus. Without that trust and hope—even as was true in the life of Jesus—the way to the passion becomes too great a burden to bear.

I see two rays of light that God sends us in these periods of deepest night. I see them already present in this Church of ours, and they are real and palpable and strong. The first is the new appreciation that the faithful have for the good and holy priests who serve them. God's people, saddened by the few who may have failed, are turning to the many whom they know through personal experience to be striving for holiness and they are supporting them in their lives and in their labors.

Secondly, in the wonderful paradox of divine grace, this day God is calling strong and dedicated young men to priestly vocation and even against the background of scandal and disappointment, courageous and generous examples are multiplying of those who are willing to accept the challenge of priestly service and to pour out their young lives in the ministry of divine love.

As I am thinking of you and of them, I want to call all of us to confidence in the God who loves us and in his gift to us of shepherds who, even in the midst of storms, are ready to serve the people. Do not lose heart—this Jesus whom we trust and worship has overcome the world.

The Peace of Easter
April 4, 2002

I don't remember a year in which I looked forward to Easter as much as I have this year. It has been a difficult Lent. Problems in the world, problems in the Church, continuing problems in our own area where the fallout from 9/11 has still not totally left our local economy—all these continued to put us "on edge" as we waited for the return of the "alleluia" and the new life that the springtime of Easter can bring. But the challenge is to let the new life in—and not to remain buried in the empty tomb of yesterday.

You and I know that it is possible to live in the past, just as it is possible to live for tomorrow. There are many people who never seem to be able to put the past behind them, to turn off the trials of yesterday and to reach out for the present moment. The folks who do that come from many different psychologies. There are those who only remember the good things of yesterday and enfold themselves in the happy memories of the past. Older people tend to do that, and it provides a shield from the sometimes threatening problems of today. Such an attitude is understandable, but it limits one's ability to rise and shine in the light of a new day and it focuses one only on "the good old days," which probably were never really as good as they want to remember them.

There are those who only seem to live for tomorrow. They try to ignore the burdens of yesterday and the realities of today. They tend to spend their lives planning for tomorrow and often forgetting that the challenges of every day have to be met before the fragile bridge to the future can be crossed.

Most of us try to live from day to day. We reflect some-times on the past, both with happy memories and at times with melancholy. We do make our plans and look forward to tomorrow, but depending on our ages, the vision can take many forms. Usually we accept the wisdom of the scriptures that each day has its own troubles and its own rewards and we are called to take them one at a time. It is when the for-mer seems so numerous and the latter so sparse that we find ourselves longing to be at peace.

Well, be of good heart. Easter has come and the new life is here, even if reading the papers and turning on the news doesn't always give you that confidence. Believe that the Lord has come and that he brings new life with him. Even the birds and the flowers know it. Even the sun sends its light ahead much earlier to call us to the challenge of the new day. "Christ has risen" the world seems to shout to people of faith! Trust him. You are in good hands. Be at peace. He is thinking of you and he loves you. After all, did he not give his very life for you? Listen to him say "Peace be with you" and pass it on today.

Catholic Education
April 11, 2002

Last week I had a great experience. I had been invited to give the keynote address to the annual convention of the National Catholic Educational Association (NCEA) and I would talk to almost twelve thousand Catholic educators. The NCEA is the umbrella organization representing just about every part of Catholic education in our country, from the parochial school and the catechetical programs in parishes to great Catholic universities and seminaries. I was really honored by the invitation and it gave me a chance to talk about something that is close to my heart.

The reason I'm telling you about it now is that I was able to speak about our own Archdiocese of Washington and to give examples to the others of what we are trying to do here. In a sense we have a microcosm of the whole country here in our own backyard.

We have the challenge of the inner city to make sure that we are offering excellent value-centered programs to the youngsters in the disadvantaged neighborhoods of this nation's capital. We are challenged to reach out to our growing Hispanic population and to make sure that they, too, will have the benefits of a Catholic education to prepare them for leadership in our community and in our nation. We have the challenge of burgeoning suburbs in the northern areas of our diocese and we need to provide more schools to care for their increasing Catholic school-age population. Finally—and for me also critically important—we have the rural areas of Southern Maryland where special circumstances demand our attention to preserving our Catholic schools and making them even better.

I didn't even get into the important necessity of campus ministry in both our Catholic and non-Catholic educational institutions, but I was able to speak to all these other issues from some real, although limited, experience. From the reaction of the listeners, I believe that they shared the same concern both from the point of view of the schools themselves to the equally huge challenge of constant improvement in the quality and effectiveness of our catechetical programs stretching all the way from pre-K to adult education.

Catholic education is really a family affair. It demands the attention of mothers and fathers as an essential part of the process. They are, as the Church has always taught, the first teachers of their children, especially in the ways of faith. Therefore, both by example and by instruction, mothers and fathers must pass on the great treasure of our Catholic faith to their children, together with the warmth and joy that they themselves should feel in the Lord. The role of the Catholic school and the parish catechetical program is to help parents accomplish this vital task.

This is my real reason for focusing this column on Catholic education. I truly believe that one of the greatest gifts you can give your children is to send them to a Catholic school. I realize how difficult that can be financially, as we continue to work for elementary justice from our governments making it economically possible for Catholic fathers and mothers to exercise their right to send their children to a non-public school. I believe it is worth the effort and I pledge to do my best to try to help rising costs from making Catholic education too difficult for our poor and working-class families to afford.

So you see, wherever I am and whatever audience I am called to address, I am always trying to think of you and your concerns and doing my best always to make them my own.

Extraordinary Women
April 18, 2002

Mark Zimmermann, the editor of the *Catholic Standard,* who in my opinion is one of the finest newspapermen I have ever met (I shouldn't have said that—the secular press will try to steal him now), did me a big favor the other day. I had asked him to list the subjects of the almost seventy columns I've been really privileged to write for you since I came to Washington in January of last year. As I looked over all the areas that we have shared in those fifteen months, I realized that I have never written about sisters and specifically about women's vocation to the religious life. I want to make up for that now.

A couple of weeks ago, when I was preparing my talk for the National Catholic Educational Association, I thought back to my early days in parochial school at Incarnation Parish in uptown Manhattan. That was the first time I really met a nun. Of course I had seen sisters in church sometimes when my mother would bring me to Mass and I always marveled at their composure, their deep attention, and their obvious prayerfulness. When I met Sister Mary Paula, the first grade teacher—we didn't have kindergarten in those days—I was awed by her and probably terrified. She was probably terrified too, since she was very young and there were seventy-two of us in that one classroom!

Most of my grammar school teachers were sisters. They all lived in a large convent a few blocks from the school and walked together—almost in procession—every school day, rain, snow, or shine, about fifteen minutes before school started. Some of them were very strict—and feared by us little kids—but most of them were extraordinary women who loved us and taught us patiently and truly touched our lives. Later on, as a teenager, I came to know nursing sisters, great missionary sisters, and the dedicated sisters whose lives were spent caring for the poor.

I thank God for the sisters in our Archdiocese of Washington. We would be lost without them. It is not just the work that they do for God's people here, but more than anything their witness of faith and love and sacrifice that their presence brings to our faithful, including to our priests as much as to our lay people! I pray that God will bless the young women of this local Church with many strong vocations to religious life. We could double the number of our sisters here in our parishes and schools, our nursing homes and institutions. I know that I give you so many intentions to pray for, but pray along with me for this intention too.

Last but assuredly not least, I think of the cloistered monasteries that shine like brilliant diamonds here in our area. Only God knows the blessings that come to us from their lives of prayer and solitude! I usually try to visit them when my own cross becomes heavy and I always feel renewed by the evident joy and peace that surrounds them. Their lives are not easy. They are directed to deepest prayer and silent work, to the service of the Lord whose tender love invites them to discover the power of his presence here in this world so that they might help us all to serve him in the world that has no end. Pray for them and get to know them if you can. Like your bishop, they too, are always thinking of you.

A Moving Experience
April 25, 2002

It's not what you think. The title of this column has not much to do with emotion, but with a very prosaic fact. Most

of you know by now that on Sunday I will be going with
the other American cardinals to Rome (I am writing this
on Saturday) to the meeting on sexual abuse of minors. I
thought for a moment of writing again on that topic, but I
decided against it. We all have heard and read so much on
that subject over the past few weeks that little new can probably be said. Besides that, I believe I have had almost twenty
media interviews on the same theme in the past week and I
am really somewhat burned out on it. When I get back from
Rome, I will bring you up to date again. So let me talk about
my moving experience instead!

I am moving back into town. In a certain sense, the archbishop always has his canonical residence at the cathedral
and I know that I am always at home there, but I have been
staying at the Archdiocesan Pastoral Center all this time and
have gotten quite comfortable there. Except that I have no
storage space here—and some of my things are still "under
the bed!"—this is a beautiful place to live. Many of you have
been to the Archdiocesan Pastoral Center and so you know
it is now located in a kind of park in Hyattsville right at the
district line. But since I have arrived here, so many people,
both in the Church and the civil society, have been saying
to me in one way or another "the archbishop of Washington
should live in Washington." I think that they are right.

There is a building owned by the archdiocese that makes
this possible. Happily for me, the top floor of the building
was never finished and we are now able to do that with the
help of some friends of mine from New Jersey. (I didn't want
to put the burden of fixing it up on the archdiocese; you
know by now how cheap I am!) I think it will be very comfortable and efficient when we get it done. Bishop Francisco
Gonzalez is now serving as pastor of the Parish of Our Lady,
Queen of the Americas and so I will be living with him and
his associate pastor, as well as with Bishop Farrell and my
priest secretaries. I'll still go to work at the pastoral center

and it will be a good thing not to live right across the hall from my office.

I hope to be able to move during the summer and I'll keep you posted. It will just be another place where you can be sure that I'm thinking of you.

La Plata
May 2, 2002

You all know how much I love Southern Maryland, that magic land that is so filled with history and beauty for me. It will therefore not be a surprise to you how much I was really shaken up by the terrible disaster that hit that area of our archdiocese last Sunday evening.

I had come back to my residence from a busy Sunday schedule around 6:00 p.m. amid dark and lowering skies. I had been listening to the weather reports on the radio as we drove back home. Actually, I turned on the weather channel to get an update, but it didn't seem to be focusing at that time on our part of the country. I heated up some supper that our cook had left for us and then got caught up in paperwork. Since I had been away in Rome for most of the past week, I had much to read over and try to handle. About 10:00 in the evening, as I began to close up shop for the day, I turned on the news again and heard the beginning story of the devastation that hit La Plata. I knew I had to go there early the next day.

Monday morning I began to try to make contact with the pastor to get a sense of the danger. The rectory there had suffered little damage, but the pastor's windows had been blown out. Thank God Father Matt Siekierski was not in his room at the time. I finally reached him on a cell phone since the difficulty of the phone lines was very real. I was thankful that he and his associate were all right, but there was a crack in his voice when he told me, "Archbishop, we lost the school." Archbishop Neale School is one of the jewels of the Arch-diocese of Washington. It has more than five hundred fifty youngsters from the central part of Charles County, and we have just finished building an addition to it. To make mat-ters worse, we didn't know where the two sisters who staff the school were. Their convent was still standing but no one had seen them. Thank goodness, after a harrowing experience they had taken refuge in a convent in Clinton. I also called the Carmelite nuns at Port Tobacco—a few miles away from La Plata—and they assured me that they were all right, but described hailstones the size of tennis balls. (Later that day, I was to see the side of a wooden house totally disfigured and pock-marked by the impact of dozens of these hailstone projectiles.)

Thanks to the state police and Father Karl Chimiak, their chaplain who is also a pastor in Southern Maryland, I could see for myself the awful effects of this monster tornado as it zigzagged through the area, totally destroying one house and leaving its neighbor completely undisturbed. I stayed in La Plata all morning, talking to people and meeting with local officials. The latter, by the way, were most impressive as they quickly organized the relief operations to rebuild this lovely old town after the destruction of an F5 tornado. As I offered the midday Mass in Sacred Heart Church there, I prayed for all those who had lost so much, and thinking of you and them, I begged the Lord to keep us always safe in his loving hands.

Come Back to the Table
May 9, 2002

As I may have told you, a few months ago I was invited to attend the World Economic Forum in New York. One of the highlights of the three-day meeting for me was a luncheon to which the religious leaders present were invited to discuss the worsening situation in the Holy Land. Shimon Peres, the Israeli foreign minister, and the Egyptian foreign minister who serves as the current president of the Arab League both spoke and outlined their positions and their hopes for the future.

I was invited to say a few words and my words were the ones that I used as the title of this column. "Please, for the sake of God and for the welfare of millions of innocent people, come back to the table and solve this impasse by dialogue and negotiation." I seem to recall that everyone applauded my plea, but no one really listened to it and the situation has deteriorated so terribly since that time.

I have hesitated to write on this subject, partly because it is so complex and I am sure that I do not understand it completely, and partly because my words could be misunderstood as not seeing the "big picture" or being swayed by the desperate stories that come to us from the news media. The tragedy of the Holy Land continues to haunt me, however, and I feel I must share my sorrow and disappointment with you who are my family here in Washington.

Too many innocent Israeli citizens have suffered from the murderous hatred of terrorism, whose attacks have left dozens dead. Too many innocent Palestinians have suffered in the harsh response of the Israeli defense forces, leaving hundreds dead and thousands homeless. The stand-off at the sacred shrine of Jesus' birth is a scandal to every religious man or woman. Here, above all, is the place for reasonable people to be able to dialogue to reach an acceptable solution.

Our own government has now called for a wider dialogue, and I believe that this is an important step, although it is much too long in coming. How many more will die before it becomes a reality? How many more have died needlessly already? The Holy See has issued a strong statement on this crisis. Its strength is undoubtedly a sign of the frustration that the great powers of the world have been so powerless to stop the bloodshed and move the parties on the road to peace.

The Holy See's positions are clear and strong: unequivocal condemnation of terrorism from whatever side it may come, disapproval of the condition of injustice and humiliation imposed on the Palestinian people, respect for the U.N. resolutions guaranteeing the security of Israel and promoting Palestinian statehood, proportionality in the use of legitimate means of defense, and the duty of the parties in the conflict to protect the holy places.

Pope John Paul II has stressed that no political or religious leader can remain silent or inactive and, thinking of you as servant of this local Church of ours, therefore I see my own responsibility to repeat my call of February to all the sides in this terrible conflict: "I beg you to come back to the table and work to bring peace to the Holy Land."

Shadows and Light
May 16, 2002

Did you ever realize that it is impossible to have a shadow unless you also have some light? Now, this is not a very profound observation, I'm sure, but I just came to realize it fully the other day when I was talking to some of our priests on retreat. I was discussing the problems through which we are passing at this difficult time and I described it as a time of shadows. All of a sudden, it struck me that you can't have shadows unless there is a light present somewhere too!

This is not just a fact of physics that I stumbled on late in life, but also a truth in the reality of our own existence. Just as in the natural world, shadows are only found because of the presence of light, so, too, in the moral order, this seems to be the case. If it were not for the holiness of the Church and so many of its members, both clergy and lay, scandals would be impossible. If there is no goodness, then the absence of goodness would never be noticed.

Two things follow from that. The first is that we should never despair because there is so much good around us. Even if the pain we feel for the victims of the terrible crimes of some priests is heartbreaking, deep in our hearts also we are sure that God still loves his Church and will never abandon it. But not only that, the second reason for our confidence is that God is still sending us visible signs of that love and of his care for each one of us.

I experienced one of these signs last weekend when in two ordinations in the parishes of the archdiocese, I ordained six deacons for the service of this local Church. I am very proud of these young men. They are mature and prayerful, psychologically well-balanced and eager to serve God's people in any place and in any way that the Lord might ask. Two are from Latin America, one was born in Poland, and all of them, plus another four or five who will join them later, are real signs of hope for me for the future.

It was wonderful to see the faith of their families, willing and happy to be giving their sons or brothers or uncles to the Lord. The fact that it was Mother's Day gave me a special reason to want to thank each of their mothers for the great gift of their sons. They are all strong, faith-filled women who see beyond the present crisis to the life of service to which their sons have so generously offered themselves. The ordinations were grace-filled occasions, marked by a deep joy and touched by a powerful trust in the Lord. I was thinking of you as I put my hands on their heads and prayed. Pray with me now for them that they may always be happy and holy men of God.

Old Faithful
May 23, 2002

Sometimes you really have to get away and breathe in deeply of God's good fresh air! That happened to me last week. I think it came just at the right time. I know a lot of us are hurting now because of the terrible trauma affecting the Church these days. As a priest and a bishop, I am so grateful to God for the strength that comes to me from you, from my visits to the parishes and the chance to be with so many of you in prayer and faith. That has always been so great a grace for me—as it must be for every priest—and never more than now.

I had a few commitments out West and I was happily able to string them together and wonderfully I found myself with a day free and within driving range of Yellowstone National Park! I had never been to Wyoming—let alone to that great part of the state that boasts not only of the magnificent Grand Teton mountains, but also of the amazing field of hot spring geysers among which Old Faithful is easily the most famous. Last Thursday, between stops in Spokane and Pueblo, I drove up to see Old Faithful.

I wonder how the first explorers of that beautiful wilderness felt when they came upon this geyser shooting its stream of water high into the sky. The Native Americans had already discovered it, of course, and they, too, had to find it awesome and worthy of respect. Predictably, almost like clockwork, the geyser sends its smoking water aloft. The buffalo that graze nearby are the only creatures who have become so used to it that they do not even raise their heads, but the visitors who watch in wonder often applaud vigorously at the end as if to thank nature and nature's God for that wonderful display of beauty.

Perhaps no one knows who first called it "Old Faithful," or perhaps that is a translation of the Indian name for it, but it does give us something to ponder. Like a school bell announcing the beginning of class, or the bell that ends the trading day of the stock exchange, each eruption reminds us that time has passed and another task is to begin. As early settlers may have paced their days by the motion of these waters, so its fidelity night and day over the centuries became a legend that drew more and more to the site.

Fidelity is always attractive. Even more than that, it is always a challenge to the man or woman who longs to be true to his or her commitment and promises. We live in a world that admires fidelity, but all too often finds it too demanding a standard for our lives. And yet I am convinced that happiness lies in our striving to be faithful to our vows, to our responsibilities, to our families and friends, to our Church, and to our God. As I looked in wonder at Old Faithful and its commitment to nature's laws, I was thinking of you and praying that with God's help I will always be faithful to you.

A Break in the Clouds
May 30, 2002

A young reporter came up to me last Saturday just as I was preparing to join the procession of scores of priests and deacons to celebrate the Ordination Mass in the Basilica. He asked if he could just ask one question. Since I try to work on the principle that it is always good to shed light on what we are doing, I said okay, thinking that he wanted to cover the story of the ordination. He said: "Archbishop, what can you say about the scandal in the Church?" My initial reaction was to be annoyed.

When I got over that in a moment or so, I said to him: "Look around you! See these five deacons willing to give their lives for the Lord and the service of his people in a time of crisis and uncertainty. Look at those seminarians from Washington and other dioceses who come to support them on their journey and to take courage from them for their own self-offering to the Lord. Look at our priests, young and old, good, holy, generous men, whose priestly lives have been a story of sacrifice and generosity in caring for God's people, in the inner cities and in the suburbs, in the ethnic communities, the schools, the hospitals, and everywhere they are needed. Look at the hundreds of faithful lay people who come here with smiling, living faith to ask the Lord's blessing on these new priests and by their presence here to support them with their love and prayers."

I hope I didn't put off the young reporter with the vehemence of my reply, but this is also the context of the present crisis. It is a Church that has not lost its faith, a Church that has not lost its love for the priesthood, a Church that is still proclaiming to all those who will listen to the message that Jesus Christ is Lord!

Saturday's ordination was a special gift that God gave us in the midst of the concerns that we all face. It was a break in the dark clouds through which we could see the living presence of the Lord who promised that he would be with us always until the end of time and tells us again and again not to be afraid.

As I ordained these five good men as priests and saw there in Our Lady's Basilica about fifty more dedicated archdiocesan seminarians still on the road to that same priestly ministry, I was thinking of you and thanking God that he has not forgotten the Church of Washington.

Remembering . . .
June 6, 2002

As we celebrated Memorial Day a week or so ago, for some reason I was reminded of the old television serial called *I Remember Mama.* It was a popular and very family-oriented show, funny in parts, poignant in others. I think it would be so good if some of our young people, those beautifully alive and talented thirty-somethings and twenty-somethings could have had the chance to watch it.

Memories are wonderful things. They can be very sad when they touch a raw nerve of regret, when we think of something we should have said or done for a loved one and didn't do. They can be so uplifting when we reflect on the goodness or the courage or the joyfulness of someone who has now gone back to God. They can also often bring us to smiles and laughter when we recall those especially happy and even funny times of long ago when life seemed simpler and more straightforward, even if it really was not.

My mom died in 1966. She was only in her early seventies. Widowed more than thirty years before, in the deep days of the Depression, she went to work in an auto-parts factory in the Bronx when I was still very young. She was a very beautiful woman who worked as an artist's model in her twenties, and illustrations and paintings of her are found as far away as museums in Asia Minor. I have two of them in the house where I live.

When President and Mrs. Bush came to the residence for dinner last year, I made sure that they paused to see a wonderful watercolor of my mother that hangs in the corridor. As they both very graciously admired it, I thought that my mother would somehow know that the President of the United States and the First Lady had stopped and commented on how very beautiful she was!

Life goes on, the wise people say, and none of us can live in the past. The needs of today and tomorrow will not let us dwell in memories, but our lives are always a continuum. We still are the children, the teenagers, the young adults we used to be, and the young people of today will bring their own personalities into maturity and old age as well. We change accidentally, but we will always be who we are.

At every point in our history, we have to know who we are, as God's children, as members of one human family, as fellow pilgrims on the way back home. May we all be together with those we love at the end of the journey. These are the hopes of my memories, as I am thinking of you.

Back to Prayer
June 13, 2002

Last Saturday, I had the special privilege of ordaining sixteen very fine and mature men to the permanent diaconate. It was a special treat for me to meet their wives at a reception the night before and to see their families so excited and joyful on the day of the ordination itself. Together with the five priests and the seven transitional deacons (those who are preparing for priestly ordination next year) that we ordained last month, they do give a great deal of hope for this local Church in the years ahead.

We are blessed that permanent deacons are present in so many of our parishes. We are blessed, too, by their devotion to the service of the altar, the Word, and to charity, which makes them tremendously valuable collaborators in the work of the archdiocese. We must all thank God so much for their vocation and for their generous service.

What struck me in a particular way in the ordination was the repeated reference to the reason that the apostles gave for their desire to ask the first deacons to help them in their own responsibilities to the Church. The apostles admitted that, with all their administrative responsibilities, especially in the care of the poor, they did not have enough time for prayer and for the preaching of the Gospel, which were the most important works these first bishops were supposed to do.

After the ordination, I examined my own conscience on that challenging point that the sacred texts offered. I do preach a lot here in the archdiocese and I am really trying to take care of the poor—mainly thanks to all you do to make it possible—but I still fall very short on the measure of personal prayer. If the apostles, who were all great saints, felt that they weren't praying enough, then a weak successor of the apostles like me, who is in no way as close to the Lord as they were, needs to pray a whole lot more.

Of course, I have a lot to pray for. My first responsibility is to pray for you, both as the People of God in this Archdiocese of Washington and as individuals with needs and worries, with joys and pains. Every day someone asks me to pray for a particular intention and I do. But the challenge in the light of ordination reminds me that I have to do it more and I have to do it better.

There is a paradox here. I need to ask you to pray more for me so that I can pray more and better for you. As I head for Dallas and for that critical meeting of the bishops of our country, I especially need your prayers now for wisdom and courage and for a deeper spirit of prayerfulness in my own life. You don't have to ask. You know that I'll be praying and thinking of you.

Hard but Right Decisions
June 20, 2002

If I could come up with a phrase that might summarize the Dallas meeting of bishops that took place last week, I think I'd opt for the phrase I used on the title of this column. The gathering of almost three hundred bishops from all over the United States Catholic Church had an almost impossible job to accomplish. It had to put in order a complex, multi-faceted program for the protection of children and it had to do it quickly, simply, and well. The bishops' task was even more complicated in that it involved the greatest treasure of the Church in our own country—its children and young people—and this was the third time it had tried to solve the problem. The first two times, it didn't work.

The bishops, including me, went to the meeting with many concerns and a lot of uncertainties. We had a couple of things at the very top of our agenda. First of all, we were determined to protect children from sexual abuse. This was the most important priority connected with our meeting. Secondly, we wanted to assure victims of past sexual abuse that we have heard their cries of pain and anguish, the terrible trauma they suffered at the hands of priests. We needed to let them know that this would never be tolerated in the future and that those who had done this in the past would not be allowed ever to hurt someone else. This was the commitment we owed to them and to the Church.

I think we finally accomplished these two goals. Not only did we take a firm decision to bind ourselves to observe these new norms, but we also voted to ask the Holy See to make it an even stricter obligation by placing this policy under particular law so that there could be canonical penalties for us if we did not observe it. In this way we wrote into the charter a double accountability to demonstrate our determination to end this tragic chapter in the history of the Church in the United States.

At Dallas we listened to the heartbreaking stories of men and women who had been abused by priests as children. We assured them that we had heard what they said and we promised them that we would take action. Some of them, I know, are disappointed that we did not vote to remove totally from the priesthood any priest who had ever mistreated a young person in any way.

I believe that any true pedophile or anyone who has committed a grave crime against a child will indeed be totally removed from the priesthood, but I cannot agree that anything is gained by taking a now elderly man who has, by this new policy, been totally removed from any ministry in the Church and making it impossible for him to follow a life of prayer and penance in an environment where he will be monitored and also cared for.

I added the words "and cared for" here so I would be totally honest with you as I always try to be. I do not believe we are faithful to Christ if we put such a man "out in the street" for the rest of his life and so I will help to support him in a monastery or religious house as long as he lives. This would not be a vast sum of money, since we are basically talking about room and board, and such cases fortunately are very rare here in our local Church, but I see this as something the Lord would want us to do. I do not want to do this without you knowing about it and I pray that we will never have anybody in this category, but as I am thinking of you, I have the confidence that you will understand that this is part of the charity and forgiveness to which all of us are called.

Past, Present, and Future
June 27, 2002

Twenty-five years ago on June 29, the great Feast of St. Peter and Paul, I was consecrated a bishop in St. Patrick's Cathedral in New York by the servant of God, Terence Cardinal Cooke. Three of us were ordained as auxiliary bishops of New York on that most memorable day, the other two being Monsignor Austin Vaughn, one of the most significant American theologians and, at that time, rector of St. Joseph's Seminary in Dunwoodie, the New York archdiocesan seminary; and Father Francisco Garmendia, a warm and dedicated charismatic pastor in the Bronx. Bishop Vaughn has since died; Bishop Garmendia only recently retired as auxiliary bishop of New York.

I remember that day very specially, even though it was so full of excitement and so busy with liturgical celebration and the gatherings of family and friends. The two assistant priests were one of my classmates and the rector of the cathedral who just passed away within the last year.

I'm sure I was happy; I know I was scared. I had served Cardinal Cooke as his principal secretary for seven years and I knew the suffering and the challenges that went along with trying to be a good bishop. Even then we suspected that he was a saint—and his cause for canonization has indeed been started. I know I wasn't, and therefore the challenge to holy service of God's people as a bishop was an awesome thing. Twenty-five years later it still is.

After work on Wednesday I'm heading to Rome to celebrate the imposition of the pallium on Archbishop John Myers, my successor as archbishop of Newark. Therefore, I will celebrate the exact day of my ordination in the Eternal City, where I hope to offer Mass in my titular church of Sts. Nereus and Achilleus. That Mass will be offered for you and for all the faithful of the Archdiocese of Washington as is always my practice every day.

Last Friday, as you read elsewhere in the *Catholic Standard*, we had a beautiful celebration in the Basilica of the National Shrine. My "eldest son"—that is, the first priest I ordained a bishop—the present ordinary of Trenton, Bishop John M. Smith, preached a beautiful homily and Bishop Wilton Gregory, the president of our bishops' conference and an old friend, added a very gracious and humorous talk that captured the moment so well, while our own Father Kevin Hart, the executive secretary of the presbyteral council, spoke very eloquently on behalf of our own priests. The only family I invited were those who live in the area, to manifest the sign that you, the People of God here, are truly my family now.

What are my thoughts as I passed through this moment of memories? They are both light and shadow. I have tremendous gratitude to God for the extraordinary blessings that he has given me. He has trusted me with the care of so many of his beloved sons and daughters and assigned me a role in the Church that can accomplish so much good. On the other hand, at almost seventy-two, I know my failings and my sins, my selfishness and stubbornness, my lack of generosity in serving. In whatever years—or days—that are left for me to serve you and to serve the Church, let me listen more carefully to the call to personal holiness and pastoral service so that the promises I made at ordination will finally come true for the glory of God and the good of the faithful. I write this so that, at this special moment in my life, you should know that I'm thinking of you.

Relaxing in Rome
July 4, 2002

It is Sunday in Rome. The weekend exodus has almost emptied out this great, historic city, or so it seems. The oppressive heat of the last three days—I arrived on Thursday afternoon—has broken a little since the skies are cloudy and there is a pleasant breeze.

I'm staying at the United States seminary in Rome, the North American College. Thanks to Cardinal Hickey who was rector here in the challenging days of the 1970s, the suite named in his honor, where I am quartered, is air-conditioned and spacious. Tonight I set out on the next leg of my journey to visit projects in Eastern Europe and the Caucuses for Catholic Relief Services. But today is a lazy day, with surprisingly—for now—little to do except relax, pray, write some thank-you notes, study the briefing papers for the rest of my journey, and get this message to the *Catholic Standard* so that you can know that I am thinking of you.

The praying involves all those special intentions that many of you give me from time to time and the thank-you notes come from a very gracious reception that Cardinal Baum gave for me in honor of my silver anniversary yesterday. The relaxing, which does not really come easily to a workaholic like me, will really serve me well in the hectic days ahead.

It was good to be in Rome these days. I had come to join my successor in Newark, Archbishop Myers, as he received the pallium and to celebrate the exact date of my anniversary quietly with just a few priests in my little titular church here in Rome. Besides that, I really have had nothing else to do— for a whole three days—except continually to thank God for the blessings of the past quarter century of my life as a bishop and try to plan to do a better job of it in the time that lies ahead. Strolling these historic streets and enjoying the great meals of this city, taking in the art, the beauty, and the real piety that is always here is the perfect invitation to take it easy, so I'm going to go on for the rest of the afternoon just relaxing—maybe!

Catholic Schools
July 11, 2002

The recent decision of the United States Supreme Court regarding the constitutionality of vouchers is truly very important for our country, our parents, and our American way of life. I know that many of our newspapers and media commentators were not happy with it, although I commend the *Washington Post* for its June 28 editorial of support, but I personally rejoice in what the Court has done to redress an

injustice that has made the families who chose religious values for their children's education somewhat like second-class
citizens for a long time.

Before I try to explain what I mean, let me tell you clearly
that I am totally dedicated to the improvement and support
of our public school system here and throughout the country.
Even from a selfish point of view, most Catholic youngsters
in America go to the public schools and, therefore, I am
devoted to their receiving the very best education possible,
even though I will always regret that they cannot be taught
the values that have always been the real foundation of our
American society. Over and above this, so many wonderful teachers in the public schools are Catholic and I have
great respect for them and for their vital vocation, which is
so essential in our society. However, I believe that this most
recent decision of the Supreme Court does much to right a
wrong.

In the late 1920s, the Supreme Court recognized the right
of parents to send their children to non-public and even to
religious schools. This right, enshrined in the Constitution
and recognized by the Court three-quarters of a century ago,
enabled religious groups like the Catholic Church to develop
a remarkable school system, which became the envy of educators in most of the states of our Union. Unfortunately for
our poor families, it was a right given often in vain, since they
could not afford to send their children to parochial schools,
especially since, as all American citizens, they were rightly
required to support the continuing work of our public school
systems with their taxes.

When, shortly after World War II, it was recognized that
the federal government could constitutionally fund the GI
Bill, which allowed hundreds of thousands of veterans to go
to a college of their choice, even if it were private or religious,
many of us felt that this was the beginning of a true recogni-
tion of the right to choose a value-centered education. Of

course, the decision of the Supreme Court a couple of weeks ago will not automatically change everything. The state legislatures will have to consider legislation on the local level first. I am no prophet, but I would surely hope that in the District of Columbia and in Maryland, our legislators would find this newly opened door and have the courage and the vision to walk through it for the good of so many families.

Over the past 150 years, our Catholic families have spent many millions of dollars to preserve that great treasure of the Catholic school. They have done this by operating excellent institutions and ones that are and always have been open to people of every religion, every race, and every ethnic background. I am hoping that our legislators will remember that and help us move forward to continue these schools in service to all people in a way that makes it possible for our poorer families to afford this constitutional right that is theirs.

As I have been trying to visit our schools as well as the parishes during my second round of visitations, I am always thinking of you and hoping that this great new opportunity, especially for our poorer families, will be something that we can work on together.

Always Rejoice
July 18, 2002

There is a great line from Saint Paul's first letter to the Christians of Thessalonika. I have always felt that it sums up the Lord's counsel to everyone who tries to live the Christian life as God asks us to do it. In that beautiful letter, Saint Paul writes: "Always rejoice, pray without ceasing, constantly give thanks to God." Wouldn't it be wonderful if all of us would try to live that way—even some of the time? (Wouldn't it be great if I would do it as your bishop and give you that good example!)

The reason I'm thinking about this now is all that happened in connection with my silver anniversary as a bishop a couple of weeks ago. As you know, a few days after that very beautiful celebration in the Basilica of the National Shrine, I left for Rome to be part of the ceremony in the Vatican where my successor as archbishop of Newark, Archbishop John Myers, received the pallium—that collar of wool that is the mark of the metropolitan archbishop. Since the day of the Pallium Mass was the great solemnity of Saints Peter and Paul, early in the morning I went out to my titular church and celebrated Mass with some of the priests who have been close to me during these twenty-five years. There was a former vicar general, several former secretaries, and many good friends whose love and prayerful support have been a blessing for me in my twenty-five years as a bishop.

I do have a lot to rejoice about. My early years in New York, the twenty years in New Jersey, and the very special time here in Washington have been very good years. The priests with whom I have worked and the people I have served have been great examples to me of what I should be as a good servant of the Gospel and of the Church. As I looked back on all that has happened, I asked myself what I remember most joyfully about that quarter century of service. There are many things—the privileged opportunity of working as an auxiliary bishop with Cardinal Cooke, a man who one day may be recognized as a saint; the grace of being able to establish a brand new diocese in Metuchen, the only new diocese in the northeastern part of our country since the Second Vatican Council; the good fortune of being able to start two missionary seminaries, one in Newark and one now here in Washington, and to see some of my priest-sons working zealously and well in mission lands from Estonia to the Turks and Caicos Islands; the awesome blessing from God to have ordained more than 250 priests and eleven bishops in the last twenty-five years! All these have been great joys for me, but most of all it has been the people who accepted me as their servant and their bishop and who prayed for me and loved me even as they found me, with all my faults and sinfulness.

I know well that I have not been one of those great bishops of whom we read with reverence and awe. Most of all, I think I have always wanted to be a kind priest and I would be grateful to God who has been so kind to me if at least through his grace I have tried to be a kind bishop to those I served.

As I am thinking of you at this special anniversary in my life, I would always rejoice if that were the way I might be remembered.

Too Much!
July 25, 2002

When I first decided to use that title for today's column, I smiled to myself and wondered what you would think I would be writing about. There are so many things in the world today about which we might exclaim "Too Much!" We could say it about the crisis in the priesthood or about the unfair way some of the media has treated it. (Thank God, it seems to be starting to diminish as the Church in our country now has in place the tools it needs to handle it.) We could say it about the perilous decline in the stock market and the terrible scandals that have accompanied it, leaving so many people without retirement pensions and hurting even the ability of Churches to care for those in need as they have always been trying to do. We could say it about the escalation of violence in the Holy Land where each step seems to become more vengeful than the previous one and the lives of innocent people seem no longer to count for anything.

In an imperfect world, as you and I struggle to take care of the needs of our families, whether they are the natural family that God has given you or the family of this local Church that I am called to serve, there are so many areas where we could say to each other and even to the Lord "Too Much!" And yet, in the stark reality of our faith, we know that nothing is ever too much for God to handle; we know that he can bring good out of evil and peace out of turmoil and that, when all is said and done, his grace is enough for us.

I confess that these profound thoughts were not in my mind when I started to write this to you, although now my original intention seems a lot less important. I was going to write to you about my summer and how it has so quickly been eaten up by commitments that I really didn't see coming. Now that I face these I, too, am shaking my head and saying "Too Much!"

A couple of weeks after I returned from the Dallas meeting of the bishops, as you know, I went to Rome for a few days. Then I fulfilled my promise to Catholic Relief Services and spent ten days visiting their operations in the Caucasus and the Balkans. I came back a little weary after that journey and had a great week's vacation at the Jersey Shore—my first full week off without commitments in fifteen years! I only just returned when now I go to join hundreds of our young people in Toronto for World Youth Day where I have a couple of talks to give. Then, with most of the American cardinals, I must go to Mexico City for the canonization of Blessed Juan Diego—the holy Indian to whom the Blessed Mother appeared as Our Lady of Guadalupe. I come back for a few days after that and then I go to California for the annual Supreme Council Meeting of the Knights of Columbus. After that, I have scheduled a week in Southern Maryland, both to take it easy and to visit our priests and our people in that magic land. When that week is over I must travel to Chicago for the important Black Catholic Congress that is meeting there and then to Los Angeles for the consecration of the great new cathedral in that largest diocese of our country. By the time that is over, it is already after Labor Day, and September with all its busyness is already upon us.

I think I can hear you saying "Too Much!"—and you are right! Pray for me that I stop saying yes to things!—even though you know that wherever I am, I'll be thinking of you.

Beaucoup, Beaucoup, Beaucoup
August 1, 2002

As you probably know, the word beaucoup means "very much" in French, as in "merci beaucoup" which is "thank you very much." It was used last week a lot by the hundreds of thousands of young people who came to visit with the Holy Father in Toronto for World Youth Day.

In one of the very emotional moments of that outstanding visit, a young lady representing the young people of French Canada ended her welcoming remarks by repeating "very much" three times. It brought a smile to the face of the Holy Father and a catch in the throat for many of us who were listening. I think it was spontaneous. She was just so excited that this remarkable elderly man, obviously suffering from a debilitating illness, struggling to walk even a few steps and making an incredible effort to be eloquent in two languages not his own, the successor of Saint Peter and the Vicar of Christ was there in her own country, in her own city, so full of love and confidence in the young people of the Church.

Thank you, Holy Father, merci beaucoup, beaucoup, beaucoup!

The World Youth Day was filled with moments like that. Pope John Paul II had been given time to rest between his appearances, but even this he seemed to use to invite the young people to be with him and to talk to him. His relationship with them is real. He does not modify his strong teaching on life, on values, and on morality. He continues to tell it "like it is" and they respond to this with respect, enthusiasm, and love.

And it is catching! So many of the bishops and priests who were there mentioned the wonderful openness of the young people—from teenagers to young adults—to receive the authentic teaching of the Church and to be enthusiastic about it!

After one of my catecheses, three young people from different parts of the United States came up to me and said that they had been hesitating about vocation to the priesthood or religious life and now they had decided to apply. God grant that we can hold onto that willingness to serve—in so many ways—among the young. It was a time of grace indeed. And as I was thinking of you, I thanked God for you and for all the young people of the Church of Washington, beaucoup, beaucoup, beaucoup.

Very Moving
August 8, 2002

If you are still living in the house where you were born or if you haven't moved in twenty years, you may not understand the trauma that this column portrays. But if you are like me and have moved six times in that period, you may sympathize with the near chaos that I am about to describe.

As you probably know, I have moved into the District of Columbia. The two great challenges are the one I mentioned above—unpacking once again—and secondly, getting my head to realize that I am not living in Hyattsville anymore and therefore I have to stop telling those who drive me to get on the roads leading to 5001 Eastern Avenue where I used to live. This problem becomes more acute when I decide that we can easily drive to the National Shrine in ten minutes—as I could from my old address—and forget that I am not living at that address anymore. The other day coming back from a parish in Bethesda, I told my priest secretary who was driving that I knew a good way home. I did, but it was to my old home and I almost got hopelessly lost trying to work my way back to where I live now. It's tough to move when you get old! The mind doesn't seem to adapt as quickly. Or maybe it's just me? Do teenagers have that problem too?

But the other problem, the unpacking again, is worse. I'm embarrassed to admit that I am only now opening some of the boxes I brought down from New Jersey! I didn't have much room in my former residence and now I almost have too much room. Although people who don't like to throw things away—like me—never have too much room. I'd invite people up to see where I live if only I could straighten it all up. I've done a lot, of course—I don't want you to think that I'm that disorganized—but the thought of putting all the books in some order in my bookcase and reading all the papers and memos that I am now coming across is a time-consuming occupation, and besides I have been on the road a lot this summer.

I'm clearly writing this just to get sympathy—or maybe for a degree of protection against the priests who live with me and who are now starting to say "Oh, I see you still haven't straightened out your room!" As I look for understanding in these confusing times, I'm thinking of you and hoping that some of you might really understand that moving can be a very moving experience.

Conversations with Children
August 15, 2002

It was a family gathering and there were some people there who I really didn't know. They were distant cousins or cousins of cousins from another branch of the family tree. One youngster was in front of me in the hot dog line—a boy of eight or nine whom I couldn't place at all. I asked him the usual questions that we ungrammatical adults would phrase: "Who do you belong to?" He turned and looked at me quizzically as if he didn't understand the question. So I repeated it, as adults are wont to do. "Who do you belong to?" I said again, now conscious of the awkwardness of the English usage. He shrugged, looked blank for a moment, and then brightened up as if with a fresh insight and answered me: "I belong to God!"

Now he may have responded that way because he knew I was a priest, but I was dressed in sport clothes like everyone else at the picnic and I really had not met him. "I belong to God," he said. What an extraordinary insight at eight or nine years old. "That's the right answer," I said to him. "But I didn't expect it. Who taught you that you belong to God?" "Mother and Daddy" he said, now with a wide, confident smile. And I thanked God for the faith that this boy's parents had passed on to him.

I'm not sure that all the youngsters in my family would give the same answer, even if they understood the question in the same radical way as my little partner in this dialogue.

Most would have understood the question in the sense that I had originally intended, namely, what part of the family do you come from, who are your parents and relatives? But even if one or two saw a deeper meaning in the question, I doubt that they would have answered so simply and directly. I'm not likely to ask that question in the same words again, but you might have fun at a family party to try it out on the young people—maybe on the teenagers too!

What a grace it is to pass on the living faith that we have received from God, usually through our own parents and older siblings. How blessed mothers and fathers are when they realize that this son or daughter has caught the divine spark of faith and that it is aflame in the hearts of their children. It is like giving birth all over again, this time to a truly new life in the spirit of Jesus. To achieve that is worth effort and sacrifice and pain, and one of my most fervent prayers is that our Catholic parents will capture the grace of knowing how important faith is in the life of a young person and what a tragedy it would be to neglect that part of their education and upbringing.

That's why Catholic schools are so important and catechetical programs when a Catholic school education is not possible. Of course, when all is said and done the parents are the child's first and best teachers, and as I am thinking of you mothers and fathers, I pray with all my heart that you are teaching your children about God and that is something you will never stop doing, by example as well as by words.

Pope Pius XII
August 22, 2002

Last week when I was on my "busman's holiday" vacation in Southern Maryland, I had an opportunity to celebrate four Masses for the Solemnity of the Assumption of Our Lady: the Vigil Mass in Ridge, and masses in Medley's Neck, Solomons, and Great Mills on the feast itself. As I was preparing my homily, I remembered that the solemn definition of this doctrine occurred about fifty years ago when I was still in the seminary. For us seminarians it was a very historic day when the Holy Father, Pope Pius XII, proclaimed that the Blessed Virgin Mary, at the end of her earthly sojourn, was assumed body and soul into heaven.

Of course there was nothing new in this teaching. It had been part of the faith of the Church for many centuries, since several of the early Fathers of the Church had written about it and it had been lovingly hailed by the faithful whenever they thought about the life of Mary. This is not the place to go deeply into the theological basis for this beautiful doctrine—and my own scholarly limitations would be enough to make that difficult—but it has always seemed to me that the most fitting argument was the easiest to understand. The human body of Jesus was formed in the womb of Mary. The body that gave birth to the Son of God should not face the corruption of death or the decay of the tomb. This was part of the teaching of Pius XII when he gave the Church this formal definition in 1954.

Pondering on this historical event as I was praying over my homilies for that feast, I began to see a new reason for the proclamation of the Assumption right after World War II. This was a time in which the so-called modern world of the twentieth century lost its bearings on the subject of the dignity of the human body. The horrors of the gas chambers of the Holocaust when a godless philosophy sought to destroy a whole people—God's chosen people, in fact—the terrible dehumanization of the concentration camps, the indiscriminate killing of innocents in the wholesale destruction of cities through pattern bombing raids, the atom bomb—all these cried out for some clear and noble statement about the value of the human body. The Holy Father made such a statement when he presented the dogma of Mary's Assumption into heaven to a world that was grasping for a new assurance that our bodies were worth more than a flock of sparrows.

In his lifetime, Pope Pius XII was recognized as a brave and wise defender of the victims of hatred and persecution. I always recall the eloquent statement of the courageous leader of Israel, Golda Meir, who lamented his death with the words: "We share in the grief of humanity. When fearful martyrdom came to our people, the voice of the pope was raised for its victims. The life of our times was enriched by a voice speaking out about great moral truths above the tumult of daily conflict."

How sad that a kind of revisionist pseudo-history has come to the fore attacking him unjustly and with more innuendo than fact regarding his actions during the Holocaust. An American nun who is a most respected historian, Sister Margarita Marchione, had taken up his defense and written several excellent books that present the accurate story of the man and his times. Her latest book, *Consensus and Controversy*, has just been published by Paulist Press. As I am thinking of you and know that sometimes it is important to have the facts to counter unfair criticism of the Church and the popes, I thought I would mention her work to you as I recall this great pope of my youth.

Llano Estacado
August 29, 2002

I am looking out the window of a plane traveling across Texas from Amarillo to Houston. As you know, I had promised to preach at the closing Mass of the Eucharistic Congress in Amarillo, which commemorated the seventy-fifth anniversary of that diocese. As the date came closer, I was regretting that I had agreed to come to the celebration so far away, but now that I am returning home, I am glad that I did. The more I travel throughout our country and see the challenges and struggles of so many of the local Churches, I come all the more to appreciate how good God was to me when I was sent to Washington. Although I appreciate the courage and the faith of God's people in these truly missionary dioceses, God's blessings to us here in Washington seem truly overwhelming.

Amarillo is the diocese in the Texas Panhandle. It was divided twice in its seventy-five-year history and now covers twenty-six thousand square miles at the northern part of Texas. Even though it has more than ten times the area of the Archdiocese of Washington, it has only about sixty thousand Catholics on its books. It has, however, a relatively high number of church-goers since it is in the Bible-belt area of our country. The diocese has fewer than forty priests to cover this vast territory, but it is blessed with an equal number of permanent deacons and almost 150 women religious. The reason that I am giving you all these statistics is to hope to impress you—even as I myself was impressed and edified—by the fact that more than six thousand people attended the Eucharistic Congress! It was a wonderful sign of deep faith in a challenging environment and even though I preached to them about faith, their presence and their enthusiasm preached a much more eloquent homily to me.

I wanted to share two things with you about Amarillo. The first relates to its geography. It is almost perfectly flat. Secondly, there seemed to be no hills, no mountains, and surprisingly, no trees! There may be a couple of hundred trees in the whole city and fewer than that in the countryside. This makes sunrises and sunsets truly spectacular, since the sun rises and sets hundreds of miles away and the colors of the sky are beyond simple description. Last night, because of the setting sun's reflection, the eastern sky lit up in a multihued fantasy as its clouds received the light of the dying sun hundreds of miles away across the flatlands. Some moments later the western sky rivaled that brilliance as the sun made its way beneath the horizon.

There is also a spiritual message here. Because the land is so flat, Coronado and the other early explorers had no way to mark trails or to establish safe routes across the land. In a totally flat land, even without trees, there are no landmarks to guide one's journey. They were forced to drive stakes into the ground and these were the guideposts for themselves and for others as to travel and direction. The whole land took its name from these stakes, in Spanish, *llano estacado*, or staked-out flatlands.

I told the folks to whom I preached last night that they themselves had to be the stake-markers for the journeys of this world. I asked them how their neighbors and their children would find the Lord and the path to holiness unless they were the signs—the stakes that mark the journey—that would help to lead them. As I preached to them, I was thinking of you and of me. It has to be our job, too, to help others find the way.

Never Without Hope
September 5, 2002

As we come nearer to the anniversary of 9/11, all of us in one way or another are starting to reflect on the year that has passed. It has been an unusual year to say the least. The terrible tragedy of 9/11 has left its scars on families who have lost loved ones and on the nation, which still finds itself locked in a shadowy war against an often invisible opponent. It has left its mark on the economy too, especially here in the Washington area, which suffered both from the overall recession and more pertinently from families disrupted and employment suspended. And besides all this, for us Catholics is the added trauma of clergy abuse.

Did it leave a mark on our national psyche? At first it was a sudden blow to our sense of security that our two oceans and our advanced technological development seemed to provide. At first it brought us together above partisanship in politics or provincialism in advancing only our own particular interests. At first, it even stirred up again the basic religious foundation of our historic roots; as it became proper and fitting to turn to God and to rely once more on divine help and guidance.

Wouldn't it be wonderful if all that had lasted throughout the passing months? Sadly, it seems to me, we have "returned to normal." Our politics have once more become acerbic and partisan. Our sense of inviolability has made us again impatient of the new demands of homeland security. Our rediscovered trust in God, which filled our places of worship to overflowing those first few weeks, has generally lapsed into pre-9/11–sized congregations. Our nation, having been rightly concerned to seek moral justification for the war on terrorism—and having found it!—now begins to consider another war without really asking the same questions.

And what is the role that we should play? I believe we must try to get on with our normal lives. We should keep pushing our elected and religious leaders to work together for the common good and dialogue together honestly and clearly about whatever dangers they see from our enemies. We must try to overcome those dangers in a way that is consistent with our American tradition, reflecting on our values and the moral implications of our actions.

And I believe that we must thank God for the courage of so many whose sacrifices have kept us safe and beg the Lord to keep us so as we pass this anniversary and enter another critical year in the history of our country and the world. Thinking of you more than ever in these days of uncertainty, I am reminded that the only sure thing is the love of God, and that never leaves us without hope!

Pre-Selected
September 12, 2002

I am usually very supportive of the new security rules at our airports. I still fly a lot. Thank God, not as much as I did, but I do travel by plane once or twice a month. The only times I get really upset is when I get upset at myself for packing something that will set off the machine, like my palm pilot or a metal paperweight. (No, I don't normally bring my own paperweights with me when I travel. Bishops tend to get them as gifts or souvenirs from events they attend.) I am usually very careful to pack anything like that in the smaller bag, which I can open easily without rearranging all my carefully packed shirts, socks, and a good pair of pants.

The times I put those metal things in my suitcase always seem to be the times I have close connections. When I stopped in Houston last month on the way back from the canonization of Saint Juan Diego in Mexico, I had such a short connection. I needed to go through Customs and Immigration and then through the security checkpoint. For the first two hurdles, I successfully got into the longest and slowest lines and for the third, I realized too late that I had put a bronze medal we received as a gift back into my larger bag. I had packed it away so well that it took a couple of minutes to find it, put it on a tray, and then send the whole luggage back through the machine again. The clock kept ticking and I could imagine my flight taking off. Of course it was my own fault and that's what made me madder!

But the most interesting of all the encounters with airport security occurs when one finds that one has been pre-selected. Through a system of random sampling that has been worked out with care, a number of travelers are picked for a more intense search prior to boarding. It can happen on any flight and it doesn't matter who you are, how you are dressed, or whether or not you smile at the guard. If there is a mark by your name on the list, the security folks must do a second search of your luggage. The good thing about it is that you know you are going to make your flight. The bad thing is trying to squeeze all that stuff back without wrinkling in a tightly packed carry-on bag.

Still, the notion of being pre-selected isn't all bad. After all, God pre-selected every one of us! Out of an infinite number of possible human beings, the Creator chose you and me. What is even more wonderful is that out of all the billions of people on the earth today who do not know him, in the mystery of God's eternal love, he gave you and me faith and the knowledge of Jesus Christ. In God's eyes, we are all pre-selected and he has showered his grace upon us. How much he must love us and with a love that is strong enough to bring each of us to the eternal happiness of heaven if only we return it in the measure that we can.

The next time as I am rushing on my way to get to the gate in the airport, whether or not I'm pre-selected, I'll be thinking of you, rejoicing in the fact that all of us are pre-selected when it really counts.

491
September 19, 2002

Years ago there was a Swedish film titled *491*. I thought of it when I was preparing my homily for the Red Mass in Charleston, West Virginia. I don't recall if I ever saw the film, but I remember the story. It was based on the words of the Lord to Saint Peter when the apostle suggested that forgiving someone seven times would be a good thing. Jesus replies that you have to forgive seventy times seven times, in other words, countless times and indeed you never can stop forgiving. The 491 title was supposed to ask whether there was one time when someone did something so terrible to you that it was beyond the Lord's requirement, in other words, seventy times seven plus one. I think that the film ended with even that one last time being forgiven by the person who was hurt.

For me, that has always been a most powerful lesson. God asks us to forgive even as he forgives, without limit, without vengeance, without leftover grudges. God even makes our own forgiveness of others a test of our true willingness to receive his forgiveness. In the Our Father we pray that he will forgive our trespasses even as we forgive those who trespass against us. We are really saying to God that he should measure his forgiveness of us on our willingness to forgive other people.

It is not easy to hold a grudge for a long time, but so many of us seem to be able to do that. The worse hurt seems to be there in a family or a formerly close friend. Whenever I preach about it, and I guess I do it a lot, someone often comes up after Mass and says "Thanks. You were talking to me. I haven't spoken to my sister—or brother—or mother— or cousin—or friend—for so many years." Wouldn't it be wonderful if we could reach out to that person and bridge the chasm of anger or disappointment and try to start over again? I know that it takes two people to patch a tear in an old relationship, but unless one starts to do it, it will never be done.

Even as I know how much I need God's forgiveness, so do I recognize that I must forgive others, too. Our offenses against a God who loves us, even to a horrible death on the cross, are so much greater than the often very slight wounds that we have received from other people. When I am thinking of you, one of the things I pray for most is that you will find the happiness that comes from receiving forgiveness and for giving it, too.

Skim Milk
September 26, 2002

No, this is not going to be a food column. I'm afraid that I am no expert in cooking. I am in one of those great mystery categories that people who enjoy eating but only know how to boil water for spaghetti seem to fit into. It is not even a column about keeping slim, although one of these days I want to write about that. As we get old, some people seem to get thinner. On the other hand, I find myself getting fatter, probably because I am exercising less than before. But this column is about appearances and how sometimes they can deceive.

There is a wonderful line in Gilbert and Sullivan's operetta *HMS Pinafore* that has been swirling around in my head for a couple of days. Like so many of the Gilbert and Sullivan musical scores—which are really some of my favorite kinds of music—it is a very catchy tune. It goes like this: "Things are seldom what they seem, skim milk masquerades as cream." In our lives, that is not an uncommon occurrence. I don't mean about skim milk. I mean about life.

So often we long for the cream, the top of the heap, the brass ring on the merry-go-round. It seems always just within reach and so many of us spend so much energy in the quest of something that will ultimately satisfy all our longings and fulfill all our desires. For some of us, it's the security that we think money can buy us. For others, it is the elusive happiness that material things seem to be able to offer. For a few, it is a quest for that perfect wife or husband, a quest that often leaves us spinsters or bachelors because the Mr. or Mrs. Right never seems to come along.

In our determination to find the cream, are we really spending too much of our lives seeking "skim milk" that merely masquerades as cream? Are we blindly looking for something that is really only a shadow of reality, only a false image of what we really need to make us happy? I write to young people here in a special way. Do not set your eyes on what will quickly perish. Seek for the real happiness that does not come from things that fade away or disappear in the uncertain meanderings of an unhealthy relationship or even a volatile stock market. Things are often not what they seem. People, too, I guess. Put your trust in a changeless friend. That is what God is. Once you have found the ultimate reality in him, all other things become real in the light of his love.

I think I have meandered a long way from those lines about skim milk in the *Pinafore*, but every time that tune comes playing on in my head, I am thinking of you, as always.

A Nice Place to Live
October 3, 2002

Every once in a while someone asks me how my new home is. I told you that I was moving back into Washington during the summer and now I am pretty well settled in here in the new residence. I have three rooms once again, but now they are big rooms instead of the three little rooms I had at the pastoral center. That building had been a seminary and so the rooms were rather small. Since where I now live had been a high school, each of the rooms is almost classroom size!

The best thing about having enough room is that now I have more closets. Where I lived before, I had to store some things under the bed. That's not so bad, except that you tend to forget where you put things and, even if you remember, it's too much trouble to pull everything out just to look for it again. Closets are really great blessings, especially for people who don't throw things away. I always come back after a journey with presents, thinking that I'll give them as gifts for Christmas and anniversaries. Unfortunately, when a birthday or the celebration comes, I forget that I had bought something and so the occasion passes and I still have the souvenirs with me. I am wondering if anyone else is like that too?

Another nice thing about where I live now is that I can walk to the cathedral and I'm close enough to stores and can shop or at least walk around looking into the display windows. There are very good restaurants around here also so I can try them too. Of course, since there are six of us priests living here now—the two who care for the parish and the four of us who work at the archdiocesan center—we do have a really wonderful cook and I have not gone out to eat too often. The only trouble with having such a good cook is that he becomes frustrated with me as I too frequently tell him just to make me a plate of spaghetti or a tuna fish sandwich with a lot of onions and he is so capable of preparing much more elegant cuisine than that.

All in all, the new residence is working out very well for me. I still get up at 5:00, go to the chapel at 5:45, and start my deskwork at 6:30. I am trying to get out to the different parishes almost every morning, and then go on from there to the pastoral center office. So far it takes about twenty or twenty-five minutes to drive directly from the center to where I live, depending on the traffic and the weather, and I can pray or work in the car as we go. One great thing is that we have garage space and good parking in both the center and the residence so we never have to spend too much time looking for a place to put the car. Knowing Washington just a little bit now, I know what a blessing that is.

As I look at it all, I know that I am extraordinarily blessed to have such a good place to live and such a good place to work. I thank God for that and I thank you, the faithful Catholics of the Archdiocese of Washington for making it possible for me to have that. One of the special graces is that I no longer live right across the corridor from where I work and that has to be good psychologically as well.

Now the challenge for me is to work harder, more effectively, and to please the Lord and serve you with greater generosity. Now that I have such a nice place to do it from, I shall be thinking of you with gratitude all the time.

Violence, Life, and Vocation
October 10, 2002

Last week throughout the area of our archdiocese, there was a heightened feeling of concern and even of anxiety. The senseless random killing of innocent people put all of us on edge. As I drove through Montgomery County for two of my Masses last Saturday, I sensed in myself a feeling of uneasiness. When I celebrated Mass that evening in St Mary's in Rockville for an end to violence, I was very conscious of the concerns of our people and their special worries for the safety of their children.

In all these terrible circumstances—as in the aftermath of 9/11—our great recourse is the Lord to whom we must turn in prayer and in trust. Sometimes this is easy to say and hard to do, but it always remains the answer. By ourselves we really cannot handle these shattering events. God knew that when he made us and that is why he is there with his saving help. Unless we believe in that and trust in him, we will never find the deepest peace.

Unfortunately there is a connection between the senseless violence of our times and the increasing indifference to life that we note in our country–and maybe even in ourselves. As we move into October—Respect Life Month—it is not hard to see that a society that turns away from protecting human life in the womb is prepared not to value human life in other people. The more we in the Western world are closed to life, the less we will see our neighbors respecting life itself. The Gospel teaching on the God-given dignity of human life is threatened by the multiplication of abortions until we reach a stage where any person's life can be placed in danger if it is not convenient for somebody else.

Perhaps, somewhat surprisingly, I am going to add another note to this equation. On the positive end of the continuum of respect for life are the men and women who courageously and generously offer their lives to God in service to his people. May I end these reflections on that positive note as we celebrate religious and priestly vocations in this week's *Catholic Standard?* I thank God for the many young men and women who are listening to his voice as he calls them to give their lives as priests and brothers and sisters. May their numbers increase and may the gift of their young lives to the service of the living God be a way to return us all to a greater respect for all human life and an end to all violent attacks against it.

I write this as I prepare to go to the Red Mass at the Basilica and pray for peace and justice and for all your special intentions, continuing as always to be thinking of you.

To Come and Go in Peace
October 17, 2002

Sometimes to help me get focused when I make my meditation in the morning, I use a text from one of the other ancient liturgies of the Church. A couple of months ago in Chicago at the Black Catholic Congress, we had the privilege of celebrating Mass in the Ge'ez Rite, the Liturgy of Ethiopia, which dates back many centuries and was truly a traditional African mode of celebrating the Eucharist. Even in translation, it is very beautiful and it reflects the faith and the hopes of our sisters and brothers who lived and worshiped in the Horn of Africa so many hundreds of years ago.

Toward the end of the Eucharist in that rite, as the priest prays over the faithful, he asks God for many gifts and blessings on the assembly that has gathered for Mass. One of the petitions he makes to the Lord begs for his people the grace "to come and go in peace." It is not hard to picture the dangers that would have threatened the Christians of those early centuries, threats from enemy armies, ambushes by brigands, dangers from wild animals—and the consolation that such a prayer would be to them in their everyday lives.

As we continue to feel anxiety over the presence of that hidden assassin and his murderous attacks on innocent people, it seemed to me that this was a great prayer for all of us. As I offer my own prayers for you every day, that is surely one that I will add and I encourage you to pray it also, for yourselves, your loved ones, and for all our community.

May God give you his protection that you may come and go in peace. May that be the sign of his love for us that we may feel his protecting hand as we travel, as we shop, as we continue to live our lives as we must. May he bless our comings and our goings, and keep us safe from harm. Travelers have been praying a similar prayer from the beginning of time. Let us join them with confidence that this trial of ours will soon be over, that the victims of these senseless attacks may find a place of eternal peace with God, and that we will take strength from the fact that God has not forgotten us. Indeed, I have no doubt that he is thinking of you and loving you now more than ever as our need for him becomes more evident to us all.

The Mysteries of Light
October 24, 2002

What an extraordinary Holy Father we have! Here is a man in his eighties, frail and courageously fighting a debilitating problems of health, facing challenges to the flock he serves in so many parts of the world—and with a vision and an understanding that touches one of the great devotions of the Church and restructures it for the needs of today! I truly believe that our Church and our world are very blessed in the continuing wisdom and insight of Pope John Paul II.

The Rosary as we have it today goes back seven centuries to the time of Saint Dominic and the early friars of the Order of Preachers. For seven hundred years it has been one of the favorite prayers of the Catholic people in every part of the world. The joyful, sorrowful, and glorious mysteries have been the themes of meditation of old and young, and we learned from them the wondrous ways in which God brought about salvation to the human race through his divine son Jesus, who was born of the Virgin Mary two thousand years ago.

I would venture that no pope in history has had a greater devotion to the Blessed Virgin Mary than Pope John Paul II. His faithful dedication to the Rosary is a gift to the Church, and now he has made that gift even more powerful and more able to teach us the mystery of our salvation. The Holy Father saw that the Rosary as we have used it for our meditation over the centuries has not focused enough on the public life of Jesus and on the light that these historic events cast on the role of the savior.

He calls these new additions the mysteries of light and each one does throw new light on the wonderful journey of the life of the Lord. In the first mystery of his Baptism we are reminded of his humanity; in that of his Transfiguration, the new fourth mystery, we are enraptured by the overwhelming sense of his divinity. In the second mystery, which presents the story of Cana to us, we are reminded both of the moment when he first proclaimed his mission by the miracle of the water made wine and of the special role of intercession that Mary always plays in his life. In the third mystery we are invited to meditate on the proclamation of the kingdom of

God, with its emphasis on conversion, forgiveness, and love. Finally, in the fifth mystery of light we recall that which is perhaps closest to us of all—the mystery of the Eucharist, the institution of this great sacrament by which Jesus perfectly fulfills his promise not to leave us orphans, but to remain with us until the end of time.

I find great consolation in these mysteries as well as a great challenge to holiness that is made to us all. We do not cease to see Our Lady's presence in all of these special moments, but here we focus on her son, as she herself would always have us do. The Holy Father recommends that we choose Thursdays as the day on which we pray these mysteries of light. Thinking of you and of all the people of the Archdiocese of Washington, I would hope that many of us would do that and that it would bring much grace and confidence to our lives in Christ.

Not Without Prayer
October 31, 2002

The wonderful news of the breakthrough in the tragic case of the sniper killings last week was a credit to thorough, skillful, and persevering police work. The many law enforcement agencies that cooperated in solving the murders and in restoring peace to our community deserve our thanks and our deep respect. We all passed through a very difficult period of serious concern for the safety of all our citizens, especially our children. Now that this particular and very understandable fear has been lifted, let us never forget that it was not without prayer that it was accomplished.

Last Tuesday in Rockville, representatives from all the major religious groups of our area gathered together in common prayer for an end to the killings and a return to peaceful days. As you may remember, I was part of that gathering and called on all our sisters and brothers in every faith community here and around the country to ask the Lord to deliver us from this evil that was causing the death of innocent people and bringing the rest of us so much anxiety and fear. I know that this tragic drama ended because of the work of many men and women, but I also know that it didn't happen without prayer.

So often when something good happens in our lives and when we escape something bad, we naturally turn to God for a moment and then just as quickly forget to thank him as we really should. God does answer prayers. We who are people of faith truly believe that. We have heard Jesus tell us: "Ask and you shall receive, seek and you will find, knock and it will be opened to you." That is why we do ask and seek and knock; because we take him at his word and know that he truly is there for us whenever we call upon him with trust. It is this deep faith that makes it possible for men and women to survive in joyful hope during the perils and uncertainties of our lives.

It is never without prayer that we can reach him; not without prayer that we can express our needs and hopes and longings, because fervent prayer is simply the raising of our minds and hearts to the God who loves us, who only seeks our good and who really does deliver us from evil. At the end of a tragedy, when the rising waters of our fears begin to subside, let us not forget that his presence made the difference and that he still wants to hold us in the palm of his hands, safe from every danger and so precious in his sight. Our God will never stop thinking of you and of me in good times and in bad and carrying us across the dangerous waters to rest at last in him. This happens every day of our lives, if we only stop for a moment and realize it.

Lebanon
November 7, 2002

I have just gotten back from four days in the Middle East.
I have tried, pretty successfully, to cut back on international
travel since I came to Washington last year. It had been a
good part of my life as a bishop over the past quarter century.
But all the experience of the past catches up with us from
time to time and when the president of Lebanon asked me to
come as his guest, I agreed since the situation in that lovely
small country is very tense right now.

Lebanon is the only country in the Middle East with a
sizeable Catholic population. At one time the majority was
probably Christian, but for many reasons that population has
shifted substantially in recent years. The civil wars of the last
quarter century, the continuing presence of its neighbors on
its own sovereign territory, the present weakness of the global
economy that has hindered complete recovery from the scars
of war, the emigration of young people due both to the tensions and to the lack of economic opportunity—all this has
caused a difficult situation, which the government and the
people must face.

You will smile to know that since I was an official guest, I
had all the trappings of diplomacy, which, as you can imagine, was both interesting and a little scary. I was met at the
plane by an honor guard, escorted everywhere by two motor-
cycles and three cars, and really treated superbly. Of course,
back at home, you all treat me so well anyway, but the extra
security can be somewhat unnerving.

My visit came at the same time as the meetings of the
Catholic Patriarchs of the East, so I saw some old friends and
listened to their concerns and hopes also. On Tuesday they
had scheduled a meeting with their Orthodox counterparts, so

I was able to be present at an ecumenical summit celebration. Lebanon is the home of some of the most ancient Christian sites and a highlight for me was the chance to visit the church in Tyre, which commemorates the Lord's conversation with the woman of Sidon and the cure of her daughter.

Of course, it was mostly a visit of listening and discussion, of suggestions and encouragement. The people of Lebanon face many problems; the majority of these problems are beyond their control since they are related to the region and will not be solved until the overall problems of the Middle East are solved. It is that frustration that prompts many of their young people to seek a more secure life elsewhere. Our country has been blessed by the many Lebanese Americans who live here. I join them in their own prayers and dreams for their homeland. During these last few days, I could not help thinking of you and how blessed we are to be here in these United States.

Belonging
November 14, 2002

This is another story from the Lebanon trip about which I wrote you last week. One of the best visits I had during those four days in Lebanon was the afternoon that I drove up to the "Holy Valley." This is a mountainous area in north central Lebanon, a couple of hours by car from Beirut, up winding mountain roads and deep picturesque valleys. This was the real homeland of the Maronite Catholics during the centuries of occupation by the Turks and other rulers. Here, half hidden in the forest and glens, they preserved their heritage, their culture, and, in a special way, their faith.

The Maronite Patriarch of Antioch and All the East is the head of that extraordinary Church. It has never broken communion with the popes and always remained faithful to the Gospel. In fact, even in spite of persecution over hundreds of years, it was blessed with a rich religious life, with many vocations, monasteries, and saints! During those dark days, the patriarch lived in this "Holy Valley" and from there guided and guarded the purity of the faith and the devout lives of his people. Like the other ritual Churches of the East that are in communion with Rome—and like their Orthodox counterparts—they add to the beauty of the liturgy and the holiness of their people a wonderful link with the ancient traditions of the Church in the first centuries after the Ascension of the Lord.

My visit to the Holy Valley was memorable for me for several reasons. First of all, the natural beauty of this part of Lebanon is breathtaking. Secondly, the wonderful history of the Church and its perseverance in these hills is a great inspiration. Thirdly, because of an insight that I want to share with you.

As I stood almost dizzyingly close to the edge of the cliff and looked out at the villages that rim the canyons of the valley, I spotted a sheep lost in some brambles a couple of hundred yards away. I asked about it and was told that it had probably wandered from the flock and was now trapped there until the shepherd spotted it and climbed down to rescue it. Sure enough, a few moments later one could see in the distance a man slowly and painstakingly climbing down to the place where the sheep was bleating in fright. It was a real re-enactment of the New Testament story for me! I asked my guides whether it would not be very dangerous for the shepherd to climb down that steep slope and then try to free the poor animal. I was told, "He doesn't have a choice. He has to save the sheep. It belongs to him!"

What a powerful thought! What a perfect meditation! The Lord doesn't have a choice, either. Once we come to realize the Father's love for us, Jesus has to help us. We belong to him! I don't think I ever saw that truth so visibly and so powerfully. We truly are the sheep of his flock. It is not just that he cares for us. We belong to him!

I didn't have the chance to see the end of the story of the sheep, but since then I am rooted in this powerful truth that it teaches. When all is said and done, this is how we are related to the Lord. We belong to him and therefore he cannot let us be lost unless we reject his rescuing hands and his unending love. As I drove down from the mountain, I was thinking of you and all those who belong to God.

Aunt Edna
November 21, 2002

Have I told you about my Aunt Edna? She is my mother's youngest sister, the eighth sibling in my mother's family. Mom was the eldest of two boys and six girls, one of whom died as a child. Although the youngest of them all, Edna soon became the "manager" of the family when my two uncles married and started their own families. Edna never married and although she would work for almost fifty years for the Metropolitan Life Insurance Company, she always found time for the rest of the family, paid the bills, and, in a sense, presided over the family decision-making.

Edna is ninety-four years old now and resides at a wonderful residence in New Jersey, cared for by the Little Sisters of the Poor. For years I have tried to call her every day to see how she is doing. Now that I have been in Washington for the past two years, I try to get up to see her every couple of months. Some of my cousins and their wives have been very faithful in stopping in more often.

Aunt Edna is slowing down a little bit. She will often ask, "How old am I?" and when I tell her ninety-four, I get a big smile and she will say, "I'm pretty good for ninety-four!" She still recognizes me but can't quite fix in her memory that I now live in Washington and will often say, "Will you be coming back to see me tomorrow?" The sisters at the residence are so very good to her. They are wonderfully good to everyone there, and I have the clear sense that it is not always easy.

Lately, I haven't been able to get Edna on the phone every day. She likes to walk in the corridor and doesn't hear the phone, or she picks it up the wrong way and has her ear to the speaker. She has some good friends at the house where she lives, but sometimes complains that there are a lot of old people on her floor! She still gives me five dollars as a present every time I visit, a custom that goes back scores of years to when her nieces and nephews were little.

She gets down to Mass at the home frequently. She has a walker, which she decorates with flowers and it is her security, because, as she tells me, she doesn't stand very well anymore. Old age has its crosses and especially its limitations. It is a world of memories as well as a world of reality. Aunt Edna's memories should be very rich and rewarding, because she really lived for others throughout her long life and God will surely bless her for all of that. There are so many extraordinary people like that in all our families. As I am thinking of you and praying for you, I remember them in a special, grateful way.

The Psalms
November 28, 2002

It is early in the morning and I have just come out of the chapel. As I sit at the desk and begin to prepare this column, the words of the psalms that I have just been praying in the divine office are still with me. How beautiful they are! They are really prayers from the heart, and all the priests and religious and lay people who use them as prayer gain an insight not just into the mind and heart of the psalmist, but into their own hearts as well.

I talk to you a lot about reading the scriptures. You may remember that a while ago I asked you to spend just ten minutes a day reading in the four Gospels. I always recommend that you read the Gospels not to finish them quickly, but just to linger on the text and ask at each verse, "What is God telling me in these words?"

We Americans of the twenty-first century have the habit of picking up a book with the intention of finishing it as quickly as possible. But the sacred texts are not like that. They should be savored, like the experts advise us to do with fine wine. The object there is not to finish the bottle quickly, but to enjoy its taste and to linger over it as you appreciate its special quality. Holy scripture is very much like that. There are so many levels of meaning in the inspired words of the Bible. Each time we read a verse slowly and carefully, a new thought can come to us, a new message that we may need precisely at that moment in our lives. And that brings me back to the psalms.

There are psalms that seem to be written for times of great joy. These give us the words to express our happiness and gratitude to God. There are psalms that plumb the depths of our hearts in times of sorrow and contain beautiful sentiments of hope in God that strengthen us when we need it most. There are psalms of praise that we can use to express our own love for God when our own words don't seem to satisfy, and psalms that seem to be written for every stage of our journey through life. Each of us may find a favorite psalm to which we turn and through which God talks to us in a very special personal way.

At Thanksgiving time and during the blessed season of Advent when we listen to the words of the Old Testament as they proclaim the coming of the Messiah, the psalms become even more important as the song of those who waited over the centuries for the birth of the Lord. For me, they are a real blessing, since even as they did a few minutes ago as I prayed my breviary, they always remind me to be thinking of you at every stage of your journey with all the joys and hopes and sorrows that all of us must bear.

Sisters
December 5, 2002

Last Sunday we began the new year of the Church with the beginning of Advent. Just as we try to make personal New Year's resolutions on January 1 each year, the thought occurred to me that it would be good to think about some New Year's resolutions that we might make as the local Church of Washington. The first among those, I think, would have to be to make our local Church as welcoming as Jesus wants it to be, that we might bring back into active participation in the life of the Church those Catholics who, for one reason or another, have left the life of our diocesan family. They are still part of the family of the Church, of course; they always will be unless they publicly decide to separate themselves from us. But wouldn't it be wonderful if every parish—as we already do in so many parishes—could remember to make a special effort to bring them home? That would be my first resolution.

The second might surprise you. I think it even surprises me! During the last few months I have received communications from several young women in different parts of our area, suggesting that the Archdiocese of Washington consider establishing a new Congregation of Religious Sisters. Some of the letters have carefully thought through the whole question. Others are now, through God's grace, just sharing a call of which they feel more and more conscious to give their lives to God in the context of a community of Catholic women that would accept the great vows of poverty, chastity, and obedience and serve God's people here in this archdiocese.

Years ago in my former assignments in Metuchen and Newark I tried to establish such a community to fill a particular need that I thought I saw. In each case, I was not successful, possibly because I was not praying enough or trusting God enough to do it. This is the first time that the impetus seems to come from the young women themselves, in different parts of the diocese, and not known to each other. I must begin to ask if this is not the Lord speaking to us all here in this local Church. I believe that it may be time for us to say, "Yes, Lord, if you want this new work, give us the light and the grace and we will do it!"

The active sisters who now work in the archdiocese are special gifts indeed. They teach in some of our schools and catechetical programs, work in our hospitals and nursing homes, help in the pastoral work of parishes, play key roles in the diocesan administration, and do so many other great and holy things here. But there are not enough of them and some of our young people grow up without ever really knowing a nun. I pray—and you do too in the Prayer of the Faithful every day—for vocations to active communities and for those in this local Church who have been gifted with the marvelous vocation of contemplative prayer and sacrifice in our cloistered convents, but we still need many more vocations to religious life for women.

This is my second Advent resolution. I am asking any single woman in the Archdiocese of Washington who feels that God may be calling her into religious life for service here in this local Church to write me and tell me about it. I promise that I will answer those letters and if the result of all of this seems to be the work of God, then I will pursue this with the Lord and with those who give me counsel here in the archdiocese.

Maybe I surprised you by this column. I think I may have surprised myself, but this may truly be the work of the Lord as he is thinking of you and me as we prepare.

Saying Thank You
December 12, 2002

This Sunday in the Basilica of the National Shrine, the Church of Washington will have a wonderful opportunity to say thank you. It will be the first time that we will honor some special people with the Archdiocesan Order of Merit. I look forward to that occasion with a very special joy. You know that I'm always saying thank you when I meet you at Masses or other gatherings around the archdiocese. It is really the happiest thing I do. Ever since I arrived in Washington two years ago, I have been impressed and touched by the goodness and generosity of our Catholic people—and of so many others who are not of our faith, but who understand what the Catholic Church tries to do for the poor, or for children in our inner city schools, or for so many other groups whom we are able to help.

Since I came to Washington, I have been looking for a way to say thank you, not just in words, but in a tangible way so that you will know that the words are not just polite expressions, but really come from the heart of this local Church, as we all say thank you to some of our parishioners for the gift of their special lives. Of course, I know that we can never thank you enough for all your prayers, your love, and your sacrifices and that gratitude reaches out to people of all ages here in the archdiocese. It includes old people who offer their pains and discomfort for others, for vocations, and for peace and a better world. It includes teenagers who generously take on projects to help their parishes and communities. It includes little children who put aside part of their own allowances to support those who have nothing. It includes families of every race and culture and ethnic background who live not just for themselves but for others. As I get to see the wonderful stories of ordinary people doing extraordinary things here in Washington and the five counties of Maryland that are part of our family, I thank God so much for you and I am often embarrassed by the little I do myself.

We teach our children to say thank you. We should never forget to do it ourselves. The celebration this Sunday in the National Shrine is one small but public way of saying thank you as a diocese to people in parishes who have made an enormous difference in the lives of their neighbors through their love, their prayers, their generosity, and in a hundred other different ways. We cannot tell all their stories on Sunday, or the ceremony would last for days, but we can point out how very good our people are and how ordinary folks like us can change the world by making our own local community a better place.

I look forward to Sunday. It will be a time to say thank you from the heart of the Archdiocese of Washington and to recognize that those who will be honored by the Order of Merit this year also represent thousands of others throughout this local Church, men and women whom God blesses abundantly for their kindness to their neighbors and their service to the Church. During the ceremony I'll be thinking of you all and I'll continue to be amazed and grateful for the good people of the Church of Washington.

Christmas Cards
December 19, 2002

Are you one of those specially gifted people who have already sent out all your Christmas cards? It takes a wonderful sense of timing and discipline to be in that privileged group of folks who can now sit back and say "All of my Christmas cards are in the mail!" I'm not one of them. Oh, I guess most of my cards have already been sent out. (That's because I have a lot of smart people to help me.) But every day I seem to remember one or two people to whom I should have sent a card and now I can't remember if I did or not. And then there are the cards that come back with wrong addresses or people who moved and I don't have the new address handy. I send out hundreds of Christmas cards and every year I end up getting cards from folks who were not on my list and should have been. If you are one of these, I apologize!

This year my Christmas card was interesting—at least I think it was. It was a photo of the interior of St. Matthew's Cathedral all filled with scaffolding for the renovation that is taking place. It is the first major renovation in a hundred years, and the cathedral will truly be more beautiful when all is finished. The thought of the card was that we are all in the process of being restored to the glory that God has in mind for us, being repaired from our sins and faults and being protected by the scaffolding of God's love and grace while that process is continuing. Even as the precious body of Jesus was being built in the womb of the Blessed Virgin Mary, so must we build a place for him to come into our lives.

Of course, Christmas cards are not the essence of this extraordinary feast of God's love. They are only symbolic messages of the love we have for each other. Like the gifts we give at Christmas, they say "thank you" and "I love you" to our family and our friends. Together with the cards that proclaim the glory of the coming of the Lord, they build up the crescendo of holy sights and sounds that remind us of the message of the angels—Glory to God and peace to good people. We must never let all these very good and worthwhile souvenirs of Christmas make us forget that essential message that challenges us today even as it challenged the shepherds two thousand years ago.

As I wish you a blessed Christmas this year, I beg you to pray fervently for that peace that the angels' voices proclaimed. May it be a peace that brings justice and safety to all God's people in the Holy Land, in the Middle East, in Africa and throughout the world. May it bring peace to our families and our Church. May it bring peace to the hearts of all of us that we may truly rejoice in his coming and, with the help of his grace, build a better world in the new year. As all these special days approach, I am thinking of you and praying for you and all your loved ones. Please pray for me too. God bless you all.

Exchange of Gifts
December 26, 2002

I think there are three kinds of Christmas gifts. There are those that we ask for directly, describing them to the gift giver in great detail. There are those that come as a pleasant surprise from people who love us and have figured out just what we want. And then there are all the others that are the wrong size or the wrong color or the fourth one we received this Christmas, or the one that just doesn't fit into the décor or the plan or the space, or whatever.

When we think of the exchange of gifts, it is usually these latter gifts that we have in mind and we begin to arrange our schedules to find time to go back to the stores and see if we can get something else in their place. The only thing that makes this kind of gift exchange a little pleasant is that we may be able to find a bargain or two in post-holiday sales. Please don't think that I am criticizing this wholesome practice. As a matter of fact, I have been looking at my usually packed schedule to see if I can work out a few hours to do the same. (So, if you bump into me in one of the stores after Christmas, don't smile too broadly!)

But when we talk of the exchange of gifts in the spiritual sense, we have something else in mind. We cannot begin to count the gifts that God gives each one of us—at Christmas or indeed every day of our lives. What gifts have we given to him at Christmas? How often it seems that the only things I give the Lord are my sins, my impatience, my fears, and concerns. What a poor exchange of gifts that is. In exchange for the overwhelming gift of his Son, our Lord, Jesus Christ, what can I possibly give him in return except all that I am and all that I have, and this is still so poor and empty a return. Yet, if it is all that I have, he accepts it with love.

The wonderful thing about God's gift-giving is that it is never the wrong size or the wrong object. We always receive from him just exactly what we need. We may try to exchange it for something we think we need, but we are so much wiser to accept it gratefully from his hand. It can be joy or sorrow, health or illness, success or disappointment, but since it comes from the one who loves us best and knows us best, it will always be the very best gift we could receive. It is always that special gift that, if we use it right, turns into the grace that brings us the eternal joy of living in his presence.

As we go about either trying on or exchanging the gifts that we can touch, God is surely thinking of you and me and daily sending us the gifts that last forever.

2003

The Realism of Faith
January 2, 2003

Was it the year that just ended that Queen Elizabeth called "a horrible year"? It clearly could have been since it truly was a very difficult year. From the increasing threat of war on two fronts, to the terrible tragedy of sex abuse by clergy, to the ongoing financial crisis that has hurt so many people, to the increasing confrontations between religious groups, to the never-ending nightmare of violence in the Holy Land. The list of fears and pains and suffering goes on and on, and you will be able to add your own special concerns, I am sure.

Someone said to me as I stood greeting people after a Mass last week, "I'm glad 2002 is over. The New Year just has to be better!" It is on that note that I wanted to start this column. As you and I look to this New Year, we have the choice of pessimism or optimism with regard to the future. Let me put a third choice into the mix. Let's call it the realism of faith.

We cannot close our eyes to the problems that the world faces and to the difficulties in solving them in a way that will be just and good and in accord with those truths we hold most deeply. We know, therefore, that there are no easy solutions to the crises that lie ahead. That part of the equation we can call realism.

But the realism that is of faith puts all these problems in a new perspective. It demands that we look at them in the context of a world that ultimately belongs to God, whose love and divine providence is always present and always at work in the mystery of that presence. The prophet reminds us that "the earth is the Lord's" and that nothing ever happens without his permission. He has counted the hairs of our head and the numbers of the stars; he knows the number of the grains of sand at the shore of the sea, as well as our deepest thoughts and hopes and fears. This does not mean that we ourselves have no responsibility for our lives, but that the world is truly in his hands, and if we only will let him, he will bring peace and make justice flourish in our time.

As we open the new book of 2003, I pray that you and I will do it with the realism of faith, with our eyes wide open to the dangers and concerns, but with an unshakable trust in the God who loves us and whose powerful hand will never let us go unless we ourselves decide to walk in darkness. Thinking of you as the New Year begins, I find a great deal of hope in your goodness and your faith.

A Busy Retreat
January 9, 2003

As many of you may know, I go on retreat this week. Every year, the bishops of two regions—from Maryland all the way down to Florida—spend a week at a retreat house where we pray and listen to the retreat master challenge us to do better and to be better. You probably know me well enough by now to figure that I would prefer to have a retreat close to home. However, this year we go to Florida. It's not that I don't enjoy Florida. I do. But I really don't like to mix up my spiritual exercises and my vacation. I really need a good, solid retreat, and for me Florida can be a distraction that takes me away from the real purpose of these few days of very special conversation with God.

In the most profound theology of the ministry of bishops, the Church teaches that the bishop is to pray for his people and that God grants graces to the faithful not only individually but also through the prayer of their bishops as they plead for their own diocesan communities. Even as a father or mother will pray for blessings upon their children, so the bishop stands before the Lord and begs blessings and heavenly gifts on those who have been entrusted to his care. This is why I must try harder to become a holy person, so that I can become a more effective channel of God's grace for you. Remember me, then, this week so that the better I can be, the more I can be a good servant to all of you.

The other challenge that meets me on retreat is to try to determine our own local Church's priorities for the year— and years—ahead. Of course, this will be discussed with the different councils that are found in our archdiocese—the council of priests, the archdiocesan pastoral council, the college of consultors, the archdiocesan finance council, and several others. But ultimately, if I am to get their input, I must know what questions to ask and in that way through them, and ultimately through you, be able to get a sense of the needs and dreams and concerns of the whole archdiocese. Therefore, I must bring some ideas so that the dialogue can begin.

Beside the vocation shortage and the fallout from our region's current economic problems, two major crises that we all must carry in the year ahead, there are some other needs that stand out and for which I will pray very hard during my days of retreat. One will be the large number of Catholic people who have more or less stopped going to Holy Mass. Another intention for my prayers will be the pastoral care of strangers from other lands who are living and working here in the archdiocese, and especially for those who are poor or ill or lonely. I will pray also for two special groups of our people: the children who need so much to know and experience God's love, and the elderly who need so often to be reminded of it.

As I start writing, my mind fills up with dozens of other intentions, perhaps the most prominent among them the need to pray for the peace of the world. It does seem that I will have enough to do on retreat, so pray that I do it well, please. At least you will know that whatever I am praying for ultimately I am thinking of you.

The Morning Offering
January 16, 2003

The other day I was speaking to a group of youngsters about prayer. They were telling me all the things they pray for, and it was a very impressive list of intentions. During the course of the conversation, one of the children, actually one of a pair of twins in the group, mentioned that she was praying for her uncle to get a job. I looked at her twin brother and asked if he was praying for that too. "Oh," he replied, very self-satisfied, "I prayed for that yesterday!"

And so today I want to talk about perseverance in prayer. The scriptures tell us that we should pray without ceasing. That means two things, I think. It means that we should try to maintain a spirit of prayerfulness all the time. This comes from trying to live consciously in the presence of God. If we know that he is always with us, we will naturally talk to him informally in prayer many times during the day.

It also means that we should never give up in praying for what we truly believe we or someone else may need. It is not enough to have prayed for something yesterday. If it is really important to us, we should keep reminding the Lord about it. Too often I think I give up too soon in praying for the things I need. Sometimes that is because I conclude that if God doesn't answer right away, he has decided against it. Other times I'm afraid it may be because of my weak faith. Jesus encourages us to keep knocking on the door of heaven. He does listen and he does love us. If a parent finally gives in when a child keeps asking for a certain gift, why should we think that God will not listen if we ask in loving trust for what we truly need?

That's why the morning offering is so special a prayer. It is the very first thing I do when the radio alarm turns on at 5:00 a.m. Sometimes it's cold in the room and that's all the more reason to remember the practices of our youth and to get down on our knees and pray to Jesus through the Immaculate Heart of Mary for all the intentions of his sacred heart. Ultimately, in that prayer I pray for all our intentions, personal intentions, those of the Archdiocese of Washington and those of the Church throughout the world. This way I join with the prayers of all of you and with the Holy Father as he prays for all the needs of the world. And all the things I prayed for yesterday can still be on the list for today because the morning offering saves them all up and tells the Lord that we still need his help so much. In a very special way, it's my way of starting the day thinking of you.

What to Write?
January 23, 2003

This is one of those days! I always wonder how the folks who create the comics and cartoons every day in the news-papers can do it. Doesn't the constant stress of getting a new idea ever get them down? How can they be so funny, day after day and over the long period of years? The same would apply, I guess, to the columnists who write learned and insightful articles with equal regularity. How do they always come up with new ideas? To be absolutely honest, I asked the editor of the *Standard* a few weeks ago to make a list of all my columns over the last two years—there are more than a hundred of them now—so I could try not to repeat myself.

And here I am today. It's Tuesday morning and I must get this in before noon. Oh, you might say, he has plenty of time between 6:30 and noon to do it. But the morning is filled with meetings—a half dozen of them at least—and so, if I don't get a good idea for a theme soon, I'm cooked! So, I figured I would just share my predicament with you. It's not that I don't have a lot of ideas on what I would write to you, it's just that I can't seem to put it all together in my head. I could have tried to do a funny column, or a deeply theological one, but the funny columns—if you ever think any of them are funny—take a lot of time, which I no longer have, and the deeply theological columns are usually beyond my capability.

I could tell you about Rome, where I spent a few days at a meeting last week, but I don't know how interesting that would be. I could tell you about our ten fine seminarians at the North American College where I stayed in Rome—all of whom are doing well and enjoy the great respect of their fellow students and the faculty, by the way—but I do want to do something about vocations next week, since we have a retreat at Theological College this weekend, January 24–26, for any young men who believe that God may be calling them to priesthood. So here I am, without a lot of thoughts and the column is almost all written.

Does it ever happen to you? Do you ever want to do something well and can't seem to get started? As I get older, I think it happens more and more. What's the answer? Maybe it is just to share your frustration with yourself and your inability to produce as you would like with the people you love and the people you serve. I guess that's what I'm doing in this column. Perhaps it's a lesson for life. We all go through times when we can't seem to get things together. When that happens it's better not to keep it to yourself. Just as it is always good to share our joys and helpful to seek support in times of sorrow, so it's probably good to reach out to others when you're stuck and just assure them that you're doing your best to think of them just as now I'm thinking of you.

Help Is on the Way
January 30, 2003

When I wrote you last week, I mentioned that we were going to have a retreat for men who are considering the possibility of a priestly vocation. Well, last weekend together with Fr. Panke, our director of vocations, and Fr. Filardi, I helped to preach the retreat. You may be surprised and I am sure you will be pleased that almost forty young men signed up for these days of prayer and discussion!

They were lawyers and Marines, teachers and graduate students. They ranged in age from the early twenties to the early forties, and they came from the archdiocese as well as from states across the country. Many of them have worked or studied in Washington and most still are residing here. I was very impressed by their seriousness, their obvious faith, and their desire to grow in their spiritual lives and in closeness to the Lord. Only God knows how many will follow up on the experience of the retreat and continue to discern their vocation until they are ready to enter seminary studies, but it was a good sign to me that the Lord is watching over this blessed local Church of Washington and that he will always give us shepherds who will care for our people in this diocese. I ask you to pray for these young men as they continue that discernment. May many of them ultimately decide to say yes to a priestly vocation.

Besides these men, the vocation office continues contact with a number of others who are in various stages of applying to the archdiocese for acceptance as a candidate for priestly studies. The road is not unreasonably long, but it is demanding. A candidate must have a number of good references; his school records and parish activities are analyzed; a thorough medical and psychological examination must be completed and the archdiocese requires interviews with several priests and lay people for each applicant. Ultimately, the Archdiocesan Board of Priestly Vocations needs to study each application and then makes its recommendation to the archbishop. In this way we try to be sure that the Church of the future will have good and holy priests to care for the faithful.

You know that I pray for vocations for the priesthood and religious life every day. I do ask you to do the same. In every Mass offered in the Archdiocese of Washington, we pray for that intention in the Prayers of the Faithful so that all of us, priests, religious and laity will always have it in mind. Pope John Paul II's great letter on the priesthood quotes the scriptures in its title: "*Pastores Dabo Vobis*—I Will Give You Shepherds." We believe that God will truly always give us the shepherds we need for the future service of his people, men formed after his own sacred heart and ready to serve with courage and generosity. Whenever I'm thinking of you, this is one of the things that I think of in a special way. Pray hard with me, because the future comes so quickly.

Life, Death, and Healing
February 6, 2003

Once more our nation suffers a tragedy in the loss of seven courageous astronauts whose lives were ended in an instant at the close of an historic journey that advanced the welfare of humanity. I was going to write this column on the World Day of the Sick, which we are very privileged to host here in the Archdiocese of Washington next week. The tragic death of the astronauts, which reminds us of our frailty and the imperfection of human inventions, may be a thoughtful background for such a reflection.

There is, of course, an essential union between a consideration of life and death and a reflection on sickness and health. Life and health are what we treasure in these years of our mortal journey here on earth. Sickness reminds us of our fragility and of the certainty that this body of ours will always be subject to imperfection until after death when God calls the just to a resurrection where there will be no illness or decay or death.

We mourn for the astronauts because their daring and wondrous competence gave us hope for discoveries that will enhance the life we live here on earth. With them, we raise our eyes and our hearts to the heavens, and we entrust them to the living God, the beauty of whose creation they caught a glimpse and of whose infinite beauty we pray that they now enjoy.

As we think with sadness at the ending of their earthly lives at their prime, we think, too, of the millions of our brothers and sisters here whose lives are touched by sickness and the stark limitations of healing in a finite world. The World Day of the Sick is one of the initiatives by which Pope John Paul II has called nations to consider the care of the ill and to study how the Church and other agencies of society can reach out to help them.

Every year, on a different continent, the Church focuses on the vital apostolate of Catholic health care to raise the consciousness of all its faithful and to study the challenges and opportunities that it faces. Next week, health experts and those who are involved in the pastoral care of the sick will gather in Washington from all over the world, especially from throughout the Americas. Much of the time will be spent in discussions and commentaries, but on Tuesday, February 11, the Feast of Our Lady of Lourdes, a Pontifical Mass will be held at the Basilica of the National Shrine of the Immaculate Conception at 2:30 p.m., during which the Anointing of the Sick will take place. This sacrament is always a wonderful reminder of the Church's care of the sick, which in turn is a reminder of God's healing grace for all his children. I hope that some of you—especially older folks and those with serious illnesses—can avail yourselves of this opportunity of receiving this great sacrament during the Mass. I am hoping that there will be a large number of folks who will come and pray with us for those who are ill and suffering and for an increase in our understanding of the needs of the sick.

Of course, whether or not you can be present physically, you know that I'll be thinking of you and praying that the Lord will give you patience and peace and even the grace of deepest healing.

"Unforgettable, That's What You Are!"
February 13, 2003

You know how a catchy line from a song sticks in your head sometimes. It can be a hymn you may have sung at Mass that keeps coming back all the day and is rather like a pleasant aspiration that brings your heart back to God. Or it can be a catchy tune from a song you heard or even a melody that somebody whistled in the street. Nat King Cole's "Unforgettable" has been in my head all weekend since that most successful Catholic Charities gala last Saturday night.

His daughter, Natalie Cole, entertained the guests at that affair and naturally she sang her father's signature song with skill and feeling. As a matter of fact, at a loss on how to end my own short remarks before the dinner started, I even sang the first line and it has stayed with me since then like an old friend or a favorite sweater. (By the way, after I sang my line, I saw one of our priests and in kidding I said to him, "You didn't know I could sing so well!" to which, without missing a beat, he replied, "Archbishop, don't quit your day job.")

There are a lot of people in our lives who are unforgettable. Parents, children, brothers, and sisters, of course, always lead the list. But there are others, like a favorite teacher whose style we can't forget or a priest whose counsel in confession changed our lives, or a stranger whose act of charity or courtesy made so great an impression on us. As we get older, we collect unforgettable moments and unforgettable people, and we start to hope that for others as well we will be unforgettable too.

The one thing we know is that God never forgets us. In that great line in the Book of Proverbs he reminds us of that with absolute certainty when he likens his love to that of a mother's love for her child. "Can a mother forget the child of her womb, yes, even if she would forget I will not forget you." For our part, we must never forget his love or his forgiveness. Day after day, he challenges us to put the past behind us and to turn to his love that never forgets us. That's why he gives us the sacrament of penance and constantly reminds us in the scriptures that we must never be afraid. If we know he loves us and if we know that he will never forget us, there is no reason for any fear to enter our lives. It is easy to say this, of course, but if we have the deep faith that we need, it becomes possible and so very life-giving.

For Jesus, unforgettable is what you are. That's why it is not just your archbishop, but the living God himself who is always thinking of you.

Some Things One Cannot Do
February 20, 2003

All of us who have lived though months and months of media preoccupation on the scandal of sexual abuse of minors will never forget that there are victims who have lived many years with this trauma. I don't know anyone—parent, priest, or passer-by—who hasn't had his or her heart broken over the pain that victims have suffered at the hands of an unworthy minister of religion. For us Catholics when this crime is committed by a priest, it is so much worse because of the trust we have placed in our priests.

One of the reasons for our trust has always been the confidence we have in a priest's total and sacramental silence about anything we may say in the confessional. History is filled with stories of priests who suffered even death rather than break that solemn seal, which guarantees the penitent that the knowledge of what is said in the sacrament of penance belong only to the priest and to God.

Unfortunately I must tell you that bills have been introduced in the legislature of the State of Maryland that would make it a crime for a priest to be faithful to that solemn sacramental obligation. These bills would require a priest by law to report what he heard in confession if any kind of abuse of a child is mentioned. I am not condemning the legislators who are promoting this bill. I am presuming that they are only interested in helping children and not in attacking the Catholic Church and any other religious body that would have such protection for spiritual conversations. However what they are proposing is a grave violation of our Church's canon law and I must oppose it with whatever authority I have, and you, dear friends, need to know this.

If this bill were to pass, I shall instruct all the priests in the Archdiocese of Washington who serve in Maryland to ignore it and to indicate they are acting on direct orders from me as their archbishop and religious superior. On this issue, I will gladly plead civil disobedience and willingly—if not gladly—go to jail. Please understand that I write this to you as your servant and your friend and as one, who however unworthy, in the mystery of God's providence, is called to be your bishop. I cannot allow three state senators and eight members of the House of Delegates who are the proposers of this legislation to force our priests to violate the sacramental seal of confession. If there is a gauntlet involved in this process, then I throw it down now.

While there is still time to prevent this attack on the sacramental seal of confession, I ask you to write or phone your own state legislators in Annapolis and tell them how you feel about the proposed law and how it affects your rights as a Catholic American and a citizen of this state of Maryland. If in spite of all you do, it gets into law, I'm happy to assure you that, even behind bars, I'll be thinking of you.

Every Child and Every School
February 27, 2003

So much has happened since Catholic Schools Week—like a blizzard and a few other distractions—that I let it go by without a column or even a brief remark. I did have a chance to visit a few schools in different parts of the archdiocese, to talk to principals and teachers as well as some parents.

Of course, for me the best part of Catholic Schools Week is to talk with the children. They are funny and they are serious. They have amazing insight beyond their years, together with that delightful sense of wonder that no child should ever lose. I always come away from these conversations edified and inspired both by the things they say and the way they say them.

From the inner city of Washington to the more affluent suburbs to the rural areas of Southern Maryland, Catholic schools are doing something wonderful. They are educating young people with care, with experience, and with respect. They are giving them everything they need to be productive citizens and to make a difference in their world through the values they present and the love for neighbor which they exemplify. Every time I leave one of our schools, I am so proud of what they accomplish and so grateful to our extraordinary teachers and the families whose generous sacrifices make all this possible. I still believe that the gift of a Catholic school education is the greatest gift that Catholic parents can give their children.

Having said that, I am well aware that many Catholic families just cannot afford the tuition that our schools are obliged to charge and therefore we should continue to press for parental choice in education. At the same time, since the vast majority of our Catholic boys and girls are in the public school system, we must also press for excellence in that system as well. I want to assure all those who are responsible for public education in this area that they have an ally in us and that we will stand shoulder to shoulder with them to improve the quality of their schools too.

For us, every child is important and every school should be the best, whether it is public, private, or parochial. As I reflect on Catholic Schools Week and ask your help again to keep our excellent schools alive and thriving, I am thinking of you and am anxious to share that wider thought as well.

A Very Remarkable Man
March 6, 2003

When Pope John Paul II was my age, he had already been Bishop of Rome and the Vicar of Christ for almost fifteen years, had survived a deadly assassination attempt, had played an historic role in the transformation of Eastern Europe, and had already made his indelible mark on the modern history of the world. In the last ten years, he has continued his extraordinary service of the Church of God, and despite severe problems of health and frailty, has constantly proclaimed the message of the Gospel in season and out of season without fear or hesitation.

He has earned the love and respect of hundreds of millions of people, both in the Catholic Church and outside of it. The other day, when I was invited to talk on Vatican Radio about the present world situation, I ended my brief and probably not too profound remarks by calling attention to the fact that today, two thousand years after the establishment of our Church, at a time of serious world crisis and confusion, the leaders of so many nations from all parts of the world made their way to Rome to discuss with this elderly and frail successor of the apostle Peter their hopes and fears for the future of humanity and sought his wisdom and his prayers for their countries and themselves.

Last week, during the three days I spent in Rome, I was able to greet the Holy Father at the Wednesday public audience. Since the archbishop of Washington serves as chairman of the board of the Basilica of the National Shrine, I had promised Msgr. Bransfield, the very capable and outstanding rector of the shrine, that I would participate in the pilgrimage, which is organized every few years, bringing the United States diocesan directors of pilgrimages on their own pilgrimage to Rome. This gave me the opportunity to greet Pope John Paul II for a moment at the end of the public audience.

I found His Holiness much stronger than I had seen him in the last couple of years. His voice was clear, his step more steady, and his interaction with the thousands of pilgrims gathered in the audience hall was more vigorous and personal. Having worried about him in the past because of the enormous burdens he carries, it was a grace for me to see him now so well as he approaches the quarter century of his pontificate. (I just realized that this may sound like a plug for the Archdiocese of Washington pilgrimage to Rome in October to celebrate the Holy Father's twenty-fifth anniversary as pope and to be present for the Beatification of Mother Teresa of Calcutta! Well, that's not a bad idea. I hope many of you can come with me for that great visit.)

All this is to remind you of what you clearly know, that when I met the Holy Father last Wednesday, after I told him how much a grace it was to see him, I asked his blessing on all of us in this local Church of Washington. You would have the right to be disappointed if, at that special moment, I wasn't thinking of you.

Irish Skin
March 13, 2003

Almost everybody I talk to is anxious about what will be happening in the Middle East in the next few days. The level of violence is higher than ever in the Holy Land where the senseless killings of innocent people by terrorists and the wanton destruction of whole neighborhoods in reprisal are both actions that only raise the cycle of vengeance in that beautiful and suffering land. Around the borders of Iraq, a different waiting period grows all the more tense as each day passes and the world hopes to solve the vexing question of this evil regime by measures short of violence and war.

I really don't want to add to the preoccupations that so many of us have. So I am going to write you about something very different today—that priceless gift, that wondrous blessing that comes from being Irish.

I have to make two clarifications right at the start. First of all, I must confess that I cannot boast of being purely Irish. In the generations of my ancestors are several nationalities and races: Scottish, Polish, German, Jewish, and even—we have always believed—a touch of Native American. But the majority of my whole background is Irish. Secondly, being Irish is not a universal blessing. Besides the gifts of music and poetry, the vaunted wit and graciousness of the Gael, the beauty of her women, and so many other well-founded boasts, there is the penalty of Irish skin.

The Irish were probably destined to do their greatest works in the mist and the rain, under cloudy skies or preferably around a glowing hearth-fire—but not in the sun. For those of us who have moved from that somewhat limiting geography to the brilliant sunshine of other, less gifted lands, there is a price to pay. As I sit in my room and look out at the glorious beginning of springtime, I hear in the distance the gentle but stirring words of my dermatologist: "Be careful of the sun!"

It's too late for me, I'm afraid. After wonderful childhood summers visiting the beaches of Long Island and the Jersey Shore, not to mention eleven years on the missions in the tropics, I've had my share of burn-outs, cut-outs, and other kinds of surgery to preserve whatever is left of the original me. As the great Feast of Saint Patrick approaches, I weigh all these things together and I'm still glad that so many of my ancestors came from Ireland because from them, through

God's grace, I received the faith in Jesus, which is far more important than any other gift. As I am thinking of you who share that faith with me, let us rejoice together and give thanks to God.

The Lord Be With You
March 20, 2003

Have you ever counted the times the greeting "The Lord be with you" is mentioned in our Mass? When I was growing up perhaps we were more conscious of it since the Latin form of those words "*dominus vobiscum*" was a phrase that sounded so frequently in our ears. We find the words often at the beginning and always before the major prayers of the Mass like the Gospel and the preface and the last blessing. I would like to talk about it and reflect on it for a few minutes in this column, since it seems to be a special prayer for these days of anxiety through which we are all passing right now.

The words "The Lord be with you" are a greeting, a reminder, and a challenge. First they are a greeting. In early Christian times the faithful tried very hard to live in the consciousness of God's presence in their lives so that it was natural for them to greet each other with words that would reflect their faith. Instead of "hello," which does not immediately call God's presence to our minds, the words "The Lord be with you" clearly did and the reply "And with you also" completed the cycle of recognizing the divine presence among us all.

Secondly, it is a reminder, strong and present, that God truly is here with us every moment of our lives. He never leaves us alone. In our deepest crisis, in our most abundant joy, in times of illness and anxiety, in times of disappointment and fulfillment, the Lord is always there. That phrase is one of the most powerful realizations of our faith. "If God is with us, who can be against us?" the scriptures tell us and so those words remind us of his presence and they are powerful medicine to drive away our fears.

Finally, the words are a challenge. They call on us not to be so enmeshed in our own individual selves here on earth that we do not become conscious of something—and someone— greater than ourselves who loves us and has an interest in us. As the Old Testament assures us that God always wishes us good and never seeks to bring evil into our lives, no man—or woman—is an island off by himself or herself. The Lord is always with us and that must give us strength.

As we all very naturally worry these days about war and peace, about justice and liberty, about loved ones who may be in dangerous missions all across the globe, it is good to hear frequently the prayer "The Lord be with you." It is another way of saying that our God and Father is thinking of you and loving you and giving you the grace and strength we all need to walk in days of shadows as well as in days of light. You know that I am thinking of you too and praying that the peace with justice for which all of us long may soon be accomplished.

You
March 27, 2003

This may seem a funny title for a column, but it will become clear when you see what I want to tell you. As I look at my life at this stage of my journey, my one, overwhelming responsibility is to care for you, the priests and deacons, religious and lay people of the Archdiocese of Washington.

Nothing else comes close to that mandate which, in the mystery of God's providence, I have received from the Holy Father and the Church. I'm not supposed to prefer myself to your good. My road to holiness—on which I still seem to walk so hesitatingly—is by serving you, by proclaiming the good news of the Gospel to you and by loving you and always striving to build you up in grace and in the joy of God's presence.

Obviously, I'm not so special in having this responsibility. Every bishop has it for his own people and because of that, every one of my brother priests shares in that call to serve the people of his parish. I wanted to put this so starkly before you so you will understand how hard it sometimes is to make decisions about the things that I ought to do.

Let me give you an example that I am wrestling with right now. As a cardinal, I also have some other rather limited responsibilities to serve the whole Church. Cardinals are often named to committees of the Holy See, somewhat like the assignments of senators and congressmen to committees as part of their government responsibility. Every elected member, therefore, must serve his or her own district or state and at the same time participate in the work of the national government.

As you may remember, a few weeks ago I was named to the Pontifical Commission for Latin America, which is an important body for us here in the Church in the Western Hemisphere. The plenary meeting of this commission began on Monday, March 24 and, since it is my first meeting, I really have to attend. I believe I will be able to fly to Rome without trouble (I am writing this in what will be last week, as you read this column) but I worry about being able to get right back if, God forbid, there is danger or terrorism at home. It is not that I could be of tremendous help if I were with you, but if you are anxious or hurting, or in danger, that is where I ought to be and where I would want to be.

All of this is a long way of saying that I really am always thinking of you and hoping that I will always be there when you may need me. Pray for me to make the right decisions and let us pray together that peace and tranquility will quickly come.

Reflections on War and Peace
April 3, 2003

(Belgrade, Serbia) I have lived through many wars, from World War II to the present, and each time in a different way, depending on my age and my responsibilities, I can recall the concerns that I felt. During World War II, I was a youngster in grammar school, not understanding the complexities of what was going on, but very much aware, since some of my older cousins were at the front. I followed as carefully as I could, at first with anxiety, as Japan and Germany seemed to be unstoppable in their conquests, and then, after the tide of war turned in our favor, with great patriotic pride in the progress of the Allied armies.

We were very conscious of the danger from war then. I recall the black-outs and the sirens, the air raid wardens, and the war bonds that we were urged to buy. It was a frightening time at the beginning of the conflict, and I am glad I didn't know how dangerous it really was for us.

When the Korean War came, I registered for the draft like everyone else my age. I was in college and was not called, but I remember as I took part in the Air Force ROTC at Fordham that I was getting ready to play whatever role our country needed me to play. By Vietnam, I was already a priest and would have been glad to serve in the military, but my superiors had other plans for me and ultimately I was sent to run the Catholic University in Puerto Rico.

In all of this, I guess I never really got used to the idea of war. When I served as secretary to Cardinal Cooke, who was a military bishop at the time, I accompanied him to Vietnam a couple of times and came under fire on several occasions. I was always impressed by the bravery and devotion of our American troops, even when we stopped to see the wounded in military hospitals. I have come to know that no one prays for peace more fervently than those who serve in war.

Let us, too, pray for peace. Let us beg our heavenly Father to keep our men and women in the armed forces safe from harm. Let us also pray for the safety of the ordinary civilians of Iraq, for our faith tells us that they, too, are our brothers and sisters. As Jesus teaches us, let us also pray for our enemies, and especially for those Iraqis who are fighting for a cause in which they really do not believe. Finally, let us pray that this terrible war soon ends, without the use of weapons of mass destruction and without a great loss of human life.

Wars are different now, but people are still dying and others are suffering terrible physical and mental harm. My prayer is that peace and justice may come quickly to Iraq and to all of the Middle East, and that the world will find ways other than war to deal with weapons of mass destruction and repressive regimes.

As I reflect on these events while I am half a world away, I am thinking of you and glad that you are safe.

Cherry Blossom Time
April 10, 2003

I may have deceived you by the title of this column. I'm not going to talk about the cherry blossoms here in town, although they truly are a wonder to behold. Suddenly the city is again clothed in the beauty of nature and we take a deep breath and thank God for the beauty of his world. But the coming of the cherry blossoms also somehow reminds me of Easter and the even more awesome wonder of the resurrection of the Lord. And, that brings me to the real message of this column.

By the time you read this, Easter will be just about a week away. Lent with all of its hopes and promises is rapidly coming to a close. With more than a little disappointment, I look at my own Lenten resolutions and see how much I have failed in doing the great things I had in mind. Oh, I did cut down on some things I like to eat and I did try to find some extra time for prayer. That was all to the good, and I thank the Lord for the grace to have done that.

But how about the real determination to grow in holiness during these past few weeks, the resolution to be more patient, more trusting, more open to the Lord's presence in my life? If you are like me, let me gently make this suggestion to you.

Christian spirituality has always focused on three great foundations of growth in holiness—prayer, fasting, and almsgiving. Each one of these is a bridge that we can cross to become more pleasing to the God who loves us and who has given so much to each one of us. I often write to you about prayer, about the spirit of prayer that helps us to live more consciously in God's presence. Holy Week is such a great time to find more time to pray. Fasting is always possible, too, if we are healthy, and Holy Week is filled with opportunities to deny ourselves the food and drink we really do not need.

I add almsgiving because I know how generous you always are. An extra sacrifice now—to the cardinal's appeal, to your parish, or to the missions—still counts as a great act of charity, and charity, as we know, can cover a multitude of sins. (I mention the cardinal's appeal in a special way at this time because, as you know, every single penny that is contributed goes to the care of the poor and to the scores of programs in the Archdiocese of Washington that help people in need.)

As I'm thinking of you, I'm wondering whether your Lent—like mine—has been a little less than perfect this year. Cherry blossom time might come as a good reminder that this is the time to redeem our pledges to the Lord even as we prepare to give him thanks for the indescribable gift of our own redemption.

Rejoice in His Consolation
April 17, 2003

Do you recall the prayer to the Holy Spirit that we learned when we were children? It's the one about renewing the face of the earth. It is a beautiful and a powerful prayer, and I pray it early every morning when I get into the chapel. A few months ago, when we had some special problem that was worrying me a lot—whether it was financial or personnel, I don't recall—I started praying it more fervently because it asks for the grace to become "truly wise." I began thinking about those words and reflecting on them more carefully. The prayers we learned in youth, we tend to recite too quickly and sometimes lose a wealth of meaning as our memory slides by the words without pausing.

There is a phrase in that prayer in which we beg God to grant us the grace always to "rejoice in his consolation." It is one of those special times when we ask the Lord to give us joy. At the Last Supper, in his farewell message to the apostles before his passion, Jesus prayed that his joy might be in us, and that is the joy we ask for in that prayer to the Holy Spirit. In that particular prayer, however, we specify it in a really beautiful way. We recognize that in this world of worries and concerns, we need to find the deepest joy in his consolation.

The dictionary tells us that "to console" means to alleviate the grief or sense of loss or the trouble that wears us down. That makes sense. When we lift sorrow from our hearts, then joy can come in and take its place. That's what God does for us.

Just as the whole Church finds joy as the sorrow of Christ's passion is lifted by the wonder of the resurrection, so the pains and anxieties we all carry day by day can be lifted by the loving consolation of the Holy Spirit. Consolation is a gift of faith. It is akin to trust and hope and makes room for joy when problems try to crowd it out.

I'm glad I caught that special meaning in an old and comforting prayer, because when Easter comes and I am thinking of you and praying that God will bring you all good things, I will pray especially that you may rejoice in his consolation.

The Crowds of Easter
April 24, 2003

In fifteenth-century France there was a lyric poet named Francois Villon. His most famous poem was the one that opens with the line: "Where are the snows of yesterday?" It is a commentary on the fleeting nature of material things. After Easter Sunday, it came to my mind.

For almost every one of the great Holy Week services we had standing room only at St. Matthew's Cathedral. I believe it was pretty much the same in the Basilica of the National Shrine and in many other churches around the Archdiocese of Washington. The liturgies of Easter and of those sacred days preceding it are truly both powerful and filled with beauty. I thank God and the Church for giving us these most precious gifts of prayer and wonder. As I looked out at the faithful standing four deep in St. Matthew's Cathedral, my heart was filled with several emotions.

First of all, I was so happy that they were there, that they could enjoy the ceremony and the music, the scripture readings, the powerful, prayerful spirit—and even the homily— that they could once again find the power of the presence of a believing community united in faith and struggling to understand together the mysterious providence of God in their lives. Wonderfully, they seemed eager and anxious to join in the singing and the public prayers.

Secondly, as I know you were expecting me to say, I was troubled by the fact that they do not come to Mass every Sunday, that despite all the Church tries to do, we have not convinced them that their lives will never be completed and fulfilled without a personal commitment to public prayer. The sociologists tell us that human beings are social animals and that the deepest and most precious parts of our lives have somehow to be expressed publicly, that we really need to manifest in public what we hold most sacred in our lives.

Finally, when I ask myself why people come only sometimes, I perceive that there must always be times when the desire for the things of God, for a personal relationship with him becomes so strong that it has to find expression and this is what brings them back to Mass and to Church, even just once in a while. I truly believe that every single one of us must have a personal relationship with God, that there is a hunger for that relationship within each of us and that we will forever be frustrated until we find a way to live it out. That way, for us, is the faith which Jesus gave us two thousand years ago and which the Church has kept alive for all these centuries. As I am thinking of you, I thank God that you and I have received this gift and I pray that it will come to all who long for it, even sometimes unaware!

The Half of It
May 1, 2003

If the title of this column confuses you, it's because I couldn't fit all the words in. I wanted to write this column about my schedule as it appears in each week's *Catholic Standard* and the title I wanted to use was "You Don't Know the Half of It!" You see, as I look at the calendar of my life as our Catholic paper describes it, it seems to me that it looks as if I only work two or three hours a day. They only print the most public things I do. So, whenever people come to me and say with very gracious concern for me, "I don't know how you keep your schedule," I think to myself: Thanks for worrying about me. You are very kind, but you don't know the half of it. I am embarrassed that you might think that that is all I do.

What the calendar that appears on this page doesn't report are all the hours spent at the desk—writing, reading, dictating letters, on the phone, at the computer—and all the hours meeting with people—staff, the priests, religious, seminarians, representatives of various organizations and ministries, possible benefactors of the archdiocese, people in public office, people in the media—and on and on and on. That's what fills the empty space in the calendar—and that is really how I earn my keep!

I'm not at all complaining. It's all part of the job. Monday to Friday, I'm in the office most of the time. I get in early if I have a very early Mass in a parish or if I have a Mass later on in the day. If my Mass is at 8:00 a.m. or after, then I usually have a cup of coffee with the priests and get to the desk a little later. When that happens, I try to send in the dictation I do at home the night before or that I did after my prayers that morning. Half the time I'm out for lunch or dinner, but usually I get home by 10:00 in the evening, which is our time for night prayer at my residence.

The great part of my life is that I never get bored and really have no time to feel lonely. The best time of my life is that which I spend with people. However, years ago when I first became bishop of Metuchen, a very wise vicar general said to me, "You don't get credit for all the paperwork, but you'll get the devil from your people if you don't keep up with it!" That has proven to be a very astute observation. I know that you would like me to be out in the parishes and Church functions all the time (and that's where I would rather be), but if I don't keep up with the business of the diocese—personnel, financial, planning—you'll have the right to be upset at me.

So you can be pretty sure that you're getting your money's worth out of this poor servant of yours. Just hope that I become smarter and can work more efficiently—and pray that with it all, I can always continue to be focusing and thinking of you.

Peace in the Holy Land
May 8, 2003

The president has just released his road map for peace in the Holy Land. It has been so long delayed, but I rejoice that our country is now committed to doing something to end the terrible ordeal of both Israelis and Palestinians. I have been very troubled at the lack of attention the whole world has had toward the crisis in the land where Our Savior walked and preached. I try to speak of it and write about it often as I constantly encourage our bishops' conference to be on the record in asking for peace with justice and an end to this intolerable situation.

In my talk last week to the Anti-Defamation League, which was reported in the *Catholic Standard,* I brought it up in the starkest terms. The coverage in the *Standard* was not complete, and I feel that it could have given an incorrect picture of what I said. Let me therefore quote a few paragraphs here.

"The status quo is not tenable. The deadly cycle of violence must be ended. One of the tragedies of the current crisis is that it has so damaged prospects for the development of new attitudes of understanding and mutual respect, without which neither side will be able to achieve their legitimate goals.

"Israelis rightly see the failure of some Palestinians to demonstrate full respect for Israel's right to exist and to flourish within secure borders as a fundamental cause of the conflict. . . . Palestinian leaders must clearly and unequivocally renounce terrorist violence and terrorist acts against innocent civilians and must show the Israeli people that they are fully committed to prepare their people to live in peace with Israel.

"Palestinians see the occupation as the underlying cause of the present crisis. This becomes unfortunately more problematic when it is cemented by the growth and expansion of settlements and is maintained by force and marked by daily indignities, abuse, and violence. . . . Despite the current crisis, the elements of a just and lasting peace remain the same: real security for the State of Israel, a viable state for Palestinians, just resolution of the refugee problem, an agreement on Jerusalem which protects religious freedom and other basic rights, and implementation of relevant United Nations resolutions and other provisions of international law. This has been our consistent Catholic bishops' position over the past many years and is the position of the Catholic community.

"Another issue of grave concern to us is that of the plight of the Christians in the Holy Land. The Christians there are often forgotten. You remember the stand-off last spring at the Church of the Nativity, the second holiest site for Christians. This exemplified how precarious is the position in which they live. In some ways they are caught in the middle, between Islamic extremism and Israeli security policy. Because of this, they have suffered much during the current crisis. As more and more Christians emigrate and leave that beautiful country, we are very concerned that what we call the Holy Land will become merely a museum without any living Christian presence in the land of Jesus' birth, ministry and death."

It is because of this continuing bloodshed and violence on both sides that we must work and pray for a new day, which hopefully the president's plan can usher in. The two sides have not been able to do that alone. It still takes the strong commitment of the United States government and its patient, constant pressure to bring them both to the table, paving the way to a just and lasting peace. I think we all join the Holy Father in expressing his profound grief at the violence and bloodshed between Israelis and Palestinians, as he said in his Easter message when he appealed for an end "to the chain of hatred and terrorism." This is a goal that we all dream of because this is the land where Jesus rose from the dead and proclaimed the great message of our salvation. Thinking of you at Easter time makes me think also of that holy place.

Disappointments
May 15, 2003

You almost prayed for me last Sunday! Oh, I know that you always pray for me in the Mass in the commemoration after the consecration when the celebrant prays for Theodore, our bishop, but I had asked all our priests to ask you to pray for me especially last weekend as I headed off on a journey to China.

Actually, I was half-packed, with my tickets and papers ready, when the visit was cancelled. The cancellation probably was because of the SARS epidemic. The World Health Organization last Friday morning had released new statistics saying that the death rate for people over sixty-five had climbed close to 50 percent and that made my going to China a little too problematic.

I was all set to go. I had hoped by the journey to give a message to our sisters and brothers there of the assurance of our prayers and our concern that we have for them at this very scary time. At seventy-two and counting, every new day for me is a bonus and a blessing and so I was not afraid of getting sick. My only concern was that if I did catch the illness, I might be jeopardizing the health of people at home or that I could be quarantined and therefore not be able to preside at our ordinations this Saturday for deacons or the following Saturday for our nine new priests. When I learned that the journey was put off, I sent another note to our priests telling them this, but I added, "Please pray for me anyway!" I hope that you will do the same.

How often God changes our plans! The old Latin philosophers had a saying that a person proposes but God disposes. Sometimes the sudden changes seem to be earthshaking, such as an unexpected illness or loss, a sudden turn in an individual's financial or personal security. The lesson to be learned is simple to recognize, but often hard to understand. The best laid of our plans are subject to so many outside forces. This happens in our families, our jobs, our schools, our physical and mental health.

The one thing that doesn't change is that we are always in the hands of a God who loves us. He uses the changes in our lives to work out his providence and that providence is always for our good. If you and I could keep that always in mind, we would be happier people and the disappointments of each day would be opportunities to find him close by and to know that every moment of our lives, this all-powerful, all-present, and all-knowing Creator has never stopped thinking of you and me and guiding us along through appointments and disappointments with unceasing love.

Blessings—Old and New
May 22, 2003

It has been several months since I wrote you about vocations to the priesthood and religious life. It's not that the subject is any less important, but there have been a lot of other things that I needed to tell you about as well. Three events have reminded me of the theme of vocations this weekend in a very special way, and I decided that I ought to take up that theme once again today.

The first was Fr. Joe Durkin. I went over to Georgetown last Sunday to pay tribute to a rather remarkable man. The day before, he had opened part of the Georgetown University's graduation ceremonies by offering a beautiful invocation. A few days before that, he had made his weekly visit to a county jail to work with the prisoners there and had someone bring him to his usual visit to a nursing home so that he might continue his work with people who have Alzheimer's disease. These are not necessarily extraordinary apostolates, although they do demand a special gift of pastoral skill and understanding. What makes the whole thing very wonderful is that last Saturday, Fr. Joe Durkin turned one hundred years old and looked back on seventy years of priestly ministry! What a great gift he has been to Georgetown, to the Society of Jesus, and to the whole Church, as well as to the tens of thousands of lives he has touched.

The second reason I write about vocations is that last Saturday I ordained three deacons for the service of the Archdiocese of Washington. Please God, there will be several others who will join them in the priestly ordination class of 2004, but even though these are good men, talented, and full of faith, our needs in this local Church continue to be so great. The average age of our own diocesan priests is high and the large classes of the 1950s are now reaching retirement. The Lord promised, "I will give you shepherds," and the Holy Father used that phrase as the title of one of his finest documents just a few years ago. You and I, by our prayers and working together, must try to help create an atmosphere of faith in which more young men will hear the call to priestly service—and more of our dedicated young women seriously consider religious life.

Finally, on the bright side, there are nine men to be ordained priests for this local Church on Saturday. Almost twice as many as last year and the largest number in several years, they will be a great grace for us all. It was Cardinal Hickey who began them on this journey and I thank God for his support of priestly vocations all through the years. It will be my privilege, God willing, to ordain them and to send them into their pastoral ministry for the service of the Archdiocese of Washington. Pray for them, please, that they may be good, kind, and happy priests and that God will use them to help us all proclaim his wondrous love here in this local Church. And so, thinking of you as I pray for more vocations, I wanted to share with you these three blessings, both old and new.

My Boat!
May 29, 2003

I think I need to tell you that I have a boat. It's not a tremendously big boat, but it can fit three people in it. (One of the priests who knows how to drive it insists that it only safely fits two.) It is really a very nice boat. I got it in New Jersey when I was archbishop of Newark. The archdiocese had a place at the Jersey Shore—actually, on the bay, which I like better for fishing. Everyone except us had a boat, and one day someone gave us one. It was fourteen feet long, had two oars, and was very seaworthy—at least it never turned over while I was in it.

The problem was that I was not in it often enough. From seeing my schedule you know that I can't seem to figure out how to take days off. (I'm actually not proud of that and I certainly do not recommend that practice to anyone else.) But during the warm months, I would get down to the shore and use the boat for fishing, maybe four or five times each year. Actually, I never went out on that boat without catching something—and usually a fish! After a while, someone gave me a motor and then we traded it all in to get a bigger boat. That one was fifteen feet long and I really felt like an admiral!

Well, when I was transferred to Washington, DC, I didn't know where I could keep the boat so I gave it to the Archdiocese of Newark. I was very embarrassed to learn that after two years they still couldn't sell it, so very graciously they gave it back to me. I am surely the first archbishop of Washington to own his own boat. The new problem is that it had been lying around for a year in New Jersey and now everyone tells me that it is not going to be seaworthy anymore. I wanted to mention that in case you happen to think that this column was really just an advertisement for a used boat for sale. To make a long story short, a friend in Southern Maryland just decided that I needed a new boat. It will be the same size and the same type, but it's going to look much nicer and it's not supposed to sink. I'd invite you all out for a ride, but even I don't think that it will hold more than three people. Please pray that I get down to the Southern Maryland shore enough to use it and catch a lot of fish.

There are a lot of morals in this story. One is that I couldn't imagine having something so pleasant as a little boat without telling you about it. One always shares good news with one's family, so no matter how insignificant my new boat is, I wanted you to know about it. Another is that there really are such nice people here in the archdiocese who do worry about the archbishop and are willing to go out of their way even to make sure that I'd be okay on those occasional fishing excursions.

A final point is that, as I finish thirty months here in your service, I have started to feel like I was never anywhere else, so gracious has been your welcome and your acceptance of an old shepherd who really feels so much younger and even more spry when he is thinking of you and thanking God for your goodness, your generosity, and your faith.

The Three-Fold Challenge
June 5, 2003

Last Saturday, on the feast of the Visitation of Our Lady, I celebrated the forty-fifth anniversary of my ordination to the priesthood. I really didn't have a celebration. It was more like taking a little extra time to meditate and to look at the past forty-five years with both a grateful and a critical eye. Grateful because of all the innumerable gifts that God has given me in the years of my life as a priest, critical because of all the things I have not done or done poorly or even done without love. I tried, in my musing, to return to that Saturday in 1958 when, with thirty-one other deacons, we got on the rented bus at St. Joseph's Seminary in Yonkers at 6:15 in the morning and drove rather quietly through a sleeping New York to St. Patrick's Cathedral on 50th Street and Fifth Avenue.

The previous night had not been without excitement! Somehow, Friday's supper in the seminary had created a major health crisis for almost half of the house. Food poisoning of some type had brought ambulances to the seminary and several of the deacons became dreadfully ill. Thank God, I was spared and slept through it all, but some of my classmates were still more than a little wobbly as we all drove down to the cathedral. I confess that I do not remember that much about my ordination ceremony, except the sense of the cold marble floor as we prostrated during the litany and the fact that I forgot to blow out the candle that we presented to the cardinal as a sign of our willingness to serve. One of the masters of ceremonies had to blow it out for me with a look that said, "Will he ever learn!" Oh yes, I also do recall that the seminary professor who was assigned to help us wash our hands after the anointing greeted me with the words "Welcome, Father McCarrick" and I realized that this was the first time anyone had called me that.

Since then, I have ordained close to three hundred priests—eighteen here for the Church of Washington—and my prayer for them has always been what I have prayed for myself through the almost half century that I have been privileged to bear this awesome challenge of the priesthood of Jesus Christ. In my own life, and in my pleas to those on whose heads I have imposed my hands at ordination, it has always been a three-fold challenge—work and pray and be kind to the people. If a priest can realize those three goals, he will be a good shepherd and a good man of God.

Of course, there is more to the priestly life than those three essential elements. The priest must study; he must recreate; he must take time for family, for friends; he must find time for exercise. These are natural virtues that every human being must cultivate—and I guess so are prayer and work and kindness, but in a priest they must be so much a part of his vocation. If we do not pray without ceasing, as the apostle urges, we become sterile. I know this because there are times when it has happened to me. If we do not work to the full extent of our capacity and if we are not kind, then we end up having lost the big picture and the great challenge of holiness and service.

As I look ahead to however many more years of service that God may give me, and I look back on the forty-five exciting years that I have lived as a priest, I ask your prayers that I may finally start to pray more and better, to work "while the light lasts" and always to be kind. I like to think that you are praying for me and for vocations, since at this time in my life especially, I am praying and thinking of you.

Families
June 12, 2003

I just wrote down the word families as the subject of this column, but that theme is so very broad that I am not really sure what I am going to write to you about it. What gave me the idea was that last Saturday we celebrated the wedding anniversaries of several hundred couples here in the Basilica of the National Shrine, and that is always a day of great satisfaction for me. In a society that seems to have adopted as its philosophy the slogan: "I'll love you until next Wednesday," the presence of so many married couples in that great Church gives me encouragement and great, renewed confidence in God's care of his world.

You know as well as I do that marriage does not have as great a place in the society of today as it had in years past. The old, rather lovely joke about the little girl who, when asked what she wanted to do when she grew up, replied: "I want to be married" would not get the same reception today, I'm afraid. Many young people have decided that they might not get married at all, and many others continue to postpone it until they have "done their thing"—whatever that really means in each individual case. Why is that?

I wonder if it is not too often the fear of making a mistake. In the frenetic society in which we live, it is possible to be "going steady" with someone for a long time without ever really finding out what they believe on the deepest levels of their life. The sexual revolution of the 1960s still dominates much of our society and it tends to obscure the great gifts of married life. The Church has taught that the two great blessings of marriage are the fostering of deep mutual love by the spouses and the challenging grace of bringing children into the world. What great gifts these two foundations are, the presence in your life of someone who really cares for you as he or she cares for no one else, and the wonder of being a partner with God in bringing new life into the world!

As a priest who has known many families in my life, I still rejoice when two people make that wonderful commitment to each other and to whatever children God will give them. I have to tell you honestly that I regret the passing of the day of large families. I really believe that children learn so much about life and love from their siblings and that the challenges of living together as part of a family are the best preparation for success and happiness. My father was one of thirteen and my mother one of eight, and I know how wonderfully her sisters and brothers reached out to her—and to me—when my father died so young and the Depression made it hard for everyone.

As I read over what I have written, I think I still have a lot of things about families that I want to share with you, so I'll probably come back to this theme later on. Just know that as I invited the anniversary couples to repeat their vows again at the ceremony, I was thinking of you and all the great families of this local Church.

Middle-Eastern Paradoxes
June 19, 2003

(Tehran, Iran) Things quiet down a little bit after the middle of June, so I don't mind taking travel assignments as much now. So, I said yes when President Mohammad Khatami of Iran invited me to come with a multi-religious delegation to visit that large and important country. I'm the only Catholic priest in the group; therefore, I figured that it would be important to go. I arrived at the airport in Tehran a couple of days ago at two o'clock in the morning, so my body clock is working hard to catch up with the rest of me.

Like so much of the Middle East, there are many paradoxes here. Our delegation was invited to sit in the press section of the great Central Mosque for the Friday services. It was somewhat chilling to hear more than ten thousand people cry out "death to America" several times during the homily. At the same time, dozens of Iranians, both Moslem and not, have gone out of their way to be gracious, courteous, and friendly to us all. In fact, I am treated at the rank of a foreign minister and given all kinds of courtesies, even though the United States does not have an ambassador here because of past historical conflicts.

There is tension here since we have American troops on three sides of this country and have just invaded its neighbor to the west, Iraq. There is no love for Saddam Hussein here, but the clouds of war make people anxious. We must bring a long-term solution to the critical problems of this region. More than ever, I am convinced that the "road map" to bring peace and justice to the Holy Land and to the suffering peoples of Palestine and Israel is a number one priority and the leaders of the world, especially in our own government, must stay the course even in the face of terrorist attacks and consequent reprisals.

Last evening, I offered Mass here in a small Church of the Sacred Heart for members of the small Catholic community. While the Mass was in Italian, with a little French thrown in, the choir had learned some lovely English hymns to make me feel at home. Thinking of you, half a world away again, I prayed for the Church of Washington and for the leaders of our government that they will have the wisdom and perseverance to bring peace to this part of the world.

Uncle's Day—Again
June 26, 2003

One of my grandnephews, who is eleven (or maybe twelve), yelled across the field: "Come play volleyball with us, we need another man on the team." I presumed that he wasn't talking to me. I haven't played volleyball in years and I was never really good. But he called out again and a whole bunch of his siblings and cousins stopped and looked and joined in his plea. The original inviter added what he felt would be an inducement to my affirmative reply and said: "Our team is very good, so you can't do much harm." All the adults—including me—had to laugh at that thoughtful evaluation, but happily one of my nephews stepped in and offered to take the challenge.

It was Uncle's Day again, my extended family's annual gathering. I have written about it before in this column. I recommend it to all big families. It is really a wonderful chance to keep up with all the different families that form part of our lives. I don't see them as much as I did when I served in New Jersey, so this yearly get-together has its own special importance. It's wonderful to see how young the new grandmothers are today! It's awesome to see how fast little kids become big kids and the teenage girls become so sophisticated. (It is not so obvious in the case of teenage boys.) It's great fun just to eavesdrop on the youngsters' conversations, sometimes so profound and other times so silly.

What a treat it is to know that you are a part of their lives and they of yours, even though the real little ones have no idea of who this smiling ancient could possibly be. The parental command to a two- or three-year-old, "Give your uncle a hug" evokes very different reactions, although the little boy who always used to shout "No" and frown and run away suddenly becomes "my best friend" at four! There is a lot of love in a family and an enormous blessing, too.

I'm going to be seventy-three next month. I confess that I don't feel it most of the time, although I realize I'm beginning to slouch more and more. (I'm trying to remind myself to stand up straight, so don't you hesitate to remind me. The rest of my family doesn't.) I can put in a really full day of work, still eat just about anything, climb stairs (maybe not the Washington Monument anymore), and generally do everything I have to do—but volleyball, that's something else again.

I'm always saying that you are all my family. This family of the Archdiocese of Washington is a very real one. It is God's will that we all are part of this local Church, that we feel at home in it, with all its hopes and all its shortcomings, too. Whatever our nationality, whatever our race, whether we are young or old, sophisticated or not—nothing matters except that the faith in Jesus as revealed in the Gospel and preached by the Church calls us together in his love. I wish that all of us could feel this way about the Church of Washington. It's the way I'm always thinking of you—and, I truly believe, God is, too.

Disappointments
July 3, 2003

A long-anticipated game is rained out; an exam we were confident would yield an "A" turns out to be a loser; a job that seemed ours for the asking goes to someone else; a gift we expected never materializes—we have all experienced disappointments. They are part of every life. In a real sense they are the building blocks of greater maturity when we are young and of greater character when we are older. But that does not make them pleasant. Like a visit to the dentist, it just makes them inevitable.

Someone someday should do a study on how different people handle disappointments. There are those who seem able just to shrug them off and others who seem devastated by them. I have been reflecting on this for the past few days and wondering how I'm handling them myself. I had hoped to make a journey this week, one that might have been helpful to a lot of people, and suddenly it all evaporated. I was disappointed by it, troubled by the loss of what might have been, and annoyed at myself for having put too many of my eggs in one basket, as the old saying used to go.

Years ago a wise old philosopher wrote: "Man proposes but God disposes," and by that axiom he sought to remind us all that we cannot create our own future. "The best laid plans of mice and men, *gang aft aglay*," as the Scottish bard would sing a couple of centuries ago. And still we make our plans. We have no choice. We have to organize tomorrow or else it will come and go and be lost forever. If we do not plan for the summer, we soon find ourselves in September; if we do not plan our lives, we ultimately find ourselves wondering where all the years have gone. And the dreams of yesterday end up on the list of disappointments. The secret of it all is to do it with an eye on the ultimate tomorrow, on that final goal of all our efforts, all our hopes and dreams.

The little disappointments of every day are part of the human condition. We do not have a perfect world here. Thank God for that or we would not yearn for the world that is to come. Even the greatest of our disappointments have a role to play. They remind us that we should not put all our hopes and dreams and longings on a world that is passing away; in other words, we should not put all our eggs in the fragile basket of today and ignore the signs that lead us to tomorrow.

When all is said and done, I guess there is only one real disappointment in life. It comes at the end and it consists in not loving God enough and in not loving our neighbor enough and missing the chance to enter the eternal peace of the kingdom for which ultimately each one of us was made. Thinking of you as you and I both handle the daily disappointments of life, I hope that we can all see in them the challenge to look beyond these temporary setbacks and set our hearts on the things that never end.

All God's Children
July 10, 2003

If you have been reading the *Catholic Standard* carefully over these past few months, you have seen the publication of our complete Archdiocesan Child Protection Policy. As I said when we first presented it last March, I am convinced that it is the best and most comprehensive program in the United States thanks to the committee that put it together under the chairmanship of Shay Bilchik, the president of the nationally respected Child Welfare League of America, and thanks to the extraordinary dedication of our own Bishop Kevin Farrell. You will be pleased to know that a large number of American dioceses are using it as a norm and as a good example of what a child protection policy ought to include. I thank all those who have produced this far-reaching document and I am sure that God will bless them for their successful efforts.

We now have another opportunity to enhance the lives of children and to prepare them well for a full and satisfying career. It is in the field of education and, even though this present plan is limited to our youngsters in the District of Columbia, it responds to the basic hopes and dreams of parents everywhere. More than a year ago, as we all realized the growing need for educational excellence here in the city of Washington, some of the leaders of our community, representing the district government, the business community, and especially those responsible for our schools themselves, came up with a three-sector plan that can truly make a difference.

The three elements are the District of Columbia public school system, the district's charter schools, and the independent schools of our city, which include our own parochial schools. We believe that a plan to help all these schools will help make our nation's capital a model of excellence in education throughout the world. We believe that a rising tide should lift all boats, as the saying goes, and that we must work together for all the school children in this remarkable and important city.

Obviously, one of the newest elements in this program are federally funded K–12 education scholarships that will enable hundreds of families, especially those who are poor, to select the independent school in which they want their youngsters to be educated. At the same time, those of us who are responsible for the parochial schools realize our own responsibility to ensure that our local public schools receive the financial and in-kind support necessary to provide the best education possible for children whose parents choose that vehicle for them. This is why we are united in a common cause, with the mayor, the chairman of the Educational Committee of the City Council, the president of the District of Columbia Board of Education, and so many others. Together, we hope to achieve this great goal of a better education for all of Washington's children. Far-sighted leaders in the federal government and in the Congress have recognized this need and opportunity, and are sincerely working to make these opportunities available in a way that really has a chance to make a difference.

It is important for us in the archdiocese for three reasons. First, because so many of our Catholic youngsters are in the public school system and charter schools, we need to ensure these schools provide the best education possible. Second, this is a project that could potentially serve as an inspiration and example for education in other areas. Finally, we are supporting this initiative because it really is the right thing to do.

We believe the scholarship program is particularly important for our lower income parents, who theoretically have a right to send their children to a non-public school but do not have the means to exercise that right because of poverty. For them this will be a great opportunity. I realize that this is not perfect legislation—man-made laws rarely are—but it does open a door to greater justice and greater opportunity for the children of our poorer families and that makes it important for me to give it my strong support.

I know that there will be much written and broadcast about this coming legislation and so I was thinking of you and wanting you to understand why I am enthusiastic about it for the greater justice it gives to our parents and the greater breadth of learning opportunities the DC Parental Choice Incentive Act of 2003 will provide to children here in our own backyard.

The Shore
July 17, 2003

There is something about the shore that is very special. The sound of the water lapping on the sides of a boat has a melody that seems to calm the restless spirit. Even the thundering of the mighty waves is like a call to adventure that only the most passive heart can try to ignore. The birds that cruise the skies ever on the lookout for the unwary fish swimming too close to the surface are both a wonderful tribute to the beauty and miracle of flight and a reminder of the cycle of nature as it provides food in turn for the whole order of creation.

Forgive these philosophical ruminations of mine. I'm on vacation! I'm here for a week at the Jersey Shore where a good friend of mine from my New Jersey days has loaned me a house on the bay. Of course, it is not a complete vacation, as you have probably already suspected, now that you know me, perhaps too well. I have three talks to prepare since I promised, in a very weak moment, to give three conferences at a summer institute for priests next week and I brought a batch of other papers that I need to study. But, when all that is said, it still remains that I'm at the shore and like the bays and brooks of Southern Maryland, there is something magic about it.

Some of my priest friends from the Jersey days drop in for a couple of days at a time. The ones who can cook are always the most welcome! (The other alternative is to live on fruit and cold cuts.) And there is time to read and pray and doze off in the afternoon. As the years go by—more quickly now it seems—I welcome the time to think and plan more carefully how to make the best use of whatever days or years are still to serve. To walk these quiet rustic streets and have near-total solitude before the sun comes up is a real blessing and always an unexpected grace. It gives me time in a special way to pray for you.

Is there any lesson in this message? Not a very profound one, I'm afraid. It's just a reminder that every one of us needs some down time, some solid block of moments to be literally just with yourself. I know how hard that is for young parents—and for busy priests—but I think that we all need a space of time "to go into neutral" and to let the Lord talk to us in the quiet of our heart. These are the times when he tells you that he is always thinking of you and loving you and calling you to share with him the peace that the world cannot give.

Listening
July 24, 2003

Last week, while I was on vacation at the Jersey Shore, I was shopping at a nearby mall for orange juice and hot dogs when I saw an exasperated mother and a very noisy child. At one point, as the youngster threw a box of cereal out of the shopping cart for the third time, the mother just about lost her patience. "Are you listening to me?" she said to the child in an angry voice and, as could be expected, the child just began to cry.

"Are you listening?" How often have people said that to me over the years? It is a question that can be asked on many levels, from the ordinary query to make sure a phone line is still functioning, to a much more profound plea for understanding of another person's point of view. There are obviously some times when we don't want to listen as when we are rightly reproached for not doing the right thing or when a command is given that we don't want to obey. There are other times when we shouldn't listen, as when the speaker is using speech to hurt another person through slander or malice. But usually listening is a good thing to do.

Priests should be good listeners. The old term for their role in the sacrament of penance is "to hear confessions." A good confessor is one who is a good listener and gently, but clearly, guides the penitent. Hearing confessions and helping people make their peace with God is perhaps the most awesome kind of listening. For me, it was always a tremendous inspiration to see how good people are and how powerfully God works to bring us to holiness and to keep us in his presence.

Of course, in our own lives, the great secret of sanctity is how well we listen to the Lord. God is always speaking to us—in the Gospels, in the sacred rites of the sacraments, in the voices of our parents and our friends. Sometimes I get so busy that I'm afraid that often I stop listening and close God out of my life. I pray that you will never do that, and that listening to God will always be a special part of every day. You will find in those most awesome conversations that he is always thinking of you.

China
July 31, 2003

(From Beijing) I have always been fascinated by China. I think that is true of many of us. The history of this ancient land, whose culture and civilization predates those of Europe by centuries, is largely unknown to us, and the succession of the dynasties—Ching Ming, Manchu, etc.—they get all the more mysterious. More than one billion two hundred million people live here. It must be a miracle that they are able to feed and clothe and find work for all these people. And the Church is present here, a large part of it officially separated from the Holy Father, who desires so much to be in communion with all those who are part of his flock and who prays for China so very much.

I first went to China in the mid-1980s. For me, it was an unforgettable journey of only a very few days. What made it special was that I met Bishop Ignatius Kung, who had been in prison for many years and had only just been released. I had a long visit with him and attended his Mass the following day. He had no zucchetto, the skullcap that bishops wear, and so I gave him mine, which he promptly put on his head and smiled. A few years later, when he lived in retirement in Connecticut, he was proclaimed a cardinal by Pope John Paul II and got a red skullcap then. I should have asked him to give me back the one I gave him, since it celebrated a special moment in my life.

The last time I went to China—my fourth or fifth visit, I think—was in 1998 when I was one of three American religious leaders that the president of China invited to come and discuss the practice of religious freedom in the United States with Chinese government and religious authorities. I spent three weeks here at that time and had the really awesome opportunity to go to Lhasa, the Forbidden City, the ancient capital of Tibet. There, amid the high peaks of the Himalayas, I celebrated Mass in my hotel room as the sun came up over the great mountains and learned to drink yak butter tea with the monks!

Now I'm back in China, but only for three days; no sightseeing, only meetings. I'll see some old friends and hopefully make some new ones. Pray that my visit goes well and that I accomplish something useful. I really care about China and its people, and I pray that they may find the peace and the opportunities for grace and happiness that only God can give. As I prepare for my meetings, I'm thinking of you and already looking forward to the fourteen-hour plane ride home.

Bob Hope
August 7, 2003

There was always a New York connection with Bob Hope. In World War II, when Cardinal Spellman was not only the archbishop of New York, but also the bishop for the men and women in the military services, he and Bob would often meet at army camps and at military bases overseas. They developed a friendly, joking relationship. For example, when Bob told the cardinal that he had been so tired that he fell asleep during His Eminence's Midnight Mass homily, the cardinal replied that it was perfectly all right since he often slept through Bob's monologues. Cardinal Cooke worked so closely with Cardinal Spellman that the friendship with Bob and Dolores Hope continued after Cardinal Spellman's death. In the seven years that I served as Cardinal Cooke's secretary, I also became friendly with the Hopes and that friendship has stretched over thirty years.

I was happy to be able to celebrate Mass in memory of Bob at the Basilica of the National Shrine last Sunday. That great Church was crowded with folks who had listened to and seen Bob Hope over the years and who recognized him as a great American icon. He was funny, quick-witted, sensitive, and a master of timing—all those gifts that make a great comedian. I remember once sharing a joke that I had just heard with him. I was almost embarrassed to tell Bob Hope a joke since, I thought, he had probably already heard all the jokes in the world. Very kindly, he took the one that I told him, assured me that it was funny, and began to tinker with it. He changed a word or two here and there, added an extra element in another spot, changed an emphasis, deleted a line—in fact, he took it and made it a new and much funnier joke.

I'll never forget that moment. It was like watching a talented craftsman at work. He was a real professional and spent his whole life in cheering people up and getting them to smile. He succeeded in that work prodigiously, especially in those dangerous wartime journeys when he brought warmth and humor to the men and women in uniform.

He was received into the Catholic Church in his later years, without fanfare, because it was a very personal thing, as it always should be. His good angel was Dolores, his wife for more than sixty years. In the Hollywood of the twentieth century, what an example and witness to the values of marriage and family that was!

Most likely, the motivation of his becoming a Catholic was Dolores' great and constant example of living faith and devotion. She truly understood that love consists in giving the very best you have to the people you love. For her—as it should be for all of us—the best she had was her faith in the Lord Jesus and her love for the Church. This is so obvious in her life and it became a constant witness to Bob. We were not surprised when, finally, Bob decided to join her in the faith of the Church.

Is there a lesson in this for all of us? There surely is. Is there someone you love who has left the Church or who has never known about it? What is the best gift you can give him or her? I believe that it is to introduce them to Jesus and to guide them along the path that leads to the Church and to the Eucharist, which is its crowning glory. As I think of the remarkable life of Bob Hope and the continuing, present witness of his beloved wife, I'm also thinking of you and hoping that you and I will both learn from their example.

Rainy Moods
August 14, 2003

I'm usually reasonably upbeat—at least I like to think that I am. It would be hard to be a pessimist and be a bishop today. First of all, because the bishop as well as the priest needs to be a man of faith who entrusts himself totally to the Lord and therefore can always work to be a witness of trust in God for his people. Secondly, because pessimism leads quickly to depression and burnout and the bishop needs to be a happy man so that he can guide the faithful always to find joy in their lives as Christians.

Sometimes it seems that the work becomes overwhelming and the problems loom larger than life. These are the scary days when faith and grace must come in and strengthen us for the mission to which we are called. This obviously doesn't just happen to me and to priests and bishops generally; it happens to all of us and is part of the human condition. That's why the Lord promised to be with us always. He knows well that there are some times when we need him more than ever to show us his smiling face and to lift us up close so that we can feel his loving presence.

On a rainy day last week—I don't remember which one, I think they were almost all rainy—I was meditating on these mysteries and wondering why I was feeling down. I suddenly realized that I always feel less enthusiastic when I haven't seen the sun very much. Dreary weather really does produce in so many of us dreary moods. Once, years ago, I had to be in Moscow for a week of meetings. Each day when I woke up and looked out the window, it was snowing lightly. Each evening when I closed the window curtains to go to bed, it was still snowing lightly. In fact, every single day that week it kept snowing lightly. I was in a terrible mood at the end of that week—and so was everybody else at the meeting, except the Russians, who were so used to it that they seemed to take it all in stride.

This column is not meant to complain about the weather, but maybe to suggest a reason why you, too, may feel less than bubbling over with joy these days. The sun is a great blessing for us all in so very many different ways. It also cheers us up and gets us going and when we don't see it for a while it gets us down.

God is like that, too. When we don't feel his presence or don't seem to experience his grace, we can all get depressed. Unlike the weather, there is a cure for that. It is called prayer. It is found most abundantly in the sacraments. It is as easy to achieve as a moment's aspiration or a quick reminder that the Lord is thinking of you both in sunshine and in shadows, on good days and bad—and you know, for whatever it's worth, so am I.

Illustrious Predecessors
August 21, 2003

Last week I was in Southern Maryland. You know how much I love that part of our diocese. One of its treasures is the sense of history you find there. From the relics of our Catholic groups in the lovely old churches to the living, continually faith-filled presence of our Catholic people—so many of whom trace their genealogy back to the first settlers who arrived in 1634—I am reminded of God's constant care for his Church and his people. That history also reminds me of the blessings that I have received from my own four predecessors here in the Church of Washington and I'd like to talk about their roles in our own Catholic history for a moment.

If any bishop has ever had illustrious predecessors here in the United States, it surely is me. When Archbishop Curley of Baltimore was asked to serve the new Archdiocese of Washington in July of 1939, it added an extra burden to his already busy life. He had to divide his own archdiocese and erect a new structure for a part of it. I'm not sure he was ever convinced of the value of the division, but he put it in place and served it with loyalty and care.

In 1947, after World War II, Archbishop Patrick O'Boyle became the first archbishop of Washington to take up residence in this territory. He served it for more than a quarter century until his retirement in 1973. The stories of his years as our archbishop and later on as cardinal are many and awe-inspiring. He was truly the architect of this local Church, a leader with a pastoral heart, fearless and far-seeing, energetic and determined. He desegregated our Catholic schools even before the public schools did so. He was a great builder and a great priest. I knew him in my years as a student here since we both had been priests of New York. He was a great model for me, especially in his love for the poor.

Our third archbishop was also a wonderful example during his seven years of pastoral service here in Washington. Cardinal William Baum brought to our Church here a brilliant mind and a gentle spirit. A gracious scholar and an extraordinary leader in education and ecumenism, he built well on the foundations of his predecessor and, although his time here was cut short by his call to Rome to oversee the worldwide Catholic educational apostolate, he is remembered for his kindness and his understanding, which reached out to so many who will never forget him.

Of course, in a few sentences I can hardly do justice to Cardinal Hickey. What a blessing his twenty years of service have been for all of us. Every time I think of something that I should try to do here in the archdiocese, I realize that Cardinal Hickey has already done it and so much better than I ever could. We all owe him a debt of gratitude that we will never be able to repay for his zeal and his wisdom, his strength, and his vision. He is on my mind now more than ever, since his health has been failing, especially in these last few months. I know that you pray for him and I tell him of your prayers whenever I see him. He has been a great friend of mine for many years, and I am so blessed to be able now to try to serve in his stead.

I do have illustrious predecessors, and thinking of you, I know how very blessed we have all been in God's gift of these four special priests who have taken such extraordinary care of this local Church of ours and of all of us as well.

Civil Rights—Revisited
August 28, 2003

The fortieth anniversary of Dr. Martin Luther King Jr.'s "I have a dream" speech brought back many special memories for me. I was in Washington at the time, still serving, I believe, as dean of students at The Catholic University of America. It seemed very important to me that the Catholic Church play a role in this major moment in the civil rights movement of our country, and so I organized a group of students to come downtown and participate in it. We all carried placards. I still remember that mine called for equal rights in employment for all men and women.

As we gathered downtown at the Mall, I recall that we all felt a sense of history and, if truth be told, a bit of anxiety as well. There had been rumors that the march could break out into violence and I knew that, if it did, as a priest I would have to do my best to keep people calm. All the great leaders of the civil rights struggle were there and right in their midst, as a sign that this was a cause involving all the churches, was Cardinal Patrick O'Boyle, the archbishop of Washington. As a Catholic, I was so proud that he was there. He had paid his dues to history in so many ways as his actions and support of African Americans and all of America's minorities would testify. His presence, standing close to Dr. King, made it clear that this was a struggle in which every religious community had a role to play.

I had a great spot from which to hear Dr. King's words. As they flowed in eloquent cadence from his lips, you could feel the deep longing for equality in his message and the thousands of people who listened were both moved and inspired by the man and the moment. It was one of those special times in my life that I can never forget.

There remains one more civil rights cause from which we should not walk away, and it concerns the rights of the children of the poor. As you know, we are presently struggling for a new commitment to excellence in education here in the District of Columbia. It is a three-segment approach that will help all our youngsters in the public schools, the charter schools and the independent schools as well. Under this program, the parents of our poor families would have a choice to educate their children in a newly upgraded public school system, a charter school, or an independent school; this last group would include our parochial schools.

For more than three-quarters of a century, the law has granted our parents the right to educate children in the parochial schools, but the reality of our society has made it impossible for poor families to exercise that right because of the tuition that these schools must charge. This new legislation, while it helps all our children, gives parents the key civil right to choose the school their children will attend. As we celebrate the clear and courageous call for civil rights of Dr. Martin Luther King in our city forty years ago, let's pray that our day may see the accomplishment of another basic civil right in the area of parental choice in education.

As I think of that historic day forty years ago, I'm thinking of you and hoping that you and I may see the accomplishment of this other civil right for the parents of the poor in this nation's capital.

Health Tips
September 4, 2003

You are right if you raised your eyebrows when you read the title of this column. Although, thank God, I think I'm probably in decent health for my age, I'm surely not an expert in providing health tips—especially in recommending walking. This summer, I've tried to walk a half hour every day as the doctor recommended and I found it so helpful that I wanted to share it with you. (As I wrote in another column, a few weeks ago, we all want to share good things with our family!)

Medical people are always telling us to walk. If you can walk a half hour a day at a relatively brisk pace, it will do wonders for you, psychologically as well as physically—and maybe spiritually, too, if you can combine the walking with prayer, such as the Rosary or the Chaplet of Mercy or just some special consciousness of walking in the presence of God.

This summer I had a week at the Jersey Shore, a busman's holiday in Southern Maryland and a three-day weekend by the ocean, and I'm so proud of myself that I got long walks just about every day during those times. A good walk gets the muscles working, the mind relaxing, and the body feeling young again—or sort of young again. Even if it is along familiar roads, a healthy walk lets us see things we've never noticed before, or different sides to the same things we know so well. It's great if you can have company on these journeys, although you shouldn't lose the chance for at least some moments of quiet in which to focus on walking with Jesus on the road to the Father.

We all know that life is a journey and that one of the worst things that can happen to us is to be trapped in a dead end on our personal road to fulfillment. I truly believe that a good walk as often as possible does clear the cobwebs from our minds and help us find the perspectives we need to keep things in place and to see the priorities more clearly and the roads we must walk to meet them. This is the end of my medical advice. I only need to add what you already know, that during these walks of mine, I am often thinking of you.

Mass on Sunday
September 11, 2003

You know what is one of my greatest worries? It is the number of us who don't get to Mass on Sunday. Now, obviously, I recognize that some people are unfortunately not able to get to church on the Lord's Day or for a Vigil Mass on Saturday—the elderly, the sick, the folks whose jobs make it impossible for them to get to this great Eucharistic Sacrifice. The ones I worry about are the folks who can go and decide that it's too much trouble or that it is not enough of a moving experience in their lives. Let me talk about that a little bit in this column.

I think a lot of us forget what the Eucharist is. It is the most important way that God comes into our lives. Of course, God is always with us. He is present everywhere, at all times, to every one of us. But he himself, in Jesus Christ our Lord, has established this special marvelous presence on our altars through the holy sacrifice of the Mass. He wants us to come and worship together, calls us to be present personally as he becomes present under the form of bread and wine.

I have heard people say, "All this is just a Church thing and I pray to God quietly in my own way." The invitation to participate in the Mass is indeed a Church thing, but it is the way the Church makes it possible for each of us to obey the divine command to worship the God who made us, who saved us, who loves us, and who calls us to holiness. That command to worship God does not just come from the Church. It is part of our lives as men and women who are the creatures of a God who has given us life and sustains us in that life every moment of every day. We know that if God were to withdraw his sustaining hand for a moment, we would return to the dust from which we came. God is important in our lives and we cannot ignore him who loves us so much.

Sometimes youngsters will complain, "I don't get anything out of Mass." There are at least two answers to that. The first is to wonder what they are looking to get from it. If it is entertainment or distraction, then they don't understand the nature of this momentous event. It is prayer. Each one of us must find room for prayer in our lives. Without it, we are like the animals or the inanimate objects whose relationship to God is of a totally different level. We are related to God as part of his family, as his children. He has spoken to us and continues to speak to us, and in this divine conversation the Mass is the most important word.

The second reason is the obvious one: "What do you put into it?" If the Mass is just something we attend or watch as a spectator, then surely it cannot always compare to a TV special or a great Broadway show. If we come to pray along with a community of believers, to worship the God that loves us, to thank him for his gifts and his graces, to seek pardon for our sins, to ask him for his help—if we know that this is why we go to Mass, then it becomes an exciting, meaningful, and, of course, grace-filled time in our lives and we begin to long to pray the Mass not just on Sundays, but whenever we can.

Reflect on this with me, because it is always a concern. As I'm thinking of you today, I long so much to see you present in prayer at this Eucharistic Banquet, since it is truly the place where God wants you to be.

It's the Children, My Friend
September 18, 2003

Anyone who has paid attention to the drama of political campaigns in our country will remember the phrase that characterized a successful presidential campaign a decade ago: "It's the economy, stupid!" In the constantly changing dynamism of our constant support for the three-sector program of aid to education here in the District of Columbia—the DC public schools, the charter schools, and the non-public independent schools—it is so important that we have a similar phrase to keep us focused. When all is said and done: "It's the children, my friend!"

Whenever anyone attacks the program that we have put together and maintains that it is an imposition of the federal government against home rule, we point out that the three District of Columbia elected leaders most involved in the work of educating our children, the mayor, the chairman of the City Council Committee on Education, and the president of the Board of Education, all are in favor of it because it's for the children!

Whenever any type of antireligious bias raises its head to attack religious-affiliated schools and dismiss them, we point out that our parochial schools have stood the test of excellence in education here in the District of Columbia for more than a century because all the work and all the resources that are put into it are for one simple reason—it's for the children!

Whenever anyone protests that it won't work and that our school systems will not change, we point out that so many leaders of our business community already have committed themselves to working together to help this effort succeed and be a model for education, expanding new possibilities and priorities for one reason above all—it's for the children!

When anyone wonders why the Catholic Archdiocese of Washington has placed millions of dollars each year to provide education in the neighborhoods of our city even in the face of other growing needs and challenges, following the extraordinary example of my beloved predecessor, Cardinal Hickey, we shout out together—because it's for the children!

You who are part of the archdiocesan family may know how hard we have all worked for the success of this three-part program. We truly believe that the public schools of Washington can be developed into an innovative and superior program under their present leadership and that the charter school movement can be successful. We also continue to be committed to do our share for the education of the youngsters of the center city, most of whom are poor and most of whom are not Catholic, because of one reason alone—it's for the children.

We have reached a crossroads in elementary education here in the District of Columbia. The Congress and the federal government have continued to maintain authority and responsibility over this vital part of our future—the education of our children. As this three-sector program becomes caught up in the inevitable world of district politics, we must keep our focus clear—this is for the children, my friend, and for their future and the future of our communities and neighborhoods. As I am thinking of you, the faithful of this archdiocese, I wanted you to understand this commitment and our determination to be faithful to it as long as we can.

Reflections on Isabel
September 25, 2003

I went down to Southern Maryland last Saturday. I had been speaking to a number of the pastors and reading the news articles about the effect of Hurricane Isabel in those areas, particularly the damaged homes and property, and felt I should pay a visit to the priests and the people. There wasn't much I could do, of course, but I felt better being with them and assuring them of my prayers and concern. I stopped in at four parishes—St. Anthony's in North Beach, Star of the Sea in Solomons, St. Peter Claver in Saint Inigoes, and St. Michael's in Ridge.

North Beach had been hit badly, but, thank God, there were no deaths or serious injuries. The Church had a generator that probably saved the building from flooding. It also made it possible for Fr. David Russell, the pastor, to feed half the town because his refrigerator was still working while the town was out of power. Some streets in Solomons along the water were badly hit, but the church is high up on a flight of stairs and so it was okay. In Saint Inigoes, where the historic parish of St. Peter Claver is located, the loss of power caused the cancellation of the vigil Mass. That small but lovely church would be too dark and too hot for a 6:00 p.m. Eucharist. In St. Michael's, where I celebrated the 5:30 Mass, power was out and it was very hot. The local fire department was good enough to provide power to a couple of large fans during the Mass. (They turned them off during the homily so that people could hear me. You can imagine how that kind of pressure can enable a preacher to cut down the time he talks rather considerably!)

To be without power was something new to me. I have become used to all the comforts that air-conditioning and refrigerators and a light by my chair can give. It was not the worst thing for me to remember my childhood when we had iceboxes and only electric fans in the hot summer time. We did have light, of course, but I can't remember it being as bright as the bulbs of today. To complete the picture—which my grandnieces and nephews can never totally understand— we didn't have television, and the radio and local neighborhood movie house had to suffice for that kind of professional entertainment. Yet, we survived, and in a sense even prospered. The lack of air-conditioning forced us to open the windows and enjoy the special grace of a cool breeze drifting in from time to time. The lack of a lot of refrigeration was a real loss, yet it forced us youngsters to be ready to go to the store more frequently to buy fresh food and bring it home. The absence of TV prevented us from seeing great theater or great entertainment or the marvelous natural and man-made wonders of the world, yet they forced us to talk to one another and to relate to people in a way that now seems much more meaningful than the monosyllabic interchanges of a family captured by the tube.

It was hot in Ridge that evening and hard to be heard over the fans, but the church was pretty full and for most of the congregation it was a bit of an adventure and a sense of satisfaction that despite the inconvenience, they had made it to Mass. I found the same feeling the next morning at Little Flower in Bethesda, as scores of parents came with their children to an early family Mass in an equally darkened church. I am so proud of our people. They make do whatever the problem is in all the communities of our archdiocese.

Thank God, no one was severely hurt during the hurricane and maybe we all learned that for a few days, anyway, we can survive without the accidental embellishments of life as long as we have our faith and trust in a God who loves us, a God who always wants the best for us. Thinking of you as I reflect on the hurricane, I pray that we've seen the last one of these for a long time.

Raise Your Hands
October 2, 2003

When I was archbishop of Newark, once in a while during major celebrations in the Cathedral of the Basilica of the Sacred Heart, I would ask the people to raise their hands if this was the first time they had come to the cathedral. More often than not, the majority of the folks at the liturgy would raise their hands and be chided by me for not having visited that truly magnificent mother church of the Archdiocese of Newark before then.

On Sunday of last week, when we celebrated a Mass of Thanksgiving for the restoration of our Cathedral of St. Matthew here in Washington, I thought of that old custom and almost asked the faithful at that impressive liturgy if this were the first time that they had visited St. Matthew's. Our cathedral, although not among the largest churches of the nation, does have a grandeur and a style that merits at least a visit, more probably a Eucharistic liturgy, and even more fittingly, the custom of praying there several times a year.

The Metropolitan Cathedral of St. Matthew the Apostle is a pearl of great price, a real jewel among the downtown Washington buildings. Because of its location, rather hemmed in by large edifices, one could pass it by and thereby lose the gift of a lifetime. From the remarkable mosaics above the doors to the magnificent sanctuary, the beautiful side chapels, and now the brilliant lighting that gathers them all together, it surely offers an insistent invitation to come and pray.

We in the Archdiocese of Washington probably get into the city more than the folks in New Jersey suburbs come into Newark, but if I asked you to raise your hands if you had never visited St. Matthew's Cathedral, how many hands would go up? Now that the cathedral renovations are complete, we can be even more proud and grateful to God for the gift of this mother church of our archdiocese. Please come and see it. Pray there for all the needs of this local Church and for your own. It is really a special place, made holy of course by the presence of the Lord in the Eucharist and also by the faith and prayers of God's holy people who for more than a hundred years have found there in the midst of the busyness of the nation's capital a place of refreshment, light, and peace. As I celebrated the Mass of Restoration, I was, of course, thinking of you and praying that God would bring many graces to you and your families through the prayers said in this holy place.

Rivers
October 9, 2003

I am one of those people who have always been fascinated by rivers. Maybe the fact that my father was a sea captain gave me that innate inclination, but whatever the cause, rivers have always been very special to me. When I was a youngster growing up in Manhattan, we played by the shores of the Harlem River and sometimes took the long climb down to the banks of the Hudson, at the spot where it runs swiftly beneath the mighty George Washington Bridge. Later on, when I was sent to New Jersey to start the Diocese of Metuchen, the Raritan River and its canal were always special gifts to me. The Newark archdiocese has on its coat of arms the symbol of three rivers. We guessed that, besides the Hudson, they had to be the Passaic and the Hackensack, which irrigated the old farms of that part of New Jersey 150 years ago when the Diocese of Newark was created. Probably, however, one of those rivers on the coat of arms of Newark would have been the Delaware, which was the western boundary of that local Church back in 1850.

Here in Washington you know how much I love the Potomac as it winds around the shores of Southern Maryland and carves out bays and swamps and lesser creeks and rivers as it flows into the Chesapeake. I had never heard of the Patuxent before I lived in Washington, but I have come to see it as a friend, which I cross when I come home by car from journeys in the north. I see great beauty in the Anacostia, too, as it gives our See city another perspective from the hills of the southeast.

I was flying to Jefferson City, Missouri, last week and marveled at "the wide Missouri" as it joins with the Mississippi and brings life and growth to so much of mid-America. What great rivers our nation has and how important the role they have played in our history. From the St. Lawrence in the north to the Rio Grande on the Mexican border, what a wonderful blessing God has given this beautiful land of ours. How truly gifted we are by the riches of our natural resources and indeed by the energy and resourcefulness of the American people, both those who founded and pioneered this nation and by those here today, of all races and national origins, who keep it alive and able to reach out to other less fortunate lands.

We sing of the river of life and of the currents that continually move us onward unto the destiny that God has prepared for us. The rivers of our own lives may sometimes be marred by rapids or at others be hindered by the low tide, which can leave us for a while on a sandbar, high and dry. Sometimes we can feel that life is moving too fast for us to grab hold of it and at others that we are stuck without movement for a long while. Thinking of you as I sit watching the river from the plane's vantage point of several thousand feet, I think a little bit how God must feel as he watches this world which he loves so much and for whose salvation he sent his beloved Son. May we ask him to let the journey of our own lives always run along peaceful flowing waters until at last he brings us back home to the safe harbor of eternal life.

The Mother of God
October 16, 2003

I am in Rome with our archdiocesan pilgrimage for the twenty-fifth anniversary of the election of Pope John Paul II and the beatification of Mother Teresa of Calcutta. I was going to write this column about the Holy Father since I saw him for a moment last Wednesday at the papal audience. I was very pleased to be in the photo with him and the twenty deacons from the North American College of Rome—including two of our own—whom I was privileged to ordain the following day in St. Peter's Basilica. I'll write about the Holy Father next week since I'll be seeing him several times as the cardinals celebrate with him his twenty-fifth anniversary as Bishop of Rome and Vicar of Christ.

Today is Sunday, the Solemnity of Mary, the Mother of God, and I am in Ephesus in Asia Minor where more than a millennium and a half ago, the fathers of the Third Ecumenical Council declared as a doctrine of our faith that Mary was truly the Mother of God. There is an ancient basilica here and once a year the Turkish government gives permission for Mass to be celebrated on this very spot where all this had taken place.

How fortunate I am to be here! The archbishop of Izmir in whose diocese this part of Turkey lies, invited me to offer this Mass here today. In a real sense, all of us are blessed since you are all here with me as I offer my Mass for you and for all the faithful of our archdiocese.

The Early Church knew and believed that Mary was the Mother of our Lord Jesus Christ. They knew and believed that he was the second person of the Blessed Trinity, True God and True Man, as we proclaim in the creed. But some theologians in the early centuries tried to make a distinction and taught that Mary was the Mother of Christ only as a man. This, of course, would have divided the Lord into two different persons and that was never the teaching of the Church. This problem had to be faced clearly and directly and that happened in 431 here in Ephesus when the council fathers proclaimed without a doubt that since there is only one person in Christ and Mary is his mother, she must then be recognized as the Mother of God, that is the great dogma that we celebrate today as I entrust all of you, the faithful of the Church of Washington under her protection and into her loving hands. Thinking of you now I pray Holy Mary, Mother of God, pray for us now and at the hour of our death. Amen.

The Holy Father
October 23, 2003

(Rome) It is late Saturday night in the Eternal City. I have just come back to the North American College—our United States seminary in Rome—from a reception at the residence of the American ambassador to the Holy See. The ambassador lives in a lovely villa not far from the college and from here you have a breathtaking view of Rome (or you could have, if it was not raining so hard this evening). We all worried about the beatification of Mother Teresa tomorrow morning. Everyone will be drenched if it is raining then as hard as it is now. We are worrying about all the pilgrims—almost three hundred of them from Washington—and we are worrying about the pope.

I have seen Pope John Paul II a number of times since I came here last week to ordain the deacons. Twice I have exchanged a word with him. He is very frail as you have seen on the television. It is very hard for him to walk or even to stand without terrible pain. Yet he still works so hard and forces his body to do what should be almost impossible.

Do you remember the poem "If" by Rudyard Kipling? There is a line in it that goes: "If you can force your heart and mind and sinews to serve their turn long after they are gone." The poet is making the point that an extraordinary man can do this and John Paul II is that kind of a man.

I have known him slightly for almost thirty years, since he first came to New York to stay with the servant of God, Cardinal Terence Cooke, during the Eucharistic Congress of 1976. We all remember well the strong, athletic, eloquent bishop who was elected pope twenty-five years ago. His body has suffered the wear and tear of bullet wounds and illnesses, of broken bones, and the side effects of strong medicine. His heart is still strong and his will is still great. What an example he is for all of us, what a special inspiration for the sick and the physically challenged. What a truly great man this is.

During the past ten days since I came here, I have spent a lot of time with the media. They always ask what this pope's great legacy has been and I always reply that his legacy is not over, but as long as he lives—and may it be a long time, God willing—he will always be a Holy Father of whom the whole Catholic world can be so proud. Perhaps more than anything else his legacy will be found in his tremendous love and care for the poor, his determination to teach the Church in season and out of season in fidelity to the Gospel, and his love of the Blessed Mother. I am sure that one day they will call him John Paul the Great, so remarkable have his accomplishments been. Thinking of you and me and of all those who have lived under his pastoral care these past twenty-five years, I believe that we can thank God for that great blessing.

The Top of the Desk
October 30, 2003

There are many beautiful and historic sites in this world of ours. We can see them in paintings and photos and now the high definition TV. But the greatest gift of all is to see them in real life. You may remember that I got to see Old Faithful, the famous geyser, last year and the historic ruins of the Basilica of Ephesus a couple of weeks ago in Turkey. I have never seen the Grand Canyon except from a high flying plane, but I am sure it is breathtaking, and some day I hope to get to see Mount Rushmore. I was moved to see Mount Kilimanjaro majestically crowning a sea of clouds and to sail into the Stanley Pool on the Congo River. I have been privileged to see the Dalai Lama's Palace in the Forbidden City of Lhasa and the Sphinx of Europe. All of these wonders are truly extraordinary, but nothing equals the joy of being able to see the top of my desk!

Let me explain before you think that your archbishop has finally lost it. I came home last Thursday from two weeks away. That is the longest I have ever been absent from the archdiocese since I came here almost three years ago. The ordinations of the deacons at the North American College, our own pilgrimage in Rome—by the way, we had the largest group from the United States—and finally the consistory of cardinals that the Holy Father called added up to fourteen days away. When you are away from home that long, the mail, the faxes, the memos, the printout of e-mails don't stop. They all pile up one on top of the other until you really can't see the top of the desk anymore.

When I came back and saw my desk last Thursday, it was completely covered with all these papers and only after hours and hours of reading and writing and dictating and sending e-mails out could I come to that most happy sight, the top of the desk! I suspect that all of us have something like this happen when we are away for longer than anticipated. We are always happy to come home, but the discouraging part of it is to see all the work that has accumulated since we've been gone. That can almost take away the joy of the journey.

It is good to have caught up now, but, of course, it never lasts long. Each day brings its own share of challenges, problems, and opportunities. The volume of mail that comes in is really enormous and I am so blessed that most of it is able to be handled by some of the other archdiocesan offices or in the parishes and other institutions of the archdiocese. Thank God for Bishop Farrell, for the other vicar generals, the chancellor and, in a special way, my secretaries, who make it possible for me to try to keep up to date. The Archdiocesan Pastoral Center is really filled with extraordinary, dedicated people who know so much more of the details of this Church of Washington than I will ever know and who are truly devoted to the service of our people. I can never really thank them enough, and I do thank God for the way they care for the archdiocese with generous dedication and even a great deal of joy.

So here I am, sitting at the desk and grateful to the Good Lord for getting me home safely after my journey and able once again to get out to the parishes to celebrate Mass and to have a chance to visit. I really ought to nuance that first paragraph of this column. As good as it is to get to see the top of the desk, the great part is to be home and see again the sites of Washington and the faces of all God's people who—in his mysterious providence I am privileged to try to serve. And being home makes it easier to be thinking of you.

Holiness
November 6, 2003

We are going to have our convocation of priests this week. It is a wonderful time for all the priests of the archdiocese to get together for a couple of days of prayer and study, fellowship, and fraternity. It will bring some of our oldest priests together with some recently ordained and give us all a chance to renew old friendships and make new ones and to create a new spirit of unity and collaboration in the work of this local Church.

I have every hope that it will be a special time of grace for us all, that we will learn much from each other, develop new ways to serve our people better, and grow in our love of Jesus who is the one eternal priest, and in whose priesthood all of us have a share.

Many of our parishes will be covered by some of the religious priests who serve in the archdiocese, but some will not have a daily Mass on one or two of the days of the convocation. I am sorry that this will be the case, but it will remind us all of the blessings we have in this Church of Washington where we still have enough parish priests to cover our needs. Many parts of the United States do not have priests for that daily sacramental care. Hopefully, these days will make us more sensitive to the need to pray and work for vocations!

As I prepare for this historic gathering of all my brother priests, I think of all the goals to which we must recommit ourselves during this special time together with the Lord. What is the most important of all the works we do with and for our people? It is at one and the same time both clear and complex. Everything we do, all the works we undertake, all the preaching and teaching, the sacramental life, and the parish meetings, all must be focused on one goal. We must strive to call you and ourselves to holiness. In every work of charity, in every chance encounter, at every formal and informal gathering, one on one or before a hundred, our role is to proclaim that Jesus Christ is Lord and to live that message out to the fullest. May this week's convocation remind all of us priests of that in the most powerful and joyful way. Pray for your priests, dear friends. We have great and good ones here in Washington! Be sure that as we get together all of us will be thinking of you.

Priests
November 13, 2003

Priests are on our minds these days. As we read the statistics of child abuse in our area, we mourn the tragic flaws of some few of our brothers who have abused children. We thank God that there have been only twenty-six over the past fifty-seven years since the beginning of this Archdiocese of Washington, compared with more than a thousand others who have served faithfully and well. Of course, we know that even one case is a terrible shame, and our hearts go out to those whose youth was so hurt by someone who was trusted as a man of God. We know, too, that this is a societal problem and, although it has hurt us all, we take some comfort in knowing that the Catholic Church is the only institution in the United States that has made so thorough and transparent an investigation of this terrible problem and that it now has in place the strongest program to protect children in the future.

Let me talk about the hundreds and hundreds of great priests who serve this local Church of ours. You know how good they are and with what generosity and love they have served you and your families. For every one who has failed, there are scores of others who have always been there for you when you needed them, in sickness and in health, in joy and in sorrow, without seeking either riches or power in this world, but interested in your welfare and in your growth at holiness.

I was with 260 of them last week at the first convocation of priests we've had since we began to serve the people of Washington and these five counties of Maryland. Except for a small number of priests who could not be with us because of age or illness or unchangeable commitments, they were all there at a hotel on the Eastern Shore whose rates in the off-season made it economically possible for us to gather. We had great talks, we prayed for you and for so many good intentions, but the greatest gift of all was the brotherhood and the fellowship we found. From those in their twenties to those in the eighties there was an evident sense of family and a recommitment to serve the Lord and our people. It was a

joyful time and a time of grace, and you can truly be proud
of the priests of this Archdiocese of Washington.

The only shadow—beside the lingering sorrow of the past
weakness of the few—was that we were in such great need of
more vocations to continue the work that the Lord has given
us. As the larger classes of fifty years ago begin to seek a respite
from their labors, we are conscious that the numbers of newly
ordained are fewer and the road of pastoral service that lies
ahead will be difficult because of our smaller numbers and
your growing needs. Pray to the Lord of the harvest—as Jesus
told us to—that he will send us the laborers we need and be
active yourself in promoting vocations!

I can say it again. We have so many good and holy priests
here. Thank them once in a while for their generous service
and know that like me, they are always thinking of you.

Bishops
November 20, 2003

I know that a lot of people criticize us bishops—and certainly some of that criticism is right on target—but I'd like
to say a word in favor of us fellows and the work we try to
do. We had the annual plenary meeting of the bishops of the
United States last week and it brought all these criticisms
to my mind. I really believe that for every bishop who may
sometimes be insensitive to the needs of his priests and his
people, there are dozens of others who really try to live only
for the Lord and for the Church he gave us as the instrument
of his peace and salvation. The bishop's job is really an almost
impossible mixing of so many different responsibilities and
can only be successfully accomplished through the grace of
God. He must be a loving father to his people, a faithful

brother to his priests, a heroic champion of the poor, a man of vision who plans for the needs of tomorrow, a talented fundraiser so he can ensure the resources for the work of the apostolate, a solid theologian so that he can teach the faithful with clarity, and a leader who is respected enough in the secular community that he can represent the Church there with honor.

Now that I have written all this down and read it over, I think I ought to examine my own conscience, since I will never be able to do all those things—and in my heart I know that you need someone who can. There is one characteristic that I do have, thank God, and it is that the bishop should be smart enough to surround himself with clergy and laity who have all these gifts and who will help him to guide the local Church in the proper way. Now I do feel better, since by God's generous grace, I do have these kinds of people around me who do all the work and even make me look much smarter than I am! And I have all of you to pray for me! So, with all my shortcomings, you all carry me along.

In the deepest theology of the Church, the bishop of a diocese represents the faithful people in front of the Lord. When I pray, it is almost never for myself, except that whatever grace God gives me is given for you that I might serve you better. When I celebrate Mass, even when I offer the Holy Sacrifice in some faraway place, it is always for you and for your welfare and blessing. The holier a bishop is, the more grace can flow through him to his people, and even a weak and sinful man like me will, in God's mercy, serve as a channel for the grace that he wants to come to you.

So you can see the bishops have a real role to play in your lives as Christians, and therefore when I ask you for prayers for me and for all the bishops, it is with this deep theology in my mind, that this poor old bishop of yours is always praying for you because he can't stop thinking of you wherever he might be.

A Walk Around the Block
November 27, 2003

Do you know that I have had thirty-one priest secretaries in the past twenty-three years since I became a diocesan bishop? Actually, I have had five in the three years that I have been in Washington. Now don't jump to conclusions. I'm not really that terrible a person to work for—or at least I hope I'm not. The reason I change so often is two-fold. It is first that I don't want someone to have to live my life—as a good secretary does—over too long a time. The second is that having worked in a bishop's office for a while, a priest really gains a very profound idea of the workings of the diocese and it helps if a number of our priests have had that experience. Of course, I've had two secretaries at a time since 1986 when I went to Newark as archbishop. Sometimes I try to do it with just one, but since I am a workaholic I seem to generate too much work for just one person.

The average length of time is two years, although sometimes I need to ask a secretary to take a special responsibility and that cuts the time shorter. Only two of my former secretaries have been on the job for three years and the longest-serving one gets to keep a pair of wooden figurines from Ireland that depict a bishop and a scribe. The present holder of that trophy is a pastor in Hoboken, New Jersey, who serves as well as vice chancellor of the Archdiocese of Newark! I am very proud of the "alumni," among them there are a vicar general, diocesan chancellors, rectors of seminaries, and two directors of development, as well as a number of episcopal vicars, consultors and distinguished canon lawyers, scripture scholars, and theologians.

There are also ten pastors of very important parishes. There are so many of them that I think of them by the numbers, a thing that always brings an amused grin to their brother priests.

As some of you will remember, I was secretary to the servant of God, Cardinal Terence Cooke, for seven years in the 1970s. He was a workaholic, too, but being a saint as well, he could inspire us all to work as hard as we possibly could. The other secretary, who was my partner, was a very holy man as well. He ultimately became a bishop in the military archdiocese and died very young of cancer. We worked well together and were a great team. There were months in which we never got a day off and when the cardinal traveled one of us always accompanied him as a working secretary. The other had to tend to the office back home. My present two secretaries generously take on a second job. Msgr. Knestout continues to serve Cardinal Hickey with great affection and care, and Fr. Filardi has been so helpful in our vocation work.

The title of this column comes from a wonderful experience with Cardinal Cooke many years ago. I happened to be working late in the office. We lived and worked in the same building behind St. Patrick's Cathedral. It had been an unusually busy day and I was really beat. His Eminence came into the office looking for something and noticed that I was very tired. Solicitous and kind, as always, and yet oblivious to everything except that total gift of self to the Lord that was his life, he said: "Ted, when you really feel tired, you should stop working, put on your coat, and walk around the block. A walk around the block is as good as a day off!" I have often told this story to my secretaries—with only limited results!

And yet, it's hard not to keep working when I'm thinking of you and all the challenges you face to live joyfully in the presence of the Living God.

Without a Song
December 4, 2003

How I wish that today's young people would hear and enjoy the great music of the light operettas of years ago. There were such wonderful melodies in those fascinating musicals. The story lines were not always gripping, to say the least, but the catchy music carried them along and I remember they were great entertainment.

One powerful melody has been in my mind for the last few days. I'm referring to the title that is the heading of this column: "Without a Song." I don't remember who sang it—perhaps Nelson Eddy—or what operetta it was from, and I don't even remember many of the words, but I can hear the music even now and feel the urge to try at least to hum it.

That's my problem. I have a bad case of laryngitis and I am not just without a song—I'm almost without a voice at all. I started to get it on Thanksgiving Day. That must be the worst time of year to lose your voice. For three days running all I did was visit my different families in New Jersey and New York and on each occasion faced the natural questions about how I was and how was Washington. It's wonderful to have people who love you ask all about your life. It's awful when you know you shouldn't talk and try to answer. I think it's even worse when the very little ones open wide their eyes in anguish and some dismay that you sound so different now.

I'll get over the laryngitis, please God, and have my normal voice back again soon. I hope I'll have my songs again—to sing off-key as usual—but not being able to talk or sing reminded me of the scripture about the new song that we should all sing to the Lord. We don't even need a good voice to sing that song, only a heart that is full of love for God and for each other. That is the new song that we shall all sing together in heaven. It is the new song of faith and trust in the God who loves us that we must sing with love here on earth as well. To be without that song is to be mute indeed. Well, since I have to be silent for a couple of days, I can be thinking of you with fewer distractions, I guess. So it can even be a blessing to be without a song once in a while.

Living for Others
December 11, 2003

I was in the western part of the archdiocese on one of my usual traveling Mass stops on a Sunday. I had celebrated an earlier Mass that day and I needed to get back to my residence for another commitment. The people who brought up the gifts in the offertory procession were a family of five, mother and father, two little boys, and a girl. All of them carried something to present, except the littlest one, whose name was Matthew, and who was carrying a little truck with which he seemed totally enamored. I watched them come up the aisle and I saw that, except for the parents, the youngsters were a little anxious. Well, I received the gifts from the parents and then went down on my knee as I often do, to welcome and receive the gifts from the youngsters. The children presented me with the bread and wine and the parents had the chalice and the ciborium, as I recall. Matthew was studying me intently and so, after thanking the parents, I thought I would say a word to him, too. In jest, I asked him if he had brought up anything to offer to the Lord like his brother and sister did. In the twinkling of an eye, Matthew offered me his truck. I didn't accept it, of course, but I was moved by it since it was all that he had with him.

Somewhere I read that by the time a youngster has reached a certain age—I seem to recall that it was the sixth grade—he or she has somehow imperceptibly made the decision either to live primarily for himself or herself or to live for others. From that decision come teachers, doctors, nurses, priests, social workers, and all the like kind of vocations. I'm not sure it is a universal projection for the future, but experience seems to bear it out even unscientifically. There are certain young people who seem at an early age to be drawn into the caring and helping professions. There are others who give the impression that they will always be loners, or very competitive people, or people who are attempting to put themselves first. Little Matthew in my story is a good example of that generous type that we mentioned first. When the opportunity was offered him to give of himself, immediately he gave the only thing he had, the little toy he liked so much.

I wish I were that way. I wish all of us were! What a wonderful world it would be if it were filled with people who look out for others, who love without wanting return, and who serve without even waiting for a thank you. I truly believe that if anyone has made the less generous decision about what they will do with their lives, they will find the chance to do it over as they grow older and see the need for love and generosity in our world. I think there is hope for everybody, even for someone at seventy-three, like me. When I pray for the Lord to give us the gift of priestly vocations among the young men of our diocese, I think of this story of Matthew and I beg the Lord to send us very fine young men who long ago made the decision to live at the service of others and who have never changed their mind. I am also open to those who started off on the wrong foot and then saw how much more happiness there is in living generously.

May the Lord bless Matthew and his family and all those who open their hearts to other people. I remember that line from *Les Misérables* that we've all quoted so often: "To love another person is to see the face of God." As I'm thinking of you all the time and asking God to bless you, this is one of the blessings for which I ask.

"To Be Very Humbled"
December 18, 2003

Have you ever heard a person say at the beginning of an introduction something like "I'm very humbled in the presence of x, y, or z"? I hear it a lot of times, possibly because I say it myself sometimes and, in those cases, I really mean it.

Last Sunday I was very humbled in the presence of almost three hundred of our sisters and brothers from this Archdiocese of Washington who gathered at the National Shrine with so many family and friends, priests and deacons from all over this archdiocese. They were the folks nominated by their pastors and parishes to receive the Archdiocesan Order of Merit for extraordinary service to the Church and to their neighbors.

There were secretaries and cooks, accountants and gardeners, teachers and catechists, young and old. I was so pleased that the African American community was well represented, befitting their historic place in this local Church of ours. There was a good number of honorees from the Hispanic community, too, a wonderful sign that this overwhelmingly Catholic population is beginning to play a vital role in the life of our Catholic community here in Washington

Three of our priests were honored as well, receiving the title of monsignor from the Holy Father. Although these honors come directly from Rome, it was very fitting that they could share in this general celebration of generous service and outstanding effort. The many different nationalities and races represented were an indication of the many faces of our local Church itself and celebrated our unity in faith and generosity. All in all, it was a wonderful day for the archdiocese in spite of the snow and the rain that accompanied it.

When I congratulated them at the ceremony, I thought of the wonderful, often silent and unknown service that people give to the Lord and to the Church. Every day I hear of the goodness and generosity of our people, sometimes in truly heroic situations. So many of our faithful do wonderful things for their families, their neighbors, their country, their Church. They do it without counting the cost or weighing the difficulties, just because in their hearts they know that it's the right thing to do.

I am truly humbled when I salute them on the occasion of this archdiocesan honors celebration, but indeed, every day when I am thinking of you, I know that there are so many of you who deserve much more praise than I can ever give you. I thank God that he knows it, too, and his reward will be eternal.

A Child Is Born for Us
December 25, 2003

For anyone who listens to the stirring music of Handel's *Messiah*, this verse from the sacred lyrics always has to have a certain special power. The wonder of the incarnation, the mystery of the virgin birth, the awesome fulfillment of the ancient prophecy—all that is woven into the powerful words made even more stirring by the musical crescendo that accompanies them.

May I share with you two lessons that I find here? The first is the story of Christmas, the sacred history of the God who loves us so much that he sends his Son to become like us in all things but sin so that he may achieve our salvation and open for us the path to the happiness of eternal life, a path that we had closed by our sin. The Child who was born of Mary was truly man and truly God. We will only understand this mystery totally when we see him face to face in heaven, but this is what we believe because he himself has revealed it to us who can neither deceive nor be deceived.

This is the joy of Christmas. A child is born, Mary's Son and God's Son, a holy child who will grow up to proclaim the good news of our deliverance from sin and give his life to obtain it for us. In faith we know that it is the intimate connection between the incarnation and the resurrection of Jesus after his passion and death that truly is the reason for our joy. We who are Christians are drawn by our faith to marvel with love at his birth, but in the deepest recesses of our humanity, do we not always rejoice whenever a child is born for us?

In so many parts of the Western world, we are losing that special moment of joy as children are becoming fewer and fewer. The large families of children, so common in generations past, are rare today in a so-called developed world. The great nations of Europe, which contributed so brilliantly to the cultural history of our world, are in danger of disappearing as birth rates sink lower and lower in Italy, France, Germany, and Spain. We must thank God for immigration in our own country or we, too, would face such demise. Maybe Christmas is a time to reflect on this.

Of course, the Church teaches responsible parenthood, but she also sees Christian marriage both as a gift for the mutual love and support of husband and wife and the unique way in which God has chosen to bring children into the world. If the choice of a new car or a new house means the choice not to have a new child, then the natural joy of parenthood is frustrated and the wondrous realization in our own lives that a child is born for us will never resound in the deepest chords of our humanity. Thinking of you at this joyful time of Christmas, I ask young couples to pray with me over that thought and maybe for the generosity that is involved in those choices.

2004

Year In, Year Out
January 1, 2004

Someone said to me, "What kind of a year did you have?" I was a little bit surprised by the question. Actually, to tell the truth, I guess I felt a little put-down. I was going to say, "Well, you live here in the archdiocese, you know everything that I've done in the last twelve months, so you have to know what my year was like." But I didn't say that. I answered something like this.

Well, there have been good things and bad about 2003. We have been at war both with Iraq and with the forces of world terrorism. We had to live with orange and yellow codes of danger. We have had so much rain that farmers have had trouble with crops. For much of the year the financial markets have been lagging and many folks can't find decent jobs. The violence in the Holy Land, the wars in Africa, and the persecution of believers in so many parts of the world have marred the international scene. The terrible poverty of so many millions around the world, together with the pandemic of AIDS and the fear of SARS, has painted a grim picture of the year that is ending. Here in our own country, the Church has only now pulled itself together after a terrible scandal caused by a small number of our clergy. So, looking back, there will be a lot of tough things that this year will bring to mind.

On the other hand, there are good things, too. The major military phase of the war in Iraq was over quickly and there is hope that we can help the Iraqi people find a better start for their future. New jobs seem to be coming and the economy is improving. New medicines seem to be helping in the struggle to heal and prevent age-old diseases. New voices are being raised calling for peace with justice in the Holy Land and throughout the Middle East. The Holy Father reached the historic milestone of twenty-five years of his papacy and the Church in our own country has now developed stronger programs to guarantee the protection of children. So there were both good and bad in our world during the past twelve months.

But—and here is the point of my ramblings—whether the circumstances of our own lives were good or bad, one thing was absolutely certain in 2003. Day in and day out, the signs of God's love for us were present if only we would look for them. This is because, year in and year out for the past twenty centuries, the Eucharist has brought us the bread of life, the sacraments have given us the grace to survive and grow in holiness, and the good news has always consoled and strengthened as well as challenged us to rejoice in God's unending and unchanging love.

Year in and year out, this has been true for those who have faith. That's not a bad doctrine to hold onto and, thinking of you, it should bring peace and courage to face the year ahead.

Telling One's Age
January 8, 2004

The priests of the archdiocese are very good to me. They show me great respect and I think they know my own profound respect and affection for them. In a diocese, the priests are like a family. That's why it was so good that almost all of us could be together for that convocation last October. They are from very different backgrounds and have many different talents and personalities, of course, but they have put their lives in the hands of God and all that they have in the service of his people. They may have differing views on the accidentals that surround our ministry—depending on age and experience and often where they studied—but they truly believe in what they do and, although I admit to some prejudice on behalf of these brothers of mine, they do it well!

From time to time, I get constructive advice from them. That's what happens in a family. I hear a lot of good suggestions like: You need a haircut; you are starting to slouch again; you look too tired; when are you going to visit my school; you need to get a new pair of shoes (I did that last during the sales after Christmas, by the way); you don't exercise enough; and so on. All these comments are excellent, and if I followed them all, I would be healthier and probably have a much better disposition. But the one I am talking of today is one that I hear from time to time: "Don't keep telling everyone how old you are."

Now I confess to doing that a lot. I think it's something a lot of men do. (There are mysterious rules that guide women in this area and I want to stay far away from that today.) I probably do it for a number of reasons. First of all, I'm happy to have lived this long. My dad died before forty. Secondly, I'm glad I'm still healthy enough to keep working reasonably hard at my age. Then also, my age is often on my mind since I know there are not too many years—or days—left and I must try to accomplish something in your service and at the same time get ready to go home to the Lord. It is not morbid; it's just realistic.

Since all this is in the back of my mind, it just naturally comes up in my conversation and in my preaching, too. Besides all that, in a lot of ways it's fun to be seventy-three. It would be tough to have to do it all over and if I were 103 it would be hard to do much at all. I may not be like the electric rabbit that keeps going all the time in the commercial, but please pray for me—and for all your priests, young and old—that we may never stop thinking of you and dedicating ourselves to your salvation at every age along the way.

Friends
January 15, 2004

When does a person most need a good friend? I was thinking about that question quite often during the Christmas
holidays when I was reminded of the kindness and constant
caring of a lot of people whom I have had the privilege to
call my friends. It started me thinking about my own life
and how important it has been at every stage of my journey
to have some special people who were and are my friends. So
many of them are also members of my family, and it must be
a great tragedy for anyone who cannot count close relatives
in that group of faithful and loving friends. (May I digress
for a moment? If anyone who is reading this column would
find himself or herself in that situation where there is a close
relative who is no longer a friend, wouldn't it be a great thing
to make a phone call—or send an e-mail—to a relative who
has dropped out of the picture and just seek once again to
build up a friendship rooted in those special bonds of flesh
and blood?)

We need a friend most in time of deepest joy and in time
of deepest sorrow. I know that in all the happy moments of
my life I need to share my joy with others. Whenever anything especially nice happens, you really can't keep it to yourself. There is a natural urge to tell a friend, to share it with
someone who will also find joy in it and thus increase your
own joy as it is reflected in the face or the voice of another
person who wishes you well. I think the need to share joy is
built into the human psyche and it helps us survive the problems by enhancing the times of joy.

Of course, there is so special a need for a friend at the
time of sorrow or of anxiety. That's what wake services are
really all about. When we lose a loved one, it is too hard to

grieve all alone. The tears we share with others are tears that help to wash away the normal pangs of grief, and the sense of loss is not as great when others are there who understand. The terrible cross of anxiety that all human beings carry as we prepare for a serious operation or a long period of recovery or a loved one going off to war or a challenge that seems beyond our powers—all those are carried better when they are not carried alone.

There are two points I want to make. First of all, in the order of nature, how important it is to have friends and, as the wise old saying goes, you can't have a friend unless you are willing to be a friend. So let us all try to reach out to others and share ourselves with them, knowing that if we do we may gain the great treasure of a good friend. There is, of course, a supernatural side to this, too. It comes in the words of that lovely old Protestant hymn: "I have a friend in Jesus." We surely do have a friend in him who understands us, saves us, and always loves us, even when we make it hard by our selfishness and sin. He is the best friend we can ever have, and if we do not find that divine friendship in our lives, nothing can take its place. This is what I hope for you as I'm thinking of you today; may Jesus be your best friend in good times and in bad, and in your heart you already know: he is and always will be.

A Baby
January 22, 2004

As we get ready once again for the March for Life here in Washington, our thoughts naturally turn to the whole history of abortion in our country and especially since the *Roe v. Wade* decision of the 1970s. So much has been written and spoken about this question, so many legal briefs, legislative actions, court decisions, and media communications that it is surely possible to lose the basic truth on which our position is built. When all is said and done, it is not a conflict over women's rights or parental oversight or medical ethics, it is much simpler and much more direct than any of these important considerations.

We believe that there is a baby in the mother's womb!

The more we learn about anatomy, physiology, medicine, and biology, the easier it is for us to see that the process of human life begins at conception. Just as the little girl and the grown-up woman thirty years later are the same person, by the differences of size, in physical development and in mental capacity, so we believe that the little fetus in the mother's body is the same person that will grow up to be the little girl and the grown-up woman later on.

As one of my little grandnephews once assured me, pointing at his pregnant mother's extended girth, "We think there is a baby in there!" It's more than just thinking. We believe it with every fiber of our being, and that's why we don't want anyone—for any reason—to put it to death. That's why we try to support pro-life activities, to encourage legislation that protects unborn and pre-born human life, and to come together in prayer and purpose to persuade our society to choose life as the sacred scriptures urged us so many centuries ago.

We may differ as to the precise ways to do this. For example, I would much rather we moved our March for Life to the springtime when so many more people could join us and when the flowering of our beautiful world would remind us of the beauty of life as it begins. But our unity as to the final goal is clear. It may be a long journey still to go, but we move step by step with the help of God and the support of so many people of good will of every religion, race, and nationality. Thinking of you as the pro-life rally approaches, I pray to the Lord of life that he will help us keep all these little babies alive and safe in their mother's womb.

Bravo!
January 29, 2004

For more than a year, many of us in Washington have been working hard on a three-sector proposal for the better education of children here in the District of Columbia. The three sectors are the District of Columbia public school system, the charter schools, and the non-public or independent schools here in the city of Washington. About two years ago I sat down with the then Superintendent Paul Vance and told him that he would have my complete support if ever he needed help from the congress to improve the quality of our public schools here in the district. My assurances were, as I told the superintendent, not just altruistic. Most of our Catholic youngsters are actually in the public schools and therefore I was determined to help those schools become the best providers of public education in the country.

With the extraordinary support of many business leaders in our city who both realistically saw the need for well-educated young people for the workforce of our area, and who, with a wonderful sense of justice, saw the poorer families falling behind in the struggle for a good education for their children, we launched the campaign. We could not have taken the first step if it weren't for the leadership of Mayor Williams, Councilman Kevin Chavous, and Peggy Cafritz, the president of the DC Board of Education. These far-reaching and courageous public officials saw in the three-sector approach the way to that rising tide that lifts all boats. When the federal government, through the Department of

Education, offered the possibility of a five-year pilot program for our area, we knew that the moment had come for us to make this happen.

The list of folks who put this project together is long and impressive, but it was the families of the district themselves whose voices were raised above the political din of special-interest groups that were the real heroes and heroines of the campaign. Mothers and fathers of grammar-school children were the mainstay of our program and their eloquence and courage really won the day.

This is not a victory for parochial schools or for a voucher program. It is a victory for poor families who now have a choice in the education of their children. The monies that will come for education in Washington will strengthen the public schools and the charter schools. It will make it possible for independent schools such as our Catholic parochial schools to continue to offer excellent education and even to make them stronger. Obviously, there are challenges we will all have to face in bringing this three-sector program to fruition, but we will work together on this as we have worked together to bring it about.

Bravo to our elected officials who courageously saw and supported this new chance for the families in the District of Columbia! Bravo to those remarkable leaders of business and government here in Washington who never forgot the poor and were determined that their children would have a better chance for excellence in education! Bravo to the parents and families of our area who never gave up hope that together we could make this happen! Bravo to the hard-working and brilliant staffs of educators and think tanks who pulled the three-sector program together, and bravo to the District of Columbia, which now has the chance to become the finest place in the nation to educate its children!

Thinking of you—and not forgetting the children in other parts of our area—I truly believe that we all took one historic step forward last week.

Decline and Fall
February 5, 2004

Do you recall studying in history class Gibbon's great historical work, *The Decline and Fall of the Roman Empire?* As I remember it, the famous scholar found many reasons for the collapse of that extraordinary power that ruled the known world for several centuries. One of the most significant of the causes of its decline was the moral decay of Roman society, which lost its values and its internal strength because of that.

At a certain point in time, internal division, barbarian invasions, and the growing moral decay signaled the end of a mighty empire and the beginning of what historians would call the Dark Ages. The great heroes of integrity and outstanding strength of character gave way to emperors who ceased to lead their people in the pursuit of honor and glory, and the citizens of Rome lost the brilliant examples of piety and patriotism that had made them so remarkable. Values such as civic responsibility, modesty, and devotion to duty gave way too often to a quest for pleasure, selfish advancement, and a false concept of liberty.

Sound familiar? Enron, the value-challenged state of the media, the growth of violent crime, especially among young people, the ominous decline of the birth rate, the subtle and now court-supported attacks on the survival of marriage and the family, pornography and drugs and political correctness— if these are not signs of trouble ahead, then the sun won't rise tomorrow. The Super Bowl halftime show should not have been surprising. It's just another element in the decline and fall of a culture that made this nation great and its people an example of decency and industry for the rest of the world.

Am I exaggerating? I hope I am, but I see enough signs around me to make me really worry. What is the most disturbing of all is that I see really wonderful young people falling for this pernicious anticulture and losing their ideals and their values, with the resulting danger to our nation and our society. What is the answer? Let me oversimplify it. God is the answer, a return to the principles of faith and hope and love. All the values and the virtues come from these fundamental building blocks of a strong and sane society.

In the breviary one morning last week, Saint Paul's Letter to the Thessalonians reminded me that we were all made for holiness and not for immorality. Thinking of you and recognizing the temptations we all face today, that is a good thing to remember.

Sacred Silence
February 12, 2004

Do you talk more than you listen? Does the funny saying about people never getting a word in edgewise relate to you? Do you find yourself saying "Are you listening to me?" more often? If you answered yes to any one of those questions, then this column is for you. (I confess that it is also for me, too, since I do talk a lot!)

There is something very beautiful in chosen silence, and I think something very healthful, too. I'm not just talking in the context of the high-decibel quality of the car radio when the young people find the music station. I mean the choice of stillness and the quiet time when the communion of heart and mind is not interrupted by the sound of busy voices. I mean the silence of nighttime when only the wind breaks the stillness of the stars or the quiet of the desert in the midday heat or the sound of water gently lapping on a boat moored close to shore. Even more wonderfully, the hush of a congregation when the words of consecration are pronounced by the priest.

That for me is the silence that moves me most, since it seems to open hearts and minds to mysteries that no words can picture or resolve. In the recently printed General Instruction for the Liturgy of the Mass, which provides guidelines for the Mass, a lot is written about silence. Quiet breathes a time for meditation, for reflection, and for peace. It is a calm for the nerves, for the anxieties, and for the soul. As I celebrate Mass, I have started to pause a little longer after Communion to let you sense the quiet presence of the Lord within you. We have tried to make sure that there is always a brief pause of silence after the readings so that we can listen to God talking to us in the depth of our hearts. I urge you to pause for a minute or two when you enter your pew in church to recognize God's presence in the tabernacle and to set your mind on the awesome mystery of the Eucharist that we are about to join.

I am sure that little additions of sacred silence will do wonders for our peace of mind. God will often talk to us in his own way during these moments of silence. They make us more aware of his presence and consequently of his love. The pace of the world is more hectic now than ever. Taking a moment of quiet time brings a sacred silence to our lives and reminds us that listening can be as great a gift as speech. Thinking of you in the stillness can even be a more powerful way to keep in touch.

Violence
February 19, 2004

(Kosovo) Like so many of us who live in or around this great city of Washington, I have fallen in love with its beauty, its grandeur, and its national location. More than that, I've fallen in love with its people. Some of the brightest and the best live here in the district and in the surrounding counties that make up the Archdiocese of Washington that I have come to know so well.

For me, some of the very best of our people are the very poor who work so hard to keep a family together, to bring up their children in an often hostile society, and whose honesty, determination, and courage are truly an inspiration for the rest of us who do not face the challenges that they do every day. I pray that the new school choice legislation will be a help for them in selecting the way they want to educate their children without the need to work three jobs or more to help pay the cost of that education.

It is because your heart breaks when you become aware of their valiant struggle that the stories of violence in the schools and neighborhoods of our community that we have seen in the past few weeks are so tragic. Much of what torments our city has its roots in drugs and poverty and fear, and we all have to do our best to reach out to our sisters and brothers who struggle with these realities every day and try their best to live and raise their families in the midst of this violence that surrounds them.

I thank God for the churches and other places of worship that give light and hope and to the many agencies like our Catholic Charities, which are working every day to help. In the name of our Catholic people of all races, ethnic groups, and neighborhoods, I pledge a continuing effort to be part of the solution. These past few days, traveling for Catholic Relief Services in the midst of the violence of Kosovo and other Balkan areas, I am thinking of you at home and confident that the solid steps of peace building that I see over here will have an echo in what we do at home for one another.

Looking for Saints
February 26, 2004

(Belgrade) I had gone into the chapel of the nunciature in Belgrade where I am staying. It was very early in the morning and I probably wasn't working on all cylinders yet. As I began my morning prayers, I looked for the sanctuary lamp—the candle that is always lit when the Blessed Sacrament is present. At first, I didn't see it and I started to look around to see if it was placed on another wall as sometimes happens. Finally, I saw it behind some flowers that had been placed near a statue of Our Lady. It is always a special grace to know that the Lord is there and to make again the powerful act of faith in the real presence of the living God in every tabernacle throughout the world. (I reminded myself to urge you all to take up the custom of visits to the Blessed Sacrament as often as you can, even daily, especially as a resolution during Lent!)

To get back to my story, when I began my prayers, my thoughts focused on the fact that I had not noticed the altar light because it was half hidden from my sight. How often does it happen that we do not find what we are looking for because we look in the wrong place? That brought me to the thought that I want to share with you about looking for saints. Last Thursday when I stopped in Rome for two days of meetings, the Holy Father called a special consistory in which he announced the upcoming canonization of six new saints. Any cardinal who is in Rome is expected to attend. We all had been advised earlier by mail of the report of the Roman congregation, which studies the causes of the saints, that in these particular cases all things were in readiness. That included both an intense study of the individual's life and work and the necessary medically approved miracles. We had already sent in our votes and the Holy Father now invited us to be present as he indicated that all was in order for the canonizations to proceed and set the date for them this coming May.

There were six very different people, four men and two women. One was very famous, Luigi Orione, an Italian priest who is well known for his works of charity and the care of the poor. Another, a Spanish priest, is important to us in the Archdiocese of Washington since he founded the religious congregation of the Sons of the Holy Family, which is present in our archdiocese and to which our own Bishop Gonzalez belongs. One of the women was a widow who raised a family and then, after her husband's death, started a congregation of sisters to work with the poor. The other woman was perhaps the most interesting for us. She only died in 1962 and her husband is still living and hopefully will be able to come to her canonization! She was a medical doctor whose life of holiness was recognized by her patients and associates and now, in this most solemn way, by the Church itself.

The pope continues to teach us that the saints are not the stuff of centuries ago. They live in our own time and place. They are often like the sanctuary lamp, which we may not always notice and can often miss. There are saints among us here, dear friends. Some, please God, are among our priests and religious and deacons. Many, I am sure, are the mothers and fathers of families, seemingly ordinary people who love God and their neighbor in an extraordinary way. They may not work miracles in their earthly life, although their virtues of patience and trust and charity may have in fact already inspired us. Some of you who read this column may be in their number. If you are, I hope you will pray for the rest of us and especially for me, who in this cold early morning in the Balkans is praying for and thinking of you.

Meeting the Press
March 4, 2004

I have to confess that one of the scariest things I do is the encounter with the TV media when the subject of the conversation is controversial. It's not that I worry about telling the truth. That's the only thing I can ever do. But the two problems always are first, to be sure that I know all the facts and, second, that I speak clearly and with love. It is easy to get rattled by the questions, to lose the point of what you want to say, and to say something in a way that could be hurtful to another person or group. This is, of course, most difficult when you are on a live interview—although many of the more professional folks prefer that, since in a taped interview the point that you are trying to make may be lost in the editing.

This is especially true when the question of sex abuse comes up, as it has during the past week, since the publication of the two studies that the bishops of our country asked to have done. The sorrow and the deep concern that we all have for victims overshadows even the numbers and the statistics. This has truly been a painful time for the Church, and it is certainly proper that once again we offer a deep apology to all who have been hurt and to their families and their parishes.

Speaking to the media about it in the more than half dozen such interviews I had over the last few days moves me also to see the need to bring it once again to the Lord in prayer as a Church and a diocese and a people called by God to holiness. As the report of the National Review Board says so clearly, this is a societal problem, not just a Church problem, and we who have now properly put all our facts on the table for everyone to see must now somehow help others to confront this scourge that seems to touch our nation and maybe the whole world since the sexual revolution of the 1960s. As our own burden is heavier because of the trust that priests should always have, so perhaps our responsibility to help the rest of society face this crisis and overcome it may be equally great.

In the Archdiocese of Washington, therefore, I am going to ask all the people of our local Church to accept another day of penance and prayer, with fasting and outreach to the poor, as a sign of sorrow and repentance for this terrible problem that we have had to face in the Church and now must face as well in our society. I realize that it is we who must shoulder the blame, but in the deepest solidarity of faith and love, I ask you to join in such a day of atonement on the Tuesday of Holy Week this year. It is always good to pray together and we are strongest when in prayer and trust we kneel before our Father in heaven and beg the grace of pardon and his forgiving love through his beloved Son, Jesus Christ, our Lord.

One more point before I end this column. It brings me back to the media. A couple of years ago, I had a luncheon with the editorial board of one of our prominent newspapers. The lunch looked delicious, but I had no chance to eat it since through the entire meal the reporters kept asking me questions about the problems which the Church was facing in the sex abuse crisis. At the end of the lunch, having got-ten hold of a cracker for nourishment, I turned to our host and asked if I could make a brief statement. Graciously, he agreed, and I said: "In the midst of all this turmoil and all this crisis and sorrow, I want you to know that the Catholic Church here in Washington continues to care for the poor and the hungry, the homeless and the hopeless. We continue to educate tens of thousands of young people, to provide psychological help for people and families in trouble. We continue to try to call ourselves and our people to holiness and to build up a society that is based on the love of God and neighbor." The folks who were there at the luncheon acknowledged that, and I want to make the point here in a special way. In the midst of all the turmoil and concern, the Catholic Church continues to serve God's people in many wonderful and grace-filled ways. Be proud of your Church and of all the things that you enable it to do. Be grateful to God for this family of faith that is the Catholic Church. It is a Church of saints and sinners, but it provides the sinners the way to become saints. Thinking of you in these difficult days, I want you to know that from my heart.

Talking with God
March 11, 2004

I was going to call this column "Talking to God," but I realize that was not what I really wanted to tell you about. We talk to God whenever we pray. We talk with him when we enter into the deep conversation where heart speaks to heart.

As I was preparing my Sunday homily, I began to think that this was a subject I wanted to share with all of you. The readings of last Sunday's Mass presented us with two divine conversations. One is in the Old Testament when God talks with Abraham, our father in faith, and the other is the wondrous conversation between Jesus and the two great figures of Israel, Moses and Elijah. In each of these extraordinary narratives, we see what a wonderful grace it is to have a real relationship with God, to enter into his life and, even more wonderfully, to allow him to enter into our own. Mother Teresa's great line, "Give God permission" comes to mind here as we feel ourselves called to allow the Lord to take control of our lives, or as the modern expression has it, to "Let go, let God!"

I think children do this more easily than the rest of us. Maybe that's part of the reason God has such a special love for them. They seem to talk to him more easily, and to listen to him more comfortably. As we become older and more self-conscious or more sophisticated, talking with God seems to get harder. Children may not always understand the profound truths of faith, but so often they possess a deep sense of faith and their openness to the presence of God within them is a grace for which we all must strive.

Our Catholic faith is a Eucharistic faith. By that I mean that the real presence of the Body and Blood of Christ is so central to our relationship with God. This should make it easier for us to talk with the Lord since we can receive him in Holy Communion and be made alive by his presence within us. That presence challenges us constantly to lift up our minds and hearts to him and, with him, to speak of those things that give us joy in this life and the hope of eternal life to come. And in that mysterious conversation, whether we are conscious of it or not, he is always thinking of you and me and reaching out in a love that cannot be measured.

Madrid
March 18, 2004

I want to talk about Spain and the terrible tragedy of last week. For so many of us, it was 9/11 revisited. Is there anyone in this city or this area who did not have the feeling that the people of Spain are reliving the trauma that shook us all so badly three years ago? As I listened to the voices of families and saw the television coverage of that awful murder of innocent people, the scenes of the Pentagon and the Twin Towers came back hauntingly again. Those of us who carry personal scars from that terrible day are drawn back into the desolation and the helplessness we felt that day.

I spoke to the Spanish ambassador to express my condolences and that of the Archdiocese of Washington. He is an old friend and a distinguished representative of a great country whose closeness to us in these days of growing Hispanic populations is akin to the feelings we have for the English-speaking world because of our own early history. The attacks seem to have had political repercussions at home and that may also have been the aim of the murderers who planned and carried out those highly coordinated acts of savagery.

Certainly this tragedy reminds us that those who hate us are still able to strike out and cause enormous damage and loss of life. It also apparently was intended to warn those who joined in the war against terrorism that they will be targets, too.

Yet, are there any alternatives? I don't see any. Either we work together to defend the dignity of all human life from every kind of terror, or we sit back while the enemies of life and human values take over the world. In that last scenario, the world becomes a jungle and civilization begins to decay.

The free world cannot just turn over and surrender. We can't let the terrorists win.

Where do we go from here? I think first of all we must take prudent precautions as individuals and as a nation and not expose ourselves recklessly to danger. Next, we must continue to live our lives courageously, generously, and with confidence and never stop in our quest to build up a just and peaceful world where all people can enjoy the fruits of their labor and work in harmony for a better life for themselves and for their children. Finally, and this is the most important of all, we must bring our needs and hopes, our dreams and concerns to the living God who loves us and who has told us that his will is for our good and not for our harm.

As we live through these critical times we can take solace and strength in the faith-filled knowledge that he who is Lord of all is very aware of our history, past and present and to come, and is thinking of you and me with love as we move from day to day.

The Movie
March 25, 2004

I finally did get to see *The Passion of the Christ.* Actually, I saw it last Sunday afternoon with our vocation directors and some young fellows who are discerning a priestly vocation. I knew that I was going to write you about it, so from the very beginning I tried to keep track of my thoughts and emotions. I really wasn't able to do that, since I found myself swept up in the awesome story of love and sacrifice that we all know so well and that was portrayed so movingly.

After the film is over, there is a long series of credits, mentioning just about every name of anyone who was involved in the production. I was glad for those few minutes. They gave me a chance to come back from the emotions of that awesome narrative and as the house lights went on again to relocate myself in the world of today. I found the presentation of the passion of Jesus to be powerful and moving. For anyone who has meditated on the events of those terrible hours, it was a meditation come to life.

I cried a little; I closed my eyes at the somewhat overdone scenes of the brutality of the Roman soldiers; I followed the wonderfully sensitive portrayal of Mary with concentration and affection; I was deeply touched by the portrayal of the centurion's conversion at the cross. All of us came away from the theater silent and reflective and needing time to sort out our thoughts.

I did not find it anti-Roman or anti-Semitic. I would be very troubled if anyone went away from the film with hatred in his heart. As many Catholic reviewers have already said, the movie invites all of us to see our own guilt and sinfulness in the redeeming death of Christ. It is true that the depiction of the role of some of the Jewish leaders was harsh and critical, but they are presented more as angry and suspicious individuals rather than as representatives of a race or an ethnic group. Someone who left the film with a grudge against anyone except himself would have missed the whole point of the picture and indeed the whole point of the Gospel. What a terrible denial of God's love that would be. I found myself saying during the portrayal of Christ's suffering, "Lord, I have done this to you. Be merciful and forgive me."

Although I would not recommend it for children because of the extreme cruelty that it portrays, it was a good meditation for me. Since I had been thinking of you as I was watching it, you can be sure that I thanked the Lord many times over for his passion and death by which you and I are released from sin and given the grace to live a good and holy life.

The Ides of April
April 1, 2004

I'm not even sure there is an "Ides of April" but it sounds ominous enough to convey the anxiety with which I write about my taxes! It's not that I haven't been paying them to the full. I have and, of course, I always will since archbishops ought to give good example, but the problem I have is getting all the paperwork together and gathering it all on time.

To the best of my appreciation of those things, my taxes should not be complicated. I don't take a salary, I don't have dependents, I try to give as much as I can away, and most of my income comes from pooled income funds or charitable remainder trusts to which I have contributed so that the archdiocese will not have to pay me anything when I retire. As long as you all give me room and board, I'll be in great shape to live comfortably without too many expenses.

So why am I troubled at tax time? It's simple. I can't find all my papers! Every year around this time—it's always around this time that I procrastinate—I go to look for all the information I'll need to have my taxes prepared. And every year around this time, there are a couple of items I can't find. The obvious solution is to contact the folks who send them out in the first place, but if you happen to be a male over fifty—and I'm over seventy—you tend not to do that obvious thing. Instead, you waste at least a week or so trying to find what you think you have misplaced.

At the end of it all, I'll contact the ones who can help me, but by then the Ides of April are coming dangerously close. Of course, there is the constant temptation to ask for an extension, but you don't want to do it this year in case you have to do it next year—if you know what I mean. The great-est victim in all of this is the good and patient friend who does my taxes for me. Thank God, he knows what he's doing. I'm not sure you can say the same about me!

It's spiritually rewarding that tax time comes during Lent. If anything helps to keep one focused on the challenges of life, that does it. And isn't it great that we have a God who bestows on us so generously so many gifts and graces and asks only that we turn to him in prayer and trust and he will do the rest? Thinking of you at tax time, I acknowledge his goodness and mercy and his abiding patience overall.

Time for the Sequel
April 8, 2004

A couple of weeks ago, I did my column on the movie, *The Passion of the Christ.* Some of you have told me that it was helpful and, of course, I'm glad of that. The terrible story of the suffering of our Lord and his heroic tolerance of the hatred of his enemies is a wonderful lesson for us all. It teaches us about his indescribable love for us men and women and his obedience to the great mystery of the Father's will. It is truly not just useful but essential for the faithful Catholic to meditate on the passion so that we may find in it the strength to take up our own crosses and carry them. We know in the most profound understanding of our faith that God does not ask us to carry them alone. He is there beside us on the journey with his grace, his strength, and his love.

But the story of our salvation does not end on the cross. It would be wrong if our spirituality never moved from Good Friday. In a certain sense, we need a sequel to the narrative of the passion. We are a people of the resurrection, a religion built on the Risen Christ, who has overcome death and sin and now lives with us forever. Glorious and immortal, we proclaim him, king of kings and lord of lords.

Our hearts are filled with sorrow when we contemplate the passion, and rightly so, for it was our sinfulness, mine and yours, that caused his cruel suffering. Christ indeed died for us to free us from sin, but he has also risen from the dead that he might walk with us in this present time and life of ours and bring us to the joy and glory of everlasting life. We cannot understand the passion unless we understand the resurrection. Without the resurrection we are overwhelmed in the defeat of the crucifixion. But that can never be the end of the story. That was never to be the Father's will. Jesus rose, and in the deepest mystery, we will rise again as well.

I can hear in my mind the stirring and powerful melody of the hymn that proclaims "We will rise again!" That is the anthem of our holy religion. Saint Augustine proclaims that we are an Easter people and Alleluia is our song. Even as the springtime signals the rebirth of the life of nature, much more surely has the resurrection proclaimed that Jesus Christ is Lord. He has manifested his power, which is stronger than all the forces of sin and death and, in the most basic insight of our faith, he has shown that he desires to be your friend, your guide and your brother. Trust him. Love him. Do not be afraid to put your life in his hands. He has manifested his love for you and even at this moment in time he is thinking of you and preparing a place for you to live with him forever. Augustine was right. That confidence surely deserves an Alleluia.

Happy Easter to you all!

Too Many Thoughts
April 15, 2004

You may remember one of my columns here in the *Catholic Standard* some time ago, when I complained about not having any thoughts about which to write to you. It was a kind of writer's block or just the temporary paralysis that comes to all of us when we know we have to put something down on paper and can't figure out what to say. In my experience with nieces and nephews, I know that this malady affects teenagers frequently when they have to do a term paper or an essay for school.

Today the challenge is different. In fact, it is just the opposite. I have so many things I want to tell you that I can't decide which of them I would like to share with you this week. You would think that I would be wiped out of thoughts after Holy Week when I was so blessed as to be able to preach to the people eleven times in seven days, but each time when I finished my homily, it left me filled with other things I wanted to tell you also.

This week I'd like to share my concerns about peace and justice and the menacing increase of violence in the world. I'd like to talk about the Holy Land where our fellow Christians, as well as Israelis and Palestinians, suffer so much. I'd like to write about the rising level of what I believe to be an increasing amount of anger and hostility in our political parties in this election year, leading to a lowering of the level of public discourse that doesn't serve the people well. I'd like to talk about a new call to religious leaders—Moslem, Christian, and Jewish—to join again in condemning violence and hatred justified in the name of religion.

So you can see that there is so much on my mind these days that I would like to share with you and I really don't know where to begin. Well, perhaps in the coming weeks I will get a chance to develop some of these subjects. For now, let me just tell you how impressed and delighted I was at the crowds of the faithful who filled our churches in the days of Holy Week. The Lord had to be pleased at the number of men and women, young and old, who came to worship at the liturgies of those last few days. As I preached and prayed and celebrated with you, I could not help but be thinking of you and your own faith and asking the risen Lord to make this for you an Easter of unending joy.

Passionately
April 22, 2004

No, this is not another column on the movie, not even directly on the Lord's passion. It's about living passionately.

Let me explain. So many people—and unfortunately, I am too often in that group—seem to live each day as if it were just another burden to be passed through. Theirs is a humdrum existence, usually uneventful because they do not seek great events or challenges, except on rare occasions. They may be just passive people who often seem to let life pass them by. They tend to live in a rut that gives them security or protection from surprises, but never calls them to reach up for excellence or to reach out to touch a neighbor's need.

God knows, I am not condemning folks like that or even trying to put them down. Sometimes people are motivated either by personality or circumstances to live that way. "I don't want to get involved," they might say. "It's not my problem," would be the mantra of their lives. "Keep your head low," they frequently advise. They always vote for staying out of trouble by staying out of the limelight.

I am sure there are saints among this group of people, but they so often miss the excitement of life, the challenge of great expectations, the wonder of great hopes. They settle for less than they can do or be by avoiding the potential dangers that come from throwing oneself into the hurly-burly of life. Now please note that there is a difference between living passionately and living dangerously. The latter is foolhardy and should be avoided. It is the road of those who dabble in drugs or cut corners with justice. To live passionately is different. It is to live genuinely, courageously, filled with great dreams, and not held back by fears. It is to think of others and their needs before you think about your own, to do what you do with enthusiasm and with a joyful spirit giving yourself without holding back to a great cause or a great challenge.

Each of us knows people who live passionately. They are not just the Mother Teresas or the Francis Xaviers of the world, but a devoted teacher or a tireless doctor or a zealous priest, a parent who sacrifices herself for her children, a youngster determined to emerge from the shackles of poverty. People who live passionately change the world—even if it is only the limited world of their own family or neighborhood or ward.

I pray every day that God will bless those men and women who live passionately, knowing that they are the ones who will serve Jesus best. He himself prepared for the terrible passion that led to his death by living every day of his life passionately devoted to the glory of his Father and the salvation of all of us from sin and darkness. Thinking of you as we continue to reflect on Easter, I ask the Lord to help more of us to live passionately in his grace.

Ad Limina
April 29, 2004

The two Latin words that are the title of this column are very important for the Church throughout the world. They mean, "To the Threshold" and they signify the visit every five years or so that all the diocesan bishops of the world must make to the places where Saint Peter and Saint Paul are buried and, at the same time, pay their respects to Peter's successor, the Bishop of Rome.

The *Ad Limina* visits have, of course, been more formal over the centuries. Today, they involve not only celebrating the Eucharist in the great Basilicas of St. Peter in the Vatican and St. Paul's outside the walls, but also visiting the Holy Father and the offices of the Roman Curia, which are set up to help and serve the needs of the diocesan Churches. This year is the time set aside for the bishops from the United States, as well as a number of other nations. Since we have about two hundred dioceses in our country, the American bishops go in geographical groups, so I will be in Rome with the bishops from Maryland, Delaware, Virginia, West Virginia, and the Virgin Islands.

Pope John Paul II changed the pattern of these visits when he was elected Bishop of Rome and Vicar of Christ about twenty-six years ago. He really wanted to spend as much time with the visiting bishops as he could, realizing that this might be the only time he would get to be with them for another five years, unless his apostolic travels would bring him to their local Churches. For that reason, at the start of his pontificate, the *Ad Limina* visit involved not just a private visit with the pope, but Mass with him, a joint meeting with the bishops together with him, and even a lunch where a dozen of us could share a meal in his own private dining room. This year, because of the Holy Father's frailty, we will still have the private visit and the group session, but the other elements are not expected to take place.

In preparation for the visit, each diocese must prepare a full report on how we are doing. We sent our own report over several months ago so the different bureaus could look at it and make suggestions or comments when we arrive. It will be a good week for me. It is always good to spend time, however short, with the Holy Father and I will be with Bishops Olivier, Farrell, and Gonzalez, too, and that is a special joy, as well. We will also see a number of old friends who work in Rome and hopefully learn many things that will help us back home. I will, of course, be telling you all about it and meeting with our council of priests, as well as with the Archdiocesan Pastoral Council when I get back, so that the whole Archdiocese of Washington will share in this important moment.

I will miss you all, and especially miss visiting the parishes every day until I get back. I will be gone for almost two weeks, since I join the Knights of Malta from our area on their pilgrimage to Lourdes for a few days and then go back to Rome for the annual meeting of The Papal Foundation, of which I am still the president. At least you know that I will be thinking of you many times each day and celebrating all of my Masses for your intentions, as I always do. Please pray for me and all the other bishops that the *Ad Limina* visit of 2004 will be a time of grace and learning for us all.

Signs
May 6, 2004

Have you noticed how oftentimes a lot of nice things happen unexpectedly? All of us come across particular moments

when God seems to give us a special sign of his presence
in our lives. We need to be very aware of those particular
moments and see in them the caring hand of a loving God.
I want to tell you about two of these occurrences that happened to me during a journey I had to make to England and
Ireland, a few months ago. Actually, I wanted to write to
you about this earlier, but there were always other subjects I
needed to share with you.

First of all, I have to admit that for each of us the signs
and the way we read them may be different. I tend to see
God's providence in so many things, probably because I'm a
priest and God is always my mind. Maybe I sometimes
read more into the ordinary occurrences of life, but God
surely does touch our lives where we are, as he finds us in the
moments of joy and in the depths of sorrow. The important
thing is that he reaches into our ordinary, everyday lives and
makes us conscious of his presence there. The point I want to
make is that these signs come into the lives of each and every
one of us and we should take the time to see in this a special
instance of God's presence and his ever-present love.

I was in Dublin some weeks ago at the meeting of the
World Faith Development Dialogue, a gathering of religious
leaders and well-known financial experts who gather to
talk about how to help solve the terrible needs of the poor
throughout the world. One day during the meeting, I had
left the hotel very early in the morning to walk to St. There-
sa's Church on Grafton Street in Dublin. I was delighted that
I had found a church so close to where I was staying and a
convenient Mass that I could celebrate with the priests there.
The pastor was all ready for me, since the archbishop had told
him that I was coming. What a surprise it was when he told
me that in Ireland on that day they were celebrating the great
feast of Saint Brigid. Saint Brigid is one of the most popular
of the Irish saints and actually was the name of one of my
grandmothers. For that reason, I always had a special devotion

to her and, because she is not on the calendar of saints in our country, this was the first time I could offer Mass in her honor. As I offered the Mass, for all of you, as always, it was a special gift to me to be reminded of my family's roots in Ireland.

Two days later, I was in London celebrating Mass in the chapel of the archbishop of Westminster's house. Cardinal Murphy-O'Connor is an old friend of mine and had offered me hospitality for the one day that I was in Great Britain. As he invited me to be the celebrant of the Mass that morning, he told me that in England, because of the ancient and venerable history of the Church there, I would be celebrating the feast of the three early archbishops of Canterbury who followed Saint Augustine, the apostle of England.

Once again, how delighted and surprised I was to learn that the names of these three saintly archbishops were Lawrence, Dunston, and Theodore! I had heard of Saint Theodore, the fourth archbishop of Canterbury, but never had an opportunity to celebrate Mass in his honor until that day. Here, in this historic chapel, I was touching history once again and in such a personal way. It was something of a special reminder that I should work harder to become a holy archbishop, too. I'll never be like my namesake, but like all of us, I must continue to strive to grow in God's grace so that I might serve you better even as Saint Theodore of Canterbury served his people.

Two little moments in my life reminding me of God's presence. You have them, too. Look for them and thank God for them. They really show that he is thinking of you.

If the World Loves You
May 13, 2004

There is a saying that has its roots in the tenth chapter of St. John's Gospel. It reminds us that we should not look for the love of the world, but strive only to find God's will and do it with all our hearts. There is a good chance that if we are never criticized by others, we have missed the mark of being faithful to the teachings of the Gospel. If the world loves you, you are probably always saying what the world wants to hear.

In light of that simple but very profound truth, I hope you were not upset at the criticism of your archbishop in an advertisement that has appeared in some places lately. I appreciate the zeal of those folks who are critical, but I do not agree with them, and during my recent *Ad Limina* visit to Rome, it was clear that so many of the highest authorities in the Church are in agreement with my position.

As you probably know, I have had a consistent position on the obligations of every member of our Catholic family to follow the teaching of the Church on the gravely important issues of our time. Certainly, the defense of life from the moment of conception to the moment that God calls us home is the primary of these issues, since without life no other human rights are possible. I have also been consistent in teaching, as our Holy Father does, that the care of the poor, the weak, and the stranger, as well as the protection of peace and justice must be an essential part of our commitment as Catholics.

The disagreement that I have with the folks who are annoyed at me is that I disagree that in this instance we should use denial of the Eucharist as a public sanction. As a priest and bishop, I do not favor a confrontation at the altar rail with the sacred Body of the Lord Jesus in my hand. There are apparently those who would welcome such a conflict, for good reasons, I am sure, or for political ones, but I would not.

At the same time, I feel it is important for each of us to understand our own personal responsibility when it comes to receiving the Eucharist. I realize that in modern times, perhaps even more since the 1960s, some Catholics have fallen into a new and false understanding of the blessed sacrament, one that does not recognize the awesome nature of the Eucharist and our need for great respect in the way we approach it. In the days when we had to fast from all food and drink from the previous midnight in order to receive Holy Communion, our sense of the wonder of the Eucharist was enhanced. When the Church, in order to encourage us to partake of the sacrament, relaxed those rules, some people may have incorrectly concluded that the rule about being in the state of grace was relaxed as well. Maybe the presence of this controversy is itself a special grace to give us a chance to clarify what our personal dispositions must be in order to receive the Eucharist worthily.

In this light it may be good to recall Pope John Paul II's words to the bishops of the United States during his second visit to our country in 1987. The Holy Father spoke very clearly as follows: "It is sometimes reported that a large number of Catholics today do not adhere to the teaching of the Church on a number of questions, notably sexual and conjugal morality, divorce, and remarriage. Some are reported as not accepting the Church's clear position on abortion . . . it is sometimes claimed that dissent from the magisterium is totally compatible with being a 'good Catholic' and poses no obstacle to the reception of the sacraments. This is a grave error that challenges the teaching office of the bishops of the United States and elsewhere. I wish to encourage you in the love of Christ to address this situation courageously in your pastoral ministry. . . ."

I am asking the *Catholic Standard* to reprint the statement about the worthy reception of the Eucharist that appears in the missalettes and that was authorized by the United States Conference of Catholic Bishops. Basically, it places on the individual Catholic the need to make a judgment as to whether he or she can properly come to receive Communion. One must not be conscious of any serious sin that has not been absolved in the sacrament of Penance. One must be striving to live as a good Catholic, keeping the commandments of God and of the Church, especially those two great commandments to love God and neighbor. This would exclude from Communion anyone who would hate his neighbor or harm his neighbor, in particular when that neighbor is a little unborn baby in its mother's womb. This doctrine by which the Church places a particular personal responsibility concerning the decision to approach the altar on each individual, protects the holiness of the Eucharist, and challenges its children to holiness as well. It places the decision to approach the altar on the informed conscience of the individual Catholic—informed by the truth of our teachings—and, therefore, each one of us must not presume to approach Holy Communion if we are not, in our informed conscience, already with the Lord and in Communion with the teachings of his Church.

This is what the Church teaches and, as your bishop and your servant and your friend, this is what I teach, too. Thinking of you, as I come back home to Washington, I pray that each one of us will never approach this most holy sacrament of the Eucharist without the necessary disposition to receive its awesome grace.

Now for the Good News
May 20, 2004

I have two things to wish to thank the Lord for. The first, of course, is for our new bishop whom I will be privileged to ordain on July 2 in our great Cathedral of Saint Matthew. The second is that our much beloved Bishop Lenny Olivier will be continuing to stay with us in his now beginning years of retirement.

Let me say a word about Bishop Olivier first. I have known him for many years, both through Cardinal Hickey and especially through Bishop Joe Francis, who was my auxiliary bishop in Newark and a dear friend and fellow religious of Bishop Lenny. It was, however, actually only since I came to Washington that I was really able to get to see this wise, warm, and holy man up close. Until his retirement, also just announced, he was the senior active bishop in our country. His service to our people here in the Archdiocese of Washington has been a labor of love since the day he arrived. He has made so many friends here through his gentle humor and cheerful graciousness that his departure to other climes would have been similar to a national catastrophe. Thank God, Bishop Olivier will be staying with us, hopefully for many, many years.

Bishop-elect Martin Holley, like Bishop Olivier, comes to us from the South. He brings the same graciousness and deep faith that has always characterized the Church in that part of the world. I had not met him until a few days ago, but I already feel that I have known him for years.

He will fit right in and become part of the team whose one goal is to serve God's people here in the district and in the five counties of Maryland that are entrusted to us. Above all, he will be a pastoral bishop, concerned about the poor, zealous in the work for vocations, experienced in the spiritual care of young people. We are all very blessed to have him and I pray that all of you will take him to your hearts. I have no doubt that in a short while he will always be thinking of you, even as all of us who serve the Church of Washington always do.

Please thank God with me for this great gift that he has given us through our beloved Holy Father, Pope John Paul II.

The Sound of Music?
May 27, 2004

I was originally planning to do this column on one of the more serious themes that we ought to talk about someday. Or perhaps I should be writing about vocations and ordinations since this is that time of the year. Well, while I was trying to decide what to write about, I became aware of a haunting melody—even though it all seemed to be on one note— that was coming to me from the trees. I figured that next week I could write about vocations, but now I had to share my thoughts on our new visitors, the ever-present singing cicadas! I don't recall where I was throughout the summer of 1987, but wherever it was, I am sort of glad I wasn't here in Washington!

Right now I'm at home, here in the district. I live four floors up and there is hardly a tree anywhere near by, but the drone of these charming little fellows is as loud as if I were walking through the park. (Maybe the rain will turn them off?) Now that they are starting to fly around, the stories are beginning to multiply. Most of these tales have to do with their effect on animals, like the poor little dog who was chased by a couple of them and ended up in a baby carriage, or the cat who thought to escape them and climbed up a tree only to be totally surrounded by a bunch of them! (Only Garfield in the comics could handle that kind of a situation.) Little kids have different reactions to them. Some find them fascinating. These are the future scientists. Others find them horrible. These are probably the future landscapers. Yet everybody has something to say about them because you can't not notice that they are around.

The point of the column is a simple one. Whatever we are trying to do—even writing a column to you—the sound of these creatures is ever present. Almost wherever we are outdoors, we can hear their humming or whatever that sound really is. I guess we get used to it after a while and will miss it for a few days after they are gone, but while it's here, it is a factor in our lives. The wonderful thing is that God's voice is always there, too. Wherever we are, indoors or outdoors, the Lord is always speaking to us. His voice is not complaining about our faults, never interfering with our freedom of will, but he is present in our lives; in a sense, like the humming sounds of these days. The difficulty is that we have grown so used to him that we often tend not to pay attention.

Wouldn't it be wonderful if we could become always conscious of his voice? It is the real sound of music with a melody like no other. It is the catchiest tune we will ever hear because it is written just for each one of us. Unlike the hum of the cicadas, it doesn't distract us from what we are doing unless what we are doing is bad for our life. The sound of God's voice calls us to happiness, to joy, to the real things of life, to friendship, to love, and ultimately to salvation. Every time I hear the voice of these little ugly visitors calling out from the trees that they are there, I start thinking of you and hoping that this sound may really be a special grace, giving you and me a chance to remember that God is here, too, and reminding you and me of his presence, not just every seventeen years, but always.

The Priesthood of Jesus Christ
June 3, 2004

Not too long ago, I questioned one of the young men of the archdiocese who is applying to the seminary in order to study for the priesthood in our local Church. I asked him why he was looking forward to serving as a priest in these days when scandal and media bias against the clergy was so abounding. He looked me in the eye and said, "Obviously, it's not for the prestige. It isn't there anymore. And it's not for the money—that was never there—but in these days the people need more priests who will serve them and love them and be balanced, normal, happy men striving to become holy and serving with joy. That's what I want to try to be."

You can't find a better answer than that: balanced, normal, happy men striving to become holy and serving with joy. Every day I pray that God will give us men like that. They don't have to be saints yet or rocket scientists or even the most talented men on the block—although many of them really are—but if they fit that young seminarian's description, they will be great priests and great servants of God's people.

Last Saturday, I ordained eight men like that. Oh, how I wish I had eighty rather than eight! But these eight will serve you well. Pray for them and for the others who will be coming along in the years ahead.

The liturgy of priestly ordination is beautiful and powerful. For those who witness it for the first time, it is always unforgettable. When the men to be ordained prostrate themselves before the altar during the Litany of the Saints, you can see their total gift of themselves to a loving God. In the imposition of my hands on their heads—followed by the same gesture by all the priests who are present—both the powerful coming of the Holy Spirit and the unity of the priests serving in a diocese is highlighted and made present before our eyes.

As they take off their deacons' stoles and put on the chasuble of the priesthood, they may look different—and, indeed, in the deepest spiritual sense they are—but they are still our sons, our brothers, and our friends. But now, they are chosen to serve us as never before in the things which pertain to God. Priestly ordinations for me are both wonderful and terrifying because by my action as a bishop these men are empowered to celebrate the Eucharist, forgive our sins and bring their lives as a total offering to the service of the Church. No one appreciates more than I the powerful role of the laity in the Church. The Second Vatican Council has made that so clear. But the more our lay men and women appreciate their responsibility in the Church, the more they will need priests to serve them and to guide and sanctify them along the road to eternal life. Thinking of you, as I pray for more good and holy priests to come from God's people, I ask you to pray for that same intention with me.

"The Sacred Body of the Lord Jesus in My Hand"
June 10, 2004

A few weeks ago, in my column on the USCCB Task Force on Relations with Catholic Politicians, I wrote that I was not in favor of a confrontation at the altar with the sacred Body of the Lord Jesus in my hand. That column has been widely circulated and some have found it very helpful, while others less so, but when all is said and done, maybe the most important words I used that day were those words in which I spoke of the Holy Eucharist as "the sacred Body of the Lord Jesus in my hand." Whether folks would agree with my own position or not, many were struck by that expression. There are many who have said to me that it made them think more deeply.

As I look back on it, I know that I chose the words carefully, but I did not foresee the importance that my choice of words might have had. It would not have been the same if I had spoken of the consecrated host, or the Eucharistic bread, or just Holy Communion or any number of other alternatives. It was precisely in the stark reminder of what Communion really is that makes us stop and consider what it is that each of us believes. The host I hold in my hand looks and feels and tastes like ordinary bread. It is not ordinary bread. It is truly the Body of Jesus Christ in sacramental form.

Over the last few decades, many Catholics have sadly moved away from the mystery of the Eucharist. Sometimes under the pressures of the secular media or of friends whose faith is weak or nonexistent, they have adopted a pseudo-anthropological or "politically correct" approach to the great sacrament of the altar. They call it merely a symbol of the presence of Christ, or something reminding us of the presence of Christ, or a poetic way of speaking about the Lord. All of this is false and harmful and it obscures the whole point of our Eucharistic faith. It is indeed the Lord, the sacred Body of Jesus.

To believe is to affirm with conviction the truth of a fact or state of affairs. In a religious context, it is one of the strongest words in the English language and, in the case of the Holy Eucharist, it is most appropriate and necessary. There are few things in our faith that are clearer than the teaching of Jesus about his sacred Body and Blood being present in the blessed sacrament. Listen to his words: "This is my body given for you . . . this cup is the new covenant in my blood poured out for you" (Lk 22:19, 20). "If you do not eat the flesh of the son of man and drink his blood you have no life in you" (Jn 6:53). Those who heard him speak were well aware of his meaning. Some of them walked away because they would not accept it. Remember how he asked his apostles, "What about you? Do you want to go away too?" (Jn 6:67). And one of the truly great moments of the Gospel is when the apostle responded, "Lord, to whom shall we go? You have the message of eternal life . . ." (Jn 6:68).

I believe that this controversy about receiving the Eucharist will give us two most important gifts. First, it will remind us clearly of what the blessed sacrament really is—the very Body and Blood of Christ. Secondly, it will remind us that we should not approach the altar if we are not properly disposed by the way we live our lives. Unless we are deeply in communion with the Lord and his Church, we should not receive his sacred Body and Blood in Holy Communion. In my responsibility to teach the good news of Jesus here in our local Church, I'm always thinking of you and praying that I will teach it well.

Peace in the Holy Land
June 17, 2004

I realize that I have written about peace in the Holy Land before. It is something that has always troubled me since the Christmas of 1971 when I went to Jerusalem with Cardinal Cooke. The war in Vietnam was going on at that time and the cardinal was preparing to make his annual Christmas-time visit to the men and women in the armed forces in his responsibility as military ordinary of the United States. He decided first to make a pilgrimage to Bethlehem to beg of the Prince of Peace an end to that terrible conflict that took the lives of so many young Americans, as well as Vietnamese.

Bethlehem, with its refugee camps, and Jerusalem, with its tensions, presented a picture that I would never forget.

As the years go on, and the attempt to find a just and lasting solution to the problems of the Holy Land seem to fade, a new and more terrible element enters the picture, the scourge of terrorism with its acceleration of attacks against the innocent. A cycle of repeated violence has begun in recent years and so much blood has been spilled on both sides. A suicide attack by terrorists kills Israeli passersby and innocent children and in the reprisal a neighborhood is destroyed and other innocents are killed. Each day it gets worse instead of better and no end appears in sight.

Last year, President Bush presented a "road map" solution that could start to move the region along the road to peace with justice. Many of us, myself included, applauded that initiative and urged our government to move forward. Suddenly, it was shelved right at the time when it seemed most likely to start the process of peace rolling. I'm not enough of a diplomat or a global strategist to know all the reasons why, but I am a pastor who sees people killed and homes destroyed and knows that there has to be a better way. Sometimes a government official will say, "We must wait until there is peace on both sides before we start to work for peace." Doesn't that really beg the question and more seriously, doesn't it give the veto over peace to the terrorists? If you say you cannot start substantive conversation until the violence ends, aren't you giving a veto power over peace directly to the hands of those who do not want peace?

I believe that Secretary Powell sees this clearly, but the decision to wait until everything is calm before we even try the road map is wrong. We are all on the same page, but some of us believe this is the time to turn that page and press on for a just peace now. Achieving just peace in the Holy Land may indeed also be one of the major keys to ending the violence in Iraq and other parts of the Middle East.

I don't often write you on subjects like this, but as I think of so many people caught in the labyrinth of violence that has gone on for decades, I was thinking of you and hoping that you will join my prayers for the peace of Jerusalem.

Unity
June 24, 2004

One of the most quoted statements of Jesus in the scriptures is his call for unity in the Gospel of Saint John. He prayed to his heavenly Father that all might be one. This prayer is at the heart of the Catholic Church's outreach in ecumenism to our sisters and brothers in other Christian Churches, as well as to our efforts to continue to build bridges of understanding and love with the Jewish community, with Islam, and indeed with every other community of faith.

Unity is such a key concept, not just in religion, but everywhere else in our world. The fact that the founders of our nation chose to call this nation the United States speaks volumes about our understanding of what kind of a republic we wanted to be. The sad tragedy of war between the states challenged that fundamental idea of our existence. Today, the organization that seeks to keep the peace and heal the problems of our world is dubbed "United Nations"—another example of how unity is such a longed-for goal in our society. Unity brings the strength that leads to peace and stability and ultimately even brings happiness and progress.

I have just returned from the bishops' meeting in Denver. This is basically the usual gathering of the Catholic bishops of our country each June, except that every five years or so the meeting is longer and focuses in a spirit of reflection on a particular pastoral need. This year, as you know, one of the points on the agenda was the question of Holy Communion being given to those in public life who oppose the teaching of the Church, especially with regard to human life and abortion.

Since I serve as the chairman of the task force studying this question, I was very involved throughout the discussions. In my words to the bishops, as I presented the final draft statement, I said that there are times when the values of manifesting and promoting unity may outweigh other considerations and that this may be one of those critical moments.

I went on to assure the bishops that the statement protected the rights of those bishops who felt the pastoral need in their own dioceses to take a certain stand with regard to Catholic politicians and the Holy Eucharist, but at the same time the statement makes clear that the majority of the bishops—who do not judge such actions as necessary—are perfectly within the pastoral and canonical traditions of the Church as they follow another course of action. Ultimately, the statement reaffirms the absolute unity of our teaching in condemnation of abortion and all attacks against the life and dignity of the human person.

The fact that the statement was overwhelmingly approved by a vote of 183 to 6 makes it clear that this is truly the teaching of the bishops of the United States.

I know that you have seen and heard other positions raised sometimes loudly in our Catholic society. For that reason, I was thinking of you and happy that the position which your own bishop has taken has been so overwhelmingly ratified.

Brilliance
July 1, 2004

I could have entitled this column "I wish I had said that!" because it's about the many people around us whose wisdom or skill or grace makes us stand back and admire. The older I get, the more I am fascinated by people who have great thoughts or great ways of expressing them or whose gift of graciousness and love just leaves us filled with awe.

You can meet such people anywhere and everywhere if you know how to look and listen. They show up—thankfully, in some abundance—when men and women of faith gather for a Mass or a meeting. You find them in government—and not always in the highest leadership posts—you recognize them in the arts—where their exquisite insights mold words into a poem of beauty or a discussion of elegance, in the sciences where innovative genius erupts into a new and fascinating form of physics and chemistry and where the once-rejected ideas of a limited past somehow become the seeds of new adventures.

All this is wonderful and a testament to the way God made us all, but my point is still to be made. I find these extraordinary gifts are equally present if we would look for them right around us and they are able to sustain, motivate, and challenge us every day of our lives. Have you never thought when some relation or friend would come up with a statement that said it all with class and insight, "I wish I had said that!" Have you never been stopped in your tracks by a most profound comment coming from the lips of a child? Have you never been touched by a line in a country ballad that made you hum the melody all day long, not just because of the tune, but because it expressed what was so deeply in your own heart?

Genius or wisdom or prophecy and grace are all around us. They are the special gifts of a God who lets us catch a glimpse of his loving presence in the things of our every day. I put the title "Brilliance" to this column, not just because it reminds me of the wonderful insights and talents that people around us really have, but because those special moments light up the ordinary give-and-take of our lives. We need to look for these brilliant gems in a world that is too often filled with clouds of dark grey and the problems of getting through the trials of life. The moments of great insight are like moments of great affection. They really are present in each one of us, but we must make ourselves more aware of them and more fascinated by their frequency. That's why we are so special and that's why we are so loved by God.

As I watch you at Mass, or at other times of prayer, as I listen to stories of your kindness to other people and your care of all your own, I am thinking of you and thanking God for the brilliance that is truly around us and that God has given so abundantly to this local Church.

Time Marches On
July 8, 2004

You probably won't remember my funny remark three and a half years ago when I first arrived in Washington as a servant of this local Church. I quipped then that, as everybody always says, "Life begins at seventy!" I find myself this week at another special moment in my life. This week I turn seventy-four and thus begin my seventy-fifth year, at the end of which I am required to send in my resignation to the Holy Father. Now, one is never sure when it will be accepted, since very often cardinals have been asked to stay on for a time beyond their seventy-fifth birthday and this, of course, could happen again.

It is still a bit traumatic to realize that one is just a year away from sending in that letter! Two questions come to my mind—and to the minds of those close to me, like all of you are—when I ponder this fact of life. The first is what do I want to do in the time that's left and the second is what will I do afterward? Of course, the afterward is always in God's hands and every time I pray for my classmates who have died, I realize how one's hold on this life becomes more tenuous as the years go by.

I think that I've told you in the past that whenever a new bishop comes to a diocese, he should have two goals for when he leaves. Will he leave enough great priests to care for the people and will he leave them with sufficient resources to do their work well? It is in answering that first goal that we have all tried to encourage priestly vocations so much—and, with God's blessings, with some success since we now do have close to sixty fine men studying in our seminaries. With your help and your prayers, we need to keep working on this with hope and confidence in the years ahead.

The second goal is the reason for our upcoming Forward in Faith capital campaign that will, please God, give us the resources to continue and strengthen our apostolates in education, in the care of the poor, and in pastoral services. I am so moved by the generosity of our folks already, since so far the quiet phase of our campaign has done so well and the seven parishes that are in the pilot phase have all gone well over goal and each one will keep at home for their own parochial needs many tens of thousands of dollars! May the Lord continue to bless us with that same generosity in all our parishes!

As to what I might do after retirement, it's really too early to have any solid plans. Just please pray for me that I'll keep trying to do what God wants me to do now and that I'll try to do it better. I'll let you know how my planning goes, of course, since you know that whatever happens, I'm always going to be thinking of you.

Pulling Together
July 15, 2004

I'm down at the Jersey Shore, taking my week's vacation. I had to go to Rome for a meeting on third world debt sponsored by the Pontifical Council for Justice and Peace, of which I am a member. I added a day for some visits to take care of some business in Rome and returned last Saturday for a family Baptism. Two little grandnephews were waiting to become Christians, one of whom was given Theodore as his middle name, and so I had no choice but to be there! Then I came down to the shore where some friends from my New Jersey days were kind enough to lend me their home on Barnegat Bay for the week.

This morning, as I looked over this picturesque little "inland sea," lying quiet and peaceful in a steady but refreshing rain, I saw a couple of fellows paddling along in a kayak. They were trying to figure a way to paddle together, but try as they did, they never could get it right and for a time the kayak kept going round and round in circles. I was tempted to call out, "Just pull together and you'll be fine," but I knew they couldn't hear me.

I think it was Benjamin Franklin who said to the other members of the Continental Congress at the start of the American Revolution: "If we don't all hang together, we will all hang separately." It was a clear and powerful call to unity without which the thirteen original English colonies would never have found a way to become a new nation as the United States of America.

You all know where I'm going with these stories. In our country, in every family, in the Church, we will never move forward unless we all pull together. There is, of course, room for differing opinions about most things in life, but the basics, the foundations of our culture and our society must always be present. Our faith, the love of God, the teaching of the Gospel, the golden rule, the law of charity—these are always going to be the essentials of our lives. They provide the glue that holds us all together, the solid steel on which our lives are built. Without them, we have no unity and without such unity our world can come crashing down.

And so, as I am thinking of you, I pray for that unity in this archdiocese, in our country and wherever good people gather together and I ask the Lord to keep us together when the going gets tough that we may always know how to pull together as one family in the Lord.

The Wasteland
July 22, 2004

Do you remember that years ago someone spoke of television as a "vast wasteland"? I had never really believed that since I have seen so many wonderful programs on TV over the years. Well, I had some time last week when I was on vacation—and it was raining so much of the time!—to watch television more than I can do when I'm at home. Usually, I watch the news or the History Channel when I get on my treadmill—and I confess that I don't get to do that exercise every day. So, it was with something of a surprise that I watched television last week.

It really hit home. What has happened to American morality? Have the great values of married life, responsibility, chastity, and respect completely disappeared? Is what is portrayed
on the TV screen really a mirror of what is happening in our
families, in our homes, schools, and offices? Maybe my head
is in the ground like an ostrich, but I can't believe that what
is presented as an example of ordinary American life truly
resembles what actually takes place in most of our society.

Many prime time programs can't seem to fill a half hour
without drugs and infidelity, casual sex, and broken promises. I've been a priest for forty-six years and I think I know
something about the reality of sinfulness in the world, but I
also know a lot about good people, mothers and fathers living
heroic lives of virtue and young people striving to follow a
way of life that can truly lead them to happiness. So much of
TV seems not to be trying to capture the reality of life, but
to change it by portraying as natural and normal behavior
which—although we know it exists in our society—is not
and cannot be the norm for the way we live our lives.

When infidelity and selfishness and a lifestyle of total
promiscuity are portrayed pretty regularly as the norm of our
actions, the danger is that we could all start thinking that
they are the way that most people live and are expected to
live. When values of honesty and responsibility, of faithfulness and respect for others are belittled or only portrayed by
characters who are weak or strange, we are getting a message
that is really way off the mark. And if we watch these TV sce-
narios of violence and promiscuous sex a lot, we can start to
think that this is the only way to live. The great danger is that
we really can take these things for granted and believe that
they are the ordinary way of life. The channels of television
can become the teachers of morality. God save us from allowing them to set an unworthy norm for truly human life.

I'm glad I don't have time to watch much TV if what I
saw is the norm. Thinking of you, I hope you watch it with

discretion and care not to let the "wasteland" be your teacher on what is right and wrong. Obviously, I surely don't want to condemn the good programs on television, but I was very troubled to see that there seems to be a certain sense of a new morality that is not what we truly believe as the way we ought to live.

The Presence of God
July 29, 2004

When I was young, in some schools of the Christian brothers, a student had the responsibility of calling out at specific moments in the day, "Remember that we are in the presence of God." What a great tradition that was! How wonderful it would be if in the hurly-burly of our lives as parents, as workers, as professional people—and as priests—someone would remind us every once in a while that we live in the presence of God.

It would certainly cut down on sin, and on unkindness and selfishness, and probably on violence and anger, as well. Wouldn't it be great if we all had a reminder at fixed moments in our day that we are never really alone and that God's grace and love and his forgiveness is always there, always present, always active in our lives?

When I am really conscious of God's presence with me, it changes the way I think and the way I act. I don't lose my temper. I swallow the harsh word that I was going to say when something didn't go my way. I don't let things "get to me" as they do at other times. I worry less and smile more. I'm probably easier to get along with than usual, and all this simply because I sense the presence of God.

Wouldn't it be great if in families, one of the children was assigned each day to call out "the presence of God" every couple of hours, to call the other members of the family to a few seconds' reminder of the reality of the Lord's presence in the home and in our hearts? It's hard to do it in a workplace, I admit, but I have an idea for that, too. I fixed my digital watch to beep every hour and that little call to attention of the time passing by reminds me also that God is here and now is with me. It helps me through the work of the day and the quiet of the evening. I don't notice it at every hour, I admit, but as often as I do, I think of Him who guides me and who loves me and carries me along. (In the interest of always being honest with you, I ought to tell you that it wasn't me who fixed the watch, but my secretary, since you all know that I am very mechanically challenged, to say the least.)

One last note about God's presence. Of all the places in our life, he is present most powerfully in the Eucharist. Unfortunately, being human beings, we can come into his Church without even acknowledging his presence there. Before we even make our act of reverence to the tabernacle, we sometimes wave to a neighbor, become fascinated by Mrs. So-and-So's new hat, wonder who that is sitting with Sally, trying to see if the family next door is coming today, plan our "escape" to reach the parking lot before the crowd, check who is advertising in the bulletin, and become anxious lest the Mass make us late for the soccer game—need I go on? If you see yourself anywhere in that description, it's time for you to call out quietly to yourself, "I am in the presence of God." I'll wager that in a few seconds you will find yourself more peaceful, less troubled, and joyfully conscious that he whose sacred presence is enclosed in the tabernacle before you is every moment thinking of you with love and grace beyond all telling.

Twenty-Four Hours
August 5, 2004

It was a beautiful summer day. The kind that warms you both physically and spiritually without excessive humidity or the constant threat of a dark thundercloud overhead. It was the kind of day that makes you feel good about life and helps you to forget for a moment all the cares and worries we all carry around with us.

But it was also a day on which a young teenager with her whole life ahead of her was killed in a drive-by shooting, a day in which another youngster was viciously beaten up by a rival gang, a day on which a drug sale to young people trapped another group of teenagers in a cycle of addiction from which some might never escape. That same day left many memories. Some remembered how nice it was to be alive. The following day's news told us that for too many people that day would always bring back other kinds of memories, those of violence and of evil and of death.

As Catholics who have been taught to love our neighbor, we are caught up in the mystery of hatred and violence and greed, which is all around us. We recognize it and we regret it and deep down we know that we must try to do something about it.

I am so grateful to those of us who work so effectively, sometimes against all odds it seems, to make a dent in the growing violence of some of our neighborhoods and the really terrifying mindlessness of many gangs. Our parishes and schools in the inner city, our Catholic Charities' programs, our Spanish Catholic Center, and innumerable other agencies of the Archdiocese of Washington work very hard to bring the peace and security that are so very necessary for families to function and for little children to grow up in peace.

Thank God there are signs of hope like the youth recreation center, for which I was able to break ground last month in Anacostia, and our projected Mother Teresa Center in Langley Park, but it will take all of us working together to turn around this problem. It will take us working with other religious communities, other faiths, and with so many private and public agencies to get to the root of the problem and to turn it around. We know that these problems are rooted in poverty, which causes family instability, which leads to the despair, which is the father of anger and the mother of violence. Truly, only good, solid families where father and mother accept their responsibilities with love and courage can ultimately turn our community and this world around. As I am thinking of you and of your families, I encourage you to make sure that you are always very present to your own children, that they know how much you love them, and that they even understand that love will sometimes come with a "no" rather than a "yes" and with a mutual openness that cuts down on sad surprises.

The Quiet Car
August 12, 2004

I was on my way back to Washington from the episcopal ordination of the two new auxiliary bishops of Newark, both very fine priests with whom I had the privilege of working during my fifteen years as archbishop there. To get to Newark from Dallas, where the annual convention of the Knights of Columbus was taking place, I had to leave at 4:30 in the morning. Thank God, the planes were all pretty much on time and so I arrived right at the beginning of the ceremony. (If you'll allow me some pride as archbishop of Washington— I was really delighted that three of the seminarians who had been chosen to take part in the episcopal ordination Mass were Washington men studying at Immaculate Conception Seminary at Seton Hall for service here in our archdiocese. The fact that three of our own young fellows were chosen for such an important ceremony really can make us all very proud!)

To get back to my story, I stayed in New Jersey overnight, having had dinner with some of my priest friends from the Archdiocese of Newark, and then took the 8:15 train back home. The train came right on time on Thursday morning and I headed for the "quiet car." This is the car, usually up front right after the first-class coach, where cell phones and loud talking are discouraged. Folks like me who do work or get some praying in during our travel prefer the quiet car, since it allows us to think and work and pray along the way. (In the usual interest of full disclosure, sometimes I do read a mystery novel on the way, but last Thursday I just had too much to do.)

A couple came in at Metro Park. They apparently knew each other from business and had met as the train pulled in. I guess they were talking and apparently didn't realize that they had entered the quiet car. As soon as they were seated— unfortunately, just a row ahead of me—the lady made a cell phone call to her office and gave instructions to her associates in a very loud voice. Following that, she began to explain to the man who was with her and then began a long and rather loud conversation about business, family, and a lot of things that the rest of us were not really that anxious to know. You could feel the rising uneasiness of the people sitting around them. Some of us looked around to see if we could change our seats for a different section of the car where it would be quiet. Others looked around and hoped that one of the conductors would walk through, notice these two folks in their animated conversation, and admonish them. The conductor did walk through, but another passenger asked him a question and so he did not become aware of the talkative folks down the aisle. Every time the train stopped at a station, we passengers looked up with hope that our two friends would be leaving the train. Unfortunately, there was no luck and they seemed to be with us until the end of the line.

I wondered if I should say something to them myself, but I held back not wanting to become involved in a dispute. Finally, at Wilmington, the man sitting next to me could hold back no longer and he went up to them to complain. They protested that they didn't realize it was the quiet car and they remained very still for the rest of the journey. You could almost feel the release of tension all around with everybody smiling a thank you at the man who brought it about.

Two lessons for me and for all of us. The first is the need we all have to take a stand on behalf of what is right. Of course, we have to do it in the proper way, with prudence and courtesy and love. But when we do it that way, it can make a difference in our immediate environment and even beyond as we affect other people's attitudes and lives. Secondly, it taught me again the wonderful value of quiet. As our world seems to find a way to become more and more frenetic and demanding, the basic human need for a little time to be silent and undisturbed becomes more and more evident. I worry about the teenagers and their ever-present multidecibel music. Oh, I realize that it may be needed to get them through a difficult school day, happily moving along with a melody. But doesn't it have to be sometimes balanced with a certain amount of quiet time and once-in-a-while periods of reflective silence and even some moments for deep conversation with God, if not also maybe even a few friendly conversations with parents?

All these thoughts come from a crowded railroad car now more peaceful because one man spoke up, thus giving me a chance once again to be thinking of you.

Charley and Me
August 19, 2004

I spent a lot of time with Charley last week. At times he was an exciting companion. From time to time, however, he caused me some anxiety as I watched his dark clouds approach and cover the horizon. At other times he was just an inconvenience, such as the presence of a shaggy dog that has just come out of the pond and seems to be waiting until he gets close to your good trousers before he shakes the water off.

Charley was more of a concern in Southern Maryland, where I still am as I write this, concluding my annual visitation to which I always look forward with joy. Low-lying roads that might flood and trees that could fall and block a country road are always hazards that I worry about as I travel to the different churches for Mass. Thank God, by the time Charley reached us in St. Mary's County, he didn't do any more terrible damage and we were left pretty much just with rain and wind.

My heart goes out to the folks in Florida who were so badly hurt by the force of a Category four hurricane. It reminds all of us of our fragility in spite of all we have learned and developed in these modern days. Let us pray for our sisters and brothers in the south who have suffered so much. Maybe we will be able to help them through Catholic Charities as their needs become clearer.

This year's visitation in Southern Maryland was good, as always, in spite of Charley. It has given me an opportunity to visit fifteen parishes and to spend some time with our priests and people. It also gave me a chance to see what is taking place in these three southern counties—their development, their progress, and their problems. (I did get about five hours on the boat and I hope for one more chance. I also got two good quick swims between the rainstorms, not to mention all the crab cakes, stuffed ham, and other wonderful dishes!)

You all know how much I love to go to Southern Maryland. I wish all our people could get a chance to visit this beautiful area and to see its great Catholic history and its continuing active Catholic life. In St. Mary's County, some of our faithful folks with a deep sense of Catholic roots are rebuilding—brick by brick—the first Catholic church erected in the thirteen colonies. When completed in the mid-1600s, it was the tallest and grandest building in our part of the world, a tribute to the place that religion had in the lives of our Catholic ancestors. As I visited the project and spoke with these men and women whose dedication is so inspiring, I was thinking of you and the Catholics of the Church of Washington today and praying that the future will remember us as the builders of a Church that was always alive and joyful and proclaiming the good news with grace.

An Historic Journey
August 26, 2004

When you get to read this, I'll be off on a very interesting and really historic journey. Since I always take you all with me wherever I go, I thought I should share my real excitement as I prepared to leave on Monday. It is a journey of two parts; each in its own way has a special wonder and significance about it and it is both strange and wonderful that I am privileged to be involved.

To give you the basic details, I will fly out on Monday evening to Rome and arrive there on Tuesday morning. I always have enough work to do in the Eternal City and so I will use my time well that first day, visiting the offices in the Vatican. (Most people in that part of Europe take their vacation in August, so I'll probably not be able to see as many as I would like on this visit.) On Wednesday, together with Cardinal Kasper, the president of the Pontifical Council for Christian Unity, I will receive from the hands of the Holy Father the mission of returning the sacred Icon of Kazan to Russia.

The icon will be placed in St. Peter's Basilica for public veneration on Thursday, and then on Friday our delegation will travel to Moscow to present it to the Russian Orthodox Patriarch, Alexy II. The whole story of my involvement in finding the icon, which is one of the most sacred objects of the Russian Church, is too long and too complex to tell you in this short column, but it is truly a grace for me to accompany Our Lady of Kazan to Russia and to ask her prayers for all of us here in the Church of Washington. On Saturday, we will make the formal presentation to the Patriarch and the following day celebrate Mass in the Catholic Cathedral of the Immaculate Conception in the Russian capital. We will return to Rome on Monday and then I'll be back home the following day.

But this is only part of the adventure. As if that is not enough of the sharing in history, during my three days in Rome before leaving for Moscow I have another journey to make. I have been invited by Cardinal Jean-Marie Lustiger, the archbishop of Paris, to celebrate Mass with him on the sixtieth anniversary of the liberation of Paris in World War II. The cardinal is asking the archbishops of Berlin, Westminster (London), Ottawa, and Washington to celebrate together with him in the great Cathedral of Notre Dame on Thursday, August 26, as part of the national observance of that historic day. This, too, is a special grace and I am grateful to God for it. I will be thinking of the men and women in that "greatest generation" of Americans who gave their lives in order to help make Paris free again. I will remember all of your relatives who played a role in that extraordinary struggle.

So, get ready to come with me to Rome and Paris and Moscow! You'll be there with me in all those times of prayer and historic celebration. Pray for me, too, that I acquit myself well to be a credit to this Church of Washington. Be sure that in all these special moments of grace, I'll be thinking of you.

The Field of Martyrs
September 2, 2004

(Moscow) This is Sunday morning and our hosts from the Russian Orthodox Church, who have helped to plan this historic visit for the return to Russia of the sacred Icon of Our Lady of Kazan, have brought us here to a quiet place in the country some miles from Moscow to show us the site of one of the great tragedies in the modern history of this extraordinary land. Like Srebrenica in Bosnia and the only-now discovered killing fields of Saddam Hussein's Iraq, this is a place of the martyrs.

It was here in the 1930s that Stalin launched his great attack against religion as a part of his misguided determination to remake Russia and the entire Soviet state. Here, in a ditch one hundred meters long and four meters wide, seven bishops and hundreds of priests were buried where they fell from the bullets of special troops recruited for that purpose.

In this place, clergy, religious, and lay people, whose faith was somehow a threat to their Communist rulers, were killed and quickly buried. There may have been thousands of them altogether, yet still a small part of the twenty million people of the Soviet Union who met their death in the 1930s.

I asked the guide how those were chosen from death among the other priests of the country. There was really no one universal reason. Some were killed because they were heroes who spoke out against the God-less regime. Others may have offended an official during a sermon or through some other innocent slight. Still others were caught up in the different roundups of believers without any cause except that they were believers. Part of this madness was the anxiety of knowing that your time could come any day at any time and you had no chance to plead against it.

As I walk around this holy ground, the same questions form in my mind and I cannot drive them out. What would I have done if I were the priest in a village of Russia at this time? What would you have done if you were among the faithful there and then? Would we have been brave and so committed to God and the Church and shouted out our faith like the martyrs of old? Would we have closed our eyes with a confident prayer that God would be with us to shepherd us through the night, or would we have broken under a burden that we could not bear? As I walk around the unmarked graves of this cemetery, I do not seek the answers, only to reflect on the questions and to thank God for his marvelous gift of hope.

Almost half a world away, I was thinking of you and of the extraordinary blessing that God has given us all, as well as asking him to continue to keep each one of us in the palm of his hand.

Questions and Answers
September 9, 2004

One of the things I worry most about, as servant of this Church of Washington, is whether our Catholic people really understand the faith that we profess. There are so many reasons why this is a problem in our country at this time. First of all, the number of our faithful who have had the benefit of a Catholic school education has gone down considerably in the last two generations. Secondly, catechetics has often not been able to keep pace with this resulting increase in numbers as well as the new emphasis and insights we gained from the Second Vatican Council. Thirdly, our culture—always tending to be hostile to the Gospel and its teaching—has played down the importance of knowing one's faith and our Catholic people have frequently been trapped in that web of downplaying religion in favor of a secular society.

Just between us, are you up for a little quiz? You won't get marked on it and it won't affect your standing in class—or in church. You can take it whether you are in second grade or are a grandparent of a second grader. The questions aren't hard, but I have the suspicion that a lot of our people may not know the answers. Here's the test:

Can you explain what a sacrament is or even what the seven sacraments are? Can you name them? How about the Ten Commandments? Or even the commandments of the Church? Do you know what the three theological virtues are and why they are important in our spiritual lives? Do you remember what Jesus called the greatest commandment? Do you know who wrote the four Gospels or what is the difference between the doctrine of the virgin birth and the doctrine of the Immaculate Conception? Could you name three important results of the Second Vatican Council? Do you know what we mean by Catholic social thought?

If you had some trouble with any of these questions, then you are one of the folks that I am concerned about. Of course, I know that it is more important to love God and your neighbor and to reach out in help to those who are in need than to be able to reply in ready made answers to the questions I just asked. On the other hand, the Lord tells us that we need to have a reason for the things we do in faith, and that reason must be based on our understanding of the Lord's revelation in the Gospel and in the tradition of the Church. Whether we are fourteen or seventy-four, all of us are challenged to act on what we believe and therefore our knowledge of what we believe is so important a motivation for what we do.

What would I recommend? For the youngsters, the answer is, of course, to make sure that they receive religious instruction at home and at their parish or their school, and for adults I'd recommend our archdiocesan program of adult faith formation or at least that all of us get a copy of the *Catechism of the Catholic Church* and determine to read at least a page or two every day. The story of your religion is one of the most moving and meaningful stories you will ever read, and it is truly worth the challenge to learn more about who we are and who is this God who loves us so much. I truly hope that you will think about this seriously. For me, it is a personal thing because when I'm thinking of you I would love to know that you are thinking about the Lord and his Church and learning more about him every day.

Preaching
September 16, 2004

I want to talk about preaching. Many of the priests and deacons of the Archdiocese of Washington are truly fine preachers. I know how they have inspired our people and called them to holiness Sunday after Sunday and I thank God for that special blessing in this local Church. There are two points I would like to make about preaching. The first is that it is really a challenging opportunity, and the second is that the listener has a role to play in it as well.

Last weekend is an example from my own life. I relate it to you not to tell you that I work hard—I really could work much harder—but to give an example of the life that your own priests live week after week. Last weekend I had the privilege of preaching five times and each time a different homily to a different kind of congregation. If you look at my schedule, you'll know that it was a busy weekend even for me. I preached to a high school gathering, a national pilgrimage in the Basilica, the celebration of two hundred years of apostolic service of a religious congregation—the Sisters of Notre Dame de Namur, who established Trinity University, a regular Sunday parish liturgy, and the annual Labor Mass. Each of these homilies needed to be tailored to a different group of hearers. "Boiler plate homilies" won't work and they don't satisfy what God demands of preachers to whom he has given the care of his people.

I am convinced that prayer and preparation are the essential prerequisites of a good homily. I confess—as you already know—that I don't manage to do all this preparation every time I preach. I know I should, every preacher knows he should, but our lives are often crowded with other demands that come from the pastoral care of our faithful. The truth is, however, that the homily at Mass is so very important since it is usually the only opportunity most of our Catholic people have to be catechized and challenged to holiness.

The first essential part of a homily preparation is prayer. Unless the preacher takes the time to ask the Lord in prayer for guidance, his words may be beautiful, but they will not touch the heart. The second element is sufficient preparation. This is really hard when you must preach to different congregations, but deeper insights into the scriptures, the needs of your people, and the teachings of the Church can make the preparation of a homily a source of light for the priest as well as the hearing of it does for the people.

What should the faithful bring to the homily? First of all, the desire to listen and to learn. I tell with a smile, but also with real sorrow, the old story that in certain foreign countries most of the men leave at homily time to stand outside the church for a chat and a smoke while the priest is preaching! God can talk to you through the words of the preacher even if he is not eloquent. Sometimes it is a simple thought, a word, or a phrase that strikes home and changes a misunderstanding, an attitude, or a lifetime! Just as the preacher must pray for guidance and inspiration as he prepares his homily, so should you approach the homily with an open heart and a mind ready to be touched by God.

I always pray that the Lord may use me to say something you need to hear. It would be wonderful if you would also ask him for that special grace. As I am thinking of you every time I sit down to prepare the homily, what a great blessing it would be if you come to listen and reflect that God can use even poorly chosen words to change a life!

"*Unless* . . ."
September 23, 2004

Last week, at the meeting of the Presbyteral Council—the group of priests that is elected by the priests of the archdiocese to help me in the pastoral care of all our people—we were discussing the Eucharist. We are all concerned by the number of our Catholic people who do not attend Mass every Sunday. As you know, last spring, this was a topic that I asked all our parish pastoral councils to discuss, and a committee of the Presbyteral Council had prepared a very thoughtful and helpful summary of that discussion. (I will be sharing that with you shortly.) One of our fine young pastors spoke up at the meeting and told us that he often preaches on the Lord's words: "Unless you eat the flesh of the son of man and drink his blood, you do not have life within you" (Jn 6:53). He reminded us that the Eucharist was not only the way we worship God as he has asked, but the strength of our lives both here on earth and in the life to come. All of us know this, of course, but it is essential to be reminded of it in our lives of prayer and in our struggles to become the holy people God wants us to be.

Unless we come to the altar of the Eucharist, we who are believers will not have the strength we need to serve the Lord well. Obviously, we must have the proper disposition to receive the sacred Body and Blood of Christ. We must be free of grave sin and determined to live in the state of grace. Obviously, as well, those who do not have the faith we have in the Eucharist are not condemned because of their ignorance, but God in his mercy, and always through the glorious resurrection of his Son, somehow will find other ways for them to grow in holiness. But those of us who have faith and know that the bread and wine we see before us after the consecration of the Mass has been really and substantially changed into the Lord's Body and Blood, must constantly hear the words of Christ calling us to the Eucharist and telling us that the strength of this sacrament is the strength we need to live good lives and to find peace and joy in our hearts in spite of the trials of this valley of tears. "Unless you eat the flesh of the son of man and drink his blood, you do not have life within you" (Jn 6:53).

How I would love to see all our Catholic people celebrate Sunday—the Lord's Day—by prayerfully participating in the Mass! Our lives would truly be better and we would live in greater harmony with each other, bear our burdens with greater courage and find the joy of living in the presence of God. When I am thinking of you and praying for you—as I do every day—that is one of the greatest intentions that I bring to the Lord.

Get a Flu Shot!
September 30, 2004

This is not a medical bulletin. It's just a cry of someone who has come down with one awful autumn cold. I was in Germany last week for some meetings and I took the opportunity to go and pray at the Shrine of Our Lady of Altotting, the famous pilgrimage place in Southern Bavaria. We are going to have a replica of that famous Madonna in the Basilica of the National Shrine next year, and I wanted to see it and to spend some time there. It was a time of prayer for our priests and seminarians and, in a particular way, for all of you. Praying for you in these special places is a real blessing for me. I can spend some real quality time undisturbed by all the concerns I have at home, and really talk to the Lord and to his Blessed Mother about the Archdiocese of Washington and about all of you.

Somehow while I was doing all these good things, I came down with a terrible cold—one that I can't seem to shake even with the Z-PAK they give you. The worst part was that as soon as I came home, I had a lot of talks to give, like the homily at the Closing Mass of the Eucharistic Congress last Saturday and the keynote address in Chicago for the Diocesan Finance Directors Conference, plus a lot of other little things to do. Walking around with a handkerchief in my hand and a bunch of tissues in my pocket, coughing and sneezing and not sleeping at night, wondering if your voice is going to hold out for a talk or a meeting or a homily—these are the things that really get you down.

Having a cold also is reminding me that it's the time of year to think of getting a flu shot. So get your flu shot, please!

I just realized that I may be guilty of practicing medicine without a license. So let me rephrase what I just said. Talk to your doctor about getting a flu shot soon, please!

I am in Chicago now for the annual retreat meeting of the board of trustees of The Catholic University of America, sitting in my hotel room and getting ready to go down to the first meeting. I'll be a big hit with my watering eyes and my coughing. Maybe I'll just sit in a corner so they won't be afraid that I'm catching. I am usually not a whiner, but I have had this cold for so long that, as I'm thinking of you, I want to encourage you not to get it, too—and to take care of yourself in all ways this winter.

To Be or Not to Be
October 7, 2004

What can I say? I was raised in New York City and everyone in my family was a Yankee fan. Even though Giants Stadium at the Polo Grounds was only a couple of miles from where we lived in Washington Heights, we were all Yankee fans.

I confess that for a time in my youth, unknown to my closest buddies, because he had the same first name as I did, I thought of Ted Williams with awed admiration. I will never forget the time he put his incredible 400 batting average on the line when he had the chance to pull out of a lineup. He told the manager he would play as usual and actually brought his average up even higher! I have always admired that decision. It spoke of self-confidence and a willingness to play the game according to the rules without an exception.

Of course, when Ted Williams retired from active play, I dropped the Red Sox—I hadn't really been a real fan of the team, just of my namesake, anyway—and came back home to the Yankees. In the years I worked in Latin America, I still followed the Yankees and when I was assigned to New Jersey, I was again surrounded by fellow Yankee fans, although I admit that some of my associates preferred Philadelphia or the Mets. I forgave them that error because they didn't have the deep connection that real New Yorkers are always able to cherish.

During my first life in Washington, when I worked at Catholic University and earned my doctorate, we had the Senators and I followed them casually, but my baseball heart was always in the Bronx.

During these past four years, however, I have really become a Washingtonian—and a Southern Marylander! I have become part of this city and this area, its hopes and dreams, its fears and its concerns, its excitement and its frustrations. And now I really rejoice that it has its own major league baseball team once again. With everybody else, I'm wondering what the team name will be, and like the rest of us, I have a lot of good ideas, too.

But when the crucial question comes, I guess that after all these years, I'll have to become a former Yankee fan, and a faithful, active, and enthusiastic fan of the Washington "whatevers" and hope that I will still be around when they win the pennant!

On a more serious note, it is good for all of us to have the distractions of healthy sports and clean entertainment as well as the habit of good reading. These are some of the things that fill out our personalities and prevent us from taking ourselves too seriously—as long as we never fall into the trap of taking them too seriously. The game of life, the wise man said, is the only game we all must play and the prize of victory is everlasting life. I thought of that, as I am thinking of you, and wanted to share both the light and serious sides of last week's good news.

Respect Life Month
October 14, 2004

As we get deep into this month, I wanted to remind all of us in a very special way that October has always been Respect Life Month. There are three areas that I would like to bring to your attention: abortion, euthanasia, and stem cell research.

All we have learned about human life and its beginnings underlines the fact that there truly is life in the womb from the moment of conception. One of the most powerful photos

I have ever seen is that of an incredibly small hand trying to hold on to a doctor's finger as he attempts a remedial surgical operation on a little fetus. The baby—for that indeed is what it is—naturally reached out to a protecting adult as if to say, "Hey, here I am, don't let them lose me!" How can anyone kill that baby—or even worse, when the infant is in the third trimester and you destroy it half-born by terrible violence! It is not always easy to be pro-life in today's society, but we who believe have no choice.

Secondly, the question of assisted suicide is something we must think about. This was never an issue when I was a young man. We believed that God determined how long we were to live and with our freedom of will we determined what kind of life we would live. Killing oneself is, I guess, the next step from taking the lives of other people, either through violence or capital punishment or anything else that fosters a culture of death. I know that pain is often so hard to bear, but as a priest who has sat at many sick beds, I know, too, that those who bear it for the sake of others can be filled with the deepest sense of satisfaction that enables them even to find joy in their suffering and release from their fears. Assisted suicide is always a slippery slope and the old, the poor, the handicapped, and the disadvantaged are ready targets. What society must do is reach out to help those in need and in pain, not to develop ways to get rid of them.

Finally, I want to talk about stem cell research. I truly believe it is a phony issue. The Church is not opposed to adult stem cell research. As a matter of fact, that kind of research has already helped hundreds of thousands of people. It should be encouraged and supported by public and private funds alike, because it has proven to be useful and beneficial to human beings. Fetal stem cell research does not have that kind of track record. It really has no track record at all. It has become the darling of the abortion lobbyists and of the already billion-dollar abortion industry. Do not take their exaggerated claims for granted. Ask the right questions and learn the difference between fact and fiction. Adult stem research has only now begun its healing work. So far, it looks as if it can do the trick in so many ways of curing people's diseases. Let us not snuff out the lives of little babies just to try to enrich the lives of other people. Enriching the lives of other people is a good thing to do and the wonderful part of it is that we already have started to do it through adult stem cell research.

Respect Life Month reminds me to be thinking of you and to call your attention to all the things we need to see clearly.

One Bread, One Body
October 21, 2004

The best thing I do for you is offer Mass for you almost every day. I say almost because once in a while I do offer Mass for a special intention. For example, at a funeral or some parish anniversary or when one of our priests is very sick or passing through a crisis of one sort or another, or sometimes when I offer Mass in atonement for my own failings and sinfulness, but almost always my Masses are for you, the faithful of the Church of Washington.

That is why I really love to be with you in the morning at Mass in the parishes. I think I have been in every territorial parish at least twice and in some places six or seven times in the last four years that I have had the privilege and the special grace to be sent here to serve. (Once again, in a spirit of total honesty—lest I get a phone call from St. George's Island in St. Mary's County—I have only offered Mass at St. Francis Xavier Church there once, since it's only open during the summer for one vigil Mass on Saturday night. Next summer,

I'll make it a special priority to be there for the Eucharist, God willing!)

The Holy Father has just proclaimed a special Holy Year of the Eucharist. It began last Sunday at the close of the International Eucharistic Congress in Guadalajara in Mexico. I was there for part of the congress and really was carried away by the profound faith of the people of Mexico. It was in that part of the country, in the state of Jalisco, of which Guadalajara is the capital, that the great martyrs of Mexico—priests and lay people alike—were present in great abundance. More than a dozen priests of the Church in Guadalajara offered their lives in martyrdom during the terrible persecution of the 1920s and 1930s. I think I told you that, as a youngster at the children's Mass in my home parish more than sixty years ago, I was moved by a visiting priest from Mexico who preached about the extraordinary courage of the Church and the people there. Maybe, in God's providence, that was a seed of my own vocation.

As the great Eucharistic procession passed along the streets of Guadalajara—a city of more than nine million people—it was estimated that some four million people watched the Eucharist pass by on a flatbed vehicle. They sang and danced and cried out in adoration as the Lord passed by. I have no doubt that this act of faith will bring them many blessings and that their own joy in the presence of God will be even more enlivened. As I walked along with other bishops in front of the blessed sacrament, I could sense the people's awareness of the presence of God in the Eucharist and I implored the Lord to give us that same sense of his loving presence in our lives, too.

We must plan how this Eucharistic Holy Year can best be observed in the Archdiocese of Washington. I would hope that the pastoral councils in all our parishes would talk about this with their pastors and discuss some ways to set our hearts on fire with the love of the God who became man so that he might win our salvation and our eternal happiness, and who continues every second of all our time to be thinking of you and of me and offering us in the Eucharist the awesome miracle of his Body and Blood.

"And for James, Our Bishop"
October 28, 2004

It was about 4:00 in the morning on Sunday when the phone rang. I had spoken to the folks at the nursing home the night before. They told me that His Eminence was failing rapidly. I asked if I should come over right away, but they said it did not appear imminent and they would call me. Bishop Lori, who had served the cardinal so well for so many years as his secretary, vicar general, and auxiliary bishop, was on the other line. With predictable generosity and affection for his former boss, he had come down from Bridgeport that afternoon after the sisters had called to tell him that His Eminence was coming close to the end. He called to tell me that the sisters now had the sense that death was coming close. I told him that I would be there in a half hour.

I called Bishop Farrell and woke him from a sound sleep. He had volunteered the night before to go with me to the nursing home whenever the call came. We left at 4:30. We were there with the cardinal and these extraordinary Little Sisters of the Poor, who serve and care for the elderly at their Jeanne Jugan Residence across the street from the Basilica of the National Shrine. Bishop Lori was waiting for us and we began once more the prayers for the dying. A short time later, Msgr. Barry Knestout arrived from his new parish of St. John the Evangelist in Silver Spring. He had succeeded Bishop

Lori as secretary and had worked with such dedication and devotion to take care of the cardinal.

We read the prayers again, prayed the Rosary, and whispered the short aspirations into the cardinal's ear. I read somewhere that the sense of hearing is the last one to go and, even though His Eminence gave no sign of understanding what was taking place, we continued to hope that he would hear and take comfort from the prayers that we offered. Around 6:10, his labored breathing seemed to become more peaceful and a few minutes later it stopped altogether. The priest and bishop who had served this local Church of Washington so well for twenty years had gone back to the Lord who had sent him to us as our shepherd and our friend.

He was always very good to me, always ready to help or to give me some good counsel whenever I asked, but never negative or critical, even when I made my mistakes. I tried to get to see him every week, and I will miss him. Often, he seemed not to recognize me, but sometimes that great Hickey smile and an unexpected funny comment came to give me hope that he was still aware of the world around him. I am sure that he was very often thinking of you. May he rest in peace.

Thank You
November 4, 2004

I would like this column to serve in a certain personal way to say thanks to the multitude of folks who made Cardinal Hickey's funeral so very special. I will be writing notes to many of you, but it will take me awhile to get them all out. Meanwhile, I want you to know how much this extraordinary outpouring of love and gratitude for our former archbishop touched me and touched so many others here in our archdiocese and beyond.

May I start out with the media? I sometimes criticize them and blame them for different things, but their coverage of the cardinal's death and burial from the day he passed away to the day of his entombment in the cathedral was exceptional and so very much appreciated by the Catholic community and all His Eminence's many friends.

The tributes that were paid to the cardinal at the conclusion of the funeral Mass will not soon be forgotten. Bishop Pilla's gratitude for Cardinal Hickey's Cleveland days, Bishop Lori's and Msgr. Knestout's warm, funny, and endearing personal tributes, Mother Mary Bernard's humble and gracious words, and Mayor Williams' unforgettable eulogy all touched special threads of memories that will surely pass into the great legacy of a very remarkable man.

The truly extraordinary numbers of our priests and deacons, together with an impressive number of his brother cardinals and bishops, underlined the role that James Hickey played both in this Archdiocese of Washington and in the larger circle of the Church in our country and around the world. The beautiful homilies of Archbishop O'Malley and Bishop Lori, the brilliance of the choirs who truly sang their hearts out, the perfection of the liturgy at the hands of Father James Watkins and his associates, the devotion of the Knights of Columbus, and the other distinguished knightly orders of the Church whose constant standing guard at the cardinal's bier was such a powerful sign, and the thousands of people of every race and age and ethnic background who passed by as he lay in state—these are the memories that I will hold forever of Cardinal Hickey's going back to the Lord whom he served so well.

Nothing touches us so much as birth and death. That is why we can never really get over the trauma of abortion and euthanasia. The cardinal's death and his birth now into everlasting life enter the history books of this local Church, but the great memories will stay with us for a long, long time. Thank you all for the wonderful tribute to a good and humble man. I have no doubt that even now he is thinking of you and bringing all our prayers with Mary to the Lord. God bless you for your faithfulness to this good and faithful priest.

Turn the Page
November 11, 2004

One of the greatest lessons of life is contained in those three words that are the title of this column. "Turn the page" means many different things to different people, but basically it means start over, change course, don't get trapped in the problems or the fears or the worries of yesterday. Begin a new day, find confidence in yourself again, and trust in God that your life can start anew!

When the Lord gave us the sacrament of Penance through the ministry of the Church in confession, he touched the deepest roots of our human nature. We all make mistakes. When I was young, there was a saying that went "that's the reason they put erasers on the end of pencils." Maybe now the modern equivalent would be "that's why there is a delete button on your computer!"

Too many people live in the past. We smile at those who are always bragging about their past glories and memorable achievements, but we grieve about those others who have never forgiven themselves for past errors or, so much sadder, those who have never had their consciences salved by the powerful grace of a good confession and never found for themselves a transforming experience of God's forgiving love. I always pray that they may find a way to approach that great sacrament and be able to turn the page and change their lives. For me, the saddest note of our modern society is the presence of so many people who are unable to forgive, even to forgive themselves.

But what is especially on my mind as I write this column is the attitude of a lot of people at the end of this last election. It was truly a hard-fought election. We all know that. It revealed a continuing division in our country and in our own area as well. The bad part was an anger and in some cases a real nastiness about candidates and about issues. Here in the Catholic community, we tried to make our positions clear, open, and constant. We did this in many ways, especially through documents like Faithful Citizenship, which we produced long before the election took place and which we continue to support and uphold.

The election is over. We have chosen our leaders once more. This is not the time for personal hatreds or for trying to undermine the people's choice. Whatever side you may have taken, please turn the page and let us work together for the nation and for the common good of all our communities.

Turning the page is not only sometimes both wise and healthy; it is often required in a democracy to be faithful to our way of life. Thinking of you, as we all strive to find the ways to work together, I pray that we may join in building up rather than in tearing down.

Thoughts on Veterans Day
November 18, 2004

A few weeks ago, I received a letter from the father of one of our young Marines serving in Iraq. He wrote of his worries for his son as he was serving in that very dangerous part of the world. You could also read between the lines of his deep pride for his son as he accepted this very challenging duty bravely and was carrying it out with courage and honor. He paid me a compliment that brought a lump to my throat when he told me that he sent this weekly column over to his son in Iraq because he thought that the young man would find it helpful.

I thought of that good father and his Marine son on Veterans Day and of all our archdiocesan families who have lost a loved one in this conflict. I wanted to write in a special way this week to all the parents of our men and women serving in the armed forces in foreign lands, and especially to their sons and daughters. All of you are our family and not a day goes by without a prayer for you in the hope that the day is coming when you all will be together safe and sound back at home. We all ask our blessed Lord to watch over you—the men and women who serve and their loved ones here at home. We do worry about you, but we put you all in the arms of Our Lady, the Queen of Peace, and the Mother of us all.

Last week, one of our fine priests wrote to tell me that he is being re-activated and will be heading for Iraq in a few weeks. We already have a number of our Washington diocesan priests serving as chaplains, and I am so proud of his willingness to join them and to dedicate himself to the service of our troops in the field. It makes me feel like that father in the letter that I mentioned to know that another of my sons—our brothers—will be going overseas.

Washington has always had great priest chaplains serving our folks in uniform in war and peace. When I worked as secretary to Cardinal Cooke years ago, I traveled with him to military stations all over the world and got to know many priests serving as chaplains. What a great service that is! It is a special way in which we as a Church can reach out to those in uniform and make them feel a little more at home by bringing the Lord to them in a special way. I wish we had more priests in the chaplain service. We must all pray for vocations so that we can make this possible.

Of course, when we talk of chaplains and our men and women in the armed forces, the thought that is most in our hearts and minds is the hope that the end of wars and hostility and the coming of peace will not be far off. Pope Paul VI said it best: "War never, never again!" We seem to be still so far away from that goal, but let us never stop working and praying for peace and justice in our world. Thinking of you and your loved ones in the service makes this intention at Veterans Day so very special.

Greeting Cards
November 25, 2004

I know it's too early to talk about Christmas, although the day after Thanksgiving, we will be reminded of the coming of that feast with lights and sales and bunting that will penetrate the consciousness of the most distracted citizen of our planet. This will be a mixed blessing. It will be wonderful to see the world so visibly reminded of the birth of the Lord, but it is sad to realize that the Holy Family may be lost in the secular focus of our culture's celebration and hidden under the tinsel of advertising specials.

And that brings me to Christmas cards. As you have probably guessed, my office sends out a couple of thousand Christmas cards! Unfortunately, I don't get to sign most of them personally. I guess I could if I started last May, but that kind of time is a far away dream for me. In my case, the card has a simple function. It really just says, "Hello—I'm thinking about you and all our friends as we celebrate the wonder of Christmas and I hope that you remember me in your prayers as I remember you." Oh, of course, I try to make the wording a little more elegant and I try to make the picture on the card something that people might like to see, but that same thought always runs through it year after year.

Getting to choose a design and to write the message is a struggle for me. The folks who work with me—and who have so much patience with me—start reminding me in September! First, they do it by simple notes, then by cordial but non-threatening messages, soon by phone calls sounding notes of urgency, and ultimately by their frustrated question, "Have you decided not to send any Christmas cards this year?" It is that last pointed challenge that usually gets me going.

This is only my fourth Christmas card as archbishop of Washington. The first was a great photo of the three Washington archbishops together in Rome on the day I became a cardinal. The second and third were about our Cathedral of St. Matthew. The 2002 card was a depiction of the scaffolding and all the work in progress on the cathedral, and last year was a picture of that remarkable church after the restoration was complete. This year, I found a beautiful picture of the Icon of Kazan—that historic Icon of Our Lady that I was so honored to bring back to Russia in the delegation sent by the Holy Father.

I must admit that I feel good about myself having finished it before Thanksgiving, but my associates are once again somewhat annoyed at me that I didn't do it earlier. Closer to Christmas, I'll ask the *Catholic Standard* to show the card to you so everyone who reads our paper can see it. You will see the struggle to get the words right and to fit them in with the picture. In a sense, we all spend time doing that all our lives. When we talk to those we love and care for, it is more important for us to get the words right. Whether we speak to each other or to God himself, the words we choose are important and we want them to be filled with love. May this gracious God help each one of us to express our love for one another in ways that will clearly indicate that we are all thinking of each other with joyful affection even as I am thinking of you.

Violence and Life
December 2, 2004

It may seem strange to start the wonderful season of Advent, when we begin to commemorate the expected coming of Jesus, the Prince of Peace, by a column on violence. However, as we know well from history and from the scriptures, there was a great deal of violence and war at the time before the first coming of Christ into the world two thousand years ago. What is troubling to us all is that two millennia afterwards, we still find violence everywhere as humanity continues to turn its back on the message of peace that was proclaimed by the angels in the shepherds' field.

First of all, we are so conscious and saddened by the violence of war in Iraq and Afghanistan as our own sons and daughters are still locked in that brutal conflict as the war against terrorism touches us all in the heightened security of every day. The continuing violence in the very place of Jesus' birth is a scandal to all the children of Abraham—Christians,

Moslems, and Jews—and reminds us of our common failing to find a roadmap to peace in that holy land.

Closer to home, we fear the violence of our neighbor-hoods, where young people face death every day, it seems, at the hands of criminals and drug dealers who have no respect for life, and in the senseless violence of gangs which bring a new kind of slavery to young people before they have a chance to decide how to live their own lives.

There is violence, too, so desperate and heartbreaking in many families where battered women must flee with young children to shelter from physical abuse. In some of the com-munities of our own area, there are places where crime and human trafficking destroy peace and force people to live in fear when they should be able to live in harmony and find happiness.

We all try to find the key to this evil in our society. We all see it even in ourselves, where we lose self-control and let anger and revenge cause even us to forget who we are as children of God and heirs of the promise of peace that Jesus brings.

Is it because we do not value life anymore? I fear that the culture of death, of which the Holy Father has spoken so often, has touched our own judgment and made us more ready to diminish the gift of God which is life itself. We need to ask ourselves if abortion and euthanasia, assisted suicide, the penalty of death, human cloning, and scientific research that ignores the dignity of the human person have all come together to change our minds on the value of life itself as a gift from God. When that happens, then violence is a natu-ral result since we have eliminated the essential reverence we must have for our own lives and the life of our neighbor.

As we begin the Church's new year at Advent time and prepare for the coming of the child who brought with him the promise of life eternal, we need to reflect on these things and on the value of human life that God himself has taught us. Thinking of you as we call out the Advent cry: "Come, Lord Jesus" and try to realize again what his presence means in our lives.

"*I Wanna Stay*"
December 9, 2004

I was celebrating Mass in one of our parishes the other Sunday. I had preached a little longer than usual, I think, and I was afraid that some of the children were getting restless. The youngsters were all supposed to leave and go to a separate celebration of the word, explained in their own terms by a few specially gifted catechists, but it was decided at the last minute that the children should stay and hear my homily. I always enjoy preaching to young people. They are so wonderfully open to the stories of the Lord and I truly believe that they understand his loving presence in their lives often better than we do.

Just as I was coming to conclude my homily, one little boy began to make noise. I think he may have dropped something and was looking for it under the pews. As his talking got louder, his father scooped him up in one arm and immediately started to carry him to the back of the church. The little fellow began to shout, "I wanna stay, I wanna stay." His voice got louder as they approached the vestibule and now they were accompanied by tears and cries. His dad was dauntless, however, and soon the little fellow's voice was silenced behind the door at the back of the church.

When I returned to the celebrant's chair after the homily and a moment of reflection, I remarked to the congregation that I felt better that he was not shouting, "Get me out of here, he's preaching too long!" As it was, I was comforted by his crying out that he did not want to leave in case it meant that he really wanted to hear the end of the sermon!

"I want to stay" the little boy said. These are words we often use, too. We want to stay healthy. We want to stay happy. We want to stay with those we love. All those are good wishes. An even better wish is to stay close to the God who loves us, to sense his presence and his care in our lives, to feel the constant protection of his abiding grace. Too often in our lives the words can mean we want to stay in our own world of selfishness, of long-standing grudges, even of sinfulness.

The Lord is always there, waiting to carry us from the evil of the world, even though we may come with him kicking and screaming. Wouldn't it be wonderful if we would let him pick us up like a loving father and bring us to a place of peace and joy and deepest happiness where we could cry out in grateful trust, "Thank you, Lord. I want to stay with you both as long as I live and in the eternal joy you promise until the end of time." Thinking of you as we move more deeply into Advent and set our eyes on the coming of the savior who, through the Father's love, has chosen to stay with us until time is no more.

Mary
December 16, 2004

If you were celebrating the Immaculate Conception of the Blessed Virgin last week at all, your thoughts had sometimes to be focused on Mary. If you had the grace-filled opportunity to be in the Basilica of the National Shrine at noon on Wednesday, when a special papal envoy from the Vatican celebrated Mass in honor of the Immaculate Conception—or if you saw it on television—those thoughts had to be filled with the beauty of the Church's veneration of the Mother of God. I thought it would be fitting, therefore, to write to you at this Advent time about Our Lady.

Children seem to capture the joy of our devotion to Mary much more quickly and easily than adults sometimes do. They have an instinctive love for their own mothers, so when they learn about Jesus and how he was a little child, they naturally open their hearts to his Mother. Since the Hail Mary is one of the easiest prayers to learn, it too nourishes their feeling of closeness to the Mother of God as they learn it either (hopefully) from their parents or at least in school or in CCD. The great story of the annunciation with its beautiful exchange between Mary and the angel is not too hard for children to comprehend, even though the great mysteries that surround it may escape them. The little boy or girl who runs to mother when he or she is hurt, finds another mother in Mary to heal the pain, to stop the bleeding, or to clean the wound.

The wonderful thing about Mary is that since she is her Son's gift to us from the cross, she has not only the opportunity to be there when we are hurting, but in the deepest sense, the responsibility as well. As we become adults, there are still hurts from relationships that we can feel, wounds of frustration or failure or personal loss that we need to cleanse, and so often a problem of physical or mental health that seems to bleed away our energy and our happiness. And so, Mary is there! We can take the wonderful litany of Loreto— the litany of Our Lady—and find in it the best short prayers that we need to face our hurts and disappointments. There are times when we need her to be "the cause of our joy" or "the seat of wisdom" or "the health of the sick." There are moments when to cry out "O Virgin most powerful, pray for me" is a great spiritual strengthening and also a psychological support. For me, the Memorare is a favorite prayer for it calls on confidence in Mary's loving concern and steadies me when the sea of life grows rough. I hope you all have some special prayer to Mary, also. We know that our prayers never end with her, for she brings them to her beloved Son and pleads for us with him. As we celebrated Our Lady so splendidly last week, I was thinking of you and wanting to remind you to use all those beautiful prayers you learned years ago.

Where Are the Angels?
December 23, 2004

Some of the youngsters in my family were working on the Christmas tree and the crib that we would always place at its base. Somehow, the figures of a couple of angels did not seem to have been packed away properly after last year's Christmas. The older children took that in stride and began carefully unwrapping the other Christmas decorations, but the littlest one was insistent that her siblings first undertake the search for those heavenly messengers, without whose presence the nativity scene would not be quite right. "Where are the angels?" she began to ask and continued her questioning until the others had to stop unwrapping the Christmas balls and instead concentrate on the search for the figures of the angels. Happily, they were found before too long and the little one was satisfied as she spent the rest of the time deciding where to place them near the child.

"Where are the angels?" My grandniece's question fascinated me. Oh, of course, I knew that she was talking about the figurines, but there is a deeper sense in that question and it has much meaning for all of us throughout the year and especially at great spiritual moments like Christmas. We believe in angels. The *Catechism of the Catholic Church* reminds us that their existence is part of our faith, both from the numerous mentions in the Holy Scriptures and from our constant tradition. Our modern world tends to equate things that are real with only things that are visible. It is a little presumptuous on our part that we seem to feel that if we do not see something with our own eyes, it cannot be real. The presence of the angels teaches us that there is a real world which we cannot see with our mortal eyes, but nevertheless is real.

Christmas reminds us that there is a real world beyond our immediate consciousness. The world we cannot see is also real, and sometimes God allows it to become visible, as when the angel came to Mary at the moment of the annunciation and as a whole chorus of angels announced to the shepherds the birth of the Lord. We believe that the presence of angels is also a sign of God's love for us as they watch over us "to guide and guard" as the prayer we learned as children used to say.

And there is also another profound way in which the little girl's question can be answered. Just as the angels are messengers of God's love and his care, so we are called to exercise that same function in the visible world of everyday life. Christmas reminds us of how much God loved us when he sent his Son into the world to be its salvation. That same Jesus, whose birth we celebrate again, comes thinking of you and me and calling us also to announce the message of the angels giving glory to God in the highest and peace to his people on earth.

Signs of Hope
December 30, 2004

I have been waiting to tell you this story. It's a true story and it happened a couple of weeks ago. You know that I went to Argentina for a few days in early December, shortly after we celebrated the solemn conclusion of the Holy Year of the Immaculate Conception at the Basilica of the National Shrine. One of the religious congregations that is active in the Archdiocese of Washington, the Institute of the Incarnate Word, invited me to ordain their new priests and deacons at their major seminary in San Rafael, Argentina where the institute was founded a little more than twenty years ago.

This community has been extraordinarily blessed by the Lord in terms of vocations and in terms of missionary activity. They now have some three hundred priests, two hundred seminarians, and almost five hundred women religious in their sisters' community, and they have accepted missions and parishes from Greenland and Iceland to Central Asia, including eleven in the United States. In our archdiocese, they have a seminary and a novitiate as well as the care of the parish of St. James in Mount Rainier. I have been close to the Institute since I truly believe that the Holy Spirit has been with them and has guided them in their remarkable growth and service of the poor.

At any rate, after five very inspiring days of visiting and praying with them in Argentina, I took an overnight flight back to the United States. I arrived at 6:30 on a Saturday morning, since I needed to be at Mother Seton parish in Germantown to dedicate its great new church that same morning at 10:00. I passed through the immigration and the customs area in Dulles Airport without any problems and entered the large hall where new arrivals are met by the folks who are going to pick them up. It had been arranged that one of my priest secretaries would meet me.

As soon as I entered the hall, it was suddenly filled with music! Our own seminarians from Washington's Archdiocesan Missionary Seminary, Redemptoris Mater, had learned the time of my arrival. They had left the seminary, located now in Our Lady of Sorrows Parish in Takoma Park, around 5:00 in the morning to be sure to be on time for my arrival.

Many of them are Spanish-speaking, coming from several countries in Latin America, and they had decided to greet me singing Las Mañanitas, the traditional Christmas hymns that are sung in the early morning hours during the time around the feast of Christmas.

I was very surprised, to say the least! Some twenty-five of our young seminarians singing at the top of their voices, strumming guitars, and accompanying the music with tambourines and drums. The music filled the hall and people came running from other locations to see what was happening. I confess that at first I was a little embarrassed at being the center of all this loud celebration, but after a while I noticed the smiles and the appreciation of so many of the other folks in the receiving hall. Our car had been parked at the other end of the terminal and so my musical accompaniment continued for the whole length of the building. Travelers and staff alike stopped what they were doing to watch and enjoy the musical procession. I realized that it had to be a special grace for people to see some twenty-five fine young men in black suits singing with joy and enthusiasm about the birth of the Lord and the blessings that his coming means for all the human race.

How blessed we are in having these vocations to the priesthood! Of course, there are not as many as we need, but the Lord is truly blessing this local Church of ours with the dedication and the growing numbers of those who are willing to give their lives to the Lord. Please pray with me for vocations to the priesthood and the consecrated life. As I often tell you, the great priests of the larger classes of fifty years ago are now coming to a stage where they will be retiring. Our Ordination classes now are smaller and so we must ask the Lord of the harvest to give us laborers who will serve you and your children and grandchildren in the future to make sure that the work of Jesus continues to grow in our archdiocese and the powerful message of the Gospel is always preached here in Washington.

I was thinking of you as I got off the plane and this grace-filled encounter made me all the more sure that God will take care of you now and in the future.

2005

Volunteers
January 6, 2005

Did you hear the report on the radio the other day about the percentage of young people who believe that they should volunteer a great part of their time to do good things for other people? According to the radio report, the number of these youngsters is not only large, but also growing. (Incidentally, the announcer said that many of the teenagers feel that their parents do not volunteer enough!)

What a wonderful world it would be if we all took up the challenge of giving more of our time to the service of good causes. We could help the poor and the handicapped, teach remedial classes, give time as a companion to a lonely old person, cook a meal once in a while for someone who has no one to help them. We could volunteer to help children learn a trade or a sport, we could write letters for people who cannot see or read the letters that they have received from others. We could give a lift to someone who needs to go shopping but has no means of transportation, or even help someone handle a crisis pregnancy and save a baby's life. I'm just touching the surface here, and you could think of a hundred other ways of being helpful, I'm sure. The good part of all this volunteer service is that we are able to do it at our own convenience and are not tied down to a demanding schedule. Indeed, many of these thoughts could be a subject of a New Year's resolution!

Where would the world be without people willing to volunteer? I always think of the Blessed Mother as a volunteer. She was free to say yes or no to the angel's message. Her simple, humble "Yes" changed the world! Every young man with a priestly vocation, every girl who feels invited by God to consecrated life is a volunteer, accepting freely a call from God to take up a challenging responsibility in love. In a very deep sense, every young couple who says yes to marriage is a volunteer. Of course, as in the case of the Blessed Virgin Mary, the volunteering comes with it the acceptance of an obligation. It becomes an informal commitment to do something for another person, or for God himself. It ultimately becomes formalized in marriage or in ordination or in religious profession, but it always starts in a wonderful grace that allows a person to volunteer to do something good for a good cause or for someone who needs them.

Watching the television this week and seeing the terrible scenes of desolation and destruction in the lands that border the Indian Ocean, I thought of the thousands of volunteers who have given up so much to care for the survivors, to bury the dead, to find a way to put lives back together again. As I prepare to leave for the area myself, I pray that I can say something useful when I get there, not only to those who have suffered so much sorrow and loss, but also to find words of encouragement and admiration for those volunteers, who even like Mary and the saints, have said yes to an awesome challenge and who by their courage and generosity can try to make the world of the dread tsunami come to life again in a better and safer way. During this journey I will surely be thinking of you.

Unexpected Adventures
January 13, 2005

Sunday morning en route to Johannesburg. Our lives are often filled with adventures. Sometimes we don't recognize them, or sometimes one person's adventure is another one's normal experience. Love is an adventure, as is faith. But I want to talk about the uncommon adventures that sometimes accompany traveling in different parts of the world.

I am in South Africa still, traveling the highway between Rustenburg and Johannesburg. I've been in this country for three days, mostly visiting AIDS centers, where I've met hundreds of courageous people suffering from this terrible disease and dozens of extraordinary people who dedicate their lives to their care. Among the former are little babies, so many of them HIV positive, and among the caregivers are unforgettable women religious, from many countries and many congregations, working incredible hours and so obviously living all of these in the presence of God. The little ones break your heart and the nuns give you confidence that the kingdom of God is truly here.

When I return home, I'll tell you more about my visits. Your support of Catholic Relief Services (CRS) reaches to these villages and to all these people, and United States government support helps in bringing medicine and hope to so many. I was proud of CRS, of our own country's aid, and of all the splendid things that our Catholic Church in this part of the world accomplishes for the poor and the hurting.

But in the midst of all these heavy visits, there were some unexpected moments of relief. You all know my built-in resistance to taking time off. Well, it turned out that I did have Saturday afternoon free and we were close to a nature park area where we could drive among the wild animals. This is the first time in my life that I could do this and so I signed up. It was a fascinating three-hour journey. We were in an open bus-like truck, with several rows of seats and the sides protected by canvas. It was great to see the zebras, wildebeests, baboons, and giraffes up so close and for the most part paying no attention to these humans with their cameras so quietly driving by. There was one moment of near panic when we halted for a rest stop and found a lion wandering between us and the vehicle as we returned. Otherwise, it was three hours well spent, especially after a serious life-and-death atmosphere of the first part of my visit.

The unexpected adventure was driving back to Johannesburg to fly to the tsunami area this morning. Packed and ready for the two-and-a-half-hour drive, we just started on the way when a passing car warned us that there were elephants on the road. By the time we arrived, one great eight-ton male elephant had planted himself across the highway and was happily munching the foliage at the side of the road. These are wild elephants and don't necessarily react graciously to a horn or a shout. There was no room to quietly pass him by and the string of waiting automobiles behind us was growing. I was afraid that we could miss our flight to Sri Lanka, until at last, the huge creature decided to leave his eating. Unfortunately, he decided to walk up the road looking for a different clump of bushes to eat. He was walking right at us and we could not pull back because the cars were right behind us. Thank God, before he came too close he turned off the road again and we were able to move forward carefully. We passed him almost close enough to reach out and pull his tail. (I wasn't even tempted!) If he had turned around or stepped back, our car would have been crushed. It was truly an unexpected adventure! For the moment I was thinking of you and wondering if I would ever be seeing you again. I have to confess that it was one of those few times when I wasn't wishing that you were here, too.

Being There
January 20, 2005

Was there ever a movie or a TV special called *Being There*? I seem to recall those words as a title of something not too long ago. I used them myself a few days ago when someone asked me about the experience of spending last week in the tsunami areas. I told the gentleman who asked me, that just as they say one picture is worth a thousand words, being there must be worth a thousand pictures.

I had seen so much TV footage about that terrible tidal wave and its destructive force that I figured I already knew the story pretty well. I was wrong. Seeing the people on the screen and being there with them as they told you story after story of that terrible day is a very different thing. Seeing their sorrow and desolation in a photo and being conscious of their resilience and their inner strength from a personal conversation, even though through an interpreter, are two very different experiences. Driving along a road only recently cleared of massive debris and flying in a helicopter over miles of shattered homes and useless boats tells a story that no picture can adequately record.

Some of the stories don't find their way into the secular press. So I'll tell you two of them here.

There is an historic statue of Our Lady in the town of Matara on the southern coast of Sri Lanka. It is an exquisite wood carving, done probably in Belgium in the 1500s. This is the third time it has been washed away since it arrived on this island, perhaps a hundred years after it was carved. The first time it happened was in a flood that roared through the church in which it was venerated. The second was when it was recovered and sent back to Europe to be repaired. At that time, it fell overboard during a storm at the beginning of the journey. The tsunami was the third time, when it disappeared into the raging tidal wave that ripped it from its pedestal.

Each of these times, perhaps miraculously, the statue was found again close to home. This third time, it was found by a Buddhist farmer clearing his land four days after the storm had passed. I saw it in a room at the Cathedral of Galle, a hand broken off the Christ Child and some damage to the

Madonna's arm, but its exquisite beauty still retained and its message of hope to people of faith still reaching out with comfort. Its third reappearance only renews the people's feeling that God has sent his Mother to reassure them that they are not forgotten.

The other story that I want to share is very different. It took place in a church in another part of this island-nation. Mass was being celebrated there on that Sunday morning, December 26, when the large wave hit. Survivors told me that it was at Communion time when they saw an automobile come crashing into the center aisle of the church, propelled by the power of the tsunami that tore its way through the building. An elderly nun was distributing the Body of Christ at that moment. She was standing at the altar rail while the faithful came up to receive. As the water hit them all, it carried her away, and she disappeared from sight, as the power of the water bore her with it.

Obviously they searched for her, as for all the others who were carried off from the church by the power of the angry waters. Two days later, they found her body under the rubble. She had been carried a good distance, but to everyone's amazement, she had never let go of the little ciborium from which she was distributing the Body of Christ. I could not learn if the sacred hosts were still within the vessel, but this remarkable old woman had never let go! This tells so much about the faith in the Eucharist of this woman and those she served.

I'm glad to have come back safely to the comfort of home and the pleasant security of these familiar surroundings. The eleven-day journey left me a little exhausted, but also left me so proud to be a person of faith among those very special people, who may not know as much about God as I know, but who really love him and sense his presence in a way that I still must learn to achieve. As I prayed before the thrice-found Virgin in Matara, I was surely praying for and thinking of you.

The Year of the Eucharist
January 27, 2005

By now, I think everybody knows that the Holy Father has proclaimed this year as the Year of the Eucharist. I know you have been discussing this in your parishes, in the pastoral councils and in the different societies. On the diocesan level, we have considered it at the Presbyteral Council and the Archdiocesan Pastoral Council, as well.

I truly believe that this special year will bring great graces to all of us in this local Church of Washington. Many wonderful recommendations have already been suggested by our priests and our laity as to how we can observe this Eucharistic Year. Let me mention some of the ideas that I think are most important for us to take the greatest advantage of this time of grace.

First of all, we have been mentioning the idea of increasing the opportunities for confession in the different parishes. Sometimes it is difficult for our faithful to make use of this great sacrament of Penance because the times for confession are not always convenient. When I was a youngster, confession was always celebrated on Saturday afternoons. In those days, that was a convenient time for most people. I hope that our parish councils will work with our priests to make sure that, as much as is possible, the faithful can find the most convenient time for scheduling confessions, given the shortage of priests in many of our parish communities and the increasing complexity of modern day life. Perhaps several parishes could join together and make an evening of confession available once a week in different parishes so that many more people will be given the opportunity. No one should be impeded from receiving the Holy Eucharist because they could not find a satisfactory time for going to confession.

Secondly, we should all consider some new, personal way of expressing our devotion to the blessed sacrament in our daily program of life. Could we get to daily Mass more frequently? Perhaps we could even do it every day? Or at least some days every week? If Mass is not possible, could we stop in to visit the blessed sacrament on the way to work or school, perhaps at lunch hour, or as we head home at the end of each day? Many of us have lost the habit of visiting the Lord in his Eucharistic presence in our churches. Wouldn't it be a grace to renew that wonderful, old custom to make a visit even for five or ten minutes every day?

Finally, and these further suggestions are only a few of so very many, could we work with our pastoral councils and with our pastors to plan a weekly holy hour, concluding with the benediction of the blessed sacrament and permitting us to use this more formal and beautiful way to join together as a worshipping community to pray for all our needs as individuals, as a parish, or even as a nation? Again, here, several parishes might join together in that a different parish in each deanery might schedule this holy hour during the week. In some places it may mean perpetual adoration of the blessed sacrament, even during the hours of the night.

I appreciate that these suggestions will depend on the availability of our priests whose time is so often committed to their parish and sacramental duties, to meetings, and to the ordinary pastoral care of the people, as well as the family needs and other needs of their parishioners. In a similar sense, this also affects our permanent deacons who give themselves so generously to parish work. Within the realm of possibility and the help of God's grace, we can and really should do more during this special grace-filled period.

In the year 2000, it was the dream of Cardinal Hickey to have a great archdiocesan Eucharistic Congress here in our local Church. I know what a wonderful success it was and how the entire archdiocese came together for prayer and worship. Maybe we could plan one again during the autumn months of this Eucharistic Year? So here I am, thinking of you and putting down on paper my thoughts as to how, with God's help, we can continue to build up the Church of God here in our archdiocese, to give glory to the Lord and to implore his constant blessing on us all. It occurs to me that some of these ideas would be great Lenten practices that we might have the opportunity to continue throughout the whole year of Eucharistic celebrations.

Faith-Based Initiatives
February 3, 2005

(Dublin) My columns are becoming travelogues, I'm afraid. After more than three years of rather successful avoidance of overseas travel, I now find myself trapped in too many meetings out of the country. I only just returned from my journey to South Africa and Sri Lanka when I had to set off for three days of meetings in Dublin and a day of talks in London. All of it is important, as for instance, I am attending this meeting of the World Faith Development Dialogue here on behalf of the Holy See. This is a gathering of representatives of many different religious communities, from Buddhist and Hindu to Muslim, Christian, and Jewish to discuss the ways in which we can reach out to help the poor in the developing countries of the world. On Wednesday I fly to London for a number of talks relating to the same topics. I probably am here since I do have experience in this kind of work and hopefully I can make a positive contribution.

I am increasingly troubled by the poverty of so many children who can only look forward to growing up in a world in which they will never be able to earn more than a dollar a day. This must be so hard for young people, since their future is so limited, in contrast to the youngsters in our country where even in the poorest neighborhoods, education can provide a road to a better life.

What is fascinating about this conference is that there is a deep realization from religious leaders all over the world that the road to success in the field of development is more easily found in the use of faith-based institutions. We have found in the United States, too, that the service of the poor is often much better rendered by Church-related institutions than by the purely secular agencies of government. I think of our poorest and sometimes violent neighborhoods. It is so often the local community Churches, many of them Protestant, but happily many of them Catholic, too, which can reach out to families in these areas and do what government can never do. They can get the funding to the community, but they cannot accompany that help by faith, which, we believe, is the key to changing lives and powerfully enabling men and women to overcome the terrible circumstances of poverty and social disruption in their lives.

Without entering into politics—because many legislators on both sides of the aisle have seen the value of faith-based initiatives—I want to encourage our political leaders to use these faith-based institutions in those critical areas. For years, our government often treated religious organizations as less than equal partners in the care of the poor. That was a mistake. We need to let our government know that it should not continue or repeat that mistake. As an example, I have no doubt that our Catholic Charities and the welfare agencies of other faith communities can accomplish more effectively and more humanely many of the tasks that public institutions cannot adequately handle. I pray that the Congress will support the use of our faith-based institutions at home and abroad. It would be good for America and good for the world.

In the conversations that I have had at this conference, I have learned a lot, but one thing becomes very clear. Whether you speak of poverty in Africa or poverty in Washington, faith-based organizations have a real place in fulfilling the government's mission to care for its people. Thinking of you in rainy Ireland, I thought I would share this conviction with my folks back home.

A Heartfelt Thanks
February 10, 2005

I started to write this column on the visit I made to Ireland and England last week and some of the special graces I received in both Dublin and London, but that will keep for another week. It's important now that I say a special thanks with all my heart for the thousands of our folks who have made the archdiocese's work to protect children so excellent a program in so vital a need.

The *Catholic Standard* today is publishing the report of our Child Protection Advisory Board and I am enormously grateful to Shay Bilchik, the president and CEO of the nationally respected Child Welfare League of America, who is its distinguished chairman, and who with the other members of the board has given so many hours and so much experience and expertise to help us create a solid and comprehensive program to meet this all-important need. You may remember a couple of years back, I asked a group of acknowledged experts in the field of child welfare if they would volunteer their time to help us make sure that we were doing all the things we should to keep children safe. I am so pleased that Shay and the other talented and respected members of our board agreed to volunteer their time to serve on it.

This group has worked so hard over the past couple of years and I am tremendously grateful to them for their insights, their expertise, and their commitment to making sure we are doing all the things we should do for children. I have asked them to hold us accountable and they have, as you can see in the report published in today's *Catholic Standard.*

What struck me the most in reading their accounting of the work we have done is how much each of you has done! I am proud of our pastors, our principals, our staffs, and in a special way of our parents. By working together, we have been able to accomplish so much to further child safety in a very short time.

I know it's not always easy for mothers and fathers to find time in their busy schedules to make appointments to get fingerprinted. I appreciate that it can feel pretty uncomfortable. Thank you for the sacrifices you have made. You did it because you know your children are worth it and because you want the peace of mind to know that those caring for children in the schools and institutions of the archdiocese have been checked out thoroughly. So many times, I pass you here in the pastoral center, often with your little youngsters at your side, and I say a prayer of thanks to God for the great people that make up this local Church of ours. Besides the folks I saw here at the pastoral center, I know many more went to our other sites and many others gave their time to attend our workshops to help learn how to keep children safe. Our pastors have shared with me how so many of you—nearly ten thousand people last year—made that remarkable effort with all the sacrifices it entailed.

I pray to God that no child is ever harmed again. We know and mourn the terrible abuse that has happened, sadly, by members of the clergy, and we reach out to those who have been abused. We know we must reach out to those who have been harmed. We know that we must also reach out to others who have been harmed by persons other than clergymen because, as we have sadly learned, child abuse is a problem of our society and knows no boundaries. I am told that the last case involving a member of our clergy that has been reported to the archdiocese occurred fifteen years ago. I thank God for that. By contrast, the last reported allegation against a lay person—in this case, a custodian whose employer had a contract with a school—occurred a year ago. We must—and we shall—always be vigilant to prevent harm in our schools, our parishes, and our communities.

There is no statute of limitations on criminal acts of child abuse and no one, lay person, priest, or family member, can ever escape prosecution on a criminal offense as long as they live. This hopefully is a deterrent and always will be.

As I read and reflect on today's report, please know that I am thinking of you in gratitude for your commitment to our children and to the happy future that each of them deserves.

In Cold Blood
February 17, 2005

I have never been to the Amazon, but I know how important it is to the life and the health of the world. That splendid phenomenon of rivers and lakes and jungle is probably the last bit of untouched nature on our globe. It is often called the lungs of the world. For decades, unfortunately, unscrupulous interests have been determined to destroy it. They've destroyed the flora and fauna, the vegetation and living creatures, and have tried to dispel the untold riches of its natural resources. And all this for a passing profit.

At the same time, they have succeeded in almost eliminating the human life—much of it primitive and at the mercy of modern weaponry and wiles—that has inhabited this region for centuries. When the missionaries arrived, perhaps a century ago, they became the protectors of the people, and by that very fact, protectors of the environment that gave these people sustenance and life. This created a collision course between the avarice of entrepreneurs and the men and women of God who stood in their way.

Last week, a courageous American nun, Sister Dorothy Stang, a member of the congregation of Notre Dame de Namur, which is well known here in this area, was gunned down in cold blood by the hired assassins of some of the people who could not stand the attention that she was focusing on their destructive and illegal activity. She had spoken out on more than one occasion, calling a spade a spade and a crime a crime. Her life had been often threatened, and sometimes in face-to-face confrontations, she had been told to keep her mouth shut and to leave the country. She did not have the protection of the police, who are sometimes as terrified of these economic warlords as the people they are supposed to protect.

Last week they were conveniently not around when the hired murderers came. Two bullets to the body and two to the face, and they finally silenced Sister Dorothy's courageous voice. The government has promised an investigation. Let us hope that it happens so that those who want to destroy the land may not be strong enough to corrupt the authorities.

I have written to you about this for two reasons. First of all, that you might share my horror and dismay at this murder in cold blood of a fellow American and a heroic Catholic nun. Secondly, that you and I might marvel together at Sister Dorothy's courage and her absolute, selfless dedication to the protection of the human rights of the poor people she served. May her terrible death not be in vain. May it refocus the attention of our modern society on the lungs of this threatened globe, and may we become all the more conscious of the remarkable vocation to service that our Catholic missionaries have as they proclaim the Gospel of Jesus to the ends of the earth.

I cannot help thinking of you as I write this and pray that there is in our heart and mind that same spark of courageous faith that is the only remedy to the ills of the world.

Mega-Churches
February 24, 2005

Every once in a while, the newspapers tell us about the mega-churches in our area and in the nation. They are churches whose Sunday attendance is in the thousands and because of that they are able to offer a number of special services to their congregation, ranging from wonderful music programs and splendid technological productions of sound and light, even to including valet parking! I give thanks when I read about such churches because it is always a blessing when people find peace and hope in coming to worship and in hearing about God and the works of his kingdom.

Last week, I was at a funeral in a parish of another diocese and the pastor told me that four thousand people come to Mass there every Sunday and that he is trying to figure out how to fit more Masses into his schedule. On the way back home, I started to muse about our own local Church of Washington and I realized that we, too, have a number of churches that would qualify as mega-churches, even though we do not have those special services that so often go along with that definition.

Since the newspapers usually begin to classify mega-churches as those that are congregations of two thousand churchgoers or higher, I could count more than a dozen Catholic Churches in our archdiocese that would qualify for that description and, indeed, there would be more if we counted parishes in the neighboring area! I wanted to write you about this subject for a lot of reasons. First of all, because I did not want you to think that our Catholic Church had none of these larger congregations, too. We just don't call them mega-churches since they don't have all the amenities that the media associates with that phenomenon.

Since we know that the attraction to the non-Catholic mega-churches often is an enormously charismatic preacher and other special programs that they are able to present, what is it that brings people into our own churches? In non-Catholic churches, the sermon is often the central element of the worship service and it is of unique importance for the gathering of the congregation. That, of course, is true with us as well, and this local Church of ours does have many out-standing preachers, but for the Catholic worshiper, the Liturgy of the Word is only part of the totality. It is an essential part, of course, but it is the setting of the theme, the breaking open of the scriptures, the introduction to the great mystery itself. For us, the Liturgy of the Sacrament that follows is the door to enter fully into the awesome mystery of God's love. We encounter Christ in the Liturgy of the Word. We receive him, Body and Blood, soul and divinity in the Eucharist!

For men and women of deep faith, Communion is the participation in the very life of Christ. And for us that is the most important part of our life of faith. And the good part about it all is that this can happen not only in our churches where thousands come to worship every Sunday, but in smaller churches all over the archdiocese wherever people gather for Mass, at which the Word is proclaimed and the Word made flesh is made present to feed and heal the wounds of our people and give them a new life in Christ. I am thinking of you as I ride along to celebrate Mass with the folks in Southern Maryland, and I am thanking God that his presence in even our smallest church makes it a mega-source of eternal life.

Some Great Good News!
March 3, 2005

It's time for good news! We have all been so concerned about the health of the Holy Father and, of course, I hope that you join me in constant prayer for his recovery from what was apparently a very dangerous moment in his life. The anxious news of his health has been on all our minds. Besides that, we continue to be concerned about the ongoing violence in Iraq and in the Holy Land, about the aftermath of the devastation of the tsunami and its effect on so many people, about the continuing damage to the health of the world through the destruction of the Amazon Basin—as we were so vividly reminded by the murder of Sister Dorothy Stang. All those have been the news items of concern day after day in the last few weeks.

But today, I really want to share some good news with you! It is not only the numbers that make the good news—although they, too, are impressive and I am so grateful for them—but what the numbers represent, namely, the awesome generosity of the people of the Archdiocese of Washington is what makes this great good news for me!

I just received the final report of the Cardinal's Appeal for last year, 2004. It not only held onto our hopes, but increased by almost four hundred thousand dollars over the previous year! What is even more wonderful for me is that there were more than three thousand new donors, folks who wanted to join us to help those important works of our local Church continue serving the people. That brings our total donors to more than fifty thousand. How very much I thank you for that very good news. (I cannot fail to hope that that growth in the numbers of people who give might even inspire some of our other folks to join us now and bring the number of donors even higher in 2005!)

People around the country often look at Washington and watch the currents of its political culture and social life. It is interesting that they often also watch the ongoing life of the Church here, too. For that reason, your generosity does have a ripple effect across the country and encourages our Catholic brothers and sisters to tend to imitate the same great generosity that you have. This makes your generosity even more important, because it strengthens and inspires the goodness of others!

I am so grateful to Monsignor John Enzler, Greg Gannon, and all their associates in the Archdiocesan Office of Development. The annual Cardinal's Appeal is what puts the bread on the table and the gas in the car. It is what keeps us going from day to day, and, as you know, every single cent collected goes to the needs which we announced when we asked for your help. Even the cost of the appeal itself is borne by other diocesan funds so that you can be sure that 100 percent of everything you gave will go to the people that you wanted to help.

And so today, in the midst of all kinds of other news stories, the wonderful generosity of our people moves me to be thinking of you with even greater thanks to God for the Church that he has given me to serve.

Surprise
March 10, 2005

I always thought you had to be an outstanding athlete to have a tear in your rotator cuff! Unfortunately, I now know that that is not true. I just had one myself! And I have never been a great athlete. Do you think that it may have come from forty-seven years of blessing people? That's about the extent of my arm exercise, although up to a short time ago, I did do a lot of pushups. Recently my exercise has been a half hour on the treadmill, but that wouldn't set the shoulder off.

Anyway, it's a mystery to me, although I think I'm going to pretend that it was from an old football injury. That would make it much more prestigious, don't you think, even though no one really would believe it.

Seriously, I'm writing this on Saturday morning as I'm getting ready to leave for the hospital. It's my right shoulder and since I'm a lefty, I will still be able to write. They tell me that my arm will be in a sling for three weeks or so, so there will be some things that I won't be able to do. I'm concerned about the liturgies of Holy Week that are coming up so soon, but we will cross that bridge when we come to it.

I'm going to understand much better the frustration of those wounded in the service who I visit in the military hospitals once in a while, who have lost the use of an arm or who, indeed, may have lost an arm itself. My temporary inconvenience is nothing, but hopefully it will make me more sensitive to them and to the folks with disabilities of every kind.

Please say a prayer for my patience. I don't really have a lot of it sometimes and yet the great spiritual writers say that patience is the mother of all virtues. Well, this will give me a good chance to learn patience with myself, with those I work with and with everybody else. It will be a good late Lenten penance, anyway. As I begin to be uncomfortable, I offer it up for you, for vocations and for peace in our world. Don't forget those prayers for me, too, and know that I'm thinking of you.

Patience, Patience, Patience
March 17, 2005

Here I am, with my arm and shoulder in a sling and a sheath—the latter describes the cloth that binds my right arm to the rest of my body so I won't move. Apparently, my shoulder was in worse shape than I thought and the surgeon had to do a lot more work inside it to fix it up, so I'll have to wear these things for a while longer.

A lot of new experiences! I learned how clumsy I am. I just got permission to take a shower a few days ago. It was great, except that I could only use my left arm (thank God, at least I'm a lefty) and that lets me very carefully wash my right arm and my shoulder, but I haven't figured out yet how to wash my left arm when it's the arm I'm washing with.

Thank God also for loafers (I don't mean lazy people, but the kind of shoes you wear). I confess that I still can't tie my shoelaces with one hand and I'm embarrassed to call the priests who live with me and ask them to do it for me. Maybe I could offer them a reward each time, maybe one for each shoe?

And how about trying to sleep on the wrong side every night without moving. When I turn on my bandaged side, I get a sharp reminder not to do it again. And then there's the problem of sitting down to dinner and finding a delicious-looking piece of food that obviously needs to be cut into small pieces. When I think there is no one watching, I sneak my right hand out of my sling and cut it, even though I know it only makes the time in the sling last all the longer.

I pray for patience every day—and for speedy healing. I haven't even been able to start the therapy yet—since the shoulder has to heal first. I must be very hard to live with these days. Thank God, there are six of us in the building, so I don't get on everybody's nerves all at once.

Of course, the thing that I miss the most is offering Mass at the parishes. It seems awfully strange to be celebrating in my little chapel on Sundays and with the great days of Holy Week coming up so close. The pain has truly not been bad at all. It's just the need to keep the shoulder quiet for the fastest healing possible to continue. Whatever the discomfort, physical or psychological, I offer it up in atonement for my sins and faults and for all your intentions. Thinking of you as I offer these prayers, I ask that you remind the Lord that it would be great to get me back in the saddle soon again.

Joys in Holy Week
March 24, 2005

Even though Holy Week contains the saddest day of our year, Good Friday, it is still a week of extraordinary gifts from God that have to fill every Catholic heart with joy. For me this year, there was the special joy of learning that my shoulder is healing nicely and that, although I must be patient for several months of therapy, I should have all my movement back before too long. (I do want to thank you for all your prayers for my healing. The wonder of it all was that I did not have any real pain. The surgeon had given me a prescription for pain medicine and I filled it, but thanks be to God and to you who remembered my shoulder in prayer, I never had to take it.)

But, there are other moments of joy in Holy Week much more mystical than my grateful joy in healing. The greatest joy, of course, comes through the greatest sorrow. The cruel passion and death of Jesus brings us forgiveness and redemption. Through his suffering and death, you and I are able to have our sins forgiven and enter the eternal joy of heaven, a joy that no other can ever match.

Another joy of Holy Week is the Eucharist, which is given to us at the Lord's Supper on Holy Thursday. In this Eucharistic Year, that is a special moment of joy-filled grace as we are filled with the wonder of God's real Presence in the blessed sacrament and his extraordinary desire to dwell among us as a sign of his indescribable love. The gift of the priesthood also comes to us on Holy Thursday as the apostles are made the ministers of his Body and Blood at the table of the cenacle. Finally, there is a sense in which some of the Fathers of the Church have seen the Church itself born on the cross of Good Friday and so that day of sorrow is also the moment that we can celebrate the beginning of the Church, as well.

For me, all these truly wondrous events are somehow summarized in the Mass of the Chrism, which we celebrate on the Monday evening of Holy Week. I am privileged to bless the holy oils and send them out to all our parishes as a mark of the unity of this local Church and a reminder to me of my responsibility to care for all our parishes and all our people. There, surrounded by so many of our priests and deacons, we celebrate a Mass of such great significance. It is truly a family gathering, both in the sense that we are reminded of the heavenly Father's love for us in sending Jesus to become one of us, true God and true man, and also because the holy oils remind us of the sacraments which Jesus himself gave to us as a sign of our salvation.

It has been my custom to use that special celebration to call, in a formal way, the men who will be ordained to priesthood in May, as well as the new deacons who will enter a year of living in sacred orders, prior to their own call to priesthood the following year. The sacristy of St. Matthew's Cathedral, where I give this call, rings out with the joyful congratulations of their brothers and sisters—priests, deacons, seminarians, religious, and lay people—who are gathered there for the Chrism Mass. The great Church itself is stirred as the word of this joyful event becomes known to the congregation of religious and lay, young and old, who come for this holy celebration and the sense of being part of a family as it gathers together in prayer.

The final joy of the Chrism Mass is the renewal of the promises that the priests of the archdiocese and other clergy make according to the old formulas of the Church. This, too, is a moment of great grace, the expression of fidelity to promises made, sometimes long ago, to be a faithful priest, a servant of the Lord and of the Church, a man for others, bound to the Church not by contract, but by loving service. As I take these promises and make my own, I am thinking of you for whom, in God's great and mysterious providence, all this great, good work is undertaken.

The Holy Father
March 31, 2005

Toward the end of Holy Week, someone in the Vatican said of the Holy Father that he had serenely placed himself in the hands of God and day-by-day continues to serve as

best he is able to fulfill his ministry as pastor of the universal
Church. That was no surprise, for this has been the dedication of Pope John Paul II since the moment of his election as
Supreme Pontiff more than a quarter century ago. Only God
knows how many months or years our pope will continue to
guide and sanctify the more than a billion members of the
Catholic family around the world, but we do know this, that
as long as the Holy Father has the strength of mind and will,
he will continue to be a model of dedication and love for us
all.

I first met Cardinal Karol Wojtyla when he was archbishop
of Krakow and came to the United States with a number of
other Polish bishops to attend the International Eucharistic
Congress in Philadelphia in 1976. I was serving as secretary
to the servant of God, Cardinal Terence Cooke, then the
archbishop of New York, and the Polish prelate stayed in the
cardinal's residence for several days. He was, even then, an
extraordinarily impressive figure. Brilliant, outgoing, strong,
and prayerful, all of us in the house were struck by his presence. Of course, we never dreamed that our Polish guest
would become pope. It had been more than five hundred
years since the election of a pope who was not Italian. I think
that many of us who met him then thought that somehow he
truly had the qualities of a great Holy Father.

Each time he has come to the United States since his election, I have been privileged to see him if only for a moment
with the other American bishops. Each time I have been so
pleased that he has recognized me from that first visit to New
York. "I know him, I know him," he would say to the person
who was presenting me to him in his deep voice with just a
trace of a tell-tale Polish accent. "I knew him when he was
secretary to Cardinal Cooke."

I have watched him grow in stature and in his understanding of this complex world. His mind, always strong and
quick to grasp even the most complex situations, has always

been so deeply rooted in his faith and in his total dedication to the Lord and the Church. Scripture tells us that we should teach clearly like a "certain trumpet," which constantly gives a bold and unmistakable signal to those who listen. This has been the teaching of Pope John Paul II. To the sometimes confusing commentaries on the documents of the Second Vatican Council, his voice has clearly stated what the council truly taught for the guidance of the whole Church. He did this both as a leading figure of that ecumenical council, as now with the authority of the Vicar of Christ.

As the Holy Father suffers from his illness and frailty, I am sure that his greatest suffering must come from the frustration of not being able to communicate as powerfully as he has always done in the past, and not being able to smile and share his warm and gracious personality with young and old alike all over the world. It is surely true that he preaches to us these days through his pain and his patience, but his greatest cross must be in not being able to speak to us in that clear and powerful voice that has marked his papacy over the years.

Thinking of you and thinking of him in these days of concern, I know that you pray for him and pray that God who called him to the Chair of Peter will give him the strength to serve there with grace and power until he calls him home.

Reflections from Rome
April 7, 2005

(Vatican City) I thought it would be good to share with you some reflections of this historic journey. It has been more than a quarter-century since the election of a pope and the awesome nature of a cardinal's responsibility hangs heavy upon me suddenly these days. I always knew that some day there would be the possibility or maybe even the probability of my being called to a conclave, but now that it is here, it comes with the anxiety that I will need to be prayerful enough to listen to the promptings of the Holy Spirit and help to elect the one the Church needs to be the next pope.

The first thing I want to tell you is to thank you for all your prayers. Since last Friday, when we realized that the Holy Father was close to death, wherever I went people made a point of saying, "We are all praying for you. We know what a big job the cardinals will have." The folks in the media were really wonderful. Of course, they do try good naturedly to learn more than I could possibly know and were determined to get me to speculate on the future. But their questions and their real concern for the pope and for the future of the Church were very earnest and they went out of their way always to be gracious. I was in the media a lot this past weekend—maybe too much—but I don't like to say no when there is a chance to get the message of the Gospel and the Church out to our own people and to those multitudes of good will who truly loved Pope John Paul II.

On the way to Rome, I flew Continental, since I was used to that airline company from my New Jersey days and they have a non-stop flight that gets into Rome early in the morning. This way, I could be present at the first of the general congregations of cardinals that was already called for last Monday morning. The folks at the airport and on the plane could not have been more helpful. I think they sensed the historic nature of this journey and did everything they could to make it as easy and successful as possible.

I'm in Rome now, staying at the North American College, where Cardinal Hickey was rector years ago, and there is a very comfortable suite of rooms that bear his name. In the last few years, the college has been giving me the Hickey Suite because of the connection with the Archdiocese of

Washington. It is a wonderful place to stay, close to the Vatican, and it also gives me the chance to visit our seminarians at the same time. Of course, the presence of the conclave is palpable all over Rome and especially in a seminary.

Please don't stop praying now. Remember Pope John Paul II as he returns home to the Lord and pray that all his hopes for the Church may be realized. And pray for me, as I know you do so often, that I may fulfill my own responsibility with faith-filled love. Thinking of you at this historic time in all our lives, I send you my love from the Eternal City.

His Secret Gift
April 14, 2005

(Vatican City) I've been saying to everybody I meet that we have witnessed the largest funeral in the history of the world! You probably have seen the photos of the enormous crowds at the funeral of the Holy Father. They were everywhere in the city of Rome. Someone said that they thought Rome had become the largest Polish city in Europe as millions of Poles—and millions of others—descended on the Eternal City and filled it with their own love of this first Slavic pope. The evening before the funeral, I had gone to a meeting across the city—ordinarily a fifteen-minute drive. That day it took an hour and a half, the streets were so jammed with life. It was like New Year's Eve in New York's Times Square that day.

Concelebrating the Mass on the day of the funeral was both a privilege and a time of sadness for me. We had all watched Pope John Paul II grow increasingly weaker and we knew that ultimately his illness and his failing strength would take him from us. On that Saturday afternoon, when he did pass away, I had returned to my residence after offering the noon Mass for the Holy Father in the National Shrine filled to capacity with the faithful young and old, as we all had this great and holy servant of God so much in our minds. As soon as the news of his death was announced, I decided that it would be important to have a special Mass in the Cathedral that evening. I was so pleased that President and Mrs. Bush, with so little prior notice, were both there with us at the Mass, filling a packed cathedral and paying personal tribute and the nation's respect to a man who had truly changed the world.

What was the secret gift of Pope John Paul II? How did he manage to touch all our lives and to remind us of God's presence and at the same time call us to put ourselves safely in God's hands? Maybe this little story can help to understand. I have told it on television more than once, so you may have already heard it, but I think it's worth telling again. I met a lady from Mexico here in Rome last week. She had come all the way just to be present for the funeral. She told me that she had been a little child in Mexico during the Holy Father's first visit to that country. I forget whether it was in Puebla or in Mexico City itself that the story took place. She was a little girl of nine or ten, sitting on the curb watching while the pope-mobile passed by the thousands who had gathered along the route to see the new pope. This is the way she told it to me: "You know, Father, when he passed by, and we all waved and shouted, he looked right at me and smiled at me! I can never forget that moment of joy!" The wonderful thing was that everyone in that street that day felt the same thing happening to them.

This story she told with tears welling up in her eyes, but with a great smile, too. The truth is that every single person along that route all did feel the same thing happen. "He looked at me and smiled!" Pope John Paul II had "the gift of people" more than anyone else I have ever known. He always seemed to be talking just to you, smiling right at you, listening to you and to your own message, whether it was sad or joyful. Being anywhere in his presence was an unforgettable experience and this woman never forgot it. She never forgot the pope who smiled right at her!

Next Sunday, I move into the Domus Santa Marta, the residence in Rome where all the cardinal-electors will live, totally cut off from the world. Next Monday the conclave begins. I will be thinking of you as I pray that the Holy Spirit will help me choose one who will have the same gift of people, together with that great closeness to God that Pope John Paul II had. Pray for me, too, at this time of grace.

The Holy Father
April 28, 2005

(First of all, I want to apologize for not writing you last week. It was the first time in almost four and a half years that I have not done the "Thinking of You" column. I know you understood that it was because I was totally out of communication with the outside world from Sunday to Wednesday of last week. The *Catholic Standard* did have a spare column handy—for any time that I would not be able to write you— but it was not on a subject that was appropriate for such a solemn and historic moment in the history of the Church— and in my own life, too, by the way.)

When the final announcement, "We have a pope" was made in Latin by Cardinal Medina, the senior cardinal-deacon of the college, at the central balcony of St. Peter's Basilica, I was standing at another balcony just a few yards away. My seat at the conclave was in the back row towards the front of the Sistine Chapel and so when the cardinals all filed out, the front rows of the balconies were taken. I could see the crowd from where I was pretty well, but you would never be able to spot me in the mass of red robes unless you knew just where to look. I hope you saw Cardinal Baum there in the central balcony. He was Cardinal Hickey's predecessor as archbishop of Washington and although his health has not been vigorous, he was a great example to us in the conclave and, together with Cardinal Ratzinger, was the only cardinal who had ever voted in a papal election before.

What a special time that was! I'll never forget the moment when the 114 cardinals had just elected the new successor of Saint Peter. At that unforgettable point in time, it seemed that everyone in the chapel held his breath as the question was asked of Cardinal Joseph Ratzinger if he would accept election as Supreme Pontiff of the Church. When he said, "I accept," suddenly he was no longer just a cardinal with the rest of us, but the shepherd of the universal Church.

The evening before, I had supper with him, as by accident I ended up at a German-speaking table. The next day's dinner found him, already clad in white, now sitting among the senior members of the College of Cardinals, as the protocol requires. After the meal he asked us to stay together until Mass the following day in the Sistine Chapel where he could speak to us about his hopes and dreams. This, of course, was the very place in which we had chosen him the day before. You have already seen his talks and statements since then, I am sure. I thought his homily at the Mass of Installation last Sunday was a masterpiece. It told us so much about this good man and about his sense of his mission as the head of the Church.

I hope you will continue to pray for him. I cannot even begin to imagine how difficult it must be to start one's service as pope. The beginning of the Second Vatican Council's great document on the Church in the Modern World, *Gaudium* et *Spes*, written some forty years ago, spoke of the joys and the hopes, the grief and the anguish of the people of the world, which are the challenges that the Church has to deal with.

In a very real sense, these same challenges are the ones that the pope himself must meet every day of his life. Pope Benedict XVI is a brilliant theologian and a very wise man. In the past three weeks I have also seen his holiness and gentleness, too. The Holy Spirit has sent us a very good and holy pope. Let us thank the Lord for that great gift and rejoice that he will be thinking of you and me and of all God's children every day as he prays for us to Christ, whose vicar on earth he is.

What Kind of Man Is He?
May 5, 2005

Since I came back from Rome last week, one question has been asked me repeatedly. It is not what you might first presume. Oh sure, I have been asked about the conclave, about how it felt to enter that awesome place with its equally awesome responsibility. I have been asked how much I can talk about what went on by media folks looking for a scoop and by our ordinary Catholic friends who just want to learn more about that process so deeply involved in the presence of the Holy Spirit himself. But more and more, people are asking me about the Holy Father. "Tell us about Pope Benedict XVI," they are saying. "What is he like?"

What can I tell you? I have seen him up close for three weeks every day. I have listened to him, talked with him, sat down at table to eat with him. We all knew that he was a brilliant theologian and a faithful witness to the Gospel and the teaching of the Church, but we also found him a very gentle man, somewhat shy and reserved at first, but warm and gracious and humble, with a fine sense of humor and a quick smile. Perhaps the way to answer the question is to do it in his own words.

In the first words he spoke to the great crowd at St. Peter's Square, he called himself "a simple, humble worker in the vineyard of the Lord," but he added something very touching and significant. He said he was comforted by the fact that "the Lord knows how to use insufficient instruments and, above all, I entrust myself to your prayers."

At the Mass of his installation as supreme pastor of the Church, we saw his deep humility and his trust in the Lord and in us, his people. Listen to his words again. "And now at this moment, weak servant that I am, I must assume this enormous task, which truly exceeds all human capacity. How can I do this? How will I be able to do it?"

He then refers to the Litany of the Saints, which we had all just sung, and goes on to say, "I am not alone. I do not have to carry alone what in truth I could never carry alone. All the saints of God are there to protect me, to sustain and to carry me. Your prayers, my dear friends, your indulgence, your love, your faith and your hope sustain me."

I want to encourage all of us to read what Benedict XVI is saying. It is filled with faith and hope and with a beauty that comes from a pastor's heart. Take, for example, his words about a pastor's duty.

"The pastor must be inspired by Christ's holy zeal; for him it is not a matter of indifference that so many people are living in the desert. And there are so many kinds of desert. There is the desert of poverty, the desert of hunger and thirst, the desert of abandonment, of loneliness, of love that has gone astray. There is the desert of God's darkness, the emptiness of souls no longer aware of their dignity or the goal of human life."

These are the words of a true pastor who is aware of the pain and the sorrow, as well as the joys, of his people. Do not let the "spin" of some in the media or in the self-proclaimed intelligencia cause you to think of this pope as anything but a good, humble, and holy man who loves the Lord and his Church and loves us, too.

We are blessed to have him as our Holy Father. He is the one the Lord had chosen, and we cardinal-electors became aware of that during the days of the conclave. I have no doubt that he will always be thinking of you and me and all our sisters and brothers and praying for our happiness both here and in the world to come.

The Holy Spirit
May 12, 2005

As we approach the great feast of Pentecost, my mind is filled with many thoughts of how the Holy Spirit works in our world. We call the Holy Spirit by many names: the Spirit of Truth, the Guiding Spirit, the Best Gift of God, the Advocate, the Gentle Father of the Poor, the Lord of Consolation, the Spirit of Love, and many other wonderful titles. But the truth is that most of us never pray to him enough. Oh, we know that he is the third person of the Blessed Trinity, equal to the Father and the Son in all things and that we owe the Holy Spirit our adoration and our praise, but aside from the glory be to the Father and to the Son and to the Holy Spirit, there are not too many prayers to the Holy Spirit that get into our own prayer life.

That is a shame since by the titles we give him, we remind ourselves of his actions in our lives every day. When we pray for consolation in grief or in sorrow, it is the Holy Spirit who comes as consoler. When we pray for our growth in holiness or our forgiveness from the sins we have committed, it is the

Holy Spirit who is our advocate. When we express the deep joy that fills our hearts when we do something good, it is the Holy Spirit in whom we rejoice.

Sorrows, needs, forgiveness, joys—these are all the special moments of our existence, and God, the Holy Spirit, is present in a very special way in all of them. These days I pray to him a lot. When I see the terrible violence in our streets—children being killed by gunfire, elderly ladies beaten viciously, anger and despair touching too many families—I ask the Holy Spirit for His gift of peace and gentleness in our neighborhoods and our society. When I see wars and violence still raging in so many parts of our world, poverty still grinding down so many of our sisters and brothers, downtrodden and stifled lives that could flourish and make a difference in the world, I beg the Holy Spirit to be the advocate of justice and righteousness in our time.

Join me in praying to the Holy Spirit these days. Ask him to watch over us and bring us and those we love his own gifts of grace and wonder that we may be able to live our lives in a better and happier way and inherit the blessings that God has prepared for us all. Thinking of you as Pentecost comes, I pray to the Holy Spirit that he will remake the face of the earth.

Parishes
May 19, 2005

Last Sunday, the Solemnity of Pentecost, was another one of those beautiful days that God gives me to enjoy the life of this Archdiocese of Washington. It started off badly because once again I had allowed the schedule to get away from me. It wasn't the fault of my secretaries. God knows, they try to

keep me from saying yes to everything, but as usual, I did it
to myself. I had four Masses that day and a dinner following.
(It was a blessing and maybe a miracle that my head did not
end up in the soup that evening!)

It began with a parish Mass at 9:00 at the chapel of
the retirement community in Resurrection Parish in Burtonsville. Then we raced down to La Plata for a wonderful
diaconate ordination of three outstanding young men at an
11:30 Mass there. After that, we rushed back to Washington
for the adult confirmation at a Mass at 3:00 at the cathedral,
where I had the privilege of confirming some 150 adults.
Then I was able to get home to my residence for half an hour
before I headed out to the Basilica of the National Shrine for
a very impressive Mass for the movements and the ecclesial
communities that are located here in the archdiocese. The
last stop of the day was a dinner honoring Bishop Bransfield
of Wheeling-Charleston—who had been the rector of the
National Shrine—on his ordination anniversary. All in all, it
was a wonderful—although a very tiring—day.

I am writing you about this not to pretend that I am
really earning my keep, but to focus mainly on the wonderful
diversity of this local Church of ours. From Burtonsville in
the northern part of the archdiocese to La Plata in Southern
Maryland and back to the district, there are so many great
parishes serving God's people in so many ways. Each of them
is different with its own strengths and its own challenges, but
the local parish is always going to be the center of the life of
every diocese. Cardinal Egan of New York always reminds his
people that the diocese only exists to take care of the parishes
and not the other way around. Everything we do in the central administration is justified only if it helps the parishes and
makes it easier for them to serve God's people.

When I spoke to the movements and the ecclesial communities Sunday night at the Mass in the Basilica, I spoke of
this and urged all of them to concentrate on building up the

parishes in the pursuit of their particular goals. The men and women who have received the special grace to be formed in the spirituality of those movements whose charism has been approved by the Church need to be challenged to find a fitting place for their apostolic labors in the context of the local parishes.

For centuries it has been the parish that is the first home of the Catholic people. The Church has always put its hopes and cares on the building up of parish life as the basis of Catholic identity and the apostolic mission of every Catholic man and woman. Of course, many of us are called to serve on a diocesan level or in an apostolate that goes beyond the local parish community, but it is there in our own home parishes that we should find the grace and strength to do the things that are so important to the Church itself. We find the sacraments there, the preaching of the Word there and the sense of community which gives us strength and purpose. If we do not take our nourishment from the family, we know that we can lose our way in life, and the parish is the first ecclesiastical family for us all. If the parishes are not strong, the dioceses will be weak and the movements themselves will ultimately suffer. Thinking of you, as you grow in grace and the challenges of Catholic living through the nourishment of your own parishes, I pray that they will always be the centers of our lives as God's faithful people where we prepare ourselves and our children for the wonder of life in Christ.

The Priests of Washington
May 26, 2005

This Saturday, please God, I will ordain five new priests for the service of the Church of Washington. That will make a total of thirty-one ordinations to the priesthood for our diocese since I first came in 2001. Relatively, when compared to other dioceses, five newly ordained is not a bad number. I thank the Lord and the faith of our Catholic people that we now have sixty fine men in our seminaries preparing for the priesthood for this archdiocese. This is the largest number we've had in years, and it is a sign of hope, but for a few years we will have to wait in joyful hope until they all come to ordination. Right now, however, our needs are great and the older priests who have blessed this Archdiocese of Washington with their ministry are going to be retiring in greater numbers as the years go by.

Having fewer priests to care for our people means three things. First of all, it means that most parishes will not have associate pastors to help care for the people. This puts a tremendous burden on the pastors as they must try to care for God's faithful in large parishes without other priestly associates. Thank God, the lay leadership in our parishes have always come forward with gifts of time, talent, and treasure, without which neither our pastors nor our parishes could give the care that we so want to provide.

The second fall-out for a shortage of priests is the difficulty—or even the impossibility—of giving the people all that we want them to have in the area of liturgical, sacramental, and pastoral ministry. Popular devotions must suffer, and both adults and children don't get a chance to know their priests as they should. It is hard to be a man of prayer if you must spend so much of your time in activity. It is hard to keep up on the needed study of theology and philosophy and at the same time always to be available in the confessional or in the parlor or at the sick bed of parishioners, both in their homes or in health-care facilities.

The third difficulty that too few priests will cause is the situation present here in our archdiocese at this time. We have been fortunate up until now. Our pastors are named

408*Thinking of You* ☞

for a term of six years, but when a large number of them are retiring by reason of age or illness, that starts a veritable tsunami of reassignments and, since we are stretched so thin, we struggle to find the right man for the right place. The priest personnel office and the personnel board work closely with me to accomplish this, but not having a large number of priests creates a great challenge to ensure that we are always doing the best we can for our people.

I want to thank our priests for their dedication in facing this challenging situation. This happens to be a critical year with so many retirements and relatively few ordinations. My brothers in the priesthood have been wonderfully understanding of our mutual challenge and have accepted it with great generosity and zeal for their ministry. I thank the Lord for them. They are a great example to me and, I am sure, also to you. They prove once again that the secret of holiness in the life of a parish priest is the loving care of his people, and this presbyterate of Washington both knows and does that well.

They are thinking of you always and of your own challenges, joys, and concerns, and they give their lives in your service and for the glory of the living God. Pray for them, as they pray for you and for me.

To Be Clear
June 2, 2005

Every once in a while someone writes me to inquire about something I said or someone said I said. I'm always grateful and at times even a little startled at the interest folks have in listening and wanting to know the truth. I believe that our media here in Washington have really tried to report with faithfulness the positions people take on issues. Sometimes, however, these issues are very complex or emotional and other times, folks like me may not speak as clearly as we should.

One case in point is the question of the Catholic bishops' position on immigration. I think it would be good to use that as an example. Let me bring up just three points which have confused people and try to set the record straight.

The first is the question of every nation's right to establish rules for the admission of immigrants into its territory. There is no question about a nation's right to do this. This has always been and continues to be Catholic teaching. We believe that the United States must be able to control its borders and have a clear policy as to who can enter to live and work here. We do believe that such a policy should be humane and gener-ous, as it was in times past when our own families were able to come and start a new life here. We also believe that other countries should help in patrolling their borders so that the flow of illegal immigrants can be controlled.

The second is the question of our United States immigra-tion policy. Because of many reasons, it is now no longer adequate for the task it has to do. President Bush under-stands that and has proposed changes in it, and the Congress on both sides of the political aisle has agreed and presented changes on its own. One example is that a legal immigrant with all the necessary papers and years of working here in this country still cannot legally bring his or her immediate family to the United States without many years of waiting until the quota allows them to be reunited. We believe that families are the basic strength of all our people and to keep families apart is an injustice and can, indeed, cause all kinds of social and moral problems. Several of the bills in Congress aim at fixing that weakness in our policy and we support those.

Finally, we do believe in legal immigration. (Realistically, except for the Native Americans, we wouldn't be here today if such a program did not exist when our parents or grandparents or great grandparents came to America.) If migrants who come here to work—often on our farms or in service industries—were not here, our economy would be adversely affected. We need to find a way for them to enter legally. Illegal immigration is a dangerous thing both for our own country and for those who try to immigrate. Hundreds of people die every year trying to cross our borders. They are so often abused by unscrupulous criminal elements. I agree with the Catholic bishops of Arizona that we must find a way to "allow migrant workers and their families to migrate in a safe, orderly and humane manner" that is legal and ultimately helps our own country and our economy.

This is an important issue for America today. We need a strong and clear immigration policy. It must serve our country's security and prosperity and at the same time be based on the moral values on which all our lives must ultimately rest. We must never forget the Gospel call of Jesus "to welcome the stranger" for in the face of this stranger, we see the face of Christ. As the bishops try to be clear and consistent in our teaching, I am thinking of you and always anxious that you understand the things I say and why I need to say them.

Permanent Deacons
June 9, 2005

Last Saturday, I was blessed to have another ordination. This one was different from the others, since four of the five new deacons are married with wonderful families. It was, of course, the ordination of the new permanent deacons for the service of the Archdiocese of Washington. The difference this year was the fact that all of the new deacons were Hispanic!

The Second Vatican Council gave the Church many gifts, but one of the most visible and prominent was the restoration of the Permanent Diaconate. I use the word restoration because it had not only existed, but flourished in the Early Church and most of the seven deacons ordained by the apostles, as described in the Acts of the Apostles, were probably married men, too. The ordination in St. Matthew's Cathedral last Saturday raises the number of our deacons from minority communities and gives us the chance to reach out to all our Spanish-speaking sisters and brothers, even as the goodly number of our African American deacons helps make the Church present in the lives of our African American people, Catholic and non-Catholic, alike.

A permanent deacon is not someone on the road to the priesthood. His ministry was spelled out clearly in the beautiful words of the apostles themselves. It is a ministry of the word, of the altar, and of charity. I presume that most of you who read these words are acquainted with permanent deacons, but still, let me talk a little about what their life is like.

First of all, most importantly, their obligations as a husband and father take priority over everything else, and those responsibilities may not be ignored or treated as secondary. No diaconal obligation comes from God if it threatens a man's happy marriage or his duties as a good father. Deacons are first of all committed to those other primary obligations of their lives. It is wonderful to see the way in which wives in a special way support the vocation of their husbands and both encourage it and make it flourish throughout their lives.

Deacons are assigned by the archbishop either to a parish or, less frequently, to an archdiocesan ministry. You see them preaching or assisting at the altar for Mass and the other sacramental rites. These are their ministries of the word and the altar.

A third ministry, which can sometimes escape our notice, is the ministry of charity, by which they reach out to the poor, the homeless, the handicapped, and the stranger. In this way, they perform truly grace-filled acts of loving service to those people who cannot always take care of themselves. Without the work of the permanent deacons' service in Churches and their service of charity, the archdiocese would be so much less able to do the things we all want it to do. What a blessing they have been to me here in the Archdiocese of Washington even as they were earlier when I served in Metuchen and in Newark. It would be wonderful if the next time you meet one of our permanent deacons, you would thank him and his wife for their devoted service.

Contemplating these five fine men and their families, who are about to begin a lifetime of service of their neighbors, I am thinking of you and thanking God and the Second Vatican Council for giving us this wonderful gift of an apostolate restored from the Early Church.

The Face of God
June 16, 2005

There is a wonderful story from the life of Blessed Jeanne Jugan, the foundress of the Little Sisters of the Poor. These are the sisters who direct the home for the elderly here in Washington and in many other places around the world. They are the ones who took such good care of Cardinal Hickey in the last year before he went to God. They are also the ones who took such good care of my Aunt Edna at their home in New Jersey before she died last December. Blessed Jeanne lived in the nineteenth century in France. She had the idea of establishing a community to take care of the old people who had no one to care for them. Her community has grown and it has been a great blessing for elderly people everywhere.

When Blessed Jeanne was old herself, she no longer had the responsibility of directing the community. In fact, she worked in very menial occupations around the convent. The young sisters often did not realize that she was the one who founded the community, seeing in her a gentle and gracious and hard-working elderly nun who kept to herself and prayed a great deal. One day, when one of the younger sisters waved to her and she did not return the salute, the young sister complained that she had not responded to her greeting. Blessed Jeanne smiled and replied that she had not seen the sister waving and added very simply, "As I get older, my eyes are failing and truly the only thing I see clearly is the face of God!"

From time to time in these columns I talk about living in God's presence and that story always reminds me of how important it is. Wouldn't it be wonderful if we could have this extraordinary grace of living always in the presence of the God who sees us and loves us and watches over us so carefully? We would certainly not commit serious sin and we would not be brusque or selfish or prone to anger. His presence among us would be so evident and we would be conscious of his love and his grace. We would be reminded that all our neighbors are his children, too, and treat them with greater care and kindness.

I try to remind myself of his presence many times during the day. I'm very conscious of the fact that I so often forget. When I do, the way I deal with other people often reflects unwillingness to put them first and myself second. If nations were able to live in the presence of God, there would be no wars. If families could live in the presence of God, there would be much more happiness and peace at home. If you and I could live in the presence of God, we would find so much less stress and tension in our lives and we would smile more at ourselves and at those around us.

If there is one recommendation above all that I would make to you, it would be to practice every day some way to remind yourself of God's presence in your life. It could be the ticking of a clock at the changing of the hours. It could be every time the phone rings. It could be every time you get a twinge of pain from arthritis or some joint that is not working as well as it used to. Whatever it is, I am convinced that it would make you and me more peaceful people and more able to handle the challenges and difficulties that come in the ordinary course of each day. Thinking of you as the hot summer comes upon us, I recommend this holy practice, a calming breeze into a too often overheated life.

Waking, Sleeping, and Everything in Between
June 23, 2005

When I was a young man, one of the funnier things in life was to notice how older people tended to take frequent naps at rather unexpected intervals. We always admired the way an elderly relative could nod off without a moment's hesitation while listening to music or watching television. It was somewhat more startling when they did it during conversations in which they suddenly lost interest. In those latter cases, the other parties to the discussion would turn to them for a comment and find them comfortably in the arms of Morpheus, blithely ignoring the subject and the other parties to the dialogue. "Dozing off" was a phenomenon that wasn't restricted to the very old. The popular cartoon called "Blondie" finds her husband, Dagwood Bumstead, napping on the couch at quite regular intervals in at least half of the comic strips each week. Every teacher has vast experience of young dozers who may have come to class after too much homework— or too much partying—the night before.

Actually, I am writing this column in my car coming back from a Mass in Southern Maryland. My secretary is driving and he just awakened me from pleasant dozing off to tell me that we had almost arrived at our next stop. This is a column that I'm not just writing, but living through, right now!

I must confess that I am a dozer. At first, it was only after a very hectic day of working that I might doze off once or twice while reading papers in the evening. Now it happens in the afternoon, whether or not I have had a heavy lunch. I have the habit of trying to do some dictation in the early hours of the afternoon before the meetings or appointments begin. I go to a quiet room with my machine and the scores of letters that I must answer personally. After about three or four letters I begin to doze.

The fascinating part of this story is that I don't stop dictating! The mind keeps going and I keep talking into the Dictaphone. The results are often hilarious—and my secretary, the real one, not the priests—gently asks me, "Did you really want to say that?" I apologize profusely for wasting her time, but she doesn't seem to mind. I suspect she looks forward to my sleeping comments and desperately tries to figure out what I want to say. In the middle of a serious letter to a pastor I might say something like "Don't take the wrong streetcar or you'll end up lost" or to a perfectly healthy brother bishop, "Remember to take it easy for a while after the operation or you won't be able to walk upstairs quickly."

I am wondering if you have the same lapses, too. It may come with age or maybe my brain is just slowing down. Whatever it is, it makes an adventure out of dozing, at least for my secretary who tries to figure it out.

How fascinating the human brain must be! Its many parts and chambers, its multiple and varied functions! It still contains mysteries that we do not grasp and depth of sense and feelings we have not fathomed. But the Lord who made it all understands its workings and understands us as he watches with a gracious love how we use this precious instrument to plan all our moments and all our lives. Thinking of you in my wakings and in my dozings, I thank the Lord who made us all so filled with wonder.

An Unexpected Homily
June 30, 2005

I was in El Paso last week to give a talk about migration problems. I had never been there before and was impressed by the weather. Although it was close to one hundred degrees, it was dry and easier to take than some of our own summers here. My talk went very well, I think. People tend to be kind to aging ecclesiastics, anyway, and they were all very gracious. What I remember most of all was my homily!

I really had not been prepared to preach. I knew that I was to be the celebrant, but I was under the impression that one of the Texas or Mexican bishops was to preach the homily. It was only a few minutes before the Mass was about to begin that I realized they were expecting me to be the preacher. You know how I'm always saying to our priests that it is really a sin to preach without prayer and preparation before you mount the pulpit. Well, here, with all my good intentions, I was caught. I couldn't ask one of the others to preach because they were expecting me to do it. It was really time to pray quickly and to hope that the Lord will give me some ideas. He does promise that in critical circumstances, he will give us the thoughts and the words to carry them.

Well, the final end of the story is that the homily was one of the best I think I have ever preached and I honestly could not take any credit for it. I pondered about the plight of the poor who, like so many of our own grandparents, came to this country with very little, except the dream of a better life and the faith in a God whom they loved and trusted. It was the Feast of Saint John the Baptist, and I suddenly realized that he was very much like that himself.

The Gospel tells us how poor John the Baptist was, eating locusts and wild honey as his only food and dressed in the skins of animals. He had gone into the barren dessert to find in the quiet of prayer the sacred mission that God had in mind for him. There he found the dream for which the Lord had called him, the dream of a better world, without oppression, without discrimination, without violence. That was what he preached and from all over Israel people came to hear him. How clear it was that they all longed for that same dream. John's dream was a special one, however. It was realized in his encounter with his cousin, Jesus, the son of Mary, whom he recognized as the Son of God. After that meeting, John's ministry became more profound, his preaching more powerful, his dream more vivid and now more connected to the Jesus who would truly be its fulfillment.

The strangers who come to our country often have these same characteristics. They are very poor, they have the dream of a better life for their families and themselves, and in so many cases they have the powerful faith, which strengthens them because it comes from Jesus and it is that grace alone which gives them the courage that they need in order to survive amidst all the difficulties they face. Just as our ancestors who made their long and difficult journey across the ocean to make their home in this brave new world, so are the strangers who today come looking for the fulfillment of that same dream.

I wanted to share my short homily with you, not because it was really so good, but because it did have a lesson for us all to ponder. We all have our dreams and we all have our fears, but the only way we will reach our dreams and overcome our fears is in the Lord and our confidence in his love for us. Thinking of you as I fly back after a half day in Texas, I wanted to share my dreams so that all of us might realize how blessed we are who have put our trust in the Living God.

Seventy-Five
July 7, 2005

Somehow, seventy-five seems to be a special number. My family talks about it a lot; so much so, that one of the littlest of the youngsters has started calling out "Bingo" every time the number is mentioned! It is certainly a gift from God to have had seventy-five years of life and now, as far as I can tell, to be in good health and to have enough energy to do my work. As required by the canon law of the Church, I have sent my letter of resignation to the Holy Father and for now continue to serve as I await his pleasure.

People often ask whether I have any regrets. You know me well enough by now to know what they are. I wish I had tried harder to be a holy person so that I could be a better shepherd to all of you. After forty-seven years as a priest and twenty-eight as a bishop, I should have prayed more, loved God more, been kinder and more generous, and become a better example to those whom, in God's mysterious providence, I have been called to serve. As I look back over these long years, that's the one great regret.

In a real way, I have to say honestly that the regrets are balanced by a deep and confident joy. I know that you pray for me and that my love for all of you is so often wondrously returned by so many. Because of that, I trust that in whatever years or days God will continue to use me, I will try harder to get it right—to atone for my sins and my stupidities, to beg pardon for my faults and mistakes, to rejoice in God's overwhelming grace, and to be a good father and brother and friend.

"The future is hidden from our eyes," as the beautiful old instruction at weddings used to say. We know that it will have its crosses and its sorrows, but we know too that if we bear those with a loving heart and with trust in God, we can carry them all with perfect joy. Thinking of you, as I cross the threshold of three-quarters of a century, I wish us all that same perfect joy.

Heady Stuff
July 14, 2005

We all have to pray that this business of my seventy-fifth birthday doesn't go to my head! I was counting the number of articles in the secular press about my turning seventy-five and it was very impressive. I have had so many birthday parties to celebrate this event that if each new party were to count another year I would soon be in my nineties.

On the one hand, I guess it is nice that people are aware that the archbishop of Washington has a significant birthday, but on the other hand, getting to be seventy-five is not a matter of accomplishment, but rather a question of survival. Here I am, three-quarters of a century old, and, as one of my more humorous priests keeps saying to me, "You don't look a day over seventy-four." Honestly, I don't feel a day over seventy-four, but I have to admit that I don't feel like I was in my forties anymore, either.

It has been a great few days, and I want to thank the many people who sent me birthday greetings. The priests of the archdiocese gave me a splendid bishop's ring with my coat of arms on it and I will wear it proudly, not just because it's a beautiful ring, but because it comes with their prayers and their fidelity on which I count so very much.

Next Saturday, I will be up in New Jersey to start my vacation—unfortunately, only one week this year—with our "Uncle's Day" celebration when all the family gathers around. I'm afraid there will be another birthday cake, making a grand total of eight! I think I will probably have to fast for a couple of months to get back to what I weighed at the beginning of my birthday celebrations. Thank you all for your thoughts and prayers for me at this three-quarter mark of a century that God has allowed me to walk in his beautiful world. May the gracious gestures of so many people from the media to the multitudes never go to my head.

Birthdays are always signs of growth in age. Wouldn't it be wonderful if they could also be occasions for growth in grace? The older I get, the holier I ought to become. The longer I walk on these earthen pathways the closer I ought to come to the kingdom of God. Pray for me, that I always find the right path which leads to him who is our salvation. As I go deeper and deeper into this world of aging, let me always remember the Lord who gave joy to my youth and now gives me the promise of peace and security in his love. That is what I pray for all of you, too. Thinking of you and of all our sisters and brothers in this great local Church, I count every moment that I am privileged to serve as your bishop and your friend as an extraordinary blessing and a special grace.

"Gone Fishing" and Other Thoughts
July 21, 2005

I think there is a Norman Rockwell painting—one of those many in which he portrays the wholesome and simple side of our American culture—that depicts a door of some neighborhood store with a sign hurriedly placed on the door handle that reads, "Gone Fishing." The door of my office in the Archdiocesan Pastoral Center ought to have such a sign this week! I'm on my way to the Jersey Shore for almost a whole week, with authentic hope of going fishing and getting a lot of good sleep.

Over the past few days, I have had another four birthday parties! A couple were family gatherings where the little children were present, and they are always so much fun. Almost every one of those over five tried to wheedle an invitation to go fishing with me this coming week, but prudently, I turned them down. Having a gang of six- to twenty-six-year-olds around is not the way for this seventy-five-year-old to get a lot of rest and refreshment. Even so, I can still see the disappointed faces, especially of the little ones. They don't cry or whine, but they do let you know that you let them down. Thank the Lord that they do not have long memories, for the excitement of their normal vacation time will soon wipe away their disappointment.

Wouldn't it be great if you and I could wipe out bad memories just as easily. It would happen if our trust in the God who loves us would give all of us always the sense of peace that comes from him alone.

May I go back to an old theme of mine now that I have reminisced about being surrounded by so many children? It's my usual pitch for large families. I know very well the heavy economic restraints that so many of our young parents face in this modern society of ours and I realize that one or two more mouths to feed, to clothe, and to send to school can well be a daunting proposition. Having known many families with four, five, and more children, however, and having seen how happy they are growing up and how wonderfully they tend to look after each other in adulthood, I am convinced that it is worth the sacrifice.

We all grew up to be aware of what social scientists called "the population bomb" that was supposed to destroy civilization because of too many people on earth. Now, more than ever—from the pages of news magazines and editorials in prominent newspapers—we are hearing that the world may face extinction not from too many children, but from too few. As birth rates drop all over the Western world, there is a fear that great nations may fail to reproduce themselves and thus disappear. In our own country, we might also be facing the awful problem of depopulation, if it were not for the numbers of immigrants who come to our shores each year. France, Italy, Germany, and Spain now have birth rates dangerously close to where the futures of these great nations may well be in doubt.

One of our priests, a wise man of long pastoral experience, once told me that I was not very likely to change many minds of parents by advocating larger families. That may be. But if I can just persuade one couple to have one child more, what a blessing that would be! To give the world one new life with all the potential that life can have, this is surely a worthwhile goal. Thinking of you and about those youngsters happily singing in my head, I remain convinced that the sacrifice of parenthood is eminently worthwhile. But whatever the number God gives us, let us rejoice in the children and thank God for the gift of life.

Sisters
July 28, 2005

You know that I write a lot about vocations to the priesthood. This year especially, with the extraordinary number of changes in priestly assignments caused by our smaller numbers, has made the increasingly fewer members of our archdiocesan priestly community abundantly clear.

Thanks be to God, the truth is that we are doing much better than most of the dioceses in our country. As a matter of fact, we have more than sixty seminarians. Relying on God's providence, we trust that the future will see greater numbers of young men and those not so young entering the seminary and, indeed, next year's class of ordination may well more than double the numbers ordained this year.

And so now I want to write you about vocations to religious life and in particular to religious communities of women. (I promise to do a column in the near future about religious brothers whose special vocation to teaching and to works of charity continue to make a profound contribution to holiness and apostolic life in this Archdiocese of Washington.)

The other day, I became so strikingly aware of women religious as I celebrated Mass in the Cathedral on my birthday and had the blessing of the presence of dozens of sisters who had come to pray with me and to wish me well. There were many young sisters whose joyful smiles and enthusiasm for a life of service to the Lord was apparent and beautiful, and even catching in its joyful vigor! I recall the days of my own youth—yes, I can still remember—when many nuns of many congregations exemplified the life of our Church and its powerful call to the vows of religious life.

Those days are not over!

A couple of years ago, a number of young women approached me with the idea of establishing a diocesan community of women here in Washington, which would serve the faithful of this archdiocese. I talk a lot about the diocesan priesthood and they presented the idea of a diocesan sisterhood, a group of women with the vows of religious life, living in community, praying together and accepting whatever apostolic mission the Archdiocese of Washington might require. We spoke of them going into campus ministry, pastoral service in the parishes, teaching in Catholic schools, parish visitations, and of the myriad other forms of service that could be undertaken by this group.

Two years ago, seven single women began to meet together to test this idea. It is my hope that sometime in the fall, some of them will begin living together in community while each continues her own work for a while until a program of novitiate can be established. They are teachers, social workers, professional women of different fields, but they enter with the hope of discerning God's will for them, and my prayer is that it will take the form of a new religious congregation in due time.

For young women who might sense the Lord's call to serve either in a new way, such as I have described, or in any of the many wonderful religious communities of sisters already serving in this Archdiocese of Washington, I invite you to write me here at my office in the Archdiocesan Pastoral Center. I will put you in contact with our already established religious congregations or with the young women in this new adventure of grace, as you request.

Thinking of you and of God's wondrous grace that abounds here in this local Church of ours, I pray that many will hear his voice and answer "Yes, Lord, here I am!"

The Breviary
August 4, 2005

I really love the divine office, the breviary, that priests and many religious are required to pray every day. As you probably know, it is a collection of psalms and prayers, hymns, and readings, focused on the season of the ecclesiastical year and the feasts of the saints. I think most priests feel as I do about the breviary.

Of course, for all of us there are days when it can seem like a burden on top of all the other responsibilities that we carry. Those are the days when you come home late at night from a day filled with meetings and realized that you haven't finished the breviary yet, or days when you must choose to leave another important responsibility to put in some quiet time with the breviary. Obviously, there are sensible rules for dealing with dilemmas and we all know the validity of the old rule, "No one is held to do the impossible."

Yet, when all is said and done, the office is a great gift, a special grace and a wonderful aid to every other kind of prayer. For me, it is that quiet morning conversation with the Lord, when before anything else as the day begins, I can salute him in the psalms of King David, meditate on the readings of the scriptures, and be edified by the writings of Augustine and Leo the Great and so many other fathers and Doctors of the Church.

During the hectic day, it is hard for me to gather much time for formal prayer and so the great, deep thoughts of the morning office help to carry me through. At evening time when much of my work is over, the escape into chapel for vespers or evensong—as the old English term dubbed it—is a great release from the tensions and the stresses of the day. It is not only the psalms that speak of Jesus who is to come, but also the words of the prophets, which are so often filled with hope and confidence in God. Every time I pick up this book of the breviary, I am reminded of God's glory, his goodness and love, his forgiveness for my own weaknesses and sins, his confidence in me and all that he has given me to do, and finally his trust in all of us to do the good and the right and the just with the help of his grace. The breviary makes it possible for me to keep my prayers focused on the Lord and not on myself. The short prayer of midday—which often I say earlier or later—is another moment of reminding me that God is in my life the whole day through.

I chose this time in the middle of a hot summer to write to you about this aid to prayer, since sometimes this is the season when we are least tied down to job and plans and concerns, and when we can reflect a little on what God and goodness and grace mean in our lives. Now, you don't all have to go off and buy breviaries and read them every day, but sanctifying each day by personal prayer, morning, noon and night will really focus you on things greater than yourself, indeed greater than any of us poor creatures. Just as the breviary does for priests, try to find a way in your own lives to be reminded of God's goodness morning, noon and night. If you do this, it will open your eyes to a more joyful relationship with a God who loves you and calls you every day to holiness.

Thinking of you in the middle of the summer, I wanted to write about prayer, while we all have a little more time to enter into it!

Do Your Best!
August 11, 2005

I was going to start this column with the phrase, "During the few days of my abbreviated vacation . . ." when I realized that I was complaining too much about the shortness of my time off this summer. I have no right to complain since it is all my own fault, anyway. I could have said, "no" to many of those jobs and I didn't. I guess I felt that if I was going to retire soon I might as well do all I can right now. Well, aside from all those other considerations, let me begin this column with a story.

A few weeks ago, I was watching some of the youngsters in my family playing horseshoes. One of their fathers came over to watch with me and quoted the old saying, "Coming close doesn't count, except in horseshoes." In other words, in most games of life or chance if you don't win, you lose.

There is a lot to that proverb and to the philosophy it represents. You should always play to win and put all your energies into doing the best. This is true of every individual sport and indeed, of every game we play. If you shoot for second place, you will end up "out of the money." We must always try to do the best.

But what if one does one's best and still falls short of victory? The proverb has no answer for that. Does that spell failure and the onus of defeat? In some circumstances, as in the world of sports, I guess sometimes it does. But it is not so in the challenge of the spiritual life. Thank God, there the rule is simple: "Do your best." Do you remember the old poetic saying, "It matters not if you win or lose, but how you play the game"? That is true of most of the things that really matter. It is true in the life of the spirit. How we play the game of life is more important than whether we are successful in material things. If we become a great success by hurting other people, we have accomplished nothing to win ourselves a place in heaven, but if we do our best in the life we live here, then God crowns that best with his love and with the real victory that we are all called to achieve.

Close or far from the peg does count in horseshoes. In a real sense, it counts in life, as well. If, by doing our best, we come close or far away from what we strive for, it is not the victory in the game that counts, but the victory over ourselves and doing the best we can. The only thing that really counts is to do the best we can and then to hear God's most generous invitation, "Well done, good and faithful servant; enter into the joy of your Lord." Thinking of you as summer comes rushing to its end, I pray that all of us may always try to do our best for God and for each other.

Guns
August 18, 2005

I'm at the airport, getting ready to start my journey to Berlin and Cologne, the Caucasus and the Balkans. As often happens, I am regretting all this travel even before it begins. As it was, I had to cut short my annual visit to Southern Maryland, only getting to twelve parishes instead of my usual twenty-plus! Southern Maryland was great as always, and I did get out fishing twice—fishing and not catching, to be exact, although I must have thrown a dozen little ones back.

The newspapers' headlines disturbed me. Here I'm not talking about Iraq or the Holy Land or London, but about our own neighborhoods in just about every part of the archdiocese. There are too many murders, too many crimes, too many gangs. My heart aches for parents whose youngsters have been killed or maimed or trapped in the terrible web of gang hatreds and gang warfare. I cannot avoid the conclusion that there are just too many guns around.

The government of the District of Columbia has tried to cut down on the number and types of guns that can be purchased here in Washington. Unfortunately, the House of Representatives has just overruled what seems to me to be a very reasonable and conscientious set of regulations.

I recognize that our federal constitution gives all citizens the right to bear arms and this is, of course, the law of the land. But what was important in the WILD West and the days of the open frontiers—and still may be useful in some parts of our country—doesn't seem either necessary or safe here in the nation's capital. This is also the opinion of Chief Ramsey of the Metropolitan Police and he is the one whose job it is to keep us safe. We make it hard for the chief and for all the men and women in law enforcement when criminals have easy access to guns that can end lives, not only of our courageous law enforcement agents, but also of children and old people who may be in the way.

I appreciate the reality that there are many factors that give rise to crimes, but I believe that having guns too readily available that can fall into the wrong hands is one of the greatest dangers of our society, a danger that a crowded modern city like ours could well do without. They are announcing my flight now and so I had better stop and board the plane, but I would hope that the Senate has a chance to take a good look at what the House has done because it affects hundreds of thousands of us who live in this great city and have a right to be safe from too many guns.

Thinking of you as I leave for a couple of weeks of heavy travel, I pray that no more lives will be lost back here at home because too many guns are available.

The Church Is Young
August 25, 2005

(Cologne) I think I may have told you already how powerful I found the words of Pope Benedict XVI in his homily on the day of his installation as bishop of Rome and universal pastor of the Church. As he spoke of his hopes and prayers for the future of our Church, he made the point of saying that "The Church is young!" By this expression the Holy Father gave words to our faith and our conviction that whatever comes against the Church through the evils of the world and the sinfulness of its own members, the Church will always have the vitality and the energy to rise and serve the Lord.

The youth and vigor of the Church was visible in a special way last week at the gathering in Cologne of more than a million young people. The twentieth World Youth Day was once again a time of grace and a moment to take confidence in the future. The young people—many of them in their twenties—caught the spirit of the celebration and found their joy not only in fun and new friendships, but in a recommitment to God. This is a beautiful city, with dozens of magnificent churches and during the days—and nights—of the youth gathering they were often filled with young people at prayer. The Archdiocese of Washington had more than three hundred youth and probably closer to five hundred of them in Cologne. Our country had close to thirty thousand and we all could be so proud of each one of them.

I had the privilege of leading two catecheses. These are the talks that are given on three of the mornings during the week. One of mine was in a soccer stadium where we had ten thousand young people, and the second was in a parish which was crowded with close to a thousand. (It was not I who brought out the crowds, but just the size of the place to which the different groups were assigned!) I really could feel the Lord's presence during these gatherings. I could feel it in the response of the young people filled as it truly was with awesome enthusiasm. We are going to have our own World Youth Day back home in Washington on October 1 and we must pray that the same grace will be abundant when we gather the youth there. I know that the program will be exciting and I ask the Lord to touch all our hearts that day just as he surely did in Cologne.

To give you an idea of the enormity of the World Youth Day preparations, the organizers had built a mountain on the field where the celebration was held so that everyone could get to see the Holy Father. This "mountain" was about ten stories high and from it the sight of more than a million young people with their flags and their signs and their songs was really an emotional moment. I think it must have been that for the Holy Father in a special way.

It had to be a wonderful first international journey for Pope Benedict. It was not only his first great international event, but it was also coming home for the first time as pope. His warm smile, his deep humility and prayerfulness, as well as his strong teaching, have already endeared him to Catholics and made him a strong moral and religious force in the world as well. Thinking of you all as part of this young Church, I ask God's blessings on each one of you as I pray for you in the great Cathedral of Cologne.

On the Road Again
September 1, 2005

I don't know why I do these long journeys, especially why I still do them at seventy-five! I seem to be so often, like the Willie Nelson song, "On the Road Again"! I am now on the plane heading to Dulles Airport from Vienna. I've been away more than two weeks and I dread seeing my desk when I get to the office tomorrow. Hopefully I was able to be of some usefulness along the way.

Catholic Relief Services (CRS) is the American Catholic humanitarian agency that reaches out to the poor and the underdeveloped throughout the world. CRS works in ninety-nine countries, and their mission is two-fold. At times of material and man-made emergencies—such as the tsunami in South Asia and in the wars in the Balkans—they immediately reach out to help the victims. We are all very familiar with what they accomplish in these situations and our archdiocese has tried to be helpful in special ways when these disasters strike.

It is perhaps not as well known that CRS continues to help people long after these immediate troubles are over by assisting in the development of programs aimed at giving them a chance to live a better life. These can range from programs of conflict resolution all the way to the developing of ways that support the role of women and the education of girls.

As you probably remember, I had promised Catholic Relief Services to give them some time this summer to visit some of the work of the agency. This also was to help me keep some promises I had made to see some of our old friends in the Balkans. I guess this counted as my vacation too!

During the week after the World Youth Day, when I began my journey to the Caucasus and to the Balkans, I had the opportunity of visiting some of those programs and meeting with the CRS staff that carries the love and concern of American Catholics to our neighbors all across the world. I was able once again on this trip to travel with Mr. Ken Hackett, the president of CRS, a really outstanding Catholic layman whose knowledge of and dedication to this work is a real gift to the Church in the United States.

Besides the CRS visits which brought me to meetings with government officials and representatives of several non-Catholic religions, I saw many old friends among our own bishops whom I had known when I worked for the United States Bishops Committee to Aid the Church in Eastern Central Europe.

The highlight of the second part of my journey took place last Friday in the City of Pristina in the Caucasus. Here the Catholics, who are almost all of Albanian background, finally realized their dream to begin a construction of a cathedral honoring Blessed Teresa of Calcutta who is the most famous member of the Albanian community.

I had spent much time in Kosovo during the difficult days there and they were nice enough to invite me to come back for the great privilege of blessing the cornerstone of the new cathedral. I felt close to Mother Teresa that day, there with her beloved people who have suffered so much. It was her birthday and I am sure she was pleased to take part in this historic event. You share in those prayers as you do in everything I do. In all the Masses of this long journey you can be sure that I was thinking of you and keeping you and all your loved ones in my mind.

A Time to Stay
September 8, 2005

Last Monday when the priests of the Archdiocese of Washington gathered for our annual Labor Day celebration, I shared with them the news that I had been awaiting from the Holy Father. A short while ago, I received from the Apostolic Nuncio, Archbishop Montalvo, the reply of His Holiness Pope Benedict to my letter of early July submitting my resignation as archbishop of Washington according to the norms of the canon law of the Church.

The Apostolic Nuncio informed me that the Holy Father would like me to continue in my present post of service to the Church of Washington for some time longer until other provisions are made. It seems as if Pope Benedict is disposed to have me stay on as archbishop of Washington probably for another two years or so.

I accept the Holy Father's decision with gratitude and confidence. The confidence is based on the fact that I can count on the help of God for the grace to continue to serve the people of the archdiocese whom the Lord loves so much. The gratitude comes from the privilege of working with my brother bishops and priests, deacons and religious whose generosity and zeal I have already experienced over the last four and a half years.

As I think you know, I would have been happy to receive the pope's decision to accept my resignation at this time. He has decided otherwise and therefore I ask your prayers that I may commit myself more willingly and more effectively to your service in the years ahead. As I've said to you on several occasions in the past, when a bishop comes to a new diocese, he considers what the situation ought to be when he leaves. Will the people have enough priests to care for their needs, and will the priests have enough resources to do that effectively with the help of God? That is why I have tried to work vigorously for vocations and why the Forward in Faith campaign is so important for the future of this local Church.

In the time that is left for me to be your pastor, let us come back to what has always been our first priority, sometimes unspoken but always present—the need to call ourselves and our people to holiness. Everything we do must have that as its goal. In the years ahead, may it become clearer that this is what we are all about.

As I recount the news of the decision of the Holy Father, I am thinking of you and am praying with all my strength that the time to come will be a time of grace for us all.

An American Tsunami—and More
September 15, 2005

(Biloxi) Thanks to the Marines, I was able to come over to this southernmost diocese in Mississippi. There are forty-five Catholic parishes in this area, seventeen of them have been at least partially destroyed, and in eight of those there is no hope of restoration. Naturally, I tried to compare this destruction to that of the tsunami that I saw last January in Sri Lanka. This was worse in many ways, although the loss of life was much less.

I say that Katrina was a more serious disaster than even the tsunami for a number of reasons. The tsunami was a terrible, frightening wall of water that crashed into the shore on a bright, pleasant sunny day. The hurricane came with a blazing wind that for six hours tore apart houses of cement and steel as well as wood and caused a wall of water to surge over the land sometimes thirty feet high. Secondly, the tsunami was an unwelcome visitor along the entire coastlines of several countries reaching sometimes a mile inland with its destruction. Katrina's wake was felt in towns more than fifty miles away from the shore of the Gulf of Mexico. Finally, the towns and villages left by the tsunami often were not totally destroyed and many people could return to their homes and businesses. Almost half a million people have been made homeless and jobless by the hurricane and have no hope of returning for months—or maybe years.

I can never forget the tsunami and those courageous people who put their lives back together in its wake. I will never forget the people of Louisiana and Mississippi who still have no idea where to find their lives, their families, their friends, their livelihood, and their businesses. As I flew over New Orleans and saw so many neighborhoods still under water, my concern is that this tragedy will be with us for a long time and neither our government nor our private philanthropies can afford to forget these brothers and sisters of ours.

I pray that New Orleans will rise again. It has always been one of my favorite cities for its friendliness, its lovely architecture and, especially, its great food. The Diocese of Baton Rouge to the north of the Crescent City has been extraordinary in its generosity. As a city, Baton Rouge is almost twice its size as two hundred thousand new people have taken refuge within its borders. Most of them will not come to the District of Columbia, or to any of the areas far away from home, unless they have relatives here. They want to stay close to home and hope and pray that it won't be too long until they get there again. The only problem is that their houses are gone and the places where they worked, as well. You can't blame them. We would be the same.

In the Church of St. Thomas, sadly, too close to the seething waters of the gulf, gutted and heavily damaged by the storm, I saw how its two-ton altar had been picked up by the waters and hurled like a toy against its back wall. I stood and prayed with the people of that parish and, thinking of you, I prayed also for you and for our folks at home and asked God to spare us this terrible trial and to make us grateful for his loving care.

A Nickel and a Comb
September 22, 2005

I was in an airport the other day—nothing surprising in that, since I seem to spend much of my life in those places these days. I was looking, of all things, for a plastic comb. My brother priests who read this column will surely think, "What in the world was he needing a comb for?" Some of you may be gentler in your reaction and think, "He really doesn't have enough hair to need a comb. He could do it with a washcloth."

Well, I guess it's just an old habit getting back to the days—years ago—when I did have enough hair to use a comb frequently. At least, even now, it's a good way to keep the few strands in place. That's not the real point of the story. Let me get back to it. I finally found a comb in an airport store and, since I don't like to go on a journey without one, I decided to buy it, even though it was priced above my usual budget, being as cheap as I am.

The plastic combs were selling at two dollars each. I dutifully took two dollar bills from my wallet and presented them to the clerk. He said it came to $2.05. I had no change. I never bring coins on a trip because they complicate the security inspection. All the inner core of my being cringed at the idea of breaking another dollar bill and acquiring ninety-five cents in change. It was one of those moments when one is stuck in total uncertainty about what to do. There was a couple standing next to me waiting to make their own purchase. Without really thinking, I turned to the man and said, "Do you have a nickel?"

Instead of looking at me and concluding that I was a little dotty, he smiled and said, "No, but I will have after I make my purchase and I'll give you one." His wife immediately spoke up and, opening her purse said, "I think I have one" and went about moving around all those wondrous items that are contained in ladies' handbags. She found a nickel and presented it to me. By that time, of course, I had realized how odd my sudden request had been to total strangers. It made it more embarrassing when, to my words of deep thanks to the couple, the man replied, "That's all right, Your Eminence, glad to be of help."

As I walked away, I was thinking of you all to whom I so often go for help. All the other times, of course, it is never for me but for other people and other great needs, and you always do come through with great generosity. I was so grateful to the couple in the airport who helped me in a little thing and I am so grateful to you for the Annual Appeal, for Forward in Faith, for your support of your own parishes and for all the good causes to which you give so much. All I can promise are my own poor prayers and the deep conviction that God is never outdone in generosity.

Generosity
September 29, 2005

I really don't know how to thank you, the faithful people of this Archdiocese of Washington. From the moment I arrived here almost five years ago, I have marveled at the generosity you have had for the Cardinal's Annual Appeal. The people in my former dioceses were generous, to be sure, but with a smaller number of Catholics, you have matched and exceeded all that was given in those other places!

Your wonderful generosity is also demonstrated when I have come to you for special collections, either the regular ones like Peter's Pence or the missions or the collection for Catholic University, or the special appeals that we must make from time to time like the collection for the devastation of the tsunami or the fund-raising efforts for the victims of Hurricane Katrina and other natural or man-made disasters.

I am not going to talk about the Forward in Faith campaign now, because when it ends, I want to dedicate a lot of time to telling you how much I appreciate what you have done and are doing as we go into the last weeks of the campaign. You need to know exactly the great things that are going to be possible in the archdiocese because of your special kindness and openheartedness.

I have never appealed to you in vain. I have never asked your help without seeing the extraordinary way which you respond to real needs and real opportunities. Of course, we who live here in the Archdiocese of Washington cannot help but be aware of the concerns, both spiritual and material, of so many of our neighbors. Yet I find something deeper than that here in Washington. I find a sense that we all truly are conscious of being brothers and sisters in God's one human family, the words from the servant of God, Cardinal Terence Cooke, that I quote so often.

I have no doubt that God will reward you a hundredfold for the loving generosity you all seem to have. May it never be lost in this local Church. May the future archbishops of Washington, as they come to be aware of the magnitude of your charity, thank God for it as I do and work and pray with you to continue this extraordinary witness of charitable giving with which God has blessed this Church of Washington all these years. Thinking of you as I hear the stories of other dioceses and their concerns, I know how blessed I am to be here as your servant.

An Extraordinary Memory
October 6, 2005

I am writing this on October 4. It is ten years to the day since the late Holy Father, Pope John Paul II, came to Newark and visited the great Cathedral of the Sacred Heart during my time as archbishop there. You can imagine how happy and excited everybody was to see the Holy Father for the first time in the state of New Jersey and in the old and sometimes very challenged city of Newark. It was a terrible day, raining most of the time and the weather made it very difficult for the thousands of people who wanted to greet the Holy Father and who had waited for hours to see him pass by.

After landing at Newark Airport, meeting President Clinton and major officials of the state, the Holy Father drove in a closed car to the cathedral. I was with him in the back seat and I could see how tired he was after the long trip from Rome. He arrived at the rectory of the cathedral, went upstairs to change, and then came right down for greetings of all the people that had been gathered there and for an hour-long meeting with President Clinton in my residence. Actually, it was the first time that there had been such a summit meeting in an archbishop's house in the United States and so we put a plaque up afterward!

The greatest memory of the whole trip was when the Holy Father entered the cathedral and greeted the people with a great smile and a wave of his arms. He went down the middle aisle, able to reach out his hands and let people touch him on both sides of the aisle, a great sign of his desire to be in the center of the Church and be able to reach out to all those both on the left and on the right and bring them together to the Lord. After a wonderful homily at the vesper service, the Holy Father then planned to return to the sacristy and to prepare to go to New York where he was going to stay at the residence of the Apostolic Nuncio to the United Nations.

As the Holy Father walked back to the sacristy, greeting people as he passed them, he noticed that I had placed the blessed sacrament on a side altar and placed a kneeler before it in case he wanted to make a visit to our Lord in the Eucharist. The Holy Father noticed that as he passed, looked at me and I could see the question in his eyes and I said to him, "Yes, Holy Father, the blessed sacrament is there." He smiled and immediately changed his direction and walked over to the kneeler that we had prepared. Here is the great heart of this story.

When the Holy Father arrived at the kneeler, he genuflected and then knelt down. Almost immediately, there was a hush as people realized that here was a man deeply in prayer with the Lord whom he loved so much. It had been my thought to kneel a yard or so behind him while he was making his visit. I couldn't do it. There was a palpable sense of prayerfulness about that spot and I could not invade it even to pray with him. I moved back and stood by the wall while this extraordinary man immediately entered a deep conversation with the Lord. There was noise in the back of the cathedral as the president and other high officials left, but there wasn't a sound around that chapel. The people who had gathered there also sensed the deepest concentration of the Holy Father as he knelt in prayer. For almost ten minutes the Holy Father knelt there and then his secretary, Msgr. Dziwisz, gently put his hand under his elbow and slowly Pope John Paul II returned to us. I have no doubt that he was in deepest communication with the Lord during those ten minutes. It made such a great impression on me that soon afterwards

I had a plaque put on the wall there that said, "On October 4, 1995, Pope John Paul II knelt here in prayer before the blessed sacrament." I am going up to Newark this morning on the tenth anniversary of that visit and to offer Mass at that little chapel where the Holy Father was so deep in prayer.

You know that I will be thinking of you as I offer that Mass and I remember an extraordinary moment in my life and in the life of the Church of Newark and, indeed, the Church in our country.

The Missions
October 13, 2005

When I was a boy growing up in uptown Manhattan, we were all very conscious of the worldwide mission of evangelization—although we never knew the word—which the Church had received from Jesus himself. Some of our heroes were those missionaries who would come to the children's Mass and tell us about the challenging work and their hopes and dreams for the future of those lands in which they lived and prayed and worked. Many of us caught something of that spirit of adventure. It is probably that which still prompts me to journey to far-off lands to experience the wonder of God's world and, hopefully, to try to do a little something to help make it better.

These were the stories of martyrs, real live Americans who lost their lives in foreign lands whose names we could find on our maps, and dream of how we, too, could take their places. There were stories of people whose names we had heard and of the hardships and sometimes failures they experienced in trying to change the hard lot of peoples far away. We youngsters sat spellbound there during these Masses and ran home afterwards to tell our families all that we had heard of the great adventures that the missionaries experienced. I rather think that many of us probably asked our mothers right away if we could go and work in the missions the very next day. For the sake of the missions themselves—as well as our families—it was probably good that the call to change the world for Christ was not followed by the wide-eyed youngsters we all were then. And yet, what a great dream to have and what a grace to have been touched at one point in our lives by the chance of such a calling and such a generosity that stirred us as young as we were.

Everyone needs a dream like that and wasn't it wonderful that so many years ago young boys and girls were moved by the dream of changing the world and bringing others to know of the love of God for them! For some of us, the dream lasted and we found ourselves becoming priests, brothers, or sisters, although most of us in service of the Church closer to home. But for some, including two of my childhood friends, the dream never died and they ended up in Far East Asia and in Latin America where they served with great courage and distinction for many years.

I hope that such dreams are still part of the growing up of children here in our country, dreams of serving the Lord, of helping the poor, of risking lives and fortunes for a quest that finds its origin in the Gospel challenge that Jesus gave us all. Thinking of you and of all the young people in this archdiocese, I pray that they too will find a similar dream in their lives, one that calls for deep and fulfilling generosity and helps them become "partners with God" in achieving something wonderful. It may not be a response to the call for evangelization, but if it is something that makes people happier and brings them closer to God, that will be all right, too.

It All Ties In
October 20, 2005

It was a coincidence that I wrote you about the missions a couple of weeks ago. I knew that I probably had to go to China soon, but I didn't realize how that visit would bring the missions story so clearly back to mind. Now that I have returned from Beijing and am back at my desk, trying to reorganize myself after the five-day journey to the Orient (two days to go, two days to spend in China, and one thirty-six-hour day to come back!), I would like to tell you a story about how the faith is very much alive.

It was Thursday of last week and I was eating breakfast in the hotel when a colleague of mine told me that he had gone out to jog that morning at 5:30. He had run past one of the larger Catholic churches in Beijing, a parish of the official Church not yet in total communion with the Holy Father, but having valid sacraments and a valid Eucharistic liturgy. He saw the lights on and out of curiosity he interrupted his run and went in.

The 5:30 morning Mass had just begun and the church was packed. In the standing room only congregation at that time in the morning there were young people and old, a scattering of foreigners among the crowded Chinese congregation and great singing. He was impressed by the fact that there were many altar boys serving at the altar and the overwhelming impression he received was one of a Church very much alive and filled with faith.

Even though the full communion between the official Church in China and the Holy See is not yet realized—and we must all pray very hard for that to come soon—in every Mass the name of Pope Benedict XVI is mentioned in the Eucharistic Prayer. My friend was struck by this and began to realize vividly the great seeds of faith that thousands of Catholic missionaries over the centuries have planted in that ancient land.

Later that day, as she came to fix up my room, the hotel maid saw the cross that I wear around my neck laying on the dresser. She picked it up and kissed it and then knelt down to bless herself, smiling a happy smile at me and letting me know that she was Catholic, too. I guess she had just figured out that I was a Catholic priest and wanted me to know that she was part of the family.

A couple of moments like that makes going around the world in five days a worthwhile journey, even if it is part of a long process that requires much patience and perseverance until the goal is achieved.

I recalled the story about the missions that I told you in the column a couple of weeks ago and was thinking of you as it all ties in half a world away.

Rosa Parks
October 27, 2005

I believe I only met Rosa Parks once. She was a cheerful and gracious lady and always seemed to be a little uncomfortable with all the publicity. She was one who would never seem to want to call attention to herself. And yet, she changed America and made it a better place.

Can you imagine a society in which you were not able to sit in the front of the bus? Or use any drinking fountain? Or restroom? Or go to any restaurant or theater? Or swim on any beach? Today we would find that incredible. We would rightly say it was a violation of our human dignity, let alone our rights as a citizen of a free society, but that's how it was within the lifetime of many of us.

Of course, the bad part is that there are still some people who find discrimination as part of their daily lives. There are still subtle ways in which people can be told that they are not acceptable because of the way they look or the way they talk or the color of their skin. We are blessed here in this area that, for the most part, we live in a multicultural society. We have good friends who are African American or Hispanic or Asiatic or Caucasian. Hopefully, we have learned to look beyond the accidentals and see the real person with his or her talents and gifts, concerns, joys and sorrows. We are all part of this human condition and each one of us in some marvelous and miraculous way can say to the one who made us, "You are our Father and therefore we must all be brothers and sisters in your one human family."

There are, then, two lessons that come to mind as we remember this extraordinary woman who died this week in her nineties. First of all, we are reminded that we must never allow any person to be treated as inferior or without respect. Just as we would hope to be treated for what we are and what we can do, so according to that ancient golden rule, we must learn to treat others as we would have them treat us. It was strange and yet a special grace that the history of Rosa Parks made us all remember that and so, in a certain sense, she was a prophet for our times.

The second lesson is that a simple, ordinary person with courage and a sense of her own dignity as a child of God could make such an enormous difference in the modern history of our country. I hope we put up a statue to Rosa Parks here in the nation's capital. It will remind us all of a past that by her courage and simplicity we have put behind us for the most part and of the fact that we, too, can make an extraordinary difference in our own times by being who we know we are, the children of a gracious God who loves us. Thinking of you, as I reflect on the passing of a special citizen of our country, I pray that all of us will always be conscious of our own dignity and that of our neighbor in such a way that we will continue to change the world.

The Priests of Washington
November 3, 2005

Next week, across the bay on the Eastern Shore, the priests of this archdiocese will come together for three days to talk and pray and to build up that unity in Christ that must always be the mark of our ministry. We did this two years ago and you may remember how happy I was with the result of that convocation, and more importantly, how pleased my brother priests were with the chance of getting together to share their pastoral ideas and experiences and to thank God for the great privilege of being a servant of the Lord and of all of you.

We will have some expert guides to bring us through the discussions of this brief period and I am sure that our liturgies will be filled with life and beauty and will be models that we can all bring back to our own parishes and institutions. The best part of the assembly, of course, will be the chance to share with old friends, with classmates of seminary days, and with former pastors and associates the great stories that make up the lore of this mysterious, challenging, and demanding vocation. The conversations along the walks and country lanes, the pleasant meals together, the exchange of insights and concerns, of joys and sorrows—this is what brings us together and what strengthens us to serve you and all God's beloved people in the Archdiocese of Washington.

I write you about this for two reasons. The first is to tell you that God has really blessed this local Church with truly great priests. There is not one of them who is perfectly like any other. They are all different and that is the wonderful part of it. Oh, I would be telling a lie if I tell you that they all see their ministry exactly as I do, but that is the strength of this presbyterate and it makes us able to learn from each other, to love each other and to be better able to serve you all. God has given us wise and prayerful men, learned and pastoral men, optimists and realists, serious and jovial, great preachers and great counselors and he has pulled it all together and given you the best he has. I am very proud of the priests of Washington, their dedication, their hard work, and their spirit of joyful fraternity. I am honored to be one of them.

Please pray for all of us during this convocation. Some parishes may be inconvenienced somewhat by the fact that their priests are not around. Hopefully, our absence will give you an even greater idea of what the Church would be without the priests we need to serve us. May it encourage you to pray more fervently for more seminarians. The vocations are coming, as you know, but we need many more to fill out the number adequately to serve you and your families as God wants you to be served and to care for the military and the missions. Of one thing you can be sure. During the time we are away on convocation, we will all be thinking of you, since it is for your salvation and our own that God has called us to this service.

Melancholy and the Divine Artist
November 10, 2005

Maybe it's just the Irish, but I somehow think that every-body feels a little bit of melancholy when the autumn comes. We see the days get shorter and the light seems to dim. East-ern Daylight Time cannot hold its own against the oncom-ing season and so we return to the reality of the place of the sun in the sky and what that means for our daylight and the coming of the night. The ancients used to refer to it as "the dying of the world" and I think that is where the melancholy comes from.

Poets and songwriters have described it and have pictured it in ways that are both sad and romantic, but here we are and it is November, and God knows that it can make us sad. As the leaves fall from the trees, we see another sign of end-ings. Those great branches filled with their verdant splendor are no more. The wisps of colder winds challenge us to face the winter which will surely come. God must read our minds very specially these days because he gives us a spectacular distraction to lift the melancholy and to raise our eyes and thoughts to him.

The leaves are falling, indeed, but they fall in splendid colors and we cannot really continue to be melancholy as we are overwhelmed by the beauty that God's hand can bring to the nature which surrounds us. Southern Maryland with its streams and brooks makes the waterway for the leaves to meet the bay. Driving through Connecticut yesterday, I saw the extravagant splendor of God's painting in the forest and the trees.

What does all this mean for us? Obviously, it means that the great painter continues his wondrous art and brings us radiant beauty to drive out the lonely thoughts. God always does that. It is not just his plan to renew the world and use the elements of nature to bring life through death again. He paints these scenes of beauty to remind us of his presence and his love. How could anyone walk among the autumn trees and not think of him and feel the rapture of his abiding hand? Thinking of you as autumn turns colder, I hope you, too, have the experience of a journey in the woodlands to feast your eyes on the presence of the living God.

Music
November 17, 2005

Now I don't want you to think that I have suddenly become sophisticated, but after the column of last week on the beauty of autumn, I do have to talk to you about beautiful music. Last Monday evening, in the Basilica of the National Shrine here in Washington, the orchestra of St. Luke's performed Beethoven's Ninth Symphony under the direction of Maestro Gilbert Levine. I'm no music critic, but I felt it to be tremendously moving and I wanted to share it with you.

I'm going to write like a real senior citizen now, but I have to confess that I don't understand the music that the young people prefer today. First of all, I can't make out the words and secondly, I can't pick out the melody. Some of my great nieces and nephews try to explain to me that the words aren't always important and the melody gives way to the beat and the power of the percussion. I'm afraid that the only way I ever have a chance of common ground with them is in the field of country music, which I truly love, and some of them do, too.

When their parents were younger—and I was, too—I would be driving in a car with them and listening to the

radio. We had a pact that I could listen to my music for
fifteen minutes and then they could have the control of the
radio for the next fifteen. I recall how they couldn't wait until
my quarter hour was over so they could get back to the fast
and loud music they loved so much. I guess that if I listened
to it long enough, I could get to like it, but by that time I
would probably be deaf from the high decibel level!

But getting back to the concert of last Monday, it was truly
impressive for me. Beethoven's moving music and the choir
of Morgan State College in Maryland singing the "Ode to
Joy" was very powerful. It seemed to capture a spiritual message as well as a musical one and, since I was watching and
listening up close in the sanctuary area of the shrine, I could
appreciate the intensity and the skill of the conductor and
the musicians. I have sometimes watched the rock stars on
television and I know that same intensity and talent is there
as well. Music does have the power to touch our innermost
emotion. Saint Augustine was right when he taught that you
pray twice when you sing.

Of course, I was thinking of you as I watched and listened.
I'm always thinking of you when I'm in the basilica,
since I offer so many Masses there for you and your loved
ones, for our country and our local Church. I believe that
the standing-room-only congregation in the great shrine on
Monday felt the same way and our prayer reached out to all
those we love and it made its way on the wings of song to the
God whose love brings harmony and blessing to us all.

Friendship
November 24, 2005

For the past couple of weeks, I have written to you about beauty—the wondrous beauty of nature and the lilting beauty of great music. Today I want to talk about one of God's most precious gifts to us human beings—the gift of friendship. In the Old Testament, the prophets described it as an uncommon treasure, a gift whose value is beyond price, and in the New Testament, Jesus often uses the word as he honors the apostles so specially by calling them his friends.

I think I told you years ago that my mother had what the Spanish call *"El don de gente"*—the gift of making friends. When I was growing up, I always marveled at seemingly great numbers of people who were her friends, who loved her, and often sought her counsel and her help. I do not know if I have received Mom's awesome ability, but I do thank God so much for the friends that I have. In my case, I am really blessed in that my family are among my best friends and that is a special grace, but along the now many years of my life, there are so many people—lay people, church people—who are very dear to me and for whom I pray every day. I like to think that they all pray for me as well.

Many priests are in that group. Some I have sent to the seminary, some I have been privileged to ordain to their sacred ministry. Some are priests who have served with me in the varied apostolates of my own life. Some, I truly believe, are saints and not just the old ones, but among the young as well. Many are holier than I will ever be and so I am always so grateful for their prayers. Those who have worked with me have been kind enough to overlook my faults and to keep challenging me to patience and to confidence in the Lord, who is, of course, the greatest friend of all. Many friends among the laity are truly precious to me as in their own lives I see God's powerful love and care.

Last Sunday, I preached at the twenty-fifth anniversary of a bishop who has been my friend for almost fifty years, since we were young priests studying together at The Catholic University of America. I remember how many times I became discouraged as I met a roadblock in an essay for one of my courses, and this good priest would patiently talk me through the temporary dryness and get me started on the road again. Of course, it never occurred to me that I was bothering him during his own throes of composition as he was preparing his personal dissertation. And he never seemed to mind, but joyfully turned from his typewriter to give me words of wisdom or a funny story he had just heard. It was his silver jubilee as an archbishop last Sunday and all those joyful and happy memories came back to me and to the others who gathered there as we shared the wonder of the priesthood and the gift of having good friends.

Thinking of you, dear friends of mine, who are indeed also my family in this local Church of Washington, I pray that you will always have good friends around you in times of joy and sorrow and that most profoundly you will come to the knowledge that your and my best friend is the Lord.

Day by Day
December 1, 2005

We live in a very hurried world. It seems to me that years ago it was only little children who couldn't wait until tomorrow, who wanted everything to happen all at once. I was reminded of this last week on Thanksgiving Day when I fell into the trap of asking some little children about what they wanted to be when they grew up. After some tentative replies about pilots or cowboys or TV news anchors—that's a new one—a bright little girl of eight became understandably exasperated with the questions that this elderly gentleman was asking and shot back an answer that ended the game. "I just want to be grown up" she said, and walked away, probably seeking a more mature conversation.

Even though my question was certainly prosaic, her answer was interesting in that it focused on the future that so many youngsters find irresistible. They may not have given thought to the details of the future. They just want it to come more quickly. In a very hurried and fast-moving world, adults are falling into the same category, too. People more and more are thinking about tomorrow and maybe sometimes forgetting about today. That's not all bad, of course. Prudence dictates that we plan for the future, and the scriptures tell us to think about the end of our lives so that we can be prepared to live well in the present, but I want to talk to you today about something equally important. I mean living day by day.

If each day we do our best, tomorrow will take care of itself. If we strive to do the right things today, to overcome the hurdles, to plan with prudence, to find time for joy and love, to try to live in God's presence, then we need never fear for tomorrow. Each day is like the building of a house. You have to start at the foundation. There is no way you can build the top floors first. Today is the most important day of your life—the signs used to say—since tomorrow has no other foundation on which to build. So don't wish away today. It is a special gift from God.

As we get older, we never know how many tomorrows we are going to have, but we do have today and we need to make the most of it. There is nothing entrancing or terribly new in this message, but as I write I'm thinking of you and of me and of all the folks who can't wait for tomorrow.

The One You Love the Least
December 8, 2005

A spiritual writer once said the best test of your charity is the person you love the least. Jesus once said to his disciples, "If only you love those who love you, what reward will you have? Even pagans do that." It is so easy to love lovable people. We grow up as children accustomed to that. Our mothers care for us and feed us. Our dads pick us up when we are hurting and give us a sense of security. It is easy to be loved and we learn to love back. As other persons come into our lives, we begin to make judgments as to whether they too are lovable. Sometimes, like when we get a new sibling, we must get over the threat that they will take our parents' love away from us. But little by little, we realize that in the wonder of love there is really enough love to go around.

As more people come into our lives, relations, classmates, acquaintances, and friends, we necessarily become more discriminating in our love. We choose—or are chosen by—some as our close friends and soon there is a bond that tends to put some distance to other people not so directly involved in our lives. And so, we move through childhood, teenage years, youth and maturity, with some people always close to us and others who come in and out of our circle of affection.

We gain friends and lose friends naturally as our lives change and we come into contact with hundreds of other people. Sadly, it can happen that a disagreement can become magnified into a dispute and relationships which once were the closest can be broken. It does seem that love can turn, if not to hate, yet to something which can aggravate and disturb. Almost always, although we don't like to admit it, the hurt that is caused is felt by both sides and therefore can be repaired much more quickly than we imagine. Even though we all change so much as we grow in years, the ties of love and friendship that once were strong have never really been totally severed.

Coming back to the first point of the column, a great Advent practice for all of us as we prepare to receive the greatest gift of love that God gives us on Christmas day is to think of whom we love the least and give that person a call or write a note or even send a friendly Christmas card. Life is too short to hold grudges and to let happy memories be forgotten with a cloud of angry hearts. It is all the worse, the closer the relation is, as with a sibling or even a parent. If every week we made peace with someone who once we loved, we would soon find that peace for ourselves as well. Thinking of you during one of those more thoughtful moments of my journey, I know that all of you will always try to be willing to be generous with love even to the one you love the least.

Adsum
December 22, 2005

Last Saturday I ordained three transitional deacons at St. John Neumann Parish in Gaithersburg. This completes the number of twelve deacons who, please God, may be ordained to the priesthood at the end of May. Twelve is a wonderful number for us, since it will be the largest number of ordinations since 1973—thirty-three years ago! It is a sign of God's loving care for this Archdiocese of Washington and we should all thank him for this special gift. (I don't want the Lord to think that I am not sufficiently appreciative, but I would also be grateful to him if he would give us vocations to the sisterhood, since we so critically need a congregation of diocesan sisters to work with us and to complete the extraordinary service of our other religious sisters whose apostolate is so vital to this local Church.)

Nowadays, when the names of the men to be ordained deacons are called at the beginning of the ceremony, they simply answer, "Present." In my day—yes, it was half a century ago—we answered with a Latin word, "*Adsum.*" That word is hard to define. It surely means "present," of course, but it has a deeper meaning for us. For those who were called in those old days, it said not just "Here I am," but "I have come to give my life to you, Lord. Whatever I have, whoever I am, whatever gifts or talents you have given me—I bring them all to you at this moment and I give my life to you forever."

It was for us something like the famous prayer of Saint Ignatius Loyola: "Take, O Lord, and receive all my liberty, my memory, my understanding and my will." Or, like the prayer of the newly beatified Blessed Charles de Foucauld, "Father, I abandon myself into your hands; do with me what you will." Certainly, I have no doubt that the deacons whom I was privileged to ordain last week had in their own hearts the same willingness and generosity and in their word "Present" they offered themselves to God totally and without reservation.

Why I mentioned it to you today is because that one word *Adsum* is, in a sense, a Christmas message in a very particular way.

Adsum was surely Mary's answer when the angel asked her to become the mother of God's Son.

Adsum was Saint Joseph's reply when the angel's message came to him in a dream that he should take Mary to be his wife.

Adsum is, in the great and perfect mystical sense, what Jesus himself says to his heavenly Father when he strips himself of his divinity to put on the weaknesses and limitations of our humanity so that he might save us and redeem us from our sins.

Adsum is what all the saints have said—both those who were heading for the scaffold to suffer martyrdom and those, like us, whose lives are meant to be changed and made holier by the coming of the Lord.

In the deepest sense, *Adsum* must be our answer when God asks us to love our brothers and sisters with the same love which we have for him, the love which challenges us to reach into a more perfect relationship with him.

As Christmas comes, the great time of gift giving and gift receiving, may we always be ready to offer to the Lord the gift of our joys and our crosses, and more importantly the gift of the love that carries them together. As we give the *Adsum* of our own lives, the Lord is surely thinking of you and me in the wonderful mystery of his own special love, which becomes so personal and present at Christmas. He is returning the *Adsum* in his promise to be with us every day of our lives and forever.

Happy First Christmas
December 29, 2005

The other day I said to a bishop friend of mine who had just been consecrated to that office a few months ago, "Happy First Christmas." He smiled and agreed that celebrating Christmas for the first time with the people God had placed in his care in this special way was indeed a great grace. On Christmas Day itself I met a young priest whom I ordained last year, who told me with great joy about offering Mass in his new parish on that holy day. "Happy First Christmas," I said to him. Later that day, I spoke to one of my nieces who had just given birth a few months ago. She is still in the beautiful wonder of motherhood and told me all about her child's first Christmas.

Christmas is truly a special moment in the lives of believers. It is just not like other days. The Church is so right in seeing it as special and in surrounding it with beautiful liturgy, with powerful songs of hope and praise, and with a hundred other reminders of the mystery of God's love for us, which the great feast calls to our minds and to our hearts.

Christmas is that extraordinary time when we celebrate the call to do extraordinary things. It seems to make possible moments that we wait for with special anticipation—the gathering of families around a common table, the finally placed call to a relative or a former friend from whom we have become estranged, the long-awaited photos of children whose growth is often more perfectly documented by annual Christmas cards which give rise to so much joy, especially to grandparents, uncles and aunts. It is because Christmas is so special a moment that the greeting, "Happy First Christmas," captures a time of grace in a way that can always be remembered.

In a way, every Christmas is a first Christmas for the many important events in our lives. A new job, a new home, a new relationship, a new adventure in our life—all of these take on a special character at Christmas time when they are focused on the context of God's love for us. That love was shown to us so personally as the Father sent his Son to become like us in all things but sin, so that he could save us from our sins and show us how to deal with the joys and the sorrows, the fears and the hopes that are part of every human existence.

As I am thinking of you, I am sure that for every one of us, each Christmas has in itself enough that is new so that "Happy First Christmas" can have a real meaning in some way in our lives.

2006

Five Years
January 5, 2006

Wednesday, January 4, was the fifth anniversary of my formal installation as archbishop of Washington. They have been five very interesting years for me. Sometimes I feel as if I have been here for decades and other times I feel still amazed at the new things I learn about this great local Church. I can tell you today that my heart is full of gratitude to God and to the Church for the extraordinary opportunity I have had to serve here, an opportunity I did not expect because I had already turned seventy before I was transferred from Newark.

The year 2006 is, in a sense, a special one for me. I have been an ordinary—that is, the bishop responsible for a diocese—for twenty-five years now. That's a long time to carry that responsibility, especially in the context of these challenging times, and I am grateful to those many people, both clergy and lay, who were so generous, gracious and wise in helping me over the past quarter century.

I think I may have told you once that I believe every new bishop comes to his diocese with some special goals. The first is the over-arching goal of calling his people to holiness and therefore to a greater closeness with our Lord. That is the hardest goal to measure. One tries to measure it in the participation in Mass and the sacramental life of the Church, as well as in the willingness of the people to give their sons and daughters to the Lord in ordained ministry and in consecrated life, and in the people's generosity in caring for the poor and the needs of the Church.

By those latter measures, I can thank God for these five years and for the truly amazing generosity of our faithful. By the end of May, God willing, in five years, we will have ordained forty-three priests for the Archdiocese of Washington, this last class including twelve men—the largest number for us in thirty-three years. At the same time, the Forward in Faith campaign, destined for the poor, the schools, and those specific needs of the archdiocese that we outlined in our program, has seen its pledge total go beyond one hundred and eighty-five million dollars. This latter sum is not counting your generosity in the Annual Appeal, which keeps the archdiocese up and running and which has remained steady in spite of archdiocesan and so many emergency appeals.

As I start to sense the inevitable slowing down of mind and body that comes with years, I look back on these five years as a wonderful time of grace in my life and I thank God for the enormous blessing of thinking of you all the time and trying in my very imperfect way to bring you closer to him who is the good shepherd of us all. I ask you to pray for me at this time in my life that I may be a better servant of the Church and always open to God's holy will.

God and the Weather
January 12, 2006

How often do we meet a stranger and find ourselves talking about the weather? If two people who don't know each other find themselves together in an elevator or waiting for a bus or standing on almost any line and silence becomes uncomfortable, they tend to talk about the weather. Did you ever wonder why we do that? I found myself in a couple of those situations last week and, sure enough, I started to talk about the weather.

As I tried to analyze my motivation for doing that, I came up with several reasons. First of all, the weather is a very neutral subject. The conversation about it is not likely to start an argument. A person usually does not feel passionately one way or the other on whether it is going to rain or not, or even if we did, we would probably all find such a discussion interesting and nonthreatening, unless one was a weatherman by profession!

A second reason might be that the vast majority of us would agree about the value of nice weather and the unpleasantness of bad weather. (The only exception here might be children in school for whom bad weather might produce a day off from classes—but with children we tend not to be in conversations about the weather. There are so many different kinds of topics about which one can chat with interested little ones—such as their siblings, their school, and what do you want to be when you grow up!)

A third reason would be that everyone is touched by the weather and just about anyone can adequately enter a conversation about it. It's not like having to know what the production of zinc in Siberia is or the latest discovery by the Hubble telescope, or the most popular works of nonfiction in Oklahoma. All of us can talk with some expertise about the rain yesterday or the feeling that snow is in the air or the brisk breeze outside.

Wouldn't it be wonderful if we could talk about God like that? If we could meet a stranger and start talking to him or her about eternal life! Oh, we wouldn't want to put them on the spot. It wouldn't be a conversation in which we asked about the other person's beliefs or whether they felt they were living a good life. It could just be a matter-of-fact remark such as "God is good," or "I thank God so often for His love," or, using a combination with the weather theme, "What a beautiful day God has given us!"

I know that most of us would feel embarrassed talking about God to a stranger. There is a good side to that because it shows us how very personal and special is the relationship that each person has with God. But the other side is that we may not feel that comfortable because unlike, as in the question of weather, we would wonder how the other person would react.

The apostles of Jesus were certainly not like that themselves. They spoke to everyone about God, and their enthusiasm and obvious sense of his love was catching and gave people of every walk of life a desire to know more about God and to see if they, too, could have that kind of a loving and trusting relationship with him.

Thinking of you and me both, I wish we were all able to enter into conversation as frequently about God as we can about the weather. There are so many people out there who need to know what we know and who need to believe in God's goodness and of his overwhelming personal love for each one of them. There is an old saying that advises people not to discuss politics or religion, but I truly believe that we ought to talk more about God.

Bits and Pieces
January 19, 2006

I am very proud of the *Catholic Standard* and I believe that we are blessed to have a really fine diocesan paper as this, which keeps all of us up to date with what is going on in the Church both here in our nation and throughout the world, as well as here in the archdiocese. I have to confess that I did get a smile out of the special section for my fifth anniversary. It was nicely done—better than I deserved—but it was a little bit like celebrating the seventeenth anniversary of someone's eighth date! I mean, it is really not that significant except to me. Anyway, they were nice to do it, and the folks who took

out the congratulatory ads were very gracious—and generous. I am going to write them all to say thank you.

I did like the pictures, although I seemed to look a lot
younger five years ago. That's not your fault; it's mine. Somehow, I'm allowing my hair to get thinner and my height to
get shorter faster than any of our priests, all of whom look
younger to me now than when I came here in 2001. The
folks who wrote the articles in that special section were all
friends and did find a lot of nice things to say. I am very glad
that this week's paper doesn't carry a rebuttal, listing all of the
mistakes I have made. Of course, to be honest, in my own
"Thinking of You" column last week on my actual anniversary, I only said nice things about myself, too.

In a sense, we are all that way. Instinctively, we know that
it is harmful to dwell on the dark side of life, on our mistakes,
our faults, our sins. Once we have confessed and done penance for the sins we have committed, it is the devil's work to
make us dwell on the past and not with a joyful resolution
to do better in the future. Years ago, once when I got angry
at one of my nephews who did something dumb—or at least
at the time it seemed dumb to me—he looked at me and
said earnestly, "Unk, why don't you just remember the good
things?" Our lives and our relationships are filled with ups
and downs, both lights and shadows. This is the price we pay
for being human.

God is so loving a Father that he tends to treat us like
my young nephew suggested. As a matter of fact, there is a
beautiful text in the Epistle to the Hebrews (Heb 8:12) where
the sacred writer quotes Isaiah (Is 45:23) and Jeremiah (Jer
31:34) where God says to the people who have turned away
from their transgressions, "For I will forgive their evildoing
and remember their sins no more." We must all arrange the
bits and pieces of our lives and make of them a gift to the
Lord that will recognize his remarkable generosity to each

one of us and his grace that enables us to do better if we turn with confidence to his love.

Thinking of you on the plane as I fly back to Msgr. Echle's funeral, my thoughts are captivated by the awesome goodness of our loving God.

The Second Vatican Council
January 26, 2006

These past few months, students of the Church through-out the world have been reflecting on the documents of the Second Ecumenical Vatican Council, which were signed and promulgated some forty years ago. Those of us who remem-ber the council can still recall the interest and excitement that it brought to Catholics in our own country and in so many other parts of the world where the Church plays a major role in society, as well as in mission countries, where it is much less known.

The very notion of an aggiornamento—the wonderful word that Blessed John XXIII used to describe the work of the council—was enough to spark the interest of men and women everywhere. That word inferred not that the Church would or could change its doctrines, since it had received them from Christ, its founder, but that it would try to express them in language that would be understood by the modern world.

The memorable first words of the great Constitution on the Church in the Modern World, *Gaudium et Spes*, were in fact something both of an introduction and a summary of the spirit and work of the council. Listen to them again: "The joys and the hopes, the griefs and the anxieties of the men of this age, especially those who are poor or in any way afflicted, these are the joys and the hopes, the griefs and the anxieties of the followers of Christ." In those words in a special way the Fathers of the Council expressed their desire to speak to the world of today about the things that are forever, in the light of the teaching which we have received from Jesus Christ our Lord.

All this is very much on my mind today, since one of the reasons for my going to Rome last week was to give a talk for the United States Embassy to the Holy See on the document, *Dignitatis Humanae.* This document talked about freedom of religion and based it on the foundation of the dignity of the human person. Besides, as you may recall, I have been asked to speak here in our archdiocese to several Jewish groups about the decree, *Nostra Aetatae,* which dealt with the relations of the Church with our Jewish and Muslim brothers and sisters and made an enormous impact on inter-religious dialogue.

By this time, knowing me as you do, you have probably figured out the reason for this column. Today, more than forty years later, so many of our Catholic people have never read the documents of this great gathering of the Church with the Holy Spirit. The number of American bishops who attended the council as bishops has decreased greatly. Probably not a dozen American bishops who had the grace-filled privilege to sign those wonderful expressions of our faith and teaching are still alive today. I attended the last session of the council, but not as a bishop, merely as a resource person for the bishops of Puerto Rico.

As the number of those who participated grows smaller, so much the more important it is that we all become familiar with what was written by them, through the light of the Holy Spirit. It was written for all of us, to challenge and guide us and, therefore, it is so important that we who are Catholics today be familiar with this extraordinary moment in the life of our Church and with its teaching. I really want to encourage our Catholic people, especially the younger members of this local Church, to read the documents, at least in summary form, so that they can sense the power of this precious moment in the life of the Church and learn how the spirit of Jesus continues to guide the Church in the way of teaching and holiness. The Lord is always thinking of you and me. In the Second Vatican Council once again in a special way and in our own times, he used this remarkable gathering to call our attention to his presence and his love.

Gettin' by and Livin'
February 2, 2006

Some of you will know that among all my favorite things, one is country-western music. The other day, as I was on a plane, listening to the audio track in their sound system, I heard a song that I have never heard before. Its lyrics were good and its melody catching and the message could be summed up in its short refrain: "There's a lot of difference between gettin' by and livin'." Unfortunately, I didn't find out who the singer was since that was announced before the song began and I wasn't paying attention. I did wait, listening to that same soundtrack until it would come around again, but the audio portion of the entertainment ended as the plane began its descent before I heard it played over again.

What a great message, I thought to myself! There is a great difference in how each of us lives our lives, how much advantage we each take of the opportunities that life offers across the journey of the years. Jesus tells us, "I came that you might have life and have it to the fullest." God wants us to live deeply and courageously, delving into the great mystery of his love—even as our Holy Father Pope Benedict XVI wrote us in his encyclical issued last week on charity. We need to spend our lives discovering every day the depth of God's love for us and the ways that this divine love guides us and strengthens us and challenges us to discover. The more we discover about our talents, our strengths, our frailties, and our dreams, the more we can rely on God's providence to help us through the shadows and to bless us through the joys that are part of our existence.

Some people don't really live life to the fullest. This is not something that is determined by wealth or education. I have known very poor people whose lives were so filled with satisfaction as they went about sharing the little they had with love, experiencing the excitement of living and the deep joy of family. I have known wealthy folks whose lives were empty because their wealth and the isolation it brought them was so focused on keeping what they had that they lost the wonder of reaching out to touch the lives of others. They were "gettin' by" for sure, but not living life as the Creator gave it to us to enjoy and to flourish. "Livin'" in the song I heard had a better definition. It included friendship, and hard work, and putting your heart into everything that you do.

Last week, I was privileged to preach a retreat for some thirty young men who were considering a call to a priestly vocation. I took that country western song as a theme for my talks. Priestly service here in the Archdiocese of Washington calls on those who accept it to take on the challenge of living to the full in the care of all our people. It includes challenging the young, comforting the older, encouraging the saints, counseling the sinners, consoling the hurting, rejoicing with the happy, and weeping with the sad. It is a life filled with ministering to all the people, because it must always find its strength in the Eucharistic presence of the God who calls us all to holiness and guides us through the troubled waters of every life to that place where we can find our peace in him. That's real living, not just getting by.

When I preach about priestly and religious vocations, I think of you and ask you to pray with me that many of our young people may realize that this vocation is a way to live their lives for others and so to find the fullest life of all.

The Best Gift of All
February 9, 2006

I want to return to a subject that we have discussed before. It is the extraordinary blessing of our Catholic schools. You already know how much I appreciate them for what they are and for what they do. In the outer counties they are the guarantee of our continuing presence as a Catholic community, and in the inner city they are the great bulwark that gives neighborhood communities a chance to survive and prosper and children a chance to accomplish something with their lives.

Sadly, our school system continues to be challenged by the rising cost of education and the growing competition among schools that are not able to teach the values we believe to be the underpinning of any solid educational foundation. Our Forward in Faith campaign hopefully will help in keeping tuition from spiraling out of sight for poor and working class families, but the survival of Catholic education will always depend on the generosity of the Catholic people and the willingness of Catholic families to make a sacrifice in order to ensure that their children are instructed in the principles that make life worth living.

I am happy that so many non-Catholic families are willing and eager to make sacrifices so that their children can have a learning experience in which strong moral values, parental participation and a safe and disciplined environment are present. I understand the pressures on parents whose income must be spread over so many demands, from mortgage payments to health benefits, including all sorts of expenses which have become more or less essential over the years.

My hope still remains strong that you will see in an authentic Catholic education one of the best gifts that you can give to your sons and daughters, a gift with benefits for their entire lives and can make a difference between the only ultimate success or failure—the eternal happiness that comes from living a good life.

This is why our archdiocese continues to spend so much of our budget on Catholic schools throughout the territory of this local Church—urban, suburban, and rural. This is why we worked so hard to be part of the Opportunity Scholarship Program in the District of Columbia, which gave poor families the chance to choose a Catholic school for the education of their youngsters. This is why we are so careful to make sure that any school which wants to be called Catholic is properly approved by the archbishop so that its teaching, its religious program, and its relationship with the parish schools of the archdiocese can be evaluated by the Catholic Schools Office and monitored by the relevant authorities of our Church. Catholic education in this archdiocese is so important not just for the past, but for the future. If we do not educate, both in our schools and in our religious education program, the leaders of our Catholic community in the next generation, the future ability of our Church to serve our people, our country and the Church universal would be in jeopardy.

In these days, after celebrating Catholic Schools Week, when I could see for myself the tremendous accomplishments of our principals, teachers, staff, and students, I am thinking of you and anxious to share my gratitude to God for this great gift of our Catholic schools and the families who support and enjoy them.

Reflections on a Snowy Day
February 16, 2006

For some few hours last Sunday, all the world looked white! The ugly potholes were filled, the barren trees were glistening in the wind, the houses were pasted over with a luminous coat of ermine, and even the ugly places looked fresh and clean. Children, who appreciate goodness and beauty more readily than they can describe it, sense the whitening of the world and rejoice in it, not only for the freedom from school that it promises, but from the sense of wonder that it brings.

For those few hours, we can see only the promise of nature, which reminds us of God's power and seems to envelope all of us in a mantel of purity, hiding the defects and scars of the earth around us. We can reach out and feel the snow before it hardens into the solidity of ice. It packs for a snowball and crumbles in a probing touch. For those who had never seen much snow before—some of our missionary seminarians and a visiting archbishop from Brazil—it really was a winter wonderland and a gift from God above.

It doesn't last, of course, and as I write this its clean freshness is almost gone and the marks of mankind have changed the glistening white into a gray at best and sometimes it seems littered with the debris of our evident humanity. The very young children stare with disbelief that it could change so quickly and we, who have seen the passing of the snows so often, shrug our shoulders and listen to the forecasters as they try to explain the workings of the world.

Is the life of the spirit an echo of the passing of simplicity that is symbolized by the snow? Maybe so. We all seem to start out with purity of intention and great clarity of hopes and dreams. Then the winds of our complex society come and we find the brilliant whiteness of our motivations clouded or disguised by our neglect or irresponsibility or worse. We lose the simple singularity of a snow-covered path and find ourselves walking in snowdrifts, or as the over-used proverb would have it, walking on ice.

For the world, only another snowstorm will cover the earth with white again, and for us, only the return to the wonderful vision of a new dawn of grace can make a difference. That was why Jesus came to be our dawn again. Only he can make the difference last and the world of our own lives so rich in grace that the purity of our intentions and the single-heartedness of our acts may remind us of a world not just temporarily covered with whiteness, but thoroughly changed and renewed in love.

Thinking of you on a morning after snowfall, I ask the Lord of all to make each one of us more like his gift of snow.

A Dish of Herbs
February 23, 2006

There is a wonderful text in the Old Testament's Book of Proverbs that we come across when we read the breviary this time of the year. The full quotation looks like this:

> Better a dish of herbs where love is
> than a fatted ox with hatred in it.
>
> (Prv 15:17)

I love that passage, not just because it seems to me to be great poetry, but because it conveys a special lesson in a way that is clear and simple. If you have love, you can be satisfied with very little. If you don't have love, nothing will really satisfy you.

It is a call to reach for the things that really count in life and not to spend one's time and energy in a search for things that really do not matter. When I encourage young men and women to consider if God is calling them to a life of service to him and to their neighbors, when I plead for married couples to be open to life and not to hesitate to bring children into the world, when I have asked you to be generous in your charity with the things of this world so that you might experience God's generosity to you both here and hereafter—this has been my motivation and my dream, that you might truly experience the overwhelming peace that comes from seeking the things of God, rather than being trapped in the things of earth which fade away and crumble.

Last month, our Holy Father, Pope Benedict XVI, issued his first encyclical, *Deus Est Caritas*. It was an eloquent call to love and kindness and to the care of the poor. In it, the pope writes as a clear and thoughtful teacher, as a great theologian who has learned to live what he preaches, and he challenges us to understand the overwhelming value of love, since, as Saint John the apostle tells us, that of all the great attributes of God, this is the essential one: God is love!

Pope Benedict calls us to the love of God and of neighbor in a challenge that is very clear. The pope writes that, "For the Church, charity is not a kind of welfare activity which could equally well be left to others, but is a part of her nature, an indispensable expression of her very being." He teaches us that "the Church cannot neglect the service of charity, any more than she can neglect the sacraments and the word." This is a powerful challenge and it calls every one of us to reflect on how charity must be the central part of our lives as Christians.

As I read the encyclical, I am thinking of you and thanking God that the manifestation of your generous love in this local Church continues to make possible so many kinds of help and service to young and old, to poor and sick and to the works of charity that have brought new life to so many. The words of the Holy Father have always struck a resounding echo in the lives of the faithful of this archdiocese and have provided so many with more than just a dash of herbs where love is. I thank the Lord that you have given the fatted ox with love as well.

Just in Time
March 2, 2006

I have the feeling that this year Lent has come just in time. Every day when I open the newspapers or turn on the radio or television, the news stories seem to be filled with more problems than happy stories, with more evidence of how much people dislike each other than how much we love one another. The terrible conflicts in the Middle East, the religious riots in parts of Africa, the violent demonstrations in so many parts of the world give one the impression that hate is having its day and love is being left behind. The lack of civility and a certain graciousness that used to mark our own society often seems to be a thing of the past, and a mean-spirited attitude has sometimes replaced it to the detriment of people working together in good faith to make the world and our own community a better place.

As I read what I have just written, it really seems an awfully dark view of life, especially for me since I usually do try to see the good side of things. That's why for all of us, I think that Lent has come just in time!

Lent is a time of penance for our sins and our faults. It is a time of deepest prayer for God's help, as well, a time in which we are all called to realize that without God's sustaining love, we are just dust and ashes, without reasons for hope or trust in the future. Lent is a great time of truth, when we are invited to look at things as they really are, not just as we would like them to be. It is a time for self-examination and for increased self-knowledge. It comes as a gift from God and from his Church, enabling us to take a good look at ourselves, at how we treat those around us, and, in a special way, how we are dealing with the most essential relationships of our lives—how we are relating to the God who made us, who forgives us and redeems us, who loves us as no human being ever could.

I believe that just about every religion in the world has a place for penance—for prayer and fasting and the giving of alms to the needy. Just as we all need some kind of physical exercises lest we lose the strength of our muscles, so every one of us needs a kind of spiritual exercise—something that is demanding of us, that calls us to reach beyond our comfort or convenience or indolence, that calls us to live more consciously of that other, more fulfilling life in the spirit! That is what Lent should be for us.

In that sense, Lent should never be a sad time. The Gospel tells us to wash our faces after the time of ashes is over and start becoming new and more enthusiastic followers of Christ, both for ourselves and for others. Lent is not passive. It challenges us to do something ourselves to make the world better, even if it is just the small but vital world around us that we change—the world of our own family, our community, our place of work.

Finally, Lent is just in time because it brings us closer to Easter, to the message that God loves us so much that he sent his Son to live and die for each of us! I once saw a sign in front of a little house on an isolated country road in an area where I used to go fishing. It hung from a tree branch and you couldn't miss it as you drove by. It read, "Hang in there," and it was always a welcome message toward the end of a long journey. Lent tells us all to "hang in there," and to live life to the fullest. By doing the good we are called to do, we prepare with joy for the Easter Alleluia, the sound of which will always remind us of God's extraordinary and providential love. Thinking of you, as Lent comes just in time, let us promise to pray for each other at this special time of the year.

Witnesses
March 9, 2006

Where do the crowds come from on Ash Wednesday? When you walk downtown in Washington on that day, the numbers of people who have the mark of ashes on their forehead is amazing and to this you have to add those who will fill our churches at evening Masses later that day. They are people of all ages, of different racial and ethnic groups, and of all types of occupations from the newest stock clerk to the CEO. What do they tell us by the ashes on their forehead? What does it mean to us and to the Church?

On Ash Wednesday, I celebrated Mass in the morning in the beautiful Dominican church in Southwest, where hundreds of people gathered on their way to work for the morning Masses. At noon, as always, I went to the Cathedral of Saint Matthew, where I found this great mother church of the archdiocese packed with standing-room four deep, as men and women gave up part of their lunch hour to be present for the Mass and the reception of ashes. That evening on Capitol Hill it was the same story, as people stopped in to pray and have ashes placed on their forehead before they began the journey home. As I prayed that night before retiring, I tried to understand what it meant.

Somehow, Lent seems to make a difference. Perhaps it is because we really are so conscious of our faults and sins and deep in our hearts, we know that we are called to be better. We are called to be more loving, more forgiving, more patient with ourselves and with others. The beginning of Lent with its call to prayer and fasting and generosity touches a chord in our hearts and makes us a little uncomfortable in who we are and a little more motivated to be better. Ash Wednesday gives us a chance to say that, not only to ourselves quietly, but by the symbol of ashes to acknowledge publicly that we are going to try a little harder. Perhaps the fact that so many others around us are saying the same thing through the symbol of ashes makes it easier for us.

Perhaps, too, the ashes are a witness to the world that we really are Catholic. The folks who do not get to Mass every Sunday and whose participation in the life of the Church is somewhat less than it ought to be find in the ashes a chance to make a statement about their faith, even if it is just for a few hours until they wash the mark of that witness away. For those Catholics who sadly have lost the sense of belonging to God's special family in the Church, the ashes may be a call to the rest of us to say, "I'm really with you! Call me back! Invite me in!"

Dear friends, we all know that the witness of the ashes is fleeting and that a good face washing eliminates the mark of penance. My hope is that there is a deeper mark for some of us and that it is truly a reminder that we are all called to leave our sinful ways behind and find strength in the gospel, that in the reminder that we are dust and we return to dust there is another reminder that the dust of which we are made has been sanctified by the waters of Baptism and ennobled by the Blood of Christ. Wouldn't it be wonderful if every man and woman who presents themselves for ashes would find themselves witnessing to that deeper realization that God is really present in their lives and calling them to be faithful to his challenge to holiness and to the abundant storehouse of grace that is his Church? This is what I pray for as I reflect on those extraordinary memories of Ash Wednesday and I am thinking of you and the witness that you gave that day to your trust in the living God.

Media and Message
March 16, 2006

Years ago someone told me of a questionnaire that was given to a cross-section of ordinary American citizens across the country and to leading figures in American media. I don't remember the extent of the instrument or how the "ordinary Americans" or the prominent media figures were chosen, but apparently it was done professionally by social scientists who knew their business. What was most interesting about the results of the questionnaire was how very different the answers of ordinary people were from those who controlled the different organs of American media—the TV, the radio, and the printed word.

In answer to questions concerning morality, family life, and societal values, the difference between the average citizen and the leaders of the media was extraordinary. What were proclaimed as essential elements of a positive American society by large majorities of the people were overwhelmingly rejected by those who set the tone for the media in their responses to the questions. Now, of course, it's true that the study could well have been biased or the groups incorrectly chosen, but the percentages in both classes were so large as to give at least some indication of a very real and serious divide in the way people looked at these rather important issues.

I had not thought of that questionnaire for several years until the last few weeks when the choice of the films presented as candidates for the Oscars were made by the Academy of Motion Picture Arts and Sciences. In a majority of cases what was presented to the American people were films that showed a view of life that is rather different from the Judeo-Christian values on which our own society was built. Undoubtedly, this manifests a real change in which Hollywood believes our morality is headed and which are the new important "values" we must learn and accept. The scary part of it all is that if the same questionnaire were to be given today—a generation or so later—would we find that the ordinary American has begun to lose the traditional values and has, over the interim, been coaxed or brainwashed into a new understanding of what is good and right and beautiful? It is pretty clear that for many folks in the media they have not changed, but have they made a significant change in what the rest of us hold dear?

I don't want to put down artists or writers or brilliant producers, but to make us all aware of this not-so-subtle change in what the public is presented these days and the damage it places on the values that made family life the great strength of our nation. Thinking of you as I fly back from the Holy Land, where our Judeo-Christian ethic began, I wanted you to reflect on this phenomenon with me. Being aware of the challenge should help us to strive to hold on to the values we can't afford to lose.

A Man Strong and Gentle
March 23, 2006

I was going to put a label on this column that said "For Men Only." I decided not to do it because I knew it would get me in trouble with the ladies and the men probably wouldn't read it anyway.

A few days ago we celebrated the great Solemnity of Saint Joseph, the spouse of our Lady and the guardian of the Lord. As I was meditating on the virtues of that great saint, I was reminded of the extraordinary model that he is for fathers and husbands and all men in general.

Sometime ago, in many dioceses around the country, there were special programs for the spirituality of our Catholic men. I think originally they were fostered because of the very successful Protestant and Evangelical programs called "Promise Keepers" and other similar efforts to involve fathers and sons more directly in the work of the Churches and in fostering a deeper spiritual life among them. About ten or fifteen years ago, there were programs like this all over the country. When I was archbishop of Newark, I initiated a program that was similar. Over the years, for some reason or other, many of these programs seem to have diminished in their ministry to the men in parishes and Church organizations. I'm not sure why that is. Perhaps it is because they were very successful and no longer needed—but in my heart I doubt that. We always need to remind ourselves of the call to holiness and a specific call to men is always not only useful, but probably vital for the life of the Church.

It is not that Catholic men are not religious. When I see the Knights of Columbus and their continuing growth in our country, especially now among younger men and in a particular way on college campuses, I know that men are interested in a spiritual life and in an apostolic life. By apostolic I mean a life that will reach out to others—as I guess every spiritual life ultimately must do since the love of neighbor is that second greatest commandment of the Lord.

As I was meditating on Saint Joseph around the time of his feast day, I thought of the extraordinary virtues of this remarkable man. After all, God chose him not only to be the guardian and protector of Mary, but also to be the role model for Jesus Christ, his only Son. Joseph, therefore, had to be a strong man so that the Lord would grow up with many examples of strength and fortitude and courage. Joseph also had to be a caring man and this is so beautifully demonstrated in his concern at the pregnancy of Mary and his desire to do what was right in a way that she would never be hurt. He was also a man who was always ready to do the will of God. Whether it was a message received in a dream or in any other way, Joseph always preferred the will of God to his own comforts or convenience. The stories about Joseph in the gospel, although they are few, give us that sense of a man who was always ready to do God's will.

He is, as you know, the patron of the universal Church. He is also the patron of the dying because, since he was not around during the public life of Christ, we presume that he died during the hidden life with Jesus and Mary at his bedside. There are so many ways in which the Church has honored Joseph, but probably the best way of all is by trying to imitate his virtues. As I am thinking of you and in a special way thinking of the men in our parishes and institutions around the diocese, how I would long to see all of us practice those singular virtues of the great Saint Joseph—strength of character and dedication to doing what is right, a caring, gentle approach to others, especially those for whom we have a special relationship such as within our own family and finally, a prompt and uncompromising obedience to the law of God. These are not easy virtues, especially in our own day when society prefers other and more selfish ways to live. But in the long run, these are the virtues that make a great and good man, and that is always what I am praying, that all the men in this local Church—including me—may become.

Seminarians
March 30, 2006

I was at breakfast this morning in the faculty dining room of the North American College (NAC) when one of the priest professors happened to say to me, "You have a fine group of men here at the NAC. You can be very proud of them." I replied, "You are right, and I am, and happily the same thing is true of all the Washington seminarians wherever we have sent them." In seminary after seminary—and we use seven different seminaries—the faculty congratulates the Archdiocese of Washington for the high caliber of our men. They are prayerful and devoted, balanced and enthusiastic. We are so blessed! Pray that this will always be true.

We started the school year with more than seventy seminarians. You might be interested to know that they include several former Navy, Army, and Air Force officers, a half dozen or so lawyers, bankers, accountants, and teachers, as well as many young men who have just recently graduated from college, plus about eight still in undergraduate studies. Because Washington is such a magnet, almost half of our seminarians come from other parts of the United States or even from abroad. Thank God that many of them come with a knowledge of Spanish since the number of Catholics from Latin America has grown so rapidly in our area.

Some folks think that I don't emphasize marriage or lay vocations enough. If that is true, and I hope it is not, the reason would be clear. There is not a crisis in the shortage of people entering lay vocations, nor, thank God, in entering marriage. In so many parts of the world, a priest and religious vocation shortage troubles the Church. Perhaps more than anything it is a result of smaller families, since parents with only one child understandably hesitate to encourage him to be a priest or her to be a religious sister. And yet, those of us who are privileged to know the mothers and fathers of priests and sisters can tell you how blessed they are in that sacrifice and how much they rejoice in the works of grace to which their sons and daughters have given their lives. Sadly, there are many priestly vocations that go unfulfilled, I know. Pray with me that God will give parents the grace to encourage their children's vocations.

I'm in Rome, as you probably know. The Holy Father called all the cardinals to a special gathering with him, just before the consistory to elevate the fifteen new cardinals. Almost all the cardinals, now about 190 of us all over the world, were able to come. We discussed a number of topics with the Holy Father, and I had a chance to greet him twice as well as to speak during the discussion sessions.

As I talk about vocations and seminarians to cardinals from different parts of the world one of their greatest concerns is truly priestly vocations for the future of the Church. I tell you this so you won't think it's only me who is always talking about this concern. As I talk to the other cardinals, I am always thinking of you and thanking God for you and for the great seminarians of this local Church who come because of your prayers and because you love the priesthood and the sacraments that depend on it.

Unexpected Journeys
April 6, 2006

I had not intended to be away from home for so many days this last trip. I had agreed to speak at a national celebration in New Delhi, the capital of India, to commemorate the first anniversary of the death of the late Holy Father, Pope John Paul II. It was to be connected with the celebration of the arrival of our Catholic Relief Services (CRS) in India sixty years ago when we first came to help in the terrible famine which hit Bombay in 1946. That was the first emergency in post–World War II to which our American Catholic Relief agency responded and, as you know, we can be so proud of the way they have responded ever since, not only in India, but everywhere in the world.

What turned a journey of five days to India into almost two weeks of traveling was the call from our Holy Father, Pope Benedict, to all the cardinals to be present at the consistory in Rome. I had to leave Washington on a Tuesday afternoon to be in Rome in time to attend the 9:00 a.m. meeting on Thursday. We didn't complete the work of the consistory until Monday so it wasn't worthwhile to come back all the way across the ocean to the office, only to leave again for India two days later.

I landed in Mumbai (the old Bombay) late at night on a Tuesday, and Wednesday was already filled with meetings. CRS is always dedicated to working with the poorest of the poor and trying to make their lives more meaningful and more productive. To see the dedication of the American lay professionals and their families who give years of their lives to helping people in far-off countries is a real inspiration and a witness to God's love in our own compatriots. The Indian nationals, who work with them and who have gradually taken more and more administrative responsibility in the agency, are likewise tremendous examples of loving service. I'm prejudiced, of course, but I have no doubt that CRS is the best and most effective nongovernmental organization both in responding to emergencies like earthquakes, hurricanes, and tsunamis, as well as helping to build up the civil society of the people in the nations that it serves.

When Cardinal Ivan Dias, the archbishop of Bombay and an old and dear friend of mine, learned that I was coming, he added two other jobs to my visit—a special Mass for all his seminarians and a day of recollection for the priests of the archdiocese. I enjoyed them both, although ninety plus–degree, non-air-conditioned chapels crowded with people do present something of a challenge. I also stopped in the infamous red light district of Mumbai to visit a local agency that is one of the partners of CRS and that gives shelter and a safe haven to women and children who have been rescued from human trafficking—the exploitation of young people who are lured from the rural villages or from other developing countries in the promise of a decent job and then find themselves trapped as victims of sexual abuse.

The following day I traveled by boat to a village in Kerala in the south of India where another partner of CRS and the local Catholic diocese have been preparing a group of women to become more able to make a living for themselves and their families. These self-help projects, initiated by CRS and guided by it, have really made a difference in their lives and in their ability to feel empowered to make a difference in their society. Finally, in Delhi, in the north of India, where the anniversary celebration took place, I met with a number of Indian bishops and discussed their hopes and dreams on that occasion. After the ceremony itself, at which I spoke briefly, two of the federal government ministers who were present asked if we could initiate conversations on the various themes that are so important to the Church in India. The local conference of bishops will be able to follow up on that and they seem very pleased that this new opportunity had been opened.

As I look back on the journey, I believe and hope that my presence was useful. I always tell my host that, even though I am with them in all the visits, meetings, and talks, I am always thinking of you whose patience and support make it possible for me to be that far away and to try to help just a little in their own great and constant challenge.

Easter Brings Us All Together
April 13, 2006

Sometimes I know we don't always agree on everything. The good thing is that we do agree on most things and hopefully always on the most important things. That's how it is in families—we all know that—and in spite of disagreements we can always love one another as I love you and pray for you all the time. I do try to stay out of controversies, although in today's world public policies are always entering into so much of the dialogue that goes on among our people.

Questions like the life issues—abortion, stem-cell research, euthanasia—and the issues surrounding family life are the most important of all and those which do call for our unity and clarity. Other issues will admit of different opinions, even though the weight of Church teaching does seem to be on one side. Here, questions like capital punishment and the just war theory would come into play. Finally, there are those other issues where good people can honestly have differing opinions—perhaps not so much on the principles themselves, but on the different ways to reach a generally agreed-upon goal. These issues would be, for example, our nation's immigration policy, the care of the poor, and universal health care.

There are indeed shades of right and wrong as one approaches issues like those latter ones. Although the principles are usually clear, like our need always to reach out and defend human dignity, the ways to get to that goal in each area of society can indeed be different. I guess I always tend to take the side of the poor in those cases. Perhaps that is because we were poor as I grew up in the Depression, or perhaps because some of my great-grandparents came from other countries as immigrants and might not have been admitted if today's laws were on the books then, or because when I worked as a young priest in Puerto Rico I became so conscious of the cost of medical care for the people whom I served. I do recognize that other folks who do not come from my experience will often come to a different conclusion than I have and a different way of solving these very serious societal problems.

The wonderful thing is that on those great issues of faith, we can all be together. There we are called by the wonder of God's love as we are all, each one of us, saved in the same way—by the power of Christ's Easter resurrection and truly made one family in his love. As we strive to live our lives in keeping with the good news of the Gospel, that wonderful fact of God's redeeming love for all of us keeps us together on the basics of our faith and in the love that saved us through the power of God's Son. It is this which gives us the reason to agree that the most important law of our lives is to return God's love by the way we live and to find in ourselves a genuine and abiding love for our neighbor. As Easter comes, I am thinking of you and rejoicing that the unity of the Easter message makes us always one at last.

Looking Forward, Looking Back
April 20, 2006

No, this isn't the beginning of a lesson of motor vehicle driving for beginners. I'm not sure I would be the best guide for that, anyway. It's just a chance to write to you about Lent and Easter and the time to take stock of how we did in that special period of challenge that has just concluded. For so many Catholics for whom Holy Week is rightly such an important week in our lives, the mystical journey with Jesus may be both exhausting and inspiring.

For our priests who try to give themselves totally to the pastoral, liturgical, and personal spiritual demands of their ministry during Lent and Holy Week, the great solemnity of Easter comes as a joyful crowning to many weeks of intensive labor. For Catholic people who try to be present at as many liturgical celebrations in Holy Week as possible, it can be exhausting as they come to the great culmination of Easter Sunday itself. The more intense their journey through Lent has been, the more they need the time to rest in the Lord that Easter brings. I confess that for myself, I was really tired as my last Easter Sunday Mass concluded. I guess I'm just getting old and that is a reality that even my usual energy can't overcome.

But my thought in writing to you this morning was to look back at Lent and measure our progress, yours and mine, in using that time to come closer to the Lord. If, like me, you weren't perfect in keeping all your resolutions, there is no reason why you can't continue them a little longer in Easter time. If they were good spiritual ideas on Ash Wednesday, they will still be worthwhile resolutions in April and May.

And looking forward, now that Easter is here, why not take that special grace of God's presence in our lives to express our thanks to God for the redemption won for us by Jesus by doing something concrete and specific in return. May I suggest getting to Mass more frequently—maybe several times a week—stopping in for a moment to visit the blessed sacrament, even daily when possible, inviting friends or relations who are not Catholic to come to Mass and learn something more about the Church? All these would be great Easter resolutions, whether or not we have been faithful in keeping the Lenten resolutions just passed.

Our life in Jesus is an ongoing adventure of love. Thinking of you, as I write this, I hope and pray it will be for all of us an adventure that is filled with challenge and joy as well.

One Person
April 27, 2006

I have to go to Freising in Germany next Monday. I have been there once before. It is a small picturesque city near Munich and I remember that it has an old historic abbey, which still owns a Bier-Halle where I had a great meal during my first visit! This time I go to give a talk on the missions at the invitation of the German bishops. Since I know many of them, I am looking forward to seeing old friends. As I was preparing my talk, I started to think of all of us here in the Archdiocese of Washington and to ponder how we are also vitally involved in the missionary activity of the Church.

Our Protestant brothers and sisters speak more than we do about "the great commission." By that, they refer to the command of Jesus to preach the Gospel to the ends of the earth and to make disciples of all the nations. That commission from the Lord is at the heart of who we are as Catholic Christians and it challenges all of us to be missionaries in a certain essential sense. Most of us are not going to travel to foreign countries and spread the Gospel, but every single one of us can be a true missionary and through that opportunity we can make a tremendous difference in the lives of other people—and in our own! All we have to do is touch one person at a time.

Just as I so often ask our priests and, indeed, all of you to pray for vocations to the priesthood and religious life and to bring your prayers into action by inviting one young person each year to consider whether God is calling them to such a consecrated life, I am also sure that God would be pleased if you also invited a non-Catholic friend or relation to come to church with you and to learn more about our Catholic family. There is a real parallel here. So many young men who are now in our seminaries have told me that one of the most powerful graces in encouraging them to pursue a priestly vocation came when a priest or a friend challenged them to think about it. I am sure that it is the same for so many people who hear the voice of Jesus inviting them to become a Catholic when you, yourself, have served to be his voice. Jesus uses you and me, as unworthy as we may be, to build up his kingdom in that same way.

As I read over the documents of the Church on the missions—and they range from the scriptures to the decrees of the Second Vatican Council and from the words of the Lord to the teaching of the modern popes—I am always touched by the fact that God so often uses human instruments like us to give his invitation and to be the mediators of his grace. As long as we speak with humility and love, those whom we call to Jesus to become a Christian or to become a priest or religious will at least take a moment to think about that challenge and maybe, a moment in the presence of that word is enough to change a person's life! To speak to one person each year is not an overwhelming burden, and as I am thinking of you and your own good example, I am sure that just one such invitation might change someone else's life forever.

Good Health
May 4, 2006

Have you ever stopped to think how many toasts and good wishes are centered about the question of health? When they lift a glass of wine, the French say, "*Sante!*" and the Italians say, "*Salute!*" Many other peoples always are ready to wish you good health even, like the Germans, when you sneeze. I think that is because people realize that good health is one of the most important things, materially speaking, that we can have. It is also one of the things that I worry about as the growing number of American people without health insurance is increasing. I spoke about this last Monday when I was asked to give the keynote address at the American Hospital Association. I was really honored to be asked since this is a very prestigious organization in our country, but I was anxious to speak to them about a real crisis in health care today.

If you purchase health insurance for yourself and your family, you know how expensive it is. Most large companies do provide health care coverage as part of a salary package and that is a blessing which covers most Americans. However, there are forty-eight million Americans without any health care at all and so many other millions whose health care is so limited that it doesn't drive away anxiety about health in the future at all. To make matters worse, as health care costs rise, more and more employers are going to cut back on the quality of health care they provide, just because of its spiraling costs.

One of the significant facts in all of this is more than 80 percent of the people without health care are already working people. They find themselves unable to pay for adequate health care they can afford on their salaries. Imagine trying to bring up a child without health insurance! Imagine the frustration, the fears, and even the anger that some people must have when they are faced with illnesses for which they cannot find affordable medical help!

But what about hospitals? They are also concerned about this grave problem too, since poverty drives people to the emergency room for ordinary medical care and this drives up the cost of hospital stays for everyone.

It is not fair to put the burden on the hospitals who already do so much in pro bono care for people who just cannot afford anything like the costs would be. (I know this from experience, since the Archdiocese of Newark at one time owned seven hospitals and I saw the tremendous economic challenge that they entailed.) Many hospitals that serve the poor have been closed by this problem!

I confess that I do not have an answer, but I think it is good for us all to ask the questions. As health care costs continue to rise and insurance plans cut back, I am thinking of you and hoping that together we will always be able to take care of the sick, even as Jesus wants us to do.

The Little Guy
May 11, 2006

No, thank you for asking, I'm not writing about myself, although I do seem to have become shorter in the last few years. (As a matter of fact, some of my nieces and nephews tend to refer to me as "the extraordinary shrinking person," which I think is a comic book character of years ago. I keep telling them that it is just that they are growing so fast and not that I am shrinking. Of course, it does get worse when so many of their children are now taller than I am, too!)

Actually, I want to write about the people in our society and all over the world who tend to get lost in the shuffle, the people to whom the Lord refers in the Gospel as "the least of these" or "the least of your brethren." They are really not properly characterized as either men or women or belonging to one race or ethnic group or living in one special area. It is true that they can be anyone and anywhere, although as we look at the world around us, so many of them are the very poor, women, minorities, the very sick, the uneducated, the badly fed, and the victims of persecution and hate.

In the course of my life, I have come across so many of these "little guys" and, as you know, I worry about them and try to help them and try to get those who are not "little guys" to reach out and help them, too. We all could make a list of the little guys in our society who seem always to come up last when the good things are passed around. Whether that is wealth or health, opportunity or security, enough to eat or a safe place to live.

The little guys can be the women who don't have a chance in so many cultures to develop their talents and to make their own contribution to the world, but have to stay a step down in a society that treats them like second-class people. The little guys can be the very poor in any part of the world, whose families will always be without enough to eat or to wear or to have a chance to escape from the crushing barriers of ignorance and discrimination. In the countries of the West, in a most horrible way, the little guy can be the little baby who is put to death in its mother's womb and never has a chance for life after birth!

The little guy can be the stranger in a foreign land who is trying to make a better life for his or her family, the forty-eight million Americans without health care, the hundreds of thousands of the men and women in the drought of Africa who will starve to death in this twenty-first century of progress, the women and children of Darfur and in the Sudan who have been fleeing for these many years from murder and rape and pillage, the Israeli and Iraqi, who must live in the terrible fear of a suicide bomber, the Palestinians whom the world—and our own government—seem to be willing to abandon without even the most elementary humanitarian aid, the young people in troubled neighborhoods who are left at the mercy of gangs and drugs and prostitution.

These are the little guys of our own world and our own time. And there are many others. And you and I really need to be aware of them and try to help them. All of us in our hearts do worry about the little guys of life and you have your own list to add to mine, I know. But thinking of you with deepest gratitude for all you do to help our Church reach out to help little guys here in our archdiocese, I thought that I would take this moment to remind us all that there is still so much to do. And Jesus told us that whatever we do for these little guys, we do for him.

A Very Good Man
May 18, 2006

Even though I know that some of you in your great kindness might have some feelings of sadness about my retirement, I really want to assure you that the coming of Archbishop Donald Wuerl is the best thing that could happen to this beloved Archdiocese of Washington. He is truly a very good man.

Way back in December, when I spoke to our priests at our annual Christmas gathering, I told these great brothers and sons of mine that I felt I was slowing down and starting to feel the weight of the years a bit more than before. I told them that, although I was in decent health, I was getting more tired, a little more forgetful, and once in a while not so sure of my steps as I used to be. The latter apparently was due to what now seems to be the start of scoliosis. No big deal, as the kids would say, but something to watch as time goes by. This is what I said to the priests:

> I don't want the Church of Washington to have anything but the best. For more than fifteen years, your bishops have been septuagenarians. No matter how young or alert or vigorous I may feel sometimes, this Church of ours really needs someone who can plan with you for five or ten or fifteen years ahead. I really can't do that because I do not know my future, except that I know I am going to be seventy-six this year. . . .
>
> Some of you have said to me, very thoughtfully, that I only know one way to serve as archbishop of Washington and that is working 24/7 and trying to do all these things that come across my life. That is probably true. There would be no way that I could take a lot of time off and still feel that I was serving you. Some may say that there is no way I could even take two or three hours off a day and still feel that I was doing everything I should be. Maybe that's true, and if I don't do that well anymore, it may be time.

In my statement about Archbishop Wuerl—which is included in another part of the *Catholic Standard*—I tell you how pleased and grateful I am about his appointment.

The Holy Father has given us a great priest and a very good man. He has been a wonderful friend of mine over the years, a truly excellent bishop and an extraordinary leader for the Church in the United States. I know that you will come to love him and respect him as you have supported me so powerfully over the past five and a half years.

I will still be in the Washington area for most of the time, although I will spend a couple of months a year up in the New York/New Jersey area where most of my family lives. One of the things I have missed is not seeing the little ones in my family grow up. They get very annoyed at me when I don't know all their names and I miss their birthdays.

One thing for sure you will always know. Wherever I am, I will always be thinking of you with love and tremendous gratitude. Even though possibly one or two of you may miss my regular column, you know that my prayer, my affection, and my deepest appreciation for all of you and for your wonderful kindnesses to me will always be uppermost in my heart. I look forward to watching this local Church grow and prosper spiritually, and in every other way, under the leadership of Archbishop Wuerl.

Born and raised in New York City, Cardinal Theodore E. McCarrick was ordained to the priesthood in 1958, following formation at St. Joseph's Seminary. McCarrick pursued graduate work to earn a doctor of philosophy in sociology at the Catholic University of America, where he also held several administrative positions before being selected as president of the Catholic University of Puerto Rico in 1965. Later appointed an auxiliary bishop of New York, McCarrick was named by Pope John Paul II as the first bishop of Metuchen in New Jersey, and later served as the archbishop of Newark and of Washington. He was elevated to the College of Cardinals in 2001.

Founded in 1865, Ave Maria Press,
a ministry of the Congregation of
Holy Cross, is a Catholic publishing
company that serves the spiritual and
formative needs of the Church and its
schools, institutions, and ministers;
Christian individuals and families; and
others seeking spiritual nourishment.

———

For a complete listing of titles from

Ave Maria Press

Sorin Books

Forest of Peace

Christian Classics

visit www.avemariapress.com

ave maria press® / Notre Dame, IN 46556
A Ministry of the Indiana Province of Holy Cross